# CROP PROCESSES
# IN CONTROLLED ENVIRONMENTS

# APPLIED BOTANY

## A Series of Monographs

CONSULTING EDITOR

### J. F. Sutcliffe

*School of Biological Sciences, University of Sussex, England*

# CROP PROCESSES IN CONTROLLED ENVIRONMENTS

*Proceedings of an International Symposium*
*held at the Glasshouse Crops Research Institute,*
*Littlehampton, Sussex, England, July 1971*

*Edited by*

## A. R. REES, K. E. COCKSHULL,
## D. W. HAND *and* R. G. HURD

1972

ACADEMIC PRESS – London and New York

ACADEMIC PRESS INC. (LONDON) LTD
24–28 Oval Road
London NW1

*United States Edition published by*
ACADEMIC PRESS INC.
111 Fifth Avenue
New York, New York 10003

Library of Congress Catalog Card Number: 72–8445
ISBN: 0–12–585440–4

Printed in Great Britain by
Butler & Tanner Ltd, Frome and London

# Participants

ACOCK, B. Plant Physiology Department, Glasshouse Crops Research Institute, Worthing Road, Rustington, Littlehampton, Sussex, England.

AUSTIN, R. B. Plant Physiology Department, National Vegetable Research Station, Wellesbourne, Warwick, England.

AVERY, D. J. Plant Physiology Department, East Malling Research Station, East Malling, Maidstone, Kent, England.

BOWMAN, G. E. Control and Instrumentation Department, National Institute of Agricultural Engineering, Silsoe, Bedfordshire, England.

BURRAGE, S. W. Department of Horticulture, Wye College, Ashford, Kent, England.

BURTON, W. G. Plant Division, Food Research Institute, Colney Lane, Norwich, England.

CALVERT, A. Plant Physiology Department, Glasshouse Crops Research Institute, Worthing Road, Rustington, Littlehampton, Sussex, England.

CHALLA, H. Centre for Plant Physiological Research, Wageningen, Netherlands.

CHARTIER, P. Station Centrale de Bioclimatologie Agricole, Institut National de la Recherche Agronomique, Versailles, France.

COCKSHULL, K. E. Plant Physiology Department, Glasshouse Crops Research Institute, Worthing Road, Rustington, Littlehampton, Sussex, England.

COOPER, A. J. Plant Physiology Department, Glasshouse Crops Research Institute, Worthing Road, Rustington, Littlehampton, Sussex, England.

DARBY, L. A. Plant Breeding Department, Glasshouse Crops Research Institute, Worthing Road, Rustington, Littlehampton, Sussex, England.

DICKS, J. W. Crop Protection Department, Glasshouse Crops Research Institute, Worthing Road, Rustington, Littlehampton, Sussex, England.

ENOCH, H. Z. Division of Agrometeorology, Volcani Institute, Bet-Dagan, Israel.

FRAMPTON, D. G. Frampton's Nurseries Ltd, Littlehampton Road, Worthing, Sussex, England.

GUTTRIDGE, C. G. Pomology and Plant Breeding Department, Long Ashton Research Station, Long Ashton, Bristol, England.

HAND, D. W. Plant Physiology Department, Glasshouse Crops Research Institute, Worthing Road, Rustington, Littlehampton, Sussex, England.

HARSSEMA, H. Horticulture Department, Agricultural University, Wageningen, Netherlands.

Ho, L. C. Plant Physiology Department, Glasshouse Crops Research Institute, Worthing Road, Rustington, Littlehampton, Sussex, England.

HUGHES, A. P. Plant Environment Laboratory, University of Reading, Reading, Berkshire, England.

HURD, R. G. Plant Physiology Department, Glasshouse Crops Research Institute, Worthing Road, Rustington, Littlehampton, Sussex, England.

HUXLEY, P. A. Department of Horticulture, University of Reading, Reading, Berkshire, England.

INCOLL, L. Botany Department, University of Leeds, Leeds, England.

JAMES, G. B. Botany Department, Aberdeen University, Aberdeen, Scotland.

JARMAN, P. D. Plant Physiology Department, Glasshouse Crops Research Institute, Worthing Road, Rustington, Littlehampton, Sussex, England.

JARVIS, P. G. Botany Department, Aberdeen University, Aberdeen, Scotland.

LAKE, J. V. Physics Department, Rothamsted Experimental Station, Harpenden, Hertfordshire, England.

LEAFE, E. L. Crop Physiology Department, Grassland Research Institute, Hurley, Maidenhead, Berkshire, England.

LUDWIG, L. J. Plant Physiology Department, Glasshouse Crops Research Institute, Worthing Road, Rustington, Littlehampton, Sussex, England.

MAW, G. A. Chemistry Division, Glasshouse Crops Research Institute, Worthing Road, Rustington, Littlehampton, Sussex, England.

MONTEITH, J. L. Department of Physiology and Environmental Studies, University of Nottingham, Loughborough, Leicestershire, England.

MORGAN, S. Electricity Council Research Centre, Capenhurst, Chester, England.

MORRIS, L. G. High-value Crop Project (FAO), Volcani Institute, Bet-Dagan, Israel.

NICHOLS, R. Plant Physiology Department, Glasshouse Crops Research Institute, Worthing Road, Rustington, Littlehampton, Sussex, England.

NITSCH, J. P.† Centre National de la Recherche Scientifique, Gif-sur-Yvette, France.

OSBORNE, DAPHNE J. A.R.C. Unit of Developmental Botany, University of Cambridge, Cambridge, England.

PEEL, A. J. Botany Department, University of Hull, Hull, England.

PENNING DE VRIES, F. W. T. Department of Theoretical Production Ecology, Agricultural University, Wageningen, Netherlands.

PORTER, HELEN K. Agricultural Research Council, 160 Great Portland Street, London W.1, England.

† Deceased.

RACKHAM, O. Department of Agricultural Science and Applied Biology, University of Cambridge, Cambridge, England.

RAPPAPORT, L. Department of Vegetable Crops, University of California, Davis, California, U.S.A.

REES, A. R. Plant Physiology Department, Glasshouse Crops Research Institute, Worthing Road, Rustington, Littlehampton, Sussex, England.

RUDD-JONES, D. Director, Glasshouse Crops Research Institute, Worthing Road, Rustington, Littlehampton, Sussex, England.

RUSSELL, R. S. A.R.C. Letcombe Laboratory, Wantage, Berkshire, England.

RYLE, G. J. A. Plant Physiology Department, Grassland Research Institute, Hurley, Maidenhead, Berkshire, England.

SCHWABE, W. W. Department of Horticulture, Wye College, Ashford, Kent, England.

SEXTON, R. School of Biological Sciences, Sussex University, Falmer, Brighton, Sussex, England.

SHEARD, G. F. Deputy Director, Glasshouse Crops Research Institute, Worthing Road, Rustington, Littlehampton, Sussex, England.

SMITH, H. Department of Physiology and Environmental Studies, University of Nottingham, Loughborough, Leicestershire, England.

SUTCLIFFE, J. F. School of Biological Sciences, Sussex University, Falmer, Brighton, Sussex, England.

THOMPSON, P. A. Jodrell Laboratory, Royal Botanic Gardens, Kew, Richmond, Surrey, England.

THORNLEY, J. H. M. Biometrics Department, Glasshouse Crops Research Institute, Worthing Road, Rustington, Littlehampton, Sussex, England.

TREGUNNA, E. B. Botany Department, University of British Columbia, Canada.

TREHARNE, K. J. Developmental Genetics Department, Welsh Plant Breeding Station, Aberystwyth, Wales.

WAREING, P. F. Botany Department, University College of Wales, Aberystwyth, Wales.

WARREN WILSON, J. Plant Physiology Department, Glasshouse Crops Research Institute, Worthing Road, Rustington, Littlehampton, Sussex, England.

WHITTINGHAM, C. P. Botany Department, Rothamsted Experimental Station, Harpenden, Hertfordshire, England.

WINSOR, G. W. Plant Nutrition and Soil Department, Glasshouse Crops Research Institute, Worthing Road, Rustington, Littlehampton, Sussex, England.

WRIGHT, S. T. C. A.R.C. Plant Growth Substance and Systemic Fungicides Unit, Wye College, Ashford, Kent, England.

# Preface

In recent years considerable attention has been given to studies of plants and crops in relation to their environment. Progress has been made both in controlling the plant environment and in improving the efficiency of agricultural and horticultural practice. Most factors of the glasshouse environment can be modified or controlled, but there is still uncertainty in many cases about the optimum conditions for plant growth and crop production and there is little information available about the effects of short-term deviations from the optimum on plant behaviour. As one speaker commented, the plant in its natural environment proceeds from crisis to crisis, and the grower attempts to reduce the frequency and extent of these crises.

It was the aim of the Symposium to explore recent advances in several technical and scientific fields of research on crop and plant processes with the object of revealing areas where further research is most urgently required. These include:

1. Recent developments in glasshouse technology, such as light-modulated control of temperature and carbon dioxide concentration; supplementary lighting; growing rooms; plastic houses and mini-glasshouses.
2. Micrometeorological and physical methods, increasingly used in studying field crops, which have as yet been little used in the glasshouse environment where many of the determining factors can be better controlled.
3. New developments in controlled-environment cabinets which allow precise gas-exchange studies, the independent control of root and shoot temperatures, and the use of natural light or improved artificial sources.
4. Advances in some areas of plant physiology of especial relevance to crop production including photorespiration; the biochemical control of photosynthesis; translocation and the control of accumulation of assimilates; hormonal control of growth and development.
5. The extension of computer simulation and quantitative analysis to crop processes hitherto treated descriptively.

The Symposium was conceived and largely organized by Dr J. Warren Wilson to mark the formal opening of the new Plant Physiology buildings and controlled-environment facilities on 14 July 1971 by the Rt Hon. Mrs Margaret Thatcher, M.P., Secretary of State for Education and Science. We are grateful to the Governing Body of the G.C.R.I., who underwrote the costs of the Symposium, and to the Trustees of the Underwood Fund for providing financial support to enable the organizers to invite overseas speakers. Many members of the Institute staff helped to organize the Symposium, and we should like to thank them all for their efforts. We are particularly grateful to the authors of the papers and to the session chairmen. Permission to reproduce tables and figures is acknowledged in the respective captions.

*June 1972*

A. R. REES
K. E. COCKSHULL
D. W. HAND
R. G. HURD

# Contents

† Deceased.

xi

## Section III  Environment–Plant Relations

Chairman: Professor W. W. Schwabe

## Section IV  Internal control mechanisms

Chairman: Professor J. F. Sutcliffe

*Introduction 1*

# Controlled environments

D. RUDD-JONES

*Glasshouse Crops Research Institute, Littlehampton, Sussex, England*

The scientist working in controlled environments has unique opportunities to determine the precise limits of productivity of plants. If he is working also in the interests of the glasshouse industry he is in the fortunate position that his "laboratory" is also what might be termed his "production unit"—a concept which embraces the whole plant or crop in the environment in which it is growing. The more closely the glasshouse can be made to simulate the controlled environment cabinet, the nearer it should be possible to get to maximum productivity in commercial crops. It is now accepted that yields of tomatoes in excess of $250 \times 10^3$ kg ha$^{-1}$ and cucumbers in excess of $375 \times 10^3$ kg ha$^{-1}$ can be achieved. This is five or six times the weight of apples that can be produced per unit area on a comparable dry weight basis, four or five times the weight of cereal grain, and twice the yield of potato tubers. In commercial practice full account has to be taken of the economics of crop production in controlled environments; the capital and running costs are high and become higher the more sophisticated the controls. One environmental factor only—solar radiation—is beyond the control of the scientist.

The development of experimental studies of the interactions of whole plants and crops with their environments under precisely controlled conditions has been comparatively recent. The main interests and the major advances in plant physiology in this country have been in two general areas; at the one extreme, field experiments with crops, and at the other, laboratory experiments with unicellular organisms, single cells, tissues or parts of plants.

The opening of the first Phytotron at Pasadena provided a great stimulus to plant physiologists to work in controlled environments with whole plants. Relatively unsophisticated cabinets had been used in this country

1

before the war (e.g., Stoughton, 1930; Wilson, 1937), but often for patho-logical rather than physiological research. This late development of research in controlled environments with whole plants is reflected by the long time lag in the exploitation of environmental control, and particularly carbon dioxide enrichment, to increase productivity in commercial practice. As early as 1916 in the Second Annual Report of the Experimental and Research Station at Cheshunt—the predecessor of the Glasshouse Crops Research Institute—an account (Lister, 1917) was given of the measure-ment of carbon dioxide in the glasshouse atmosphere which showed that it could reach four or five times the ambient concentration at soil level, whereas at the top of the house it was only just above ambient although during the night the concentration normally rose. Some of the first experi-ments to investigate the possibility of increasing yields in glasshouse crops by carbon dioxide enrichment were done at Cheshunt by Timmis (1923). These experiments involved the injection of carbon dioxide into the glass-house in concentrations up to ten times ambient and they were continued at Cheshunt and in association with the Research Institute of Plant Physio-logy, Imperial College, London. Owen and Williams (1923) (the latter author was specially appointed for the carbon dioxide investigations), Owen *et al.* (1926) and Small and White (1930) demonstrated increased yields of tomatoes and cucumbers in glasshouses enriched with carbon dioxide from several different sources. Bolas and Henderson (1928) ob-tained increases in the vegetative growth of cucumbers and other plants under laboratory conditions using pure carbon dioxide and Bolas and Melville (1935) showed yield increases of tomatoes of nearly 14% over the whole cropping season from enrichment with carbon dioxide produced by burning paraffin.

Experiments at the two Institutes continued up until the war. There was then a long gap until the 50s and early 60s when there were reports of increased yields of cucumbers, tomatoes and heated lettuce from several European countries (Kilbinger, 1951; Klougart, 1963, 1964) and North America (Wittwer and Robb, 1964). In Holland, Gaastra (1959) published a detailed account of the more fundamental aspects and Briejèr (1959) a more general account. The latter paper had the provocative title "An abandoned gold mine; the supplementary application of carbon dioxide". In this country Gardner (1963, 1964) demonstrated the value of carbon dioxide enrichment for heated lettuce and winter-flowering chrysan-themums at the Lee Valley Experimental Horticulture Station. The rapid developments in glasshouse engineering and control instrumentation that derived from the work of L. G. Morris and his colleagues at the National Institute of Agricultural Engineering pointed the way for much more precise and integrated control of environmental factors including carbon characters that could be turned to advantage by the breeding of varieties for particular cultural systems. This in turn might stimulate a more rational and critical examination of alternative, cheaper systems of protecting crops and of extending the variety of such crops.

The declared object of the Symposium is "to evaluate recent advances in several technical and scientific fields which have important implications for research on crop and plant processes, and to suggest areas where further research is most urgently required". It comes at an especially opportune time for the Glasshouse Crops Research Institute. The Plant Physiology Department has, over the past four years, expanded both in staff and facilities for research on environmental control, on photoperiodism and on other crop processes. There would appear to be a need now to integrate the environmental control work with developmental studies.

After a decade of intensive research with whole plants in controlled environments, in which the controls have become more and more precise, physiologists are now returning to chemical and physical studies at the cell level with plant tissues or parts of plants in parallel with the whole plant studies. This more analytical approach which is necessary in order to acquire basic information on crop processes will then have to be correlated with data on whole plants.

The organizers have attempted to provide for the consideration in logical sequence of these changing trends by arranging the Symposium in four sessions. The opening session is devoted to a consideration of controlled environment facilities, the associated instrumentation, monitoring and control of the glasshouse environment, and future trends in structures and materials for protected cropping. The sessions which follow are concerned with the environment–crop and environment–plant relations and with internal control mechanisms.

# References

BOLAS, B. D. and HENDERSON, F. Y. (1928). Effect of increased carbon dioxide on the growth of plants. *Ann. Bot. O.S.* **42**, 509–523.

BOLAS, B. D. and MELVILLE, R. (1935). The effect on the tomato plant of carbon dioxide produced by combustion. *Ann. appl. Biol.* **22**, 1–15.

BORTHWICK, H. A. (1964). Control of photomorphogenesis by phytochrome. *Abstr. Pap. 10th Int. bot. Congr., Edinburgh, 1964*, 197.

BRIEJÈR, C. V. (1959). Een verlaten goudmijn: koolzuurbemesting. *Meded. Dir. Tuinb.* **22**, 670–674.

CALVERT, A. (1968). Effects of temperature on cropping of glasshouse tomatoes. *Rep. Glasshouse Crops Res. Inst. 1967*, 52.

CALVERT, A. and SLACK, G. (1970). Effects of carbon dioxide concentration on glasshouse tomatoes. *Rep. Glasshouse Crops Res. Inst. 1969*, 61–62.

dioxide. This led to the experiments in the so-called "cuvette" glasshouse by Lake (1966) who suggested that ultimately the control of the glasshouse environment might be achieved by a system operated by a digital computer This work was paralleled at the Glasshouse Crops Research Institute by the development of the Multifactorial Glasshouse Unit in which Cooper *et al.* (1966), Calvert (1968) and Calvert and Slack (1970) have done critical experiments on the integrated control of temperature, ventilation and carbon dioxide.

Thus it has taken nearly forty years to exploit commercially the original observations of the advantages of carbon dioxide enrichment. This has been due in large part to the fact that enrichment did not become practically feasible until systems of automatic control of temperature and ventilation were generally available, and even today only about a third of the heated tomato acreage in the U.K. is carbon dioxide-enriched, although probably nearly all the early crop, which shows the greatest benefit, is treated.

By contrast with the slow development of research on the interaction of crops grown in controlled conditions with their environments, there has been a much more rapid adoption by commercial growers of growth-regulating chemicals. Although these studies stem from more fundamental work by physiologists such as Went (1957), Hendricks (1967) and Cathey (1967), it was the essentially empirical approach of Preston and Link (1958), Tolbert (1960), Riddell *et al.* (1962), Tso (1964) and Cathey *et al.* (1966) that led to the dramatic developments in the control of flowering which have now become widely adopted in commercial practice.

At the present time the practical methods of controlling daylength for chrysanthemums which have been developed scientifically are being widely used in conjunction with growth retardants. Recently, too, research on supplementary illumination of chrysanthemums undertaken at the A.R.C. Unit of Flower Crop Physiology (Cockshull and Hughes, 1968) in controlled environments has led to recommendations for commercial use which are being taken up by some growers.

The next stage must be to achieve an understanding of the mode of action of synthetic growth-regulating chemicals and of their interactions with environmental factors and with internal control mechanisms involving naturally-occurring growth hormones. At the same time there is a need to study the more fundamental aspects of photoperiodism including the role of phytochrome (Borthwick, 1964), the pigment that mediates the developmental effects of light; the possible existence of a flowering hormone should also be investigated. This could lead to a further exploitation of the glasshouse environment for increased productivity and improved quality and to a better understanding of the genetical control of physiological

CPCE—B

CATHEY, H. M. (1967). Photobiology in horticulture. *Proc. 17th Int. hort. Congr., 1966* **3**, 385–391.

CATHEY, H. M., STEFFENS, G. L., STUART, N. W. and ZIMMERMAN, R. H. (1966). Chemical pruning of plants. *Science, N.Y.* **153**, 1382–1383.

COCKSHULL, K. E. and HUGHES, A. P. (1968). First two weeks of short-day treatment are critical with chrysanthemum. *Grower* **70**, 520–521.

COOPER, A. J., HURD, R. G. and GISBORNE, J. H. (1966). The effect of ventilating the control glasshouses in $CO_2$ enrichment comparisons. *Rep. Glasshouse Crops Res. Inst. 1965*, 142–144.

GAASTRA, P. (1959). Photosynthesis of crop plants as influenced by light, carbon dioxide, temperature, and stomatal diffusion resistance. *Meded. LandbHoogesch. Wageningen* **59**, (13), 1–68.

GARDNER, R. (1963). Response differs with variety. *Grower* **59**, 813–814.

GARDNER, R. (1964). $CO_2$ for glasshouse crops. *Agriculture, Lond.* **71**, 204–208.

HENDRICKS, S. B. (1967). Photoreactions controlling plant growth. *Proc. 17th Int. hort. Congr., 1966* **3**, 381–384.

KILBINGER, A. (1951). Die Dungung mit Kohlensaure. *Technik Bauern Gärtn., G, 10th October 1951*; 542.

KLOUGART, A. (1963). Agurkkulturens kuldioxydforsyning. *Gartner Tidende* **79**, 463–468.

KLOUGART, A. (1964). Kuldioxyd-tilførsel i vintertiden virker vækstfremmende på salat. *Gartner Tidende* **80**, 18–20.

LAKE, J. V. (1966). Measurement and control of the rate of carbon dioxide assimilation by glasshouse crops. *Nature, Lond.* **209**, 97–98.

LISTER, A. B. (1917). Carbon dioxide control of greenhouse air. *Rep. exp. Res. Stn. Cheshunt, 1916*, 9.

OWEN, O. and WILLIAMS, P. H. (1923). Carbon dioxide in relation to glasshouse crops. Part II. The preparation of an atmosphere rich in carbon dioxide. *Ann. appl. Biol.* **10**, 318–325.

OWEN, O., SMALL, T. and WILLIAMS, P. H. (1926). Carbon dioxide in relation to glasshouse crops. Part III. The effect of enriched atmospheres on tomatoes and cucumbers. *Ann. appl. Biol.* **13**, 560–576.

PRESTON, W. H. Jr. and LINK, C. B. (1958). Use of 2,4-dichlorobenzyltributyl phosphonium chloride to dwarf plants. *Pl. Physiol., Lancaster* Suppl. 33, XLIX.

RIDDELL, J. A., HAGEMAN, H. A., J'ANTHONY, C. M. and HUBBARD, W. L. (1962). Retardation of plant growth by a new group of chemicals. *Science, N.Y.* **136**, 391.

SMALL, T. and WHITE, H. L. (1930). Carbon dioxide in relation to glasshouse crops. Part IV. The effect on tomatoes of an enriched atmosphere maintained by means of a stove. *Ann. appl. Biol.* **17**, 81–89.

STOUGHTON, R. H. (1930). Apparatus for the growing of plants in a controlled environment. *Ann. appl. Biol.* **17**, 90–106.

TIMMIS, L. B. (1923). Investigations upon the fertilising effects of carbon dioxide. *Rep. exp. Res. Stn Cheshunt, 1922*, 57–65.

TOLBERT, N. E. (1960). (2-chloroethyl) trimethylammonium chloride and related compounds as plant growth substances. II. Effect on growth of wheat. *Pl. Physiol., Lancaster*, **35**, 380–385.

Tso, T. C. (1964). Plant growth inhibition by some fatty acids and their analogues. *Nature, Lond.* **202**, 511–512.

Went, F. W. (1957). "The experimental control of plant growth". Waltham, Mass.: Chronica Botanica.

Wilson, A. R. (1937). Apparatus for growing plants under controlled environmental conditions. *Ann. appl. Biol.* **24**, 911–931.

Wittwer, W. H. and Robb, W. M. (1964). Carbon dioxide enrichment of greenhouse atmospheres for food crop production. *Econ. Bot.* **18**, 34–56.

*Introduction 2*

# Control of crop processes

J. WARREN WILSON

*Glasshouse Crops Research Institute, Littlehampton, Sussex, England*

## I. Control of glasshouse crop production

### A. Environmental control in the glasshouse

The annual yield of glasshouse crops is roughly three times that of field crops, expressed as dry matter per unit area of land (Table I). The contrast is greater for fresh weight yields, since glasshouse products tend to have

**Table I**

Yields, values and water contents for some crops in the United Kingdom

|  | Yield as dry matter ($g\ m^{-2}\ year^{-1}$) | Value per unit dry weight (*pence* $g^{-1}$) | Water content per unit dry weight ($g\ g^{-1}$) |
|---|---|---|---|
| Field crops |  |  |  |
| Wheat (grain) | 400 | 0·003 | 0·1 |
| Sugar beet (sugar) | 600 | 0·004 | 0·0 |
| Potato (tuber) | 700 | 0·01 | 3·0 |
| Apple (fruit) | 400 | 0·04 | 4·0 |
| Protected crop |  |  |  |
| Mushroom (fruiting body) | 34,000 | 0·4 | 9·0 |
| Glasshouse crops |  |  |  |
| Tomato (fruit) | 1100 | 0·5 | 19·0 |
| Chrysanthemum (pot plant) | 1800 | 0·6 | 6·0 |

7

higher water contents. The mushroom is somewhat comparable to glass-house crops in being grown in a protected environment; its high yield per unit land area is partly due to the stacking of trays, often in four layers.

Whereas agricultural crops are grown mainly for their nutritional value, this is of little significance in glasshouse crops, which are grown largely for the attraction of their flavour and appearance. For these qualities, the consumer pays 10–100 times as much for glasshouse produce as for the produce of field crops in this country (dry matter basis).

These high values reflect the cost of providing a large measure of en-vironmental control. Control of temperature, allowing year-round pro-duction of high value crops, is perhaps most important. In a modern glasshouse the control system can regulate temperature within $\pm 1°C$— except when ambient temperature is excessive—and the need for such precision is indicated by the estimate (Calvert, 1971) that a 1°C difference in mean temperature can alter net returns on a tomato crop by about 25 p $m^{-2}$ (£1000 per acre). Other factors which can be controlled in the glass-house are:

(a) Carbon dioxide concentration: a level of about 2 g $m^{-3}$ (three times ambient) is often used for glasshouse vegetables, and raises tomato yields by some 40% (Calvert and Slack, 1971).

(b) Water supply is independent of rainfall, and automatic irrigation can provide control of both water and nutrient supply; some control of atmospheric humidity is also possible.

(c) Daylength control, by artificial lighting and blackout covers, allows programmed production of photoperiodically sensitive crops.

More sophisticated light-dependent control systems are now available for regulating temperature, humidity and carbon dioxide concentration in relation to prevailing light (Bowman, 1972).

The degree of environmental control that is commercially worthwhile in the glasshouse depends on its cost, on the responses of the crop, and on an understanding of these responses without which optimal control settings are not known. The present need is for progress not in control engineering —efficient systems have been devised for controlling the glasshouse en-vironment—but in crop science, since knowledge of crop responses to the various environmental factors is not yet adequate for informed com-mercial exploitation of the available environmental control systems.

## B. *Limitation of crop production by daylight*

The major climatic factor not controlled in the glasshouse is light. At present supplementary artificial lighting costs too much to be commercially worthwhile except in certain marginal cases, such as in propagation and in chrysanthemum flower production in midwinter (Canham *et al.*, 1969). Accordingly, since light is the source of energy and the ultimate limitation to crop yield, it is critically important to make efficient use of daylight falling on the glasshouse. Efficiency depends on glasshouse structure, setting of the glasshouse environment, cultural practice and genotype.

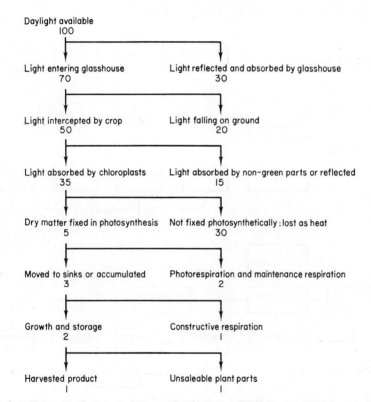

**Fig. 1.** Efficiency of use of photosynthetically-active light energy in annual production of harvestable dry matter by a glasshouse crop.

At present, glasshouse crops seldom achieve more than 1% efficiency in using light energy for the production of the energy-rich plant material that is harvested. Substantial losses occur at various stages in the process, as roughly indicated in Fig. 1. It is the task of the crop scientist to identify limiting or controlling factors at each stage and, through an understanding of the control of the chain of processes, to find ways of relieving limitations and increasing efficiency.

# II. Control systems

Thus the crop scientist seeks to understand the control systems that determine crop performance, while the glasshouse engineer is concerned with control systems that determine glasshouse environment. The operation of control systems of both glasshouse and crop can be formally analysed in the same way (e.g. Machin, 1964; Wilkins, 1966).

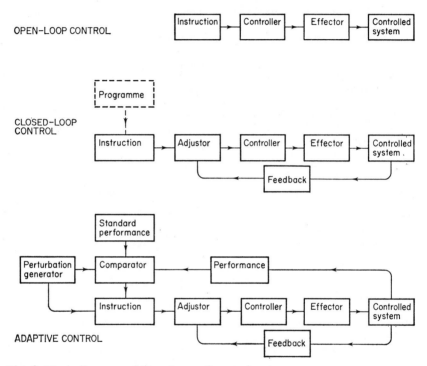

**Fig. 2.** Block diagrams of three types of control system.

Figure 2 illustrates three important types of system:

*Open-loop* control can be exemplified by the control of carbon dioxide concentration in a glasshouse by injection of carbon dioxide at a constant rate. A certain dial setting or "instruction" as to the rate and duration of carbon dioxide flow determines the position of a valve which is the "controller". The source of energy for the carbon dioxide injection may come from the storage under pressure of liquid carbon dioxide which can be distributed as a gas through pipes, and this forms the "effector", injecting carbon dioxide into the "controlled system", i.e. the glasshouse atmosphere. A limitation of open-loop control is that it will maintain a constant level in the controlled system only if there are no modifying factors. If parts of the system vary, the level will vary; in the example quoted, the carbon dioxide concentration will change with carbon dioxide pressure, valve wear, and air change rate of the glasshouse.

*Closed-loop* (feedback) control tends to counteract such variations. A feedback signal indicating the actual level in the controlled system, for example air temperature in the glasshouse, is compared with the command signal corresponding to the "instruction". This comparison by the "adjustor" yields an error signal which actuates the controller. In glasshouse heating the thermostatic control effects changes in the flow of steam or hot water, correcting for departures from the set temperature level no matter what their cause. The instructions can be modified by a "programme", for instance to give different day and night temperatures or a temperature setting dependent on prevailing light.

*Adaptive* (hill-climbing) control incorporates a "perturbation generator" which makes small changes in the setting of the instructions, and a "comparator" which compares some measure of the performance of the system with a standard performance or with the value at a previous moment; if the performance is improved the comparator incorporates the appropriate change in the instructions. Such a system has been proposed by Lake (1966) for optimizing glasshouse temperature and carbon dioxide concentration so as to maximize crop photosynthesis.

The examples quoted refer to control of environment, but the same types of control system operate widely in plants. The open-loop system is exemplified by the control of photosynthetic rate by atmospheric carbon dioxide concentration, or by the limitation of metabolic activity by substrate level. Biological complexity is so great that such open-loop systems will not usually result in control at a constant value; however, they are an important component of the whole complex. Goodwin (1963) distinguishes "weak interactions" for non-specific, open-loop control of metabolic patterns through competition for substrates, and "strong interactions" in which there is feedback control by specific substances. Such closed-loop systems may operate at the metabolic level by repression of enzyme synthesis, by end-product inhibition, or by induction (Bayliss, 1966; Lewis, 1966; Filner, 1969). The quantitative treatment of such metabolic control systems has been discussed by Goodwin and others, both for simple and for complex interacting systems, in terms of pool sizes, concentrations, equilibrium constants and rates of synthesis, using kinetic theory.

Closed-loop systems are also found operating in hormonal control. A further example is in the control of plant water status by stomatal aperture, for which a number of models have been developed (e.g. Hopmans, 1971) and have provided an explanation of observed oscillations in stomatal aperture through delays in a feedback control comparable to the "hunting" that arises in inanimate closed-loop systems. Many of the control systems in plants seem to be concerned with homeostasis, that is, the maintenance of relatively constant internal conditions and organization in spite of changes in the external environment.

Adaptive control is represented in the plant population by genetic adaptation, in which perturbations result from environmental and genetic change, and natural selection of fitter individuals up-dates the genetic instructions.

A further important type of control system in plants is involved in "determination", that is, a lasting change in character during the life of a cell, organ or plant: the induction of flowering and the induction of polarity are examples. Such phenomena can perhaps be treated as threshold or unstable control systems. They may be less common in engineering, but parallels can be found in protective cut-out or abort mechanisms.

Although this section has discussed similarities between the control systems of engineering and biology, there is a difference in approach between the glasshouse engineer and the crop scientist. The engineer designs a control system for a particular purpose, using components with known characteristics, and the success of the system can be assessed against the required performance. The crop scientist, on the other hand, seeks to identify the control systems existing in the intact plant, and to discover how they operate; he may find it hard to identify the components and characterize their properties, particularly as the techniques available are crude and tend to modify the characteristics of the components, e.g. surgery, heat, and chemical treatments. Moreover, the effectiveness of biological control systems can be assessed only in teleological terms related to homeostasis or selective advantage: no particular purpose or performance is specified as in the engineering system.

However, both engineer and crop scientist aim to understand the properties and interactions of the components in the control systems that they deal with, so as to predict behaviour under specified conditions, and so as to improve performance.

# III. Crop processes

Processes in the crop or plant can be described in terms of two basic activities:

(a) Physical transport, resulting in change in structure.
(b) Chemical conversion, resulting in change in composition.

Changes under both headings are intimately dependent on energy transfer, but this aspect is not considered here.

It is useful to distinguish between two components of physical transport:

(a) Movement within the plant, i.e. translocation.

(b) Exchange between environment and plant, e.g. salt and water uptake, transpiration, carbon dioxide exchange, and death.

The second component involves change in total plant weight, whereas the first does not.

The change in weight $M$ for a particular chemical substance in a particular part of the plant is thus given by:

$$M = E_g - E_l + T_g - T_l + C_g - C_l \tag{1}$$

representing gains and losses by influx from and efflux to the environment $(E_g, E_l)$, import and export by translocation $(T_g, T_l)$, and synthesis and utilization by chemical conversion $(C_g, C_l)$.

For example, the balance of gain and loss for carbon dioxide in a leaf will depend on carbon dioxide uptake from the air $(E_g)$ and efflux to the air $(E_l)$, a small amount of carbon dioxide imported in solution in the transpiration stream $(T_g)$, respiratory production of carbon dioxide $(C_g)$, and utilisation of carbon dioxide in chemical conversions among which photosynthesis will be dominant $(C_l)$. The rate of each process in such a balance is likely to be controlled by a number of factors.

In theory a balance of this type could be stated for each substance in each part of a plant, even down to organelle level. Obviously, the whole interacting system is exceedingly complex. For useful progress it is necessary to simplify the treatment, and various methods can be used: it can be based on net gain (or loss) through exchange, translocation or conversion, rather than on separate values of gain and loss; it can be based on major parts of the plant, or on the entire plant in which case the translocation terms vanish; it can be based on broad chemical categories, e.g. structural materials or soluble nitrogen compounds, instead of single substances; or it can be confined to certain parts of the plant or certain substances, neglecting other parts or substances.

# IV. The concept of source and sink

## A. Definitions

Discussions of crop processes sometimes employ the concept of source and sink. However, these two terms are seldom given clear definitions, they have been used in various senses, and there are no agreed units of measurement for them. This section attempts to clarify the use of these terms, and to suggest how they might be defined in a quantitative manner allowing measurement.

The terms source and sink refer broadly to gain and loss. Though applied in certain contexts to gain or loss of energy, their use by plant scientists is usually restricted to gain or loss of matter of a specified type. The terms may be applied to the respiratory gain and photosynthetic loss of carbon dioxide by air at various levels in the crop canopy (e.g. Denmead and McIlroy, 1971), or to gain and loss of any particular substances within the plant (e.g. salts: Sutcliffe, 1962); but the most usual application refers to the gain or loss of "assimilates" in a broad sense.

In the context of assimilates, three criteria seem to be used for defining sources and sinks:

*a. Transport.* Sources are regions that export assimilates, while sinks import them. An early use of these terms was by Mason and Maskell (1928), who discussed the transport of sugar down concentration gradients from source to sink. Though it is now known that translocation may involve movement up concentration gradients, the terms are still widely used in relation to the direction of translocation, especially long-distance translocation.

*b. Morphology.* Because mature leaves tend to be associated with production and export of assimilate, whereas other parts—roots, meristems, fruits and storage organs during their accumulation phase—tend to be associated with import and utilization of assimilate, the terms source and sink are applied to particular parts of the plant. Thorne (1971) equates the sink with storage organs alone. Some difficulty may arise with such morphological definitions, since a single organ may simultaneously import and export assimilate, and produce and utilize assimilate. At different stages of development, or even at different times of day, one or other process may dominate.

*c. Metabolism.* Metabolic activities underlie the above criteria. Sources produce assimilate, by photosynthesis or by mobilization of stored materials, while sinks utilize assimilate in respiration and growth (and in storage according to some definitions). This is stressed in the use of the phrase "metabolic sink" (e.g. Beevers, 1969). It is thus possible to define source and sink in metabolic terms, and this basis is implied where, for example, the sink strength of planktonic algae is discussed in relation to their photosynthetic rate (Lake and Anderson, 1970).

The results of applying these three different criteria in defining sources and sinks for assimilate are often somewhat similar, but are not always identical, and this—coupled with failure to indicate which criterion is used—may cause confusion.

In an attempt to find a definition that can be generally applied and permits measurement, it is here proposed to define sources and sinks in terms of losses and gains of a particular substance in a particular plant part.

Recognizing that a plant part may act as both source and sink simultaneously (or at least over a period of time), source–sink status is represented by sign, defining source as positive and sink as negative. Then, using the symbols of equation (1), source–sink status can be defined for a particular substance in terms of either transport or metabolism:

*Transport*   Source–sink status $= (E_1 - E_g) + (T_1 - T_g)$   (2)

*Metabolism*   Source–sink status $= C_g - C_1$   (3)

The change in weight of the substance within a given plant part is then equal to the difference

$$(C_g - C_1) - \{(E_1 - E_g) + (T_1 - T_g)\}$$

For example, in the case of a source in which the amount of substance synthesized is equal to the amount exported, and there are no other gains or losses, the change in weight is zero. Information on the net change in weight provides only limited understanding without a knowledge of the magnitudes of the components.

Because the terms "source" and "sink" have usually been applied to assimilates, some unfamiliar statements result from application of these terms—as defined above—to the metabolism of other substances. For example, a potato tuber growing on the parent plant is metabolically a sink for sugars and a source for starch and cellulose, but when the mature tuber is sprouting it is a metabolic sink for starch and a source for sugars. This extension of source–sink terminology to the metabolism of substances other than assimilates, though unfamiliar, may help to provide a framework for full quantitative description of the interaction of metabolism and transport for the various types of substance in the plant.

The treatment so far has been non-committal as to whether the symbols refer to quantities, rates or relative rates. To define the terms further, it is proposed (Warren Wilson, 1967) that:

source strength $=$ source size $\times$ source activity   (4)

sink strength   $=$ sink size $\times$ sink activity   (5)

Here "strength" refers to the absolute rate of change in weight of a substance for a plant part (or plant or unit area of stand), and "size" is measured in terms of the weight, area or other appropriate characteristic. Watson (1971) defines "sink strength" for assimilate on the basis of unit land area, but assumes a non-limiting supply of photosynthate: a situation termed "potential sink strength" by Warren Wilson (1967). Watson also proposes "sink capacity" for the integral of sink strength over the period of its activity.

In equations (4) and (5), "strength" is the relevant measure for considering the balance of gain and loss of the various plant parts, while its resolution into "size" and "activity" is useful in interpreting source–sink relations when these are defined in metabolic terms (equation 3). The same components may be helpful also when definition is in transport terms (equation 2), but in this case it may be useful to consider the flux (which, in the case of a simple system with one source and one sink, is equal in magnitude to source strength and sink strength) as proportional to the difference in "potential" between source and sink for the substance under examination, divided by the resistance to transport. This relationship is commonly applied to transport of carbon dioxide and water in the plant, and has been extended to the transport of assimilates (Mason and Maskell, 1928).

The following sections consider source–sink concepts in terms of metabolism, not transport.

## B. *A practical application*

As an example, these concepts can be applied to the case of the metabolism of assimilates in an entire plant. By considering the plant as a unit, translocation terms vanish. As a further simplification, and to allow the treatment to be related in a later section to traditional growth-analysis measures, photosynthesis and respiration are not separated but instead the dry weight gain of "net assimilation" is regarded as equal to (photosynthesis — respiration), ignoring mineral nutrient uptake.

In Fig. 3, rectangular boxes represent amounts of material, arrows represent metabolic flows, and valve symbols represent the control of flow rates (cf. de Wit *et al.*, 1970). The source of assimilates ($C_g$) is net assimilation, and the sink for them ($C_l$) is taken to be structural growth, i.e. permanent gain in the essential plant structure.

As indicated earlier, storage can be treated as a sink for assimilates; this course may well be appropriate when specialized storage organs are involved. However, the present analysis will be applied to young plants without storage organs, and storage is treated not as a sink with defined activity but as a pool of assimilates which increases when source strength exceeds sink strength and decreases when sink strength exceeds source strength.

If such source–sink imbalance results in a sufficient rise or fall in the proportion of storage to structural materials, source or sink activity will be depressed to a level at which equilibrium is regained. This statement again is a simplification, particularly in suggesting that either source or sink or neither is limiting. There may often be some limitation by both, and by the translocation system; but quantitative evidence on this point is inadequate.

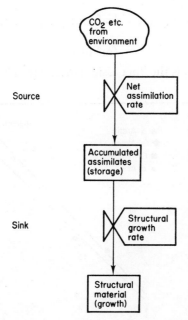

**Fig. 3.** Flow diagram of metabolic production and utilization of net assimilates.

In terms of the equations used above:

$$M \quad = \quad C_g - C_1$$

storage = net assimilation − structural growth        (6)

Warren Wilson (1967) gives two examples of the application of this balance to experimental data.

# V. Control of source and sink strengths for assimilates

## A. Source strength

Leaf area provides a generally accepted measure of the size of the assimilating system, and some justification for this lies in the dependence of photosynthesis on light interception and carbon dioxide uptake, both surface phenomena. Accordingly the general statement:

source strength = source size × source activity

can be interpreted as follows for the particular case of assimilates in the entire plant:

rate of assimilation per plant = leaf area per plant × rate of assimilation per unit leaf area

(g plant$^{-1}$ day$^{-1}$)            (m$^2$ plant$^{-1}$)         (g m$^{-2}$ day$^{-1}$)

The right-hand term is the "net assimilation rate" ($E_A$) of growth analysis.

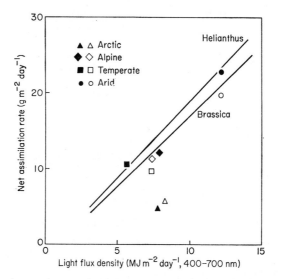

**Fig. 4.** Dependence of net assimilation rate on light flux density for young plants of *Helianthus annuus* and of *Brassica rapa* and *B. napus* grown widely spaced on nutrient culture. Regression lines are fitted to data obtained at various times of year in two localities; symbols indicate mean values at the height of the growing season for (closed symbols) *Helianthus* and (open symbols) *Brassica* in four climatic regions.

The source activity ($E_A$) depends on many internal and external factors, but the foremost of these is light flux density. Figure 4 shows near proportionality between $E_A$ and light up to the highest flux densities, for plants of two genera grown in various climates. Two points substantially below the normal relationship are for plants growing in an arctic climate; it is suggested that the cold conditions depressed sink activity to a level at which accumulation of stored assimilates depressed source activity. High sugar concentrations and other observations support this interpretation (Warren Wilson, 1966).

# B. Sink strength

There are no generally accepted methods of measuring the rate of utilization of assimilates in structural growth, or the size of the growing system. However, in the case of actively growing cells or tissues, as in meristems, it may be acceptable as an approximation to regard the whole system as being involved and to interpret the general statement:

$$\text{sink strength} = \text{sink size} \times \text{sink activity}$$

in terms of total dry matter:

$$\underset{\text{(g day}^{-1})}{\text{absolute growth rate}} = \underset{\text{(g)}}{\text{dry weight}} \times \underset{\text{(g g}^{-1}\text{ day}^{-1})}{\text{relative growth rate}}$$

A major aim of the crop scientist is to maximize the relative growth rate ($R_W$) of useful sinks. It is noteworthy that the sink activity for apical meristems of active crop plants tends to be lower than the sink activity for unicellular plants and especially bacteria (Table II), and it is interesting to speculate on possible reasons for this restriction:

(a) Transport of oxygen and metabolites by diffusion is expected to become more limiting as size increases; however, there seems to be no clear evidence that they are generally deficient in meristems of higher plants.

(b) If protein can be regarded as a measure of the growing machinery, it may be relevant that bacteria have relatively high protein contents.

(c) Differentiation within the multicellular meristem presumably requires that at least some parts of the meristem have sink activity below the potential level in the absence of organizing influences.

Table II includes values of $R_W$ for entire plants. A substantial proportion of the dry weight of such plants may represent storage rather than structural

### Table II

Comparative values of relative growth rate
(Data from Williams, 1960; Whaley, 1961; Grime, 1965; and others)

|  | Typical range $(g\,g^{-1}\,day^{-1})$ |
|---|---|
| Bacteria | 5  –20 |
| Unicellular algae | 1  – 4 |
| Root apex | 1  – 3 |
| Stem apex and young leaves | 0·3 – 1·0 |
| Embryo | 0·2 – 0·8 |
| Young plants (sun species, arable weeds, crop plants) | 0·1 – 0·4 |
| Young plants (shade species) | 0·02– 0·04 |

material, and the appropriate measure of sink activity is not $R_W$ for total dry weight but $R_G$ for the dry weight of material incorporated in structural growth.

However, when appropriate data for obtaining $R_G$ are not available, it may be permissible to accept $R_W$ as an estimate of sink activity, though only under "steady-state" conditions in which growth is not accompanied by change in plant constitution. Two points seem to give some justification for this approximation:

Firstly, provided the proportions of structural and storage material in total dry weight remain constant, $R_G = R_W$.

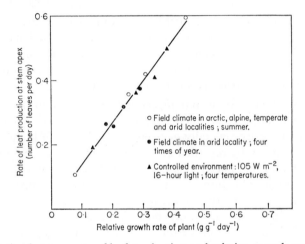

**Fig. 5.** Relation between rate of leaf production and relative growth rate for young plants of *Brassica rapa* and *B. napus* grown widely spaced on nutrient culture.

Secondly, data for young plants of *Brassica rapa* and *B. napus* (Fig. 5) show $R_W$ to be directly proportional to the rate of leaf production at the apex ("production" refers to attainment of 1 mm length). If the rate of leaf production can be regarded as a measure of the activity of a meristematic sink, this relationship supports the use of $R_W$ as a measure of sink activity. The same relationship has been found in *Helianthus annuus*. The data for both species are based on widely spaced plants in strong light. In this situation it seems likely that sink activity—whether of the apex or whole plant—is limited not by assimilate but by internal metabolic controls: it approximates to the genetically determined "potential sink activity" for the prevailing temperature.

The dependence of sink activity on temperature is stressed in Fig. 6 by the relation between $R_W$ and temperature for well-illuminated plants of

*Helianthus annuus*; the data indicate that the trend in the field is similar to that in controlled environments where temperature is the only variable.

For these plants, it seems that while light exerts dominant environmental control of source strength, temperature is dominant in the control of sink strength.

The existence of large differences in $R_W$ between genotypes (last two lines of Table II) suggests that it should be possible to breed cultivars with increased potential for growth. This is indicated also by the differences in $R_W$ observed among local populations within a species, e.g. *Phalaris tuberosa* (Cooper and McWilliam, 1966). However, comparison of $R_W$ (g g$^{-1}$ day$^{-1}$) for wild and cultivated tomatoes grown under glasshouse conditions in

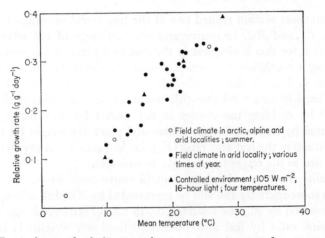

**Fig. 6.** Dependence of relative growth rate on temperature for young plants of *Helianthus annuus* grown widely spaced on nutrient culture.

summer suggests that breeding has not always achieved increase in potential for growth:

Wild

| | |
|---|---|
| *Lycopersicon pimpinellifolium* | 0·31 |
| *Lycopersicon esculentum* var. *cerasiforme* | 0·28 |

Cultivated

| | |
|---|---|
| *Lycopersicon esculentum* cv. "Eurocross" | 0·29 |
| *Lycopersicon esculentum* cv. "Kingley Cross" | 0·30 |
| *Lycopersicon esculentum* cv. "Minibelle" | 0·28 |

Higher sink activity may be associated with adaptation to higher temperatures; for example, Whaley (1961) refers to a strain of *Chlorella pyrenoidosa* which had about the same $R_W$ (1–2 g g$^{-1}$ day$^{-1}$) as other strains at their optimum temperature of 25 °C, but for which $R_W$ continued to rise with temperature up to a maximum of 6·2 g g$^{-1}$ day$^{-1}$ at 39°C. The potential for high temperature provided by the glasshouse offers a means of exploiting such genotypes with high sink strength, so long as source strength is adequate to support the sink.

# VI. Source and sink for assimilate related to growth analysis

## A. "Steady-state" plants

The previous section related two of the traditional measures of growth analysis, $E_A$ and $R_W$, to source and sink activities of the whole plant. Justification for this is simplest in the case of a plant that is conceived as containing a negligible proportion of stored assimilates. In this case the source strength (assimilates produced) is equal to the sink strength (assimilates utilized in structural growth), and the source and sink activities are obtained by dividing the change in dry matter by the "factory sizes", represented by leaf area for the source and plant dry weight for the sink. In this situation the leaf area ratio ($F_A$), i.e. leaf area/plant dry weight, can be regarded as the ratio of source size to sink size.

In reality, however, all plants contain stored assimilates. Accordingly, whereas source activity can still be represented by $E_A$, sink activity should be represented by $R_G$, the relative growth rate of structural material, and source–sink ratio by leaf area/plant structural dry weight. It has been noted that $R_W = R_G$ in "steady-state" plants in which the ratio of storage to structural material is constant; on the other hand, the presence of storage material will depress $F_A$ to a value below that of leaf area/plant structural dry weight.

This can be illustrated in terms of either leaf area/plant weight, or more simply its reciprocal plant weight/leaf area (Fig. 7a). In a simple model, the relative leaf area growth rate ($R_A$) is assumed to be equal to $R_G$, and plant weight is regarded as composed of two fractions, a basic structural fraction and a larger or smaller proportion of storage material. Then for any given sink activity $R_G$ ($= R_W = R_A$), plant weight/leaf area rises in proportion to source activity ($E_A$), owing to accumulation of stored assimilates. The proportionality varies with $R$; increased utilization in structural growth results in less storage. Limiting values of plant weight/leaf area can be expected at which stored material is at a minimum ("source limiting") or is at a maximum concentration at which further accumulation is not possible ("sink limiting").

Figure 7b expresses the same relationships for the reciprocal, leaf area/plant weight.

Obviously this model oversimplifies a complex system, but it nevertheless helps to explain certain observations. Hughes and Evans (1962) pointed out an "inverse relationship" between leaf area/leaf weight and $E_A$ in *Impatiens parviflora* plants. Since leaf weight/plant weight varies little, leaf area/leaf weight is closely proportional to leaf area/plant weight. There

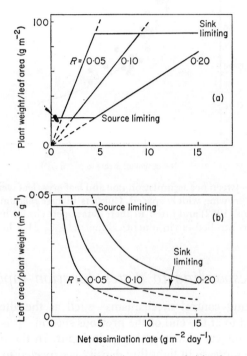

**Fig. 7.** Relations between net assimilation rate and (a) plant weight/leaf area, (b) leaf area/plant weight according to simple model proposed in the text.

is an obvious similarity between the curves in Fig. 7b and Fig. 8, which shows (a) data of Hughes and Evans, (b) an inverse curve fitted to these data and extrapolated to higher values of $E_A$, (c) additional data for plants at four light levels in controlled-environment cabinets, which agree with the curve except perhaps at low $E_A$ ("source limited"). Hughes and Evans see this inverse relationship as important in determining the comparative constancy of $R_W$ over a range of medium light intensities, but the reverse interpretation is proposed here, that differences in $E_A$ resulting from differences in light have no direct effect on $R$, with the consequence that the constancy of $R$ determines this inverse relationship through more or less accumulation of stored assimilates.

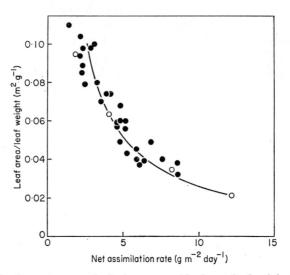

**Fig. 8.** Relation between net assimilation rate and leaf area/leaf weight for *Impatiens parviflora* plants growing widely spaced. Curve is inverse relationship proposed by Hughes and Evans (1962) and fitted to their data; open circles indicate values for plants grown in controlled-environment cabinets (14°C, 24-h light) at four light flux densities.

# B. *Plants responding to a step function input*

In investigating control mechanisms—such as the alternative control systems referred to at the end of the previous section—it is often revealing to examine the effects of a step change in input. In the present case, for example, a step increase in light flux density is expected to increase source strength without (if the model proposed is valid) changing sink strength, and as a consequence the proportion of storage material will increase. If so, the "steady-state" situation with $R_G = R_W$ which was assumed in the previous section will not apply while the plant is responding to the change.

In the experiment described below, an increase in light flux density from 11 to 75 W m$^{-2}$ was applied to young, widely spaced plants of *Impatiens parviflora* in a controlled-environment cabinet. Source–sink relations are analysed in terms of the balance in equation (6):

$$\text{storage} = \text{net assimilation} - \text{structural growth}$$

The "storage" fraction of dry weight is measured as the material removed by hydrolysis with 0·1 M sulphuric acid at 100°C for 1 h followed by washing, and the residue is taken to be the materials of "structural growth". This procedure for separating the two fractions is arbitrary and imperfect, as are alternative methods; it is comparable to the acid hydrolysis technique recommended by Priestley (1965).

Growth parameters were calculated as follows:

$$R_W = 2(W_2 - W_1)/t(W_1 + W_2)$$
$$R_A = 2(A_2 - A_1)/t(A_1 + A_2)$$
$$R_G = 2(G_2 - G_1)]/t(G_1 + G_2)$$
$$R_{W(G)} = 2(G_2 - G_1)/t(W_1 + W_2)$$
$$R_{W(S)} = 2(S_2 - S_1)/t(W_1 + W_2)$$
$$E_A = 2(W_2 - W_1)/t(A_1 + A_2)$$

where $W$, $G$, $S$ and $A$ represent respectively the dry weights of total, structural and storage material and the leaf area, and subscripts indicate initial and final values for a sampling interval of duration $t$. These linear equations were preferred to the usual logarithmic equations because (a) they are simpler, (b) for plants undergoing transient changes in components the validity of the logarithmic equations is reduced, and (c) discrepancies between values yielded by the two equations are small when short intervals result in small differences between initial and final quantities.

The results (Fig. 9 a–d) show that the seven-fold increase in light caused a step increase in $E_A$ to a new constant level about three times the original value. $R_W$ was also increased initially; however, there occurred a gradual fall in $R_W$ and $F_A$, apparently approaching a new equilibrium with $R_W$ near its original value. Such responses have been observed previously, and interpreted as an "adaptation" by which change in $F_A$ restores $R_W$.

Such an interpretation implies a closed-loop, homeostatic, control system; Hughes (1965) represents diagrammatically a negative feedback control of leaf area/leaf weight by $E_A$, maintaining an inverse correlation. The interpretation offered by the treatment in this paper is an open-loop control, in which increased light raises source activity without affecting sink activity; the resulting accumulation of storage materials depresses $F_A$ and $R_W$, since storage materials are included in the denominator of both expressions.

An attempt to simulate this response is shown in Fig. 9 e–h. Values were selected to fit approximately the experimental data: $E_A = 3.8$ and $11.2$ g m$^{-2}$ day$^{-1}$ before and after the light increase; $R_G = 0.188$ g g$^{-1}$ day$^{-1}$ and $R_A = 0.188$ m$^{-2}$ m$^{-2}$ day$^{-1}$ throughout; leaf area/plant structural dry weight $= 0.0855$ m$^2$ g$^{-1}$. The model adequately simulates the observed changes in $R_W$ and $F_A$.

However, there is some discrepancy between Figs 9c and 9g. These graphs divide $R_W$ into two components: storage materials ($R_{W(S)}$) and materials of structural growth ($R_{W(G)}$). Both experiment and simulation indicate that the step increase in light and $E_A$ was associated with a large increase in $R_{W(S)}$ but little change in $R_{W(G)}$. Subsequently, however, the observed $R_{W(G)}$ did not decline as did the simulated $R_{W(G)}$. It can be shown that this difference arises because the simple model assumes $R_A$ and $R_G$ to be unaffected by the light increase, whereas the experimental data indicate some decrease in $R_A$ and increase in $R_G$.

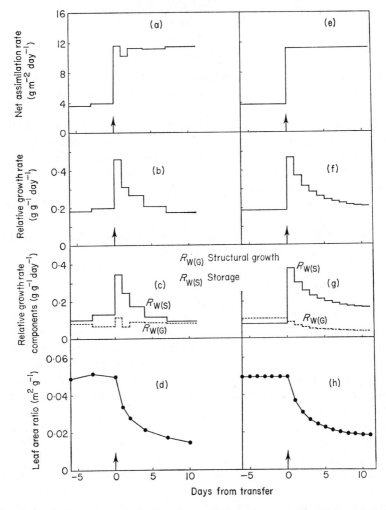

**Fig. 9.** (a–d) Growth analysis for plants of *Impatiens parviflora* in a controlled-environment cabinet (23 °C, 24-h light), transferred at day 0 from 11–75 W m$^{-2}$; (e–h) simulated growth using simple model described in the text.

The effect of this increase in $R_G$ was that by the end of the experiment, when a new "steady-state" had been approached, the storage–structural balance had nearly returned to that before the light increase.

It is uncertain how the increase in $R_G$ was achieved, but outgrowth of axillaries, increased activity of root and cambial meristems, and thickening of leaves may all have contributed. Since change in leaf area/leaf weight was roughly similar to that in leaf area/plant weight, it seems likely that "structural" material was laid down in relatively mature leaves, though it is doubtful whether this was necessary for the proper functioning of the leaves; for example, cell wall thickening in excess of that needed for mechanical support may have contributed to the substantial increase in leaf structural weight/area.

This suggests that three major categories should perhaps be recognized, even if not fully distinct in function or by chemical analysis:

(a) Essential structural materials: necessary for normal functioning of the plant; not available for utilization.

(b) Inessential structural materials: not necessary for normal functioning; not available for utilization.

(c) Storage materials: not necessary for normal functioning; available for utilization.

There may well be a case for recognizing also a fourth category, of storage materials that are necessary for normal functioning but are not available for utilization; since Priestley (1970) has stressed that a proportion of the "resources" or storage materials must not be utilized if the plant is to remain healthy.

# VII. Conclusions

The increasing use made of the source–sink concept indicates its importance. However, as it is used in more than one context—metabolism as well as transport—clear definitions are necessary. Where the concept is applied to the metabolic gain and loss of assimilates, methods are needed for measuring not only source activity (these are available) but also sink activity (these are not well developed). Information is required on the actual and potential magnitudes of both source and sink activities and on the ways in which they, and intervening transport processes, are quantitatively controlled. It may be possible to extend growth analysis techniques so as to allow formal treatment and investigation of source–sink relations.

To achieve high crop yields it is necessary to maximize source strength by efficient light interception coupled with efficient photosynthetic conversion, which can be aided by carbon dioxide enrichment and other environmental manipulations in the glasshouse as well as by breeding for photosynthetic efficiency. Also, sink strength—particularly of harvestable parts—must be sufficient to utilize fully the assimilates produced by the source, without wasteful respiration, unnecessary storage, or excessive structural deposition. Sink strength of the crop can be raised by closer spacing, by breeding cultivars with sufficient growth potential, and (in the glasshouse) by raising the temperature. However, reasoned recommendations on these matters will be possible only when more is known of the systems controlling source and sink strength and their interrelationships.

# Acknowledgements

I am grateful to Mr D. J. Fitter, Mr S. J. Rance and Mr J. Tunney for efficient assistance in experimental work, and to many colleagues— especially the editors of this book—for helpful discussion and advice.

# References

BAYLISS, L. E. (1966). "Living Control Systems." English University Press, London.

BEEVERS, H. (1969). Metabolic sinks. *In* "Physiological Aspects of Crop Yield" (J. D. Eastin, F. A. Haskins, C. Y. Sullivan and C. H. M. van Bavel, eds), pp. 169–180. American Society of Agronomy and Crop Science Society of America, Madison, Wisconsin.

BOWMAN, G. E. (1972). Principles and progress in environmental control systems. *In* "Crop Processes in Controlled Environments" (A. R. Rees, K. E. Cockshull, D. W. Hand and R. G. Hurd, eds), pp. 63–77. Academic Press, London.

CALVERT, A. (1971). Don't economise with lower temperatures. *Comml Grow.* No. 3937, 1045.

CALVERT, A. and SLACK, G. (1971). Effects of carbon dioxide concentration on glasshouse tomatoes. *Rep. Glasshouse Crops Res. Inst.* 1970, 66–67.

CANHAM, A. E., COCKSHULL, K. E. and HUGHES, A. P. (1969). Supplementary illumination of chrysanthemums. *Comml Grow.* No. 3850, 334.

COOPER, J. P. and McWILLIAM, J. R. (1966). Climatic variation in forage grasses. II. Germination, flowering and leaf development in Mediterranean populations of *Phalaris tuberosa*. *J. appl. Ecol.* **3**, 191–212.

DENMEAD, O. T. and McILROY, I. C. (1971). Measurement of carbon dioxide exchange in the field. *In* "Plant Photosynthetic Production: Manual of Methods" (Z. Sestak, J. Catsky and P. G. Jarvis, eds), pp. 467–516. Junk, The Hague.

FILNER, P. (1969). Control of nutrient assimilation, a growth-regulating mechanism in cultured plant cells. *In* "Communication in Development"

(A. Lang, ed.), pp. 206–225. Developmental Biology Supplement 3. Academic Press, New York.

GOODWIN, B. C. (1963). "Temporal Organization in Cells." Academic Press, London.

GRIME, J. P. (1965). Shade tolerance in flowering plants. *Nature, Lond.* **208,** 161–163.

HOPMANS, P. A. M. (1971). Rhythms in stomatal opening of bean leaves. *Meded. LandbHoogesch. Wageningen* **71** (3), 1–86.

HUGHES, A. P. (1965). Plant growth and the aerial environment. IX. A synopsis of the autecology of *Impatiens parviflora. New Phytol.* **64,** 399–413.

HUGHES, A. P. and EVANS, G. C. (1962). Plant growth and the aerial environment. II. Effects of light intensity on *Impatiens parviflora. New Phytol.* **61,** 154–174.

LAKE, J. V. (1966). Measurement and control of the rate of carbon dioxide assimilation by glasshouse crops. *Nature, Lond.* **209,** 97–98.

LAKE, J. V. and ANDERSON, M. C. (1970). Dynamics of development of photosynthetic systems. *In* "Prediction and Measurement of Photosynthetic Productivity". *Proc. IBP/PP technical meeting, Trebon,* 1969. (I. Setlik, ed.), pp. 131–136. Centre for Agricultural Publishing & Documentation, Wageningen.

LEWIS, D. (1966). Molecular regulation in the cell. *In* "Regulation and Control in Living Systems" (H. Kalmus, ed.), pp. 61–80. Wiley, London.

MACHIN, K. E. (1964). Feedback theory and its application to biological systems. *In* "Homeostasis and Feedback Mechanisms" (G. M. Hughes, ed.), pp. 421–445. Cambridge University Press.

MASON, T. G. and MASKELL, E. J. (1928). Studies on the transport of carbohydrates in the cotton plant. II. The factors determining the rate and the direction of movement of sugars. *Ann. Bot. O,S.* **42,** 571–636.

PRIESTLEY, C. A. (1965). A new method for the estimation of the resources of apple trees. *J. Sci. Fd Agric.* **16,** 717–721.

PRIESTLEY, C. A. (1970). Carbohydrate storage and utilization. *In* "Physiology of Tree Crops" (L. C. Luckwill and C. V. Cutting, eds), pp. 113–126. Academic Press, London.

SUTCLIFFE, J. F. (1962). "Mineral Salts Absorption in Plants." Pergamon Press, New York.

THORNE, G. N. (1971). Physiological factors limiting the yield of arable crops. *In* "Potential Crop Production" (P. F. Wareing and J. P. Cooper, eds), pp. 143–158. Heinemann, London.

WARREN WILSON, J. (1966). An analysis of plant growth and its control in arctic environments. *Ann. Bot.* **30,** 383–402.

WARREN WILSON, J. (1967). Ecological data on dry-matter production by plants and plant communities. *In* "The Collection and Processing of Field Data" (E. F. Bradley and O. T. Denmead, eds), pp. 77–123. Wiley, New York.

WATSON, D. J. (1971). Size, structure and activity of the productive system of crops. *In* "Potential Crop Production" (P. F. Wareing and J. P. Cooper, eds), pp. 76–88. Heinemann, London.

WHALEY, W. G. (1961). Growth as a general process. *In* "Encyclopedia of Plant Physiology. XIV. Growth and Growth Substances" (W. Ruhland, ed.), pp. 71–112. Springer-Verlag, Berlin.

WILKINS, B. R. (1966). Regulation and control in engineering. *In* "Regulation and Control in Living Systems" (H. Kalmus, ed.), pp. 12–28. Wiley, London.

WILLIAMS, R. F. (1960). The physiology of growth in the wheat plant. I. Seedling growth and the pattern of growth at the shoot apex. *Aust. J. biol. Sci.* **13**, 401–428.

WIT, C. T. de, BROUWER, R. and PENNING DE VRIES, F. W. T. (1970). The simulation of photosynthetic systems. *In* "Prediction and Measurement of Photosynthetic Productivity". *Proc. IBP/PP technical meeting, Trebon*, 1969. (I. Setlik, ed.), pp. 47–70. Centre for Agricultural Publishing & Documentation, Wageningen.

*Section I*

# Controlled Environments

# I.1. Phytotrons: Past achievements and future needs

J. P. NITSCH†

*Laboratory of Multicellular Physiology, C.N.R.S., Gif-sur-Yvette, France*

## I. Introduction

Since the dedication of the first phytotron at Pasadena, Calif., 22 years ago, great hopes as well as great criticism have been generated by the erection of such laboratories throughout the world. The formal opening of the new controlled-environment facilities of the Glasshouse Crops Research Institute is an excellent occasion to try to evaluate the results which have been obtained with the help of phytotrons, and to try to foresee what the future needs will be.

All plant growers know that the climatic environment plays a determining role in the development of plants. However the extent of such a control has been discovered only through the use of artificial environments. Neither Tournois, (1914) nor Garner and Allard, (1920) would have discovered photoperiodism, had they not grown plants indoors and used, at least in part, artificial lighting. The past task of controlled-environment facilities has been to determine which factors of the environment were crucial for plant growth and to devise means to control these factors at will. In the first part we shall see how far these aims have been fulfilled. The second part will be devoted to an evaluation of some needs that may develop in the future.

† Deceased

# II. The search for the environmental factors affecting plant growth and for their control

## A. Important environmental factors and their control

Climate is a complex of variables, some of which may be closely linked (e.g. illumination and the absence of rainfall), and which may have a relatively large or relatively small effect upon plant growth. In order to disentangle each factor, artificial environments in which only one factor can be varied at a time have been extremely useful. Let us examine some examples.

### 1. Nutrition through the roots

The efforts of plant physiologists over the past 100 years have resulted in the demonstration that soil as such is not indispensable for plant growth. All that is needed are certain ions which the roots can take up, a certain balance between these ions and a proper aeration for good root functioning. Based on these principles, many different techniques have been designed for feeding plants in phytotrons. They differ in three main aspects: the supply of the fertilizing elements, the type of support for roots and the method of watering.

*a. Fertilizing elements.* In rare cases, various soil mixes with incorporated fertilizers have been used. Their chief disadvantages are the necessity for sterilizing them and the lack of precise control over plant nutrition. Thus, in general, synthetic nutrient solutions have been used. In the Gif phytotron, the formula given in Table I (which does not form precipitates) has been used for 12 years now, with excellent results on all plants, from wheat to spruce and sugarcane to orchids. The solution is prepared each day in batches of about 3000 litres by mixing in the order given stock solutions as defined in Table I. The water used may be a source of problems. Rivers nowadays contain detergents which pass through deionizing columns, as is the case with the Seine in Paris. The best method seems to be to run spring water through deionizing columns. Once purified, the water, and later the nutrient solution, should come in contact only with glass, stainless steel, or inert plastic (i.e. plastic which does not release compounds such as butylphthalate). Once made, the nutrient solution should not be exposed to light as algae may develop in it.

*b. Root-support.* To support the roots, a mixture of gravel and vermiculite (expanded mica) was used at Pasadena. Since the gravel has to be washed and its composition varies with the region of the quarry from which it has been extracted, a more uniform material is used at Gif, namely a special brand of glasswool called "Verrane", which is a borosilicate glass

## Table I

Composition of the standard nutrient solution used in the Gif phytotron for all plant species. Formula devised by Dr J. P. Nitsch

| *In* mg litre$^{-1}$ | | *In* $\mu$moles litre$^{-1}$ | |
|---|---|---|---|
| $KNO_3$ | 411 | $NO_3^-$ | 12·134 |
| $Ca(NO_3)_2.4H_2O$ | 959 | $SO_4^{--}$ | 3·272 |
| $(NH_4)_2SO_4$ | 137 | $PO_4^{---}$ | 1·007 |
| $MgSO_4.7H_2O$ | 548 | $EDTA^{----}$ | 110 |
| $KH_2PO_4$ | 137 | $BO_3^{---}$ | 50 |
| $EDTA\ Na_2Fe.2H_2O$ | 41 | $Cl^-$ | 36 |
| $H_3BO_3$ | 3 | $MoO_4^{--}$ | 0·2 |
| $KCl$ | 2·7 | $K^+$ | 5·111 |
| $MnSO_4.H_2O$ | 1·7 | $Ca^{++}$ | 4·063 |
| $ZnSO_4.7H_2O$ | 0·27 | $Mg^{++}$ | 2·223 |
| $(NH_4)_6Mo_7O_{24}.4H_2O$ | 0·27 | $NH_4^+$ | 2·077 |
| $CuSO_4.5H_2O$ | 0·13 | $Na^+$ | 110 |
| | | $Fe^{+++}$ | 110 |
| | | $Mn^{++}$ | 10 |
| | | $Zn^{++}$ | 0·9 |
| | | $Cu^{++}$ | 0·5 |

In practice, the solution is prepared as follows:

1) the tank is filled with 3650 litres of deionized water;
2) the 4 stock solutions are added in the order given with constant stirring:

Solution A: $KNO_3$ (1 kg) + $KH_2PO_4$ (0·5 kg) in 10 litres of $H_2O$.

Solution B: $MgSO_4.7H_2O$ (1 kg) + $(NH_4)_2SO_4$ (0·5 kg) in 10 litres of $H_2O$

Solution C: $Ca(NO_3)_2.4H_2O$ (4 kg) + $EDTA\ Na_2Fe$ (0·15 kg) in 10 litres of $H_2O$.

Minor elements: $KCl$ (10 g) + $H_3BO_3$ (11 g) + $MnSO_4.H_2O$ (6·2 g) + $ZnSO_4.7H_2O$ (1 g) + $(NH_4)_6Mo_7O_{24}.4H_2O$ (1 g) + $CuSO_4.5H_2O$ (0·5 g) + $H_2SO_4$ (0·5 ml) in 1 litre of $H_2O$.

manufactured in fibres of 8 $\mu$m in diameter and cut to a length of 12·5 mm. We have been using the type "EV8, L2", manufactured by C.T.A., 8 Avenue Percier, Paris. Even though this material may not be totally inert, it has the advantage of being always the same, of being sterile and

CPC E—D

of being very soft to the touch, without ever causing the skin troubles insulating brands of glasswool may generate. However, since it is transparent to light (and thus allows algal growth throughout the rooting medium), we routinely cover it with 2–5 cm of vermiculite. In this way algae develop only on the surface of the vermiculite, the rest of the root medium remaining free of them.

*c. Automatic watering.* To obtain comparable lots of plants, it is necessary to give them the same amount of nutrient at the same time. This is achieved by bringing over to each pot a small tube of black plastic through which drips the nutrient solution, once a time clock has opened a solenoid valve. Large pots may, however, require several applications of nutrient solution.

## 2. Composition of the air

The Gif phytotron conditions over 300,000 m³ of air per hour of which 100,000 m³ are constituted by fresh air taken from outside. A little over 140,000 m³ are used to cool lighting panels and their ballasts. This air needs only to be freed from dust, by passing through Poelman paper filters.

On the other hand, the composition of the air which circulates around the plants should be more accurately controlled. In the first place, it should be free of toxic gases, such as the "smog" of modern cities, the ozone which xenon arc lamps generate, or ethylene which may act on various physiological processes such as flowering, abscission, senescence, etc. In fact, it has been shown that certain lacquered copper wires which are used in ballast chokes of fluorescent tubes generate ethylene when the circuit becomes hot (Wills and Patterson, 1970).

Secondly, sufficient carbon dioxide should be available for photosynthesis. With large air renewals (2 air changes min$^{-1}$) such as those used at Gif, the carbon dioxide level has been found to remain that of the outside air. The latter however drops during the day, to rise again at night, so that devices controlling the level of carbon dioxide should also be installed. These are still expensive, and they have therefore been used only in rare cases, such as that of the German phytotron at Rauisch-Holzhausen. In this installation it is possible to enrich to a level of up to 30,000 vpm but decrease below the atmospheric level is unobtainable.

Finally the percentage of oxygen in the air may also have to be controlled, as it affects the net assimilation rate through photorespiration.

## 3. Temperature

Temperature has been one of the chief factors over which a precise control has been attempted in phytotrons.

*a. What temperature should be controlled?* Ideally, the temperature which should be known and controlled is that of the plant. This, however, proves to be an impossible task, except at night. When radiations, such as those of the sun or of an artificial light-source, strike a plant, they heat it, but in an irregular fashion, which depends on the position (exposed or shaded) and on the physiological status (actively transpiring or not) of the organ under consideration. As a consequence of the difficulty in achieving a uniform plant temperature in a given room, most installations measure and control the air temperature. In fact, if the air could be changed instantaneously and could move freely around all parts of each plant, the plant temperature would indeed stay very close to the ambient air temperature.

*b. Amounts of air needed.* Temperature gradients. In both the Pasadena and the Gif phytotrons, air is changed at the rate of two volumes per minute in the rooms receiving sunlight. This necessitates a huge air-conditioning factory.

Yet, despite such a large air renewal, temperature gradients occur in the rooms. Figure 1 gives the temperature profiles of a room in the Gif phytotron. Even with an artificial light in this room, the temperature gradient is quite marked: at 10 cm above the floor (through which the fresh air enters the room), the temperature is 14°C; at 60 cm it is 15°C; in the zone between 1·1 m and 1·5 m it is 17°C; and at 1·9 m it reaches 21°C.* Thus only in a certain zone does the air have the required temperature. As long as the plants remain under 40 cm in height, they stay in the correct temperature zone. When they become taller, however, they grow out of it. To prevent the tops from touching the ceiling, pots are lowered below 1 m from the floor. Roots are then subjected to a lower temperature, and tops (if they protrude above 1·5 m) to a higher temperature, than the official room temperature. In fact, plants approaching 2 m in height have their roots at 14°C and their tops at 21°C, a gradient of 7°C!

The air velocity in the same room at various levels is given in Fig. 2. It oscillates between 0·3 and 0·5 m sec$^{-1}$. A higher velocity, for example 1 m sec$^{-1}$, would strongly reduce the temperature gradient. Thus, if feasible, a rate of air change greater than the one used at Pasadena or at Gif

---

* As measured with a Model 60 Anemotherm Air Meter, manufactured by the Anemostat Corp. of America, Scranton, Pennsylvania, U.S.A.

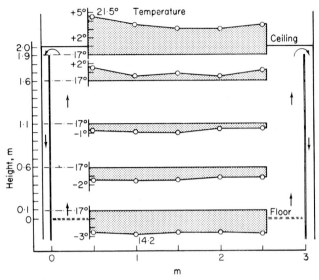

**Fig. 1.** Actual air temperatures in the 17°C room of the Gif phytotron (artificial lighting). Cross-section of the room, which is 3 m wide (abscissa). The experimental points (circles) give the measured temperatures in degrees above or below the desired 17°C at 0·1, 0·6, 1·1, 1·6 and 1·9 m above the perforated floor.

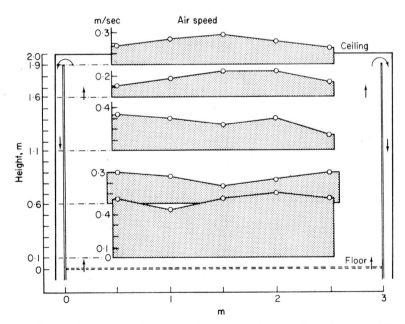

**Fig. 2.** Actual air velocities (in m sec⁻¹) at the various levels indicated in Fig. 1.

would be better for maintaining a uniform temperature throughout the room.

*c. Pattern of air movement.* To prevent draughts, the large amount of air entering each room has to be injected through a surface as large as possible, e.g. the whole floor (Went, 1957). In such a case, the floor of each room is perforated. The air ascends vertically and leaves the room through openings placed on the walls as high as possible (Fig. 3). Such a pattern of air movement tends to accentuate the temperature gradient as the shaded portions of the plants receive the cool air first.

Injecting air through the floor has other disadvantages which are due

**Fig. 3.** A view of an artificially-lit room of the Gif phytotron. (Photo courtesy C.N.R.S.)

mainly to the fact that, under the perforated floor, there must be a solid floor. Through the perforations of the first level fall water and miscellaneous debris which have to be removed. A thorough cleaning of the lower floor is often difficult to perform (as it is at Gif) and accumulations of moist debris constitute a source of pathogenic infections. In addition, the reservoir of moisture thus formed impairs the quality of the humidity control in the rooms.

A single, non-perforated floor is thus preferable, but this poses the problem of injecting uniformly large volumes of air into the room. At Wageningen, air enters the room through one side wall, moves horizontally across the room, and leaves through the other side wall. The air speed is 0·5 m sec$^{-1}$ at plant level and the temperature gradient in a room with artificial illumination has been found to differ by several degrees C on the

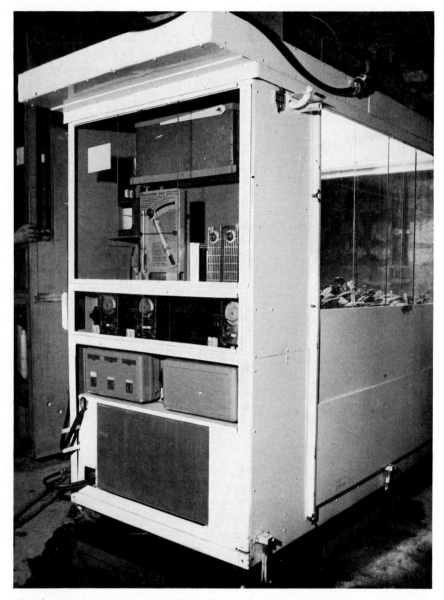

**Fig. 4.** A "microphytotron" with artificial light and vertical shutters for photo-periodic experiments.

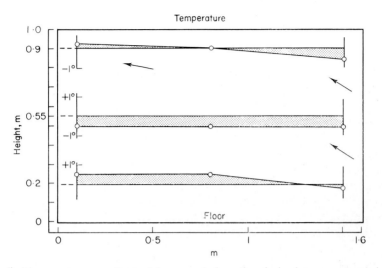

**Fig. 5.** Temperature gradients (above or below the desired temperature) in a microphytotron at 0·2, 0·55 and 0·9 m above the plant floor.

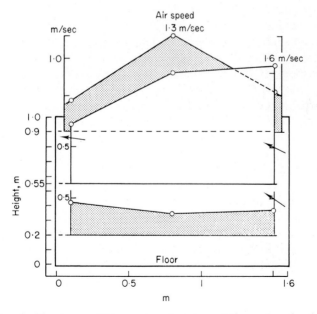

**Fig. 6.** Air velocities (m sec$^{-1}$) in a microphytotron at the various levels indicated in Fig. 5.

same horizontal plane between the side where the air enters and the side where it leaves the room.*

In the Gif "Superglasshouses", another principle is used: the air is passed vertically from the bottom to the top of the glasshouse along the vertical walls and taken out through slots in the middle of the floor. The air mixes very well, and measurements have shown a remarkable homogeneity in temperature throughout the growing space.

In a type of small cabinet called the "microphytotron" (Fig. 4), the temperature is also reasonably uniform (Fig. 5); the air velocity being high (Fig. 6).

*d. Soil and air temperatures.* The same temperature may have different effects depending upon whether it is applied uniformly to the whole plant or only to the shoot or root. Thus independent control of soil and air temperature may be necessary. This is usually achieved by placing the rooting medium in a temperature-regulated water bath.

## *4. Light*

Light, an environmental factor of paramount importance to plant growth, influences plant development through its quality, intensity and periodicity.

*a. Light quality.* Monochromatic light, such as that of sodium lamps is unable to support plant growth. A combination of various wavelengths is necessary. Sunlight provides a balanced spectrum for plants. Colourless glass transmits all the necessary wavelengths, although it cuts out more of the ultra-violet than do certain plastics such as "Plexiglas". Complete plant development can be obtained with white artificial light only, such as that produced by fluorescent, incandescent or xenon arc lamps. Following the experience gained at Pasadena, we have equipped the artificial light chambers of the Gif phytotron with fluorescent tubes supplemented in the far-red region by 15-watt incandescent bulbs. In this way sunflowers, wheat and many other plants have been grown from seed to seed without ever experiencing natural light.

*b. Light intensity.* An intensity of 80–120 W m$^{-2}$ (visible) at the plant level should be aimed at. At Gif, an intensity of 80 W m$^{-2}$ (visible) exists in all the artificially lit rooms throughout the year. A higher intensity could be obtained by using only new fluorescent tubes, but as the light output declines with time the luminous flux varies over the year. In order to have a constant intensity, a mixture consisting of $\frac{1}{3}$ new, $\frac{1}{3}$ middle-aged and $\frac{1}{3}$ old fluorescent tubes is used at Gif. Consistency of the illumination has been found to be more important for scientific work than a very high but variable light intensity.

* N. de Bilderling and J. Valognes, unpublished.

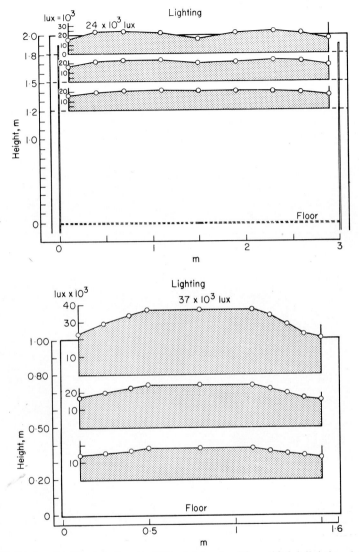

**Fig. 7.** Light distribution (lux × 10³) obtained with artificial lighting inside a room of the Gif phytotron above and a "microphytotron" below.

Another problem is that of achieving uniform illumination over the whole surface of the room: a peak occurs at the centre and light intensity drops sharply near the walls. To offset this effect, one can add lamps on the side walls, as has been done at Fukuoka, Japan. One can also transform these walls into mirrors, by lining them with aluminium foil as is done in Great Britain. Multiple reflexion then produces the effect of an infinite plant array. At Gif, a combination of white, reflective paint on the walls and the joining of the light panels in the centre of the room (which cuts down the amount of light produced there) has resulted in a homogeneous illumination (Fig. 7).

**Fig. 8.** Partial view of the air-conditioning units for the rooms with natural light of the Gif phytotron. (Photo courtesy C.N.R.S.)

*c. Light periodicity.* Since daylength controls processes such as flowering, tuber formation and dormancy in a number of species, its control is also important. In cabinets or chambers receiving only artificial light, such control is easy. When natural light is used, daylength can be shortened by raising metallic curtains over cabinets (as is done at Canberra or at Gif) or over whole sections of greenhouse (as is done in the "Superglasshouses" of the Gif phytotron).

## 5. Humidity

Provided roots are supplied with adequate amounts of water, air humidity generally exerts little influence on growth and development in higher plants. The large harvests that one can obtain in deserts by irrigation are a consequence of this fact. On the other hand, the development of pathogens is strongly influenced by air moisture, so that humidity control may be necessary for their study.

Full control of air moisture in phytotrons is difficult and costly. It is complicated by the fact that when the plants are irrigated the surplus water drips on to the floor. When air enters rooms through perforated floors, the formation of pools of water and the accumulation of wet debris under the perforated slabs negate the efforts of the machinery to reduce air moisture. Thus at Gif, despite high costs, no perfect control of the humidity was ever achieved and, at Pasadena, this parameter was left uncontrolled between the limits of 50 and 70% relative humidity.

It is relatively easy to approach 100% relative humidity by spraying mist. When a very dry atmosphere is required, the air is passed over cooling coils in order to condense most of the water before heating to the desired temperature. This may not be sufficient if very dry air is wanted, and the air may have to be dehydrated further by chemical means, e.g. passing it over lithium chloride in special "Kathabar" units which are used both at Pasadena and at Gif (Fig. 8).

## 6. Rain

Besides providing water in general, rain may have special effects such as leaching nutrients from the foliage or causing the opening of the flower buds of coffee (which remain closed unless touched by liquid water). Its control is easy.

## 7. Wind

Wind also has effects on plant growth. Special installations such as wind tunnels have been erected at Patscherkofel, Austria and at Fukuoka, Japan, in order to study respectively the effects of wind in mountains and of typhoons.

## 8. Gravity

Gravity also influences plant growth through geotropism, sometimes in unexpected manners, e.g. flowering of the pineapple can be triggered by laying the plant horizontally. Its control is more difficult to achieve, but installations exist at centres for space travel research.

## 9. Freedom from diseases

Large rooms which house many different kinds of plants at the same time are liable to contain insects and pathogenic fungi. The danger is increased when some of these plants remain there for months or years, thus acting as reservoirs of diseases. People walking in and out of these rooms many times a day help in spreading pests.

In order to avoid diseases, Went, in the Pasadena phytotron, devised a series of drastic measures to keep out insects. The whole building was first disinfected with cyanide. Thereafter, only plant material which had been fumigated with methyl bromide could be brought into the building. All persons entering the building had to exchange their outer clothing for disinfected clothes and shoes which remained permanently inside the building, to comb their hair in order to remove possible aphids, and to wash their hands with soap to eliminate possible viruses. Since cigarettes may carry tobacco mosaic virus, they could not be used inside the building unless autoclaved. Such measures were successful, on the whole, in keeping out diseases. They are such an inconvenience, however, that they have not been duplicated elsewhere. In fact at Gif, installations patterned after the Pasadena ones have never been put into operation.

Several years of experience at Gif have shown that the only serious pest is red spider (*Tetranychus*). These have caused real trouble by checking growth in many species, thus distorting experimental results. Spraying various acaricides had little effect and, at times, caused burning of leaves. A different approach was devised, using systemic insecticides of the demeton-S-methyl group such as "Metasystox". This preparation can be added once a week to the general tank in which all the nutrient solution is prepared. In this way, all the plants automatically receive the compound which they absorb through the roots. Any pest which sucks the sap is destroyed. At the active doses, "Metasystox" is metabolized by the plant without altering its growth, though not every species has the same toler-ance. A recent answer to the problem is the use of predators specific to red spider mites.

# B. Technical answers

Controlled-environment facilities have been built in many parts of the world in the form of large, centralized laboratories, such as phytotrons, or of growth chambers and cabinets. Let us briefly review the advantages and disadvantages of a few of the existing types, namely large rooms, cabinets and "superglasshouses".

## 1. Large rooms

*a. Principles.* The first phytotron, realized by Professor F. W. Went at Pasadena, California, consisted of a series of rooms which were environmentally similar, except for one variable at a time, generally temperature or light. Each room had its own machinery to maintain the temperature at the desired value. Changes were provided by moving the plants from one environment to another. Thus, with a limited number of rooms, one could make a large number of combinations.

The core of the Gif phytotron is patterned after the Pasadena one, and consists of 8 large rooms (6·5 × 5·6 m) with natural light and 12 rooms (8 × 3 m) with artificial light. The temperatures range from 9° to 40°C (day) and 6° to 31°C (night) in the naturally-lit rooms, and from −10°C to 40°C in the artificially-lit ones. The air conditioning of all these rooms requires enormous machinery (Fig. 8).

*b. Advantages.* Phytotrons with large rooms can accommodate, of course, large plants or large groups of plants. The disposition of plants on mobile trolleys offers the possibility of many different, environmental conditions which can be obtained simultaneously, provided a sufficient number of rooms with different climatic characteristics is available.

*c. Disadvantages.* The disadvantages of the large conditioned rooms are: lack of accuracy, lack of flexibility and relatively high costs.

(i) Lack of accuracy. In addition to the existence of temperature gradients (which may be rather serious in the case of large plants), the fact that people enter the rooms in which the experimental plants are growing is a source of disturbance. For example, the level of carbon dioxide changes, and pathogens may be brought in. There is also the danger of light leaks, should a door be opened at the wrong time. At Pasadena and Gif, this danger is increased by the fact that each room with artificial light is divided into compartments with different light regimes. Partitions between these compartments are opened every day and if these are not positioned correctly, light leaks may occur and ruin photoperiodic experiments.

The problem of moving the plants twice a day is also a real one. Firstly

## Table II

Comparative costs of three types of phytotrons. The three types are those represented at Gif, France, which makes comparisons more valid. They were computed in 1964. Costs are expressed per month in U.S. dollars

| | Phytotron (large rooms) | Microphytotron (cabinets) | | Super-glasshouse (conditioned glasshouses) |
|---|---|---|---|---|
| I. CONSTRUCTION: per m² of usable plant space: | 10,000[1] | 2600[2] | | 1000[1] |
| II. RUNNING COSTS: | for the whole | for one unit with: natural light | artificial light | for the whole |
| Actual usable plant space: | 328 m² | 1·5 m² | 1·5 m² | 152 m² |
| Items: | | | | |
| 1. Electricity | 7000 (500,000 kW) | 45 | 79 | 200* |
| 2. Coal | 2400 (90 tons) | 0 | 0 | ? |
| 3. Water | 470 (6000 m³) | 0[3] | 0[3] | ? |
| 4. Lamps (one replacement per year) | 2500 | 0 | 7.40 | 100 |
| 5. Nutrient solution | 120 | 0.6 | 0.6 | 6.0 |
| 6. "Verrane" and pots | 200* | 1* | 1* | 100* |
| 7. Machinery repairs | 1870* | 5* | 5* | 20* |
| 8. Personnel | 8400 (32 people)[4] | 16.80 (0·06 people) | 16.80 (0·06 people) | 840 (3 people) |
| Total: | 22,960 | 68.40 | 109.80 | 1.320 |
| per square metre of usable plant space | 70.00 | 45.60 | 73.20 | 8.68 |

* Estimated.
[1] Includes building.
[2] Does not include building.
[3] None in the air-cooled units, but some in the water-cooled ones.
[4] Including night shifts.

it requires much manpower every day, on holidays as well as on work days. Secondly, in practice, there are many plants to move at the same time and in moving, roots may be disturbed, and the leaves of large plants bruised. These movements are subject to human error since a truck can be wheeled into the wrong room, and unless the experimenter is informed he may never know what has happened in his experiment.

(ii) Lack of flexibility. Because of their size, large rooms are used for more than one experiment at a time and by more than one research worker. This means that they have to be set at temperatures which, even though they suit the majority of experiments, do not suit them all. For example, at Gif there is at the present time one room at 12°C, the next one being at 17°C. If a worker wants 15°C, he cannot use any of the existing rooms.

(iii) Costs. Table II gives an idea of the costs calculated per m² of usable plant space as they were in 1964 for the Gif phytotron. Since this phytotron has large rooms, cabinets and "superglasshouses", these three types of controlled environments could be compared directly.

The running cost of $70 per m² and per month is an average for the rooms with natural and those with artificial light. The use of natural light results in reduced operating costs for electricity but increased capital costs for the more powerful air-conditioning machinery that is required.

The main problem with large-room phytotrons is one of management. Since the amount of air conditioning is the same, whether there are many or only a few plants in a given room, the aim is to keep all of the growing space occupied by important experiments. This is not always feasible, and, in practice, space is often not used to the best advantage.

As a consequence, large phytotrons have to charge for their services. In 1965, the daily charge for one m² of plant space was $1.50 at the Madison Biotron. In 1970 it was also about $1.50 in the Gif phytotron. The result is that such phytotrons have permanent financial troubles and many workers cannot use their facilities because of costs.

## 2. Cabinets

*a. Principle.* Instead of conditioning large rooms, part of which are used for people to walk around the experimental plants, only the actual plant environment is carefully controlled. Phytotrons based on this principle operate with a large number of relatively small, independent units.

The best example of a large phytotron built on this principle is the CERES at Canberra. In this phytotron, the cabinets are themselves placed in glasshouses in which the temperature is maintained above the highest temperature desired in any one of the cabinets. Temperature regulation in the latter is by cooling only.

At Gif, a series of completely independent units known as "microphytotrons" has been devised with the cooperation of a private firm.* The "microphytotrons" can be used outdoors and are completely autonomous in that they can heat, cool and humidify the air, water the plants with nutrient solution, turn on and off the lights as well as operate automatic shutters. All they need is to be plugged into an electrical outlet. Measurements made inside have revealed that the temperature gradient is surprisingly small, in the order of $\pm 0.5\,°C$ from the set temperature. This is probably because of a high air velocity (between $0.5$ and $1.5$ m s$^{-1}$) and perhaps also because the air sweeps the plants horizontally, which is a more natural way than ascending vertically from below. With the lighted panels used, the light intensity is good, from 60 to 120 W m$^{-2}$ (visible). The reservoir for the automatic watering system only has to be filled every three days, and this means that the units can be used over week-ends with the minimum of labour.

*b. Advantages.* The advantages of small cabinets are numerous:

(a) reduction of the temperature gradient, as is the case with the "microphytotrons",

(b) complete automation (no personnel necessary during holidays, at least for the "microphytotron" type; trolley pushers are often difficult to find during holidays,

(c) greater flexibility: research workers can set the temperature cycles they want; when they are through with the experiment, other research workers can take over,

(d) ease of maintenance: should one unit break down, plants can be transferred to another unit while the first is being repaired; in phytotrons of the large room type one may have to close down a whole room or even the whole phytotron, thus interrupting many research projects,

(e) possibility of having a stand-by electrical generator in case of power failure; the C.N.R.S. has never agreed to provide one for the whole Gif Phytotron, because it would be too costly,

(f) possibility of controlling the composition of the air; in large rooms through which people go and from which plants are wheeled in and out twice every day, accurate control of the composition of the atmosphere is not possible,

(g) reduction in running costs (electricity, etc.): large room type phytotrons have to be kept running whether there are 500 plants in a room or 5; small cabinets can be turned off when not in use.

* C. Crapez—L'Humidifère, 19-Vasles, France.

*c. Disadvantages.* These are mainly of size. The cabinets are usually small, perhaps 1 m tall, 1 m wide and 2 m long. If one wants to study trees, or maize, or sugarcane past the seedling stage, they cannot be used. However, taller units have been built for these purposes at various places, for example at Canberra, at the Sugar Research Institute at Honolulu or even in the form of non-mobile "phytotronettes" at Kyoto University.

## 3. Superglasshouses

*a. Principle.* Air-conditioned glasshouses, called "superglasshouses" have been built at Gif. They have temperature control, daylength control and automatic feeding of nutrient solution.

The air is injected vertically along the lateral partitions of each of the 10·75 × 3·60 m compartments. It rises to the ceiling and then comes down, mixing very well until it reaches the evacuation openings which are located on the floor, under the benches. This arrangement has given a good distribution of the temperature, with less than a 2°C gradient around the plants in mid-summer, when the sky is overcast. When the sun is shining, differences may be greater. The air velocity around the plants varies from 0·3 to 0·7 m sec$^{-1}$.

In regions of the world where natural humidity is low, the air may be cooled very cheaply by the evaporative cooling obtained with the moist pad and fan technique which is much in use in the United States.

Daylength control is obtained by adding artificial light when days have to be lengthened and by closing automatic shutters when they have to be shortened. This is done by means of a metallic curtain which is rolled around a drum outside the glasshouse during the day and which, at the proper time, is pulled by cables to cover the top of the compartment. The sides are made light-tight by vertical sheets of metal composed of several horizontal segments which, during the day, are housed side by side between the floor and a height of about 1 m. A similar hydraulic system functions in the glass door.

*b. Advantages* include: low cost of operation; the fact that large plants can be grown, as there is space (compared with the cabinets) and no moving of plants (as in the large-room-phytotron type); the possibility of installing an automatic distribution of nutrient solution; the easy cleaning of the floors, since the air is not passed through them.

*c. Disadvantages.* The precision of temperature control is less than in true phytotrons, especially if one does not use machinery as expensive as a phytotron. Lighting is that provided by the sun under local climatic conditions and varies in intensity around the year, but supplementary lamps can be added, as at Gif in winter.

# C. Results achieved with phytotrons

Phytotrons have stimulated progress in technical, physiological and genetical areas.

## 1. Technical advances

The production of crops under totally artificial conditions, that is without natural soil and without sunlight, has been realized. This has been possible because of advances in the techniques of artificial lighting, of air-conditioning and of automatic feeding of nutrients. The result is that it is now possible—although not economical—to build underground plant factories in which any crop could be grown.

## 2. Physiological results

Many recent physiological results have been obtained with the help of growth chambers, although one cannot say that they have been gained *because* of them. One discovery, however, is almost entirely due to the use of controlled-environment facilities, namely the fact that, for many species, plants grow faster when temperature is dropped at night, a phenomenon which has been called "thermoperiodism" (Went, 1944).

Other points which have been elucidated with the help of controlled conditions are the existence of endogenous rhythms in plants and the fact that some variations in climatic conditions actually lead to higher yields than an uninterrupted optimal regime.

The conditions leading to optimal sugar production in sugar beets or to maximum alkaloid production in pharmaceutical plants such as *Datura* have been defined thanks to the use of phytotrons.

One important contribution of controlled-environment facilities has been the production of homogeneous experimental plants, and the repetition of experiments under defined and reproducible conditions. In fact, the difficulty of obtaining reproducible plant material has slowed down the progress of experimental biology in the past.

## 3. Plant breeding

Phytotrons have been used to shorten the growth cycle (four generations of wheat per year at Christchurch, New Zealand) and also to bring to simultaneous flowering species which do not normally flower at the same time. They have also served as a preliminary testing ground for new varieties (e.g. Schuster and Bretschneider-Herrmann, 1967).

## 4. Critical appraisal of the achievements of phytotrons

There is no doubt that controlled-environment facilities are necessary nowadays to physiologists and plant breeders in order to progress in their fields. Precise experiments cannot be performed unless one controls the factors of the environment to which plants are so sensitive.

The point, however, is to know whether one should group all such facilities in the form of a central phytotron or to scatter growth chambers in various research centres.

Advocates of central phytotrons have proposed that people from even distant laboratories could have research done for them at the centre. Experience has shown that research cannot be done by proxy, and that central phytotrons have mainly benefited those who were on the spot. Thus it might be sometimes more advisable to put the facilities where the workers are.

The high costs of building and maintaining large phytotrons have also favoured the development for individual workers of small units which can be turned off when experiments are completed. Symptomatic of this situation is the fact that, in the autumn of 1969, the huge and ultra-modern Biotron at the University of Wisconsin was empty, whereas pathologists, geneticists and physiologists all had their growth chambers full on the same campus.

# III. Future needs

Despite the difficulty of making forecasts, one can venture a few suggestions concerning the immediate and more distant future.

## A. The immediate future

In the immediate future several, sometimes contradictory, needs are coming to light, namely:

### 1. Technical refinements

Technical refinements are needed, for example in the control of the atmospheric environment. There is a need for gas-tight units, so that carbon dioxide and oxygen effects can be studied with precision, as well as the fixation of atmospheric nitrogen. The units being developed at the Glasshouse Crops Research Institute of Littlehampton are in line with this need.

A second need is that of the production of germ-free plants for scientific research, especially cell and tissue culture. A prototype has been built and is currently being tested by the Laboratory for Multicellular Physiology at Gif.

Most importantly, means to reduce the costs of controlled-environment facilities will have to be devised.

## 2. Areas of research

Among the numerous possibilities, special mention should be made of the search for techniques leading to an increasing plant productivity as a whole and to an improved food quality by fostering the production of a balanced spectrum of amino acids and vitamins. Means of reducing pollution will also have to be devised, as the accumulation of pesticides, fungicides and herbicides threatens to generate catastrophes.

Controlled environments will also enable scientists to raise custom-tailored plants by techniques as delicate as the nursing of single cells, whether of pollen or of vegetative parts, into whole plants. Indeed flowering plants have already been obtained by such means, especially haploid ones from pollen (Nitsch, 1969). Protoplasts, i.e. the living cytoplasm without cell wall, have also been caused to divide and to develop into flowering specimens (Nitsch and Ohyama, in press).

## B. The more distant future

As population pressure increases, the need for highly efficient means of "farming the sun" will also increase, that is the need for using photosynthesis to its fullest in order to generate organic edible matter. Then cell farming will have to be developed, namely the raising of only those cells which are useful to man. Examples of cell farming in the production of apple tissues, of protein or of sugar have been given (Nitsch, in press).

Finally, space travel will give plants new importance in the dual task of detoxifying spacecraft for humans or animals and of providing food through the capture of light energy.

Thus the plant, its study and its utilization in controlled environments will continue to have a bright future for the benefit of mankind.

## References

GARNER, W. W., and ALLARD, H. A. (1920). Effect of the relative length of day and night and other factors of the environment on growth and reproduction in plants. J. agric. Res. 18, 553–606.

NITSCH, J. P. (1969). Experimental androgenesis in *Nicotiana*. *Phytomorphology* **19**, 389–404.

NITSCH, J. P. (in press). Cell farming, the basis of a new horticulture. *Proc. 18th Int. hort. Congr.* 1970.

NITSCH, J. P., and OHYAMA, K. (in press). Obtention de plantes à partir de protoplastes haploïdes cultivés *in vitro. C.r. hebd. Séanc. Acad. Sci., Paris.*

SCHUSTER, W., and BRETSCHNEIDER-HERRMANN, B. (1967). Untersuchungen über den Einfluss von Temperatur und Tageslänge auf Wachstum und Entwicklung von Ölrettichstämmen im Phytotron mit vergleichenden Beobachtungen an Feldversuchen. *Z. PflZücht.* **58**, 383–399.

TOURNOIS, J. (1914). Sexualité du houblon. *Annls Sci. nat. (Bot.)* **19**, 49.

WENT, F. W. (1944). Plant growth under controlled conditions, II. Thermoperiodicity in growth and fruiting of the tomato. *Am. J. Bot.* **31**, 135–140.

WENT, F. W. (1957). *In* "The experimental control of plant growth". Chronica Botanica, Waltham, Mass.

WILLS, R. B. H., and PATTERSON, B. D. (1970). Ethylene, a plant hormone from fluorescent lighting. *Nature Lond.*, **225**, 199.

# I.2. Future trends in structures for protected cropping

G. F. SHEARD

*Horticulture Dept., Glasshouse Crops Research Institute, Littlehampton, Sussex, England*

## I. Conventional structures

Structures for protected cropping were first developed in northern latitudes to eliminate the effects of low temperature and wind on crop production in the open. As a consequence of protection and the resulting ability to control air temperature, light became the dominant factor limiting plant growth. Furthermore, light, already limiting outside, is reduced still further by the protecting structure.

During the last twenty years there has been considerable development in the design and construction of glasshouses, the main objective being to increase light transmission during the winter and spring months. Before 1950 the majority of glasshouses were built in multispan blocks, orientated N–S. Such glasshouses had a mean overall transmission in midwinter rarely exceeding 40% and in many cases as low as 35%. Many modern glasshouses have a transmission of 70% and it can be inferred as an approximation that a 1% increase in transmission gives a potential increase in yield of 1%.

The marked improvement in winter light transmission arises from developments in materials and structural design, from studies of roof geometry and from changing the orientation from N–S to E–W. Timber has been replaced by steel and aluminium to give structural members of greater strength and smaller size. This in turn permits the use of larger sheets of glass to give a structure with a smaller proportion of opaque material. The largest improvement in transmission comes from changing the orientation from N–S to E–W. This can only be fully exploited in single span houses but it has stimulated the design and construction of houses with spans of up to 26 m. It is difficult in N–S houses to achieve

57

a transmission in December exceeding 48% but the same house orientated E–W may have a transmission of 70%. Roof shape has a small but significant effect on light transmission. In E–W houses a high south facing side and a Mansard roof improve light transmission.

There is no doubt that improvements in design increasing light transmission increase crop yield and quality and thereby gross output. With increasing sophistication of design there has been a marked rise in the capital cost of glasshouses and the law of diminishing returns now operates. The present cost of building glasshouses ranges from £37 to 50,000 per hectare (£15–20,000 per acre) for multispan "Venlo" blocks of 3 m span, through £60,000 per hectare (£24,000 per acre) for houses in spans of 6–12 m, to £74,000 per hectare (£30,000 per acre) for single span houses of 18–24 m span. The high capital investment required for wide span houses can now only be justified for high value crops such as all-year-round chrysanthemum, carnation and certain pot plants. It is questionable for early full-season tomatoes and cucumbers and totally unjustified for low-value crops such as lettuce, late tomatoes and late cucumbers. The level of investment must be closely related to the crop and cropping system and a high level of investment in the glasshouse structure can only be justified for high-input/high-output production systems. The wheel has now turned full circle and in the immediate future at least the interest is likely to be in glasshouses of less sophisticated design and lower cost. There will be some compromise on light transmission but some improvement in the design of these lower cost houses to make them more efficient for higher value crops.

There have been attempts both in England and Holland to evaluate different designs using the crop as a yardstick but also relating yield and quality to measurements of the main parameters of the environment and in particular light. In general the results tend to show that for medium-value crops additional investment in more sophisticated designs is not economically justified. The need to use complex experimental techniques, the problems of measuring and integrating environmental factors, the need for adequate replication and the high cost make such investigations extremely difficult and some results are, to say the least, most confusing.

A factor in light transmission frequently overlooked is the deposit of dirt on glass. Even in areas not subject to pollution, reductions in transmission of 10% are commonly recorded mainly from deposition of dust. Glass cleaning is a difficult, unpleasant and expensive operation particularly on the high roofs of wide span houses. There will be increasing effort to develop better and safer methods of cleaning and to mechanize the operation.

Labour is the largest single item in the production cost of glasshouse crops. The design of glasshouses will be markedly influenced by the need to mechanize as many cultural processes as possible and to use mechanical handling within the glasshouse. There are examples of production lines for pot plants already in operation in Britain and the complete mechanization of lettuce production is being developed in Holland. Such developments could affect light transmission, directly by the use of opaque structural framework and indirectly by the need to reposition heating pipes at high level to give clear movement.

Glasshouses are cooled by ventilation when insolation increases the air temperature above the desired level. In the past, ventilation has been provided by opening ventilators in the ridge and sides of the house but the use of fans provides an alternative. Fans allow a simpler roof design, give less light obstruction and provide positive air movement. On the other hand, fans introduce temperature gradients between inlet and outlet; it is difficult to get uniform air movement through the crop and the cost of power may be as high as £1000 per hectare (£400 per acre) per year. There is a returning interest in evaporative cooling to reduce the cooling load. This may be applied externally to the roof or internally to the crop. Any development of mist spraying on the crop would have particular interest to the physiologist in relation to relative humidity and water stress in the plant.

## II. Rigid sheet alternatives to glass

The ideal shape for maximum light transmission is a hemisphere. This is impracticable for commercial cropping, the nearest usable shape being semi-cylindrical in profile. Glass cannot be readily or economically used to cover a curvilinear profile in contrast to rigid sheet plastic which lends itself to such application. Three such plastic materials have possibilities; these are resin-bonded glass fibre, unplasticized clear PVC and acrylic sheet. Of these three, only acrylic sheet has transmission properties equal to glass, indeed its optical characteristics are slightly better than glass. Resin-bonded glass fibre is not acceptable because of its low light transmission which declines with age. Neither PVC nor acrylic sheeting are sufficiently stable and durable to replace glass. All are more expensive than glass by a factor of between three and four but due allowance must be made for their load-bearing properties and the reduction in the supporting structure which these permit. Plastic sheet materials can be profiled to increase light transmission and reduce reflection. Rigid plastic is not likely to replace glass in the foreseeable future. In spite of its weight and brittleness, glass has overriding advantages in good optical properties, durability, stability, resistance to soiling and relative low cost but developments in plastics technology could quickly change the situation.

# III. Thin film

The use of thin film coverage has increased very rapidly in the last decade. Development began and is still largely confined to areas where protection is only marginally necessary, the countries with largest areas being Japan and Italy. There has been relatively little interest in countries such as Holland and Britain with a well-developed glasshouse industry. In Britain, plastic has mainly been used as low coverage on strawberries but interest is extending to high coverage and to salad crops such as lettuce and celery. The advantages of thin film structures are the minimal supporting structure and low capital cost. Disadvantages are that they are labour intensive, mechanization is not easily applied and maintenance cost in film replacement is high. The surface properties of the films used are such that the surface does not wet and condensation collects in discrete droplets. These droplets cause back reflection of incident light and markedly decrease transmission. Thin film structures are tightly sealed. This is an advantage in reducing air exchange and avoiding waste when the atmosphere is enriched with carbon dioxide but it creates problems of humidity control. Plastic clad structures are difficult to cool by natural ventilation and for sizeable structures cooling by fans is the only practicable solution. The capital and running cost of such equipment quickly offsets the low-cost advantages of thin film. Thin film lends itself to double-skin construction with consequent reduction in heat loss but again this is offset by increased cost of construction and film replacement.

Thin film plastic structures are likely to complement rather than compete with conventional glasshouses. They will probably be used to forward and extend the season of crops normally grown in the open. New entrants to the industry with limited capital could well use them to generate capital to purchase conventional glasshouses.

Economics will be the major determining factor in future trends. The cost of building conventional glasshouses is such that it is increasingly difficult to ensure an adequate return on capital. High-cost sophisticated designs can only be justified with high-value crops and where winter light is really critical. Less costly designs are more likely to be used in the immediate future. Rigid sheet plastic is unlikely to replace glass due to cost and durability. Thin film is attractive in initial cost but maintenance cost is high. Total cost over a 10–12 year period of thin film and low cost "Venlo" design glasshouses is unlikely to be materially different. Any sophistication or refinement of plastic structures quickly increases capital cost to a point where "Venlo" design glasshouses are competitive and would generally be preferred.

# Bibliography

ANON. (1969). Plastic structures for agricultural and horticultural use. Short Term Leaflet No. 86. Ministry of Agriculture, Fisheries & Food, London.

ANON. (1970). Minimum Standards for Glasshouse Construction—Loading. Short Term Leaflet No. 106. Ministry of Agriculture, Fisheries & Food, London.

ANON. (1971). Glasshouse Construction. Siting and Design. Short Term Leaflet No. 28. Ministry of Agriculture, Fisheries & Food, London.

ANON. (1971). *Rep. Efford expl Hort. Stn 1970*, 25–29. National Agricultural Advisory Service.

BOWMAN, G. E. (1970). The transmission of diffuse light by a sloping roof. *J. agric. Engng Res.* **11**, 113–123.

CANHAM, A. E. (1969). Air supported plastic structures—materials and design factors. *In: Agricultural Engineering. Proceedings of Silsoe Symposium, 1967, Inst. agric. Engng.*

EDWARDS, R. I. and LAKE, J. V. (1964). Transmission of solar radiation in a large-span East–West glasshouse. *J. agric. Engng Res.* **9**, 245–249.

EDWARDS, R. I. and LAKE, J. V. (1965). Transmission of solar radiation in a large-span East–West glasshouse. II. Distinction between the direct and diffuse components of the incident radiation. *J. agric. Engng Res.* **10**, 125–131.

FRIEND, P. D. (1965). Light and heat in a large span glasshouse. Expl. Fm. Buildings Rep. 2. Agric. Res. Coun. London.

GERMING, G. H. (1965). Comparison of Glasshouse types. *Acta Hort.* **2**, 49–54.

JONES, M. P. (1966). A survey of glasshouses and glasshouse practice. *J. agric. Engng Res.*, **11**, 113–123.

KLOUGART, A. (1970). Overhead sprinkling as a technique for better growth of greenhouse ornamentals. British Growers Look Ahead Conference Papers, 1970, 15–18.

NISEN, A. (1969). "L'Eclairement Naturel des Serres." J. Duculot, S. A. Gembloux.

SMITH, C. V. and KINGHAM, H. G. (1971). A contribution to glasshouse design. *Agric. Met.* **8**, 447–469.

VAN KOOT, Y. and DIJKHUIZEN, T. (1965). Light transmission of dirty glass and cleaning methods. *Acta Hort. Int. Soc. hort. Sci.*, No. 6, 97–108.

WHITTLE, R. M. and LAWRENCE, W. J. C. (1959). The climatology of glasshouses. I. Natural illumination. *J. agric. Engng Res.* **4**, 326–340.

# I.3. Principles and progress in environmental control systems

G. E. BOWMAN

*National Institute of Agricultural Engineering, Wrest Park, Silsoe, Bedfordshire, England*

## I. Control of aerial environment

### A. Introduction

As in many practical situations, a marked feature of the control of aerial environment in greenhouses is that measures adopted to control one factor frequently affect other factors. Table I lists environmental parameters which may conveniently be measured, control actions which are practicable in engineering terms and environmental parameters which have a direct effect upon the crop. If, for example, a deviation from the desired dry bulb temperature occurs such that it can be corrected by ventilation, then plant temperature, carbon dioxide gradient and water gradient will all be affected. Such interactions determine whether or not a

**Table I**

Environmental parameters and control actions

| | | |
|---|---|---|
| Solar radiation | Ventilate | Light intercepted |
| Dry bulb temperature | Supply heat | Plant temperature |
| Wet bulb temperature | Spray $H_2O$ | $H_2O$ gradient |
| Carbon dioxide concentration | Stir air | $CO_2$ gradient |

particular control function is physically possible, horticulturally desirable or economically justifiable.

# B. Control of air temperature

Historically, the function of the greenhouse was to provide thermal protection to delicate plants during the winter and, in considering general principles, it is convenient to take as an example the control of air temperature.

## 1. Energy balance

The instantaneous energy balance of the greenhouse can be expressed as follows*:

$$aI - (\theta_1 - \theta_0)\left\{b + cW(1 + dF^n)\right\} + H = 0$$

The constants $a$, $b$, $c$, $d$, and $n$ depend upon house geometry and cropping arrangements. In particular, the constant $a$ is the product of the solar radiation transmission factor of the house and the proportion of energy dissipated by the evaporation of water from the crop. Measurements of the solar radiation transmission have been made for several types of greenhouse of commercial importance (Edwards and Lake, 1964, 1965; Edwards, 1968) and calculations made of the light transmission of multispan glasshouses (Stoffers, 1967) and also of houses made of rigid plastics (Manbeck and Aldrich, 1967). Although the proportion of solar radiation intercepted by the plants dissipated in evaporation should theoretically be about 0·5 (Morris et al., 1957), in practice the proportion may vary from 0·3 to nearly 0·6, the higher values being associated with dense foliage canopies, high solar radiation flux densities, large water vapour pressure deficits and unlimited supplies of water to the roots (Lake et al., 1966; Walker and Cotter, 1968; Hand et al., 1970).

## 2. Thermal inertia

In considering the control of air temperature, it is not sufficient to confine the discussion solely to the instantaneous energy balance, since heat may be exchanged with portions of the greenhouse of large thermal capacity. Table II lists the water equivalent (mass × specific heat) of various parts of a modern multispan greenhouse and its contents. In calculating the water equivalent of the soil, a depth of 200 mm was assumed, the depth at which diurnal temperature changes are very small or

* Symbols used are listed on p. 75.

zero. The thermal capacity of soil depends upon soil type and upon moisture content; the values quoted apply to dry light soil and saturated heavy soil respectively, using data obtained by Morris (1954). The heating system is assumed to consist of pairs (flow and return) of 32 mm steel

**Table II**

Water equivalents of different
components in a growing system

|  | kg m$^{-2}$ |
| --- | --- |
| Soil | 56–100 |
| Crop—tomatoes | 10·2 |
| —lettuce | 5·5 |
| Heating system | 1·7 |
| Glass | 1·4 |
| Air | 0·7 |
| Roof structure | 0·5 |

pipes, containing pumped hot water, spaced 1·5 m apart. The roof structure is assumed to be aluminium alloy. Table II shows that the presence of a crop in a greenhouse may be expected to exert a considerable influence on the behaviour of the air temperature control system—especially in the case of a mature tomato crop in which the plant material has a large surface area well distributed throughout the volume of air contained in the greenhouse.

## 3. Heating

The slowest process in the control of air temperature in greenhouses is the addition of heat from a piped heating system. Traditional 100 mm diameter hot water pipes with gravity circulation are the least responsive, having a time constant of more than two hours (Hoare and Morris, 1955). Time constant is defined as the period of time required for the air temperature to reach 63% $(1 - e^{-1})$ of its final value in response to a step change or discontinuity in the rate of heat input. Measurements on 32 mm pipes containing pumped hot water gave values of less than one hour (Bowman and Weaving, 1970), whilst measurements in multispan greenhouses equipped with direct discharge air heaters yielded time constants of ten minutes or less (Heissner and Krasper, 1967). It is reasonable to assume that hot-air heating systems with air distribution by means of lightweight perforated plastics ducts would have similar time constants of about ten minutes.

Although hot air heating systems are attractive in view of their rapid response and low capital cost, they differ from conventional piped heating systems in two important respects.

(1) All the heat output is by free and forced convection and there is no radiant heating of the soil if transparent polyethylene is used as duct material.

(2) It is difficult to obtain high rates of heat supply, i.e. difficult to maintain large temperature lifts, from ducted hot air systems unless either the air is discharged at a high temperature, or ducts of large cross-section are used; neither is horticulturally desirable.

Studies on the influence of meteorological factors on the rate of change of air temperature in a large multispan greenhouse led to the conclusion that hot air heating systems gave better control than other systems when the rate of change of external temperature exceeded $6°C\,h^{-1}$ (Förtsch and Heineken, 1968). The effect of wind in cooling the greenhouse by forced convection from the external surface has been investigated by several workers (Seibert and Renard, 1962; Whittle and Lawrence, 1960a). The rate of heat loss was found to be doubled as the wind speed increased from zero to $7\,m\,sec^{-1}$ (Bowman, 1962).

## 4. Ventilating

Under most weather conditions, control of greenhouse air temperature by natural or mechanical ventilation is a rapid process, except when the external air temperature is near the desired internal air temperature. The various forms of mechanized ventilation are described in a M.A.F.F. leaflet (Anon, 1965). Under conditions of intense solar radiation and high external temperature, cooling of the greenhouse interior may be the only means of maintaining the desired air temperature. A study of air conditioning in greenhouses indicated that in the U.K. mechanical refrigeration is totally uneconomic and that evaporative cooling, with or without a heat exchanger, is not at present economic (Wolfe, 1970). With closed ventilators, some exchange with outside air takes place, depending principally on wind speed (Whittle and Lawrence, 1960b; Heissner, 1967). With open ventilators, amount of opening, position of ventilators in the structure and wind direction exert important effects in addition to the main effect due to wind speed (Businger, 1954; Renard and Stein, 1960).

## 5. Types of control system

The air temperature control systems currently in use in greenhouses rely on a thermostat, suitably aspirated and shielded against solar radiation. For this purpose, the N.I.A.E. has designed an aspirated screen, described in an M.A.F.F. leaflet (Anon, 1962). The thermostat may be a simple on/off switch or, in more elaborate control systems, consist of a resistance thermometer connected in a bridge circuit. In the latter case, the control action may be proportional, integral or derivative, or a combination of any or all of these actions. Precise definitions of these terms are

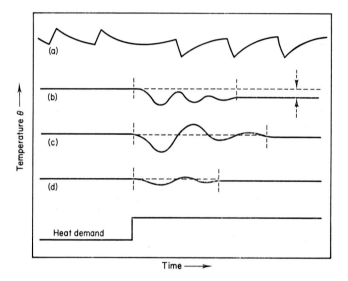

**Fig. 1.** Variation of temperature with time for different control systems.

given in the appropriate British Standard (Anon, 1967). Figure 1 shows how temperature may be expected to vary with time, under each of the four control actions, in response to a sudden change in heat demand. Curve (a) shows two-step or on/off action, in which the rate of heat supply is alternately zero and maximum. The profile of the curve changes with heat demand, as does the frequency of switching. Amplitude and frequency of the temperature fluctuations about the desired value also depend upon thermostat differential and the response time of the complete system. The frequency of switching is maximum, i.e. the control action is most sensitive, when the rate of heat supply in the "on" state is twice the demand rate; rates of rise and fall of temperature are then equal.

Curve (b) relates to proportional action, in which the controller output signal $V$ is given by

$$V = -K_1\theta$$

The constant term $K_1$ is negative because of the need for the control action to oppose any change in temperature $\theta$. An inherent characteristic of proportional action is the sustained offset which occurs, the magnitude of which is a function of the demand and the chosen value of proportional band. Proportional band is defined as the range of values of deviation corresponding to the full operating range of the output signal. Put in numerical terms, if at a given instant the temperature is $1\,°C$ above the desired value and the proportional band setting chosen is $4\,°C$, then the ventilators will be driven a quarter of the distance between fully shut and fully open. A very small proportional band setting results in the control system behaving in a manner similar to that of an on/off system. Curve (c) shows the operation of a system in which proportional and integral actions are combined, where

$$V = -K_1\theta - K_2\!\int\!\theta \; \mathrm{d}t$$

and in which the second term changes at a rate proportional to the temperature deviation from the desired value. Such two-term control eliminates the offset resulting from proportional action alone, but has the disadvantage that the amplitude and persistence of fluctuations of temperature about the desired value are greater and longer than those experienced with proportional action only. Curve (d) illustrates the consequences of adding a third term, derivative action, to the control system, where

$$V = -K_1\theta - K_2\!\int\!\theta \; \mathrm{d}t - K_3\,\frac{\mathrm{d}\theta}{\mathrm{d}t}$$

The third term introduces an output signal proportional to the rate of change of deviation of temperature from the desired value; this has the desirable result of reducing the amplitude and duration of fluctuations about the desired value.

## 6. Practical control systems

In practice, on/off control is adequate for piped hot water and steam heating systems, particularly if an accelerator heater is applied to the thermostat which should be of small mass. The arrangement of the heating pipes within the greenhouse governs the temperature distribution; uniform spreading of the pipes over the floor area gives rise to a number of convection cells, usually four, resulting in persistent temperature variations along the length of the greenhouse. This can be overcome by placing all the heating pipes on the side walls, thus promoting very rapid air circulation in the direction transverse to the axis of the house (Winspear and Morris, 1965). In the latter case, the greenhouse soil is no longer appreciably heated by radiation from the pipes, because of the small angle subtended at the array of pipes by the soil surface.

The faster response of hot air heating systems makes proportional control desirable. This may be achieved in a simple manner by the on/off operation of a valve at the condensate outlet of a calorifier (K. W. Winspear, private communication).

Since the thermal response to the movement of hinged ventilators, or the operation of fans, is even more rapid than that of a hot air heating system, proportional control is a necessity. Whilst in general the output of a heating system can be uniquely related to the position of a control valve, the rate of fall of temperature obtained by opening a hinged ventilator is not closely related to the extent to which it is opened, yet ventilator position is the only parameter which can conveniently be measured and fed back to the control system. This may lead to difficulty in the choice of a suitable proportional band setting; ideally the proportional band width for ventilation should be a direct function of wind speed and an inverse function of external air temperature.

# II. Environmental control systems

## A. The $\Delta x$ control system

### 1. Basic principles

The $\Delta x$ control system has been developed at I.T.T., Wageningen; the basic principles and control equipment have been described by van Drenth and Achterberg (1969). From considerations of energy balance (but neglecting radiation exchange with surrounding foliage) for unit leaf area it is shown that

$$Qv = \frac{1}{1 + \dfrac{cp}{csl}} \cdot I + \frac{1}{\dfrac{c}{2h} + \dfrac{cp}{2hsl}} \cdot \Delta x$$

or $Q_v = C_1 \cdot I + nC_2 \cdot \Delta x$

where $n$ is the leaf area index.

Of the terms comprising $C_1$ and $C_2$, variations in $cp$, $l$ and $h$ are negligible, $c$ is assumed constant and $s$ is determined by the crop, e.g. for tomatoes $s = 0.4$.

The object of the $\Delta x$ control system is to maintain the moisture saturation deficit in the greenhouse atmosphere at a constant and appropriate value.

## 2. The moisture sensor

Originally, an array of twenty wet- and dry-bulb thermocouples was used; the present system employs two platinum resistance thermometers, housed in an aspirated screen (Koopmans *et al.*, 1970). Figure 2 shows the arrangement of the moisture sensor bridge; an essential feature is the deliberate difference of 100 Ω between the wet- and dry-bulb resistance

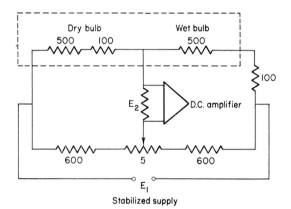

**Fig. 2.** Moisture sensor bridge for $\Delta x$ control system (after Koopmans *et al.*, 1970).

thermometers at 0°C. By this means, the output signal is made proportional to moisture deficit, rather than wet-bulb depression. Such temperature compensation is needed because at a constant moisture deficit (expressed as g water/kg dry air), wet-bulb depression varies with dry-bulb temperature. Figure 3 shows the $\Delta x$ control characteristic.

## 3. The solar radiation sensor

Besides providing control of moisture deficit, the $\Delta x$ system offers the possibility of daytime air temperature adjustment depending upon solar radiation, and nocturnal air temperature adjustment depending upon the previous daily solar radiation integral.

The sensor is a cadmium sulphide photoresistor (spectral response 450-900 nm, max. 670 nm), placed beneath a diffusing glass dome, mounted externally on the ridge of the greenhouse. The non-linearity of the sensor is reflected in the air temperature/solar radiation control characteristic (Fig. 3). The sensor is connected to an electronic controller which drives a servo motor such that the angular displacement is a linear

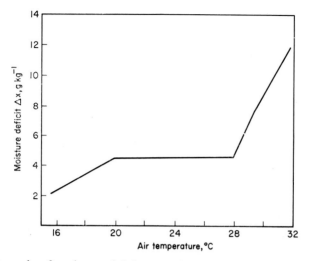

**Fig. 3.** Example of moisture deficit control characteristic obtainable with $\Delta x$ control system.

function of illumination. The servo motor shaft operates adjustable contacts used to control carbon dioxide injection and air temperature night set-back; it also rotates the wipers of potentiometers which provide signals to the control systems for air temperature, moisture deficit and heating pipe temperature, also to an indicator calibrated in mW m$^{-2}$.

# B. The N.I.A.E. light-modulated controller

## 1. Basic principles

Experiments on photosynthesis by Gaastra (1959) and by Daunicht (1961), also experiments using apparatus described by Hand and Bowman (1969) led to the possibility of controlling greenhouse environment, at different levels of natural illumination, on the basis of the response surface of carbon assimilation with respect to atmospheric carbon dioxide concentration and air temperature. If such surfaces have single maxima, then it is possible to choose optimum values of air temperature and carbon dioxide concentration in relation to illumination.

Natural illumination is the only major environmental factor which cannot be controlled (other than by shading, which would generally restrict growth). Apart from completely clear or overcast conditions, natural illumination is characterized by frequent random variations resulting from cloud movement. An analogue control system designed to respond to such fluctuations would demand frequent adjustment of the heating and ventilating equipment, causing rapid mechanical wear and wastage of heat and carbon dioxide. Control is therefore based on short-period illumination integrals, the working range being divided into several

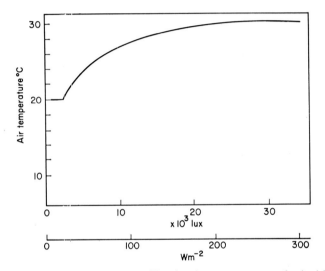

**Fig. 4.** Example of air temperature/illumination programme obtainable with $\Delta x$ control system.

equal increments or steps. Stepwise or digital operation has the following advantages:

(i) minimum actuation of heating and ventilating equipment,
(ii) several greenhouses can be controlled from one unit,
(iii) each greenhouse can have a different control programme,
(iv) either linear or non-linear relationships can be arranged between illumination and each of the other environmental factors under control.

## 2. General arrangement of the controller

A full account of the N.I.A.E. light-modulated controller, including circuit diagrams and a list of components, has been given by Bowman and

Weaving, (1970) and the apparatus is covered by British Patent No. 1 199 278.

Ideally, the light measured should be that incident on, or intercepted by, the crop. However, it is not possible to choose a truly representative region inside a greenhouse, unaffected by shadows or by internal reflections, in which to place light sensors. Since the transmission of the house was known, the sensor, a solarimeter, was placed outside the house. A solarimeter was used in preference to a photocell for the sake of reliability and stability of calibration—despite the aim to control a photosynthetic process. The proportion of photosynthetically active radiation to total solar radiation is nearly constant, depending mainly on cloudiness (Szeicz, 1968).

Solar radiation is detected by means of a thermopile, the analogue output of which is directly proportional to the radiation received on a horizontal surface. This output is integrated and converted into electrical pulses which are stored in digital counting relays equipped with readout switches. At the end of a predetermined time interval (generally 15 min, but adjustable within the range 2–20 min) the counts stored in the digital counting relays are rounded off to the nearest leading (i.e. tens) digit and a uniselector rotated to one of ten possible positions, corresponding to one of ten possible values of the solar radiation integral. The digital counting relays are then reset to zero and the integrating sequence repeated.

Using the remaining banks of contacts on the uniselector, the value of the solar radiation integral is displayed on a luminous indicator and resistors, mounted on interchangeable plug-in cards, switched in series with the air temperature and carbon dioxide concentration control circuits, thus altering their set points. Provision is made, via a solar-dial time-switch, for night set-back of air temperature. By means of a printing counter, the integrating time and value of each solar radiation integral is recorded. This record, and records from temperature integrators (Weaving, 1970), make it possible to assess the extent to which the desired control programme is achieved in practice.

Figure 5A shows the light-modulated controller housed in a standard instrument case: the luminous indicator is at the extreme left, adjoining the digital counting relays and in the centre the connections to the uniselector are visible. Figure 5B shows the plug-in cards on which the control circuit components are mounted; the card on the right is a temperature programme and arranged for increments of 0·5 °C.

A typical air temperature/solar radiation programme is shown in Fig. 6. It will be seen that, if desired, unequal increments of temperature may be obtained and that a "dead zone" is necessary between the cessation of heating and the onset of ventilation. The horticultural consequences of

**Fig. 5.** The N.I.A.E. light-modulated controller, 5A above, 5B below—see text.

employing such a programme have been described by Hand and Soffe, (1971).

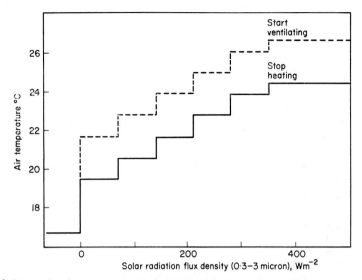

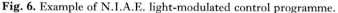

**Fig. 6.** Example of N.I.A.E. light-modulated control programme.

### List of Symbols

| | |
|---|---|
| $c$ | gradient of absolute humidity/temperature curve |
| $cp$ | specific heat of air at constant pressure |
| $F$ | percentage opening of ventilators |
| $h$ | thermal surface conductance |
| $H$ | rate of heat supply |
| $I$ | solar radiation flux density |
| $l$ | latent heat of evaporation of water |
| $Q_v$ | rate of evaporation of water |
| $s$ | stomatal index |
| $V$ | controller output signal |
| W | wind speed |
| $\theta_0$ | external air temperature |
| $\theta_1$ | greenhouse air temperature |
| $x$ | saturation deficit |

## References

ANON. (1962). Measurement and control of air temperature. *Hort. Mach. Leafl.* No. 7, M.A.F.F. London, H.M.S.O.

ANON. (1965). Glasshouse ventilation. *Mech. Leafl.* No. 5, M.A.F.F. London, H.M.S.O.

ANON. (1967). Glossary of terms used in automatic controlling and regulating systems. Part 1. Process and kinetic control. British Standard 1523.

BOWMAN, G. E. (1962). A comparison of greenhouses covered with plastic film and with glass. *Proc. 16th Int. hort. Congr. Brussels*, **5**, 551–558.

BOWMAN, G. E. and WEAVING, G. S. (1970). A light-modulated greenhouse control system. *J. agric. Engng Res.* **15**, 255–264.

BUSINGER, J. A. (1954). De invloed van raamstanden op de ventilatie van kassen. *Meded. Inst. TuinbTech. Wageningen* **28**, 897–903.

DAUNICHT, H. J. (1961). Untersuchungen zur Wirkung des Kohlendioxyd-Angebots auf den Ertrag von Treibgemüsen unter besonderer Berücksichtigung der Hydrokultur. *Gartenbauwissenschaft* **26**, 96–147.

DRENTH, A. VAN and ACHTERBERG, S. H. (1969). Regelsysteem voor het kasklimaat. *Publ. Inst. TuinbTech. Wageningen* **52**, 1–84.

EDWARDS, R. I. (1968). The transmission of solar radiation in greenhouses. *Acta Hort.* **6**, 47–52.

EDWARDS, R. I. and LAKE, J. V. (1964). Transmission of solar radiation in a large-span East–West greenhouse. *J. agric. Engng Res.* **9**, 245–249.

EDWARDS, R. I. and LAKE, J. V. (1965). Transmission of solar radiation in a large-span East–West glasshouse II. Distinction between the direct and diffuse components of the incident radiation. *J. agric. Engng Res.* **10**, 125–131.

FÖRTSCH, CH. and HEINEKEN, R. (1968). Der Einfluss meteorologischer Elemente und technologisch bedingter Massnahmen auf die Änderungsgeschwindigkeit der Temperatur im MZG 0/55 und deren Auswirkung auf eine automatische Temperaturregelung. *Arch. Gartenb.* **16**, 17–35.

GAASTRA, P. (1959). Photosynthesis of crop plants as influenced by light, carbon dioxide, temperature and stomatal diffusion resistance. *Meded. LandbHoogesch. Wageningen* **59** (13), 1–68.

HAND, D. W. and BOWMAN, G. E. (1969). Carbon dioxide assimilation measurement in a controlled environment glasshouse. *J. agric. Engng Res.* **14**, 92–99.

HAND, D. W., SLACK, G. and MACHIN, D. R. (1970). Evaporation rates of capillary-watered tomatoes in an East–West glasshouse. *J. hort. Sci.* **45**, 3–14.

HAND, D. W. and SOFFE, R. W. (1971). Light modulated temperature control and the response of greenhouse tomatoes to different $CO_2$ regimes. *J. hort. Sci.* **46**, 381–396.

HEISSNER, A. (1967). Experimentelle Untersuchung des Luftaustausches von nicht gelüfteten Gewächshäusern. *Arch. Gartenb.* **15**, 521–532.

HEISSNER, A. and KRASPER, P. (1967). Untersuchung der unstetigen Raumtemperaturregelung in Gewächshäusern. *Dt. Agrartech.* **17**, 509–511; 577–579.

HOARE, E. R. and MORRIS, L. G. (1955). The heating and ventilation of glasshouses. *J. Instn Br. agric. Engrs* **12**, 1–26.

KOOPMANS, A., VAN DRENTH, A., ACHTERBERG, S. H. and GIELING, T. H. (1970). Automatisering van installaties in kassen. *Jversl. Inst. TuinbTech. Wageningen 1970*, 50–57.

LAKE, J. V., POSTLETHWAITE, J. D., EDWARDS, R. I. and SLACK, G. (1966).

Seasonal variation in the transpiration of greenhouse plants. *Agric. Met.* **3,** 187–196.

MANBECK, H. B. and ALDRICH, R. A. (1967). Analytical determination of direct visible solar energy transmitted by rigid plastic greenhouses. *Trans. Am. Soc. agric. Engrs* **10,** 564–567; 572.

MORRIS, L. G. (1954). The steam sterilizing of soil. *Report natn. Inst. agric. Engng*, No. 14.

MORRIS, L. G., NEALE, F. E. and POSTLETHWAITE, J. D. (1957). The transpiration of glasshouse crops and its relation to the incoming solar radiation. *J. agric. Engng Res.* **2,** 111–122.

RENARD, W. and STEIN, J. (1960). Der Einfluss des Windes auf die Gewächshauslüftung. *Gartenbauwissenschaft* **25,** 134–150.

SEIBERT, L. and RENARD, W. (1962). Wärmebedarf von Gewächshäusern *Heizung, Lüftung, Haustech. Rdsch.* **13,** 101–105.

STOFFERS, J. A. (1967). Lichtdoorlatenheid van met vlakke materialen bedekte warenhuizen. *Publ. Inst. TuinbTech., Wageningen* **14,** 1–40.

SZEICZ, G. (1968). Measurement of radiant energy. *In* "The measurement of Environmental Factors in Terrestrial Ecology" (R. M. Wadsworth, ed.), pp. 109–130. Blackwell, Oxford.

WALKER, J. N. and COTTER, D. J. (1968). Influence of structural features and plant growth on temperatures in greenhouse structures with particular reference to plastic glazed structures. *Acta. hort.* **6,** 26–46.

WEAVING, G. S. (1970). An improved thermistor temperature integrator. *J. scient. Instrum.* **3,** 711–714.

WHITTLE, R. K. and LAWRENCE, W. J. C. (1960a). The climatology of glasshouses: V. The heat consumption of glasshouses. *J. agric. Engng Res.* **5,** 399–405.

WHITTLE, R. K. and LAWRENCE, W. J. C. (1960b). The climatology of glasshouses: II. Ventilation. *J. agric. Engng Res.* **5,** 36–41.

WOLFE, J. S. (1970). Feasibility and economics of conditioning recirculated greenhouse air by evaporative cooling. *J. agric. Engng Res.* **15,** 265–273.

WINSPEAR, K. W. and MORRIS, L. G. (1965). Automation and control in glasshouses. *Acta. Hort.* **2,** 61–71.

# I.4. Analysis of the microclimate in the glasshouse

S. W. BURRAGE

*Dept. of Horticulture, Wye College, University of London, England*

## I. Introduction

The plant environment is one of action and interaction, the action of the natural environment on the plant and the interaction between the plant and the natural environment. When investigating any plant microclimate the most important considerations are the exchange of energy that is taking place between the plant and its surroundings. Given a knowledge of these and of the requirements for plant growth man may be able to modify the plant environment to attain the maximum potential yield of the plant. The main fluxes of energy are those of radiation, sensible heat, evaporation and conduction and the physiological processes of respiration and photosynthesis. To determine these exchanges the principal measurements required are of radiation, temperature, humidity, windspeed and carbon dioxide. The acquisition of data from glasshouse crops follows a pattern similar to that used in investigations with field crops: comprising three stages:

"sensing"    "recording"    "evaluation"

The sensing stage consists of mounting in or near the crop instruments capable of detecting the changes in the environmental parameters, temperature, windspeed, etc. The recorder is a means of logging this information for permanent reference. Evaluation, the synthesis of these data by the computer and the analysis of this information is necessary in relation to plant growth and cultural practices.

This paper describes the system of data acquisition from the glasshouse environment used at Wye.

# II. The crop

The tomato crop was chosen for two reasons, firstly because of its commercial significance, and secondly because a commercial crop grown at the College was readily available for investigation. The observation site is a central area in a quarter-acre bay of a four-bay, one-acre modern glasshouse. The entire acre is used to grow tomatoes and air is free to flow between the four equal bays. Each bay is 9·75 m wide, 45·7 m long and 5·5 m to the ridge. The plants, "Eurocross BB", are grown on a twin-row system with 60 cm between rows, 92 cm in the alleyways and 32 cm between plants within the row. The house and rows are aligned in an East–West direction. The house is heated by 5 cm steam pipes at ground level and at 2·0 m. Ventilation is by ridge vents only, which are temperature controlled. The sensor instruments are set up within and between rows in the central region where the crop is uniform.

# III. Sensing instruments

The physical parameters monitored are temperature (air, leaf surface and soil), humidity, windspeed, radiation (short wave and net), carbon dioxide and soil moisture. Instruments are mounted at a number of levels within and above the crop, the number of instruments used being dependent upon the stage of development of the crop. Most instruments are copper–constantan thermocouple units constructed either from separate copper–constantan wires or by electroplating. A brief description of the instruments is given in Table I.

The air thermometers consist of two concentric perspex tubes 25 mm and 10 mm diameter covered with aluminium foil. Within the central tube the thermocouple is supported in a central position and aspirated continuously. The same air stream is eventually drawn into the instrument caravan alongside the glasshouse where it is analysed for carbon dioxide and water vapour. The rate of airflow through the tube is 1–2·5 litres min$^{-1}$. The inner tube is perforated behind the thermocouple allowing air to be drawn from the space between inner and outer shields. Leaf thermometers consist of five, 40-gauge thermocouples connected in series which are attached to the leaf with small clips allowing 3 mm at the tip of the thermojunction to make contact with the leaf. The thermometers are attached to the upper and lower surfaces of the leaves in zones approximately 100 cm in height. Soil thermometers were similarly grouped, five in each series, each thermocouple being sheathed with PVC. Temperature measurements are made on a comparative basis, successive depths being compared with one another and the deepest with a silicone

**Table I**

Sensor instruments used in analysis of the glasshouse environment

| Parameter | Type | Description | | Output | Sensitivity |
|---|---|---|---|---|---|
| TEMPERATURE | Air | Thermocouple (single or 5 junction units, Double screened and ventilated) | (1) (5) | 0–2 mV 0–10 mV | 40 $\mu$V deg C$^{-1}$ 200 $\mu$V deg C$^{-1}$ |
| | Soil | Thermocouple 5 in series PVC covered | | 0–10 mV | 200 $\mu$V deg C$^{-1}$ |
| | Leaf surface | Thermocouple 5 in series | | 0–10 mV | 200 $\mu$V deg C$^{-1}$ |
| RADIATION | Shortwave | Szeicz, Monteith and dos Santos (1964) | | 0–100 mV | 25–50 mV cal$^{-1}$ cm$^{-2}$ |
| | Net External | Thermocouples beneath Black and White Surfaces Tubular polyethylene covered | | 0–30 mV | 20 mV cal$^{-1}$ cm$^{-2}$ |
| | External Shortwave | Kipp Solarimeter | | 0–20 mV | 9 mV cal$^{-1}$ cm$^{-2}$ |
| WINDSPEED | Internal | Heated thermocouple Rod Anemometer | | 10–20 mV 0–1 V | 5 mV m$^{-1}$ s$^{-1}$ Non linear |
| | External | Casella Sensitive 3-cup Anemometer | | | 100 mV m$^{-1}$ s$^{-1}$ |
| HUMIDITY | Internal & External | Psychrometer, 10-unit thermopile for temperature depression, single unit for air temperature | (10) (1) | 0–5 mV 0–2 mV | 0·4 mV deg C$^{-1}$ 40 $\mu$V deg C$^{-1}$ |
| CARBON DIOXIDE | Internal & External | "Uras 2" infrared gas analysers (Hartmann & Braun) | | 0–5 V (comp) 0–5 mV (Rec) | 10 mV vpm 10 $\mu$V vpm$^{-1}$ |
| SOIL MOISTURE | Internal | Heated Thermocouple rod | | 5–15 mV | 0·5 mV bar$^{-1}$ |
| VENT OPENING | | Potentiometer | | 0–18 mV | Non linear 1 mV per 10° of arc |

rubber block buried in the soil. The temperature of the silicone rubber
block is standardized with a constant–temperature bath in the caravan.

Shortwave radiation measurements are made using tubular solarimeters described by Szeicz et al. (1964). Net radiation is measured with a
tubular radiometer, of dimensions similar to those of the solarimeter. It
consists of a horizontal blackened plate, with thermocouples embedded
in its upper and lower surfaces which measure the temperature differences
between the two surfaces. The plate is supported by two aluminium rods
parallel to the plate and held at either end in a perspex rod 25 mm in
diameter. The plate is tensioned to a horizontal position and covered by a
polythene tube 0·1 mm thick which is fixed at both ends to the perspex
rod and thus retains its tubular shape.

Windspeed within the house is measured with heated thermocouple
anemometers similar to the Poppendick type, described by Lourence
(1967). These are particularly sensitive in the 0–1 m sec$^{-1}$ range and are
not as susceptible to wind direction as the Simmons (1949) or Sparling
types (Brooks et al., 1965) when used at low windspeed. Continuous
records of the degree of air movement at various levels within the crop
are thus made available.

The soil moisture probes used are essentially the same as the anemometers but are covered with a thin film of silicone rubber, the temperature
difference ($<1°C$) between heated and non-heated junctions vary with
soil moisture utilizing the parallel changes in the thermal conductivity of
the soil.

The air from the thermometer units is drawn through 6 mm bore PVC
tubing into the caravan where it is analysed for carbon dioxide and water
vapour. Between the caravan and the glasshouse these tubes are well
insulated with polystyrene foam and supported within an outer, rigid
PVC tube. In this region the tubes are heated internally with plastic-
covered soft iron wires. Before air is drawn through the tubes their
temperature is raised above that in the glasshouse to assist in preventing
condensation forming within the tubes. Air from 20 heights within and
above the plant canopy is drawn into two gas-stream selectors. These
consist of ten three-way solenoid valves, two diaphragm pumps and a
pulse-operated rotary switch (Fig. 1). Operation of the system is as follows. Nine of the ten valves are in the off position, air from these valves is
drawn from them by pump 1, and pumped to waste. The air from the
tenth valve is drawn by pump 2 and is split into two streams, one passing
through the psychrometer, the other through the infra-red gas analyser
(I.R.G.A.). Operation of a rotary switch turns on each valve individually in
sequence and thus each of the ten air channels is sampled. The sequence
operation is carried out by a pulse from the data logger at the end of each

two-minute cycle. It is important to maintain a continuous flow of air in those tubes not being analysed; this provides aspiration for the thermometers and eliminates delays in sensing any changes in the glasshouse. Each line is provided with a flowmeter to monitor the flow rate. Airflow through the sample tube is maintained at 2·5 litres min$^{-1}$, 1·5 litres min$^{-1}$ passing through the I.R.G.A., and 1 litre min$^{-1}$ through the psychrometer. Before passing into the I.R.G.A. the air is cooled to 2°C in a refrigerator unit. This lowers the air temperature below dew point and therefore maintains the air entering the I.R.G.A. at a constant water vapour content. The I.R.G.A. ("Uras 2" model made by Hartmann and Braun, Frankfurt) is a conventional twin-tube model, with one tube filled

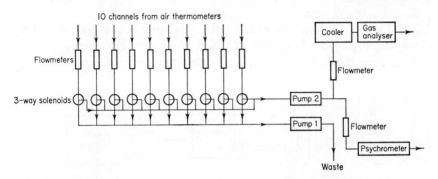

**Fig. 1.** Gas stream selection system for carbon dioxide and water vapour measurement.

with inert gas and the air to be analysed passing through the other tube. The carbon dioxide is measured, therefore, in absolute units. The calibration of the instruments is checked periodically with standard gas mixtures. Output from the gas analysers is recorded on chart recorders for an immediate visual record and on the data logger for analysis in the computer.

The psychrometers for humidity measurement consist of a ten-unit thermopile within a perspex tube. The thermopile is wound on an open perspex structure with one set of junctions covered by a cotton wick. The air temperature within the psychrometer is measured by a single junction thermocouple. The entire unit is mounted within a polystyrene box to prevent errors from temperature gradients, and airflow through the psychrometer is adjusted to give full aspiration.

Outside, the glasshouse air temperature, carbon dioxide, and water vapour are monitored with units similar to those used inside; but the windspeed is recorded with a sensitive cup anemometer (Casella) and the shortwave radiation with a Kipp solarimeter. The movements of the ventilators are also recorded by linking them to potentiometers; their position is detected by the voltage across a low resistance in series. Measurements of leaf area index are made on the leaf canopy at successive heights using a cutting and core sampling technique. Leaf resistance is determined at two-hourly intervals with an Alvim porometer.

# IV. Data logger

Output from all the sensors is fed through the field cables via a matrix board (allowing rearrangements of the inputs) to the logger. The logger is a "MBM Series 5000" system with provision for 100 analogue inputs from millivolt and volt sources with a maximum resolution of 4 microvolts. A block diagram is shown in Fig. 2. Data sampling is achieved with 100, threepole, dry-reed relays, each of which is energized or de-energized in sequence by the sampling unit. The data from each unit are routed, in

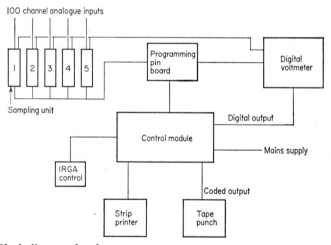

**Fig. 2.** Block diagram data logger system.

turn, to the Digital Voltmeter (D.V.M.) for measurement and digitization. Sampling sequence is from 00–99 with facility to confine channel sampling to any group of consecutive channels, i.e. 00–23 or 46–77. A programming Pinboard provides facility for programming the D.V.M. range (0·1V, 1V, 10V, 100V, or 1000V) and a scaling factor relative to each block of ten consecutive channels (0–9, 10–19, 20–29, etc.). The digitized data are displayed visually on the D.V.M. and so also are time and Channel Identity (C.I.). The "Fenlow 301" D.V.M. is an integrating digital voltmeter having an integration period of 25 ms with a total readout period of

40 ms. The digitized data are put out on tape on an "Addo-X" 8-hole punch and an "Addo-X" printer. These devices may be operated together or separately as individual units. Minimum sampling time for 100 channels is 15 sec, on "Addo-X" punch 1 min 8 sec, and on "Addo-X" printer 2 min 15 sec. The outputs on the printer and punch are in the displayed form on the logger. Time (4 digits), C.I. (2 digits), polarity (1 digit), Data (5 digits, "new line" character), C.I. (2 digits) etc. The pattern of the punch output is very important in maintaining flexibility in programming. The new line, and line feed characters at the end of each block of data are used to separate data blocks and individual data points.

Sampling periods of 40, 80, 320, 1280 and 2560 ms between individual data points with continuous 2, 10, 20, 60 min intervals between complete scans may be programmed. In general a sample time to 40 ms and a scan period of 2 min are selected. With this setting the output from the punch in 24 h is approximately 3 complete 30-cm reels of tape. Printer output is used only in setting up of the apparatus and checking for faults during the run. The data tapes are taken to the computer centre in London where the information is transferred from the punch tape on to magnetic tape for analysis.

# V. Data analysis

The main bulk of data so far analysed has been carried out with the help of the Atlas Computer Centre, University of London. Much of this work is now being transferred to the C.D.C. 66 in the University of London Computer Centre utilizing the terminal facilities with this computer at Wye College. However, the pattern of analysis is very much the same on both computers.

The programme required for carrying out the analysis is kept on a second tape. A small programme is used then to call down both data and programme tapes in the computer and instructs the computer to analyse a particular section of the data tape. The analysed data are printed out and may then be plotted.

Much of the programme for analysing the data consists of so-called "housekeeping" functions. Figure 3 shows an outline of the programme. Some of the more significant points are as follows: at A are set the times between which data are to be analysed, the number of data points to be extracted, and the deviation of the points around the mean that will be accepted. The setting of a limit to the deviation allows some of the machine errors in the data to be eliminated. To do this within the programme the previous mean for a particular data point is compared with the present reading under scrutiny; should this point deviate from that point to a greater extent than the limits set by the programme card the datum is not added into the mean and is eliminated as "wild data". The limit values set vary with the instrument used: for example, it may be as low as 500 $\mu v$ for a single junction thermocouple and as high as 5000 $\mu v$ for a solarimeter. The limit values must be so arranged that only data errors are eliminated

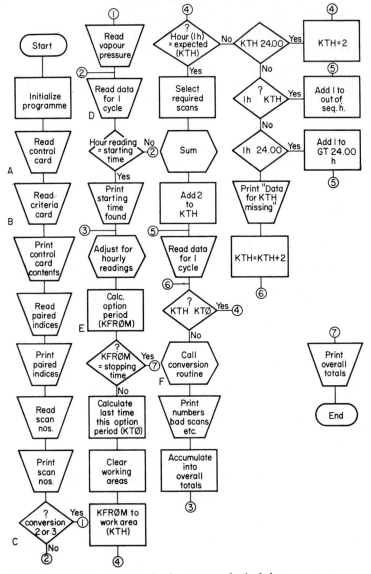

**Fig. 3.** Programme for analysis of micrometeorological data.

and all valid data are collected. At point B the starting mean for each data point is fed into the programme to set the first mean for wild data elimination. At point C the appropriate subroutine for a particular instrument is selected, each subroutine being specific to a particular form of instrument; anemometer, solarimeter, etc. At D reading begins to find the correct position (time) on the data tape, at E the period of time over which data are to be meaned is selected, 10, 20 and 30 min. At point E the data for each input are averaged and at F converted from mV to °C, m sec$^{-1}$ etc. The readings for each time period are then printed and the process is repeated until stopping time is reached. Data are plotted by hand graphically for final analysis.

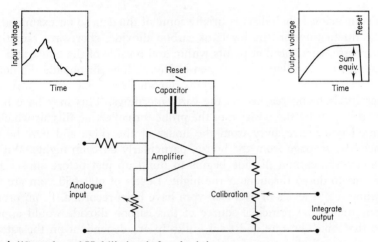

**Fig 4.** "Sample and Hold" circuit for obtaining parameter means.

There are a number of improvements which ought to be made to the existing recording system. At present, samples are taken at frequent intervals and averaged to obtain an approximation of the mean value of the particular environmental factor. The frequency of the sampling is dependent on the variability of the factor and the sampling capability of the recording equipment. At present this involves frequent sampling to satisfy the needs of the fastest changing factor, resulting in the production of large quantities of tape and a high use of computer time. This problem could be overcome if integrated means were taken instead of spot readings. This could be done relatively simply and at a lower cost than the computer time saved. Before outputs from the various sensors are read they could be fed into a "Sample and Hold" circuit; this consists of a Miller integrator circuit with a reset switch (Fig. 4). When an analogue signal is fed into the system the voltage at the output rises dependent on the gain of the system and the magnitude of the input. The gain being constant, output voltage is equivalent to the sum of the input voltages. Thus the output from a thermocouple may be translated over a set period of time to average temperature during that time, and by adjusting the gain of the amplifier the output may read as °C directly. Thus over short runs, use of the computer stage could be eliminated.

One of the more laborious tasks in our system is the final plotting of data. Programmes for the automatic plotting of data by the computer are now available and it is planned to plot all new data in this way.

# VI. Results

In conclusion I shall discuss briefly some of the data so far examined.

The fluctuations in the levels of carbon dioxide, shortwave radiation, temperature, windspeed at points within and outside of the house and the position of the ventilators are shown in Fig. 5. The air outside the house shows very little variation in carbon dioxide level (350–380 vpm), the higher levels being reached in the early mornings. This may have been affected in part by the position of the probe for collecting this air which is mounted one metre away from the house at the ridge and may be influenced by seepage from the house, particularly on calm nights. Within the house the carbon dioxide begins to build up just before sunset and continues to do so throughout the night. Levels of 600–650 vpm are not uncommon and levels of over 800 vpm have been recorded. From profile measurements the principal source of this carbon dioxide would appear to be the soil. The rate and total build-up are dependent on the rate of production and the rate of leakage from the house. This may also be seen in Fig. 5. On the night of the 28th–29th June windspeed over the house was 3–4 m sec$^{-1}$ and on the night of 29th–30th June, 1–2 m sec$^{-1}$. As one might expect, the higher average windspeed led to greater leakage and the build-up of carbon dioxide within the plant canopy during the latter period was very much greater. Depletion of carbon dioxide within the glasshouse begins at sunrise and the surplus of carbon dioxide relative to air becomes a deficit of 50–100 vpm in 2–3 h. Increasing temperature within the house brings about the opening of the ventilators, increases air circulation, and a rise in the level of carbon dioxide to a little below external air levels. It remains at this level throughout the rest of the day except when closure of the ventilators again brings depletion. This pattern is as one might expect from our knowledge of photosynthesis; profile measurements also showed that greatest depletion is in the region of the plant canopy where there is most active growth.

Observations of this type give a clearer picture of the plant environment and should enable us to develop control techniques with more certainty of success.

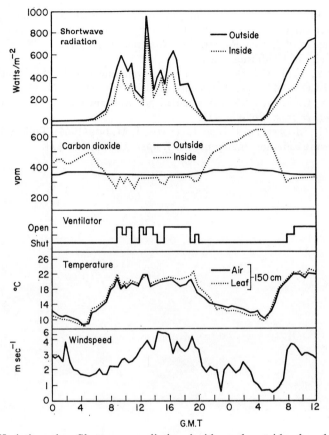

**Fig. 5.** Variations in: Shortwave radiation inside and outside the glasshouse, carbon dioxide within the plant canopy and outside the glasshouse, ventilator opening, leaf and air temperatures in the plant canopy and windspeed over the glasshouse, 29–30 June 1968.

# Acknowledgements

I should like to thank Professor W. W. Schwabe for his support and encouragement in this project and Mr F. V. Jones for much of the original work on the computer programming.

# References

BROOKS, F. A., SPARLING, C. L. and MULHOLLAND, F. F. (1965). "Calibration and Interpretation of Sparling heated-rod anemometers including change in heater current." Investigation of Energy, Momentum and Mass Transfer near the Ground. Final Report, 1965. Contract No. DA-AMC-28-043-65-G12, University of California, Davis.

LOURENCE, F. J. (1967). "Instrument development and calibration", Tech. Rept. ECOM 0447(E)-1 University of California, Davis, 11–44.

SIMMONS, L. F. G. (1949). A shielded hot wire anemometer for low speeds. *J. scient. Instrum.* **26,** 407–411.

SZEICZ, G., MONTEITH, J. L. and SANTOS, J. M. DOS (1964). Tube Solarimeter to measure radiation among plants. *J. appl. Ecol.* **1,** 169–174.

# I.5. A prototype, airtight, daylit, controlled-environment cabinet and the rationale of its specification

B. ACOCK

*Glasshouse Crops Research Institute, Littlehampton, Sussex, England*

## I. Introduction

Commercial glasshouse operators have an opportunity, unique among cultivators, for controlling their crop environment. For the Plant Physiology Department at G.C.R.I. to perform properly its function of research on the cultivation of glasshouse crops and enabling glasshouse operators to make best use of their facilities, it must be able to simulate reliably the full range of environmental conditions encountered in glasshouses. It has therefore been provided with controlled environment facilities varying from glasshouses and cabinets with simple temperature control to airtight, daylit and artificially-lit cabinets with provision for controlling temperature, humidity, airflow, daylength and the composition of the gaseous atmosphere.

In the course of acquiring these facilities, a survey of commercial plant growth cabinets available in the U.K. was conducted. Also a great deal was learned about factors to be considered and procedures to be followed in deciding which growth cabinets to purchase and where to house them. The knowledge gained in the course of these activities is neither peculiar to G.C.R.I. (A.I.B.S. 1971), nor appropriately discussed under the present heading. Nevertheless, it is expected to be of interest to intending purchasers of cabinets and has been included as an appendix to this paper. The primary purpose of this paper is to describe a protype, airtight, daylit cabinet recently built at G.C.R.I., and to discuss the rationale of its specification.

# II. Daylit cabinets

Daylit cabinets differ from glasshouses in having refrigeration and forced air circulation. A number of daylit cabinets of varying degrees of sophistication have been built during the past two decades and references to the accounts of their design may be obtained from the C.A.B. Annotated Bibliography on Controlled Environment Facilities (Query File No. 5170). The cabinets designed by Schwabe (1957) and by the C.S.I.R.O. (Morse and Evans, 1962; Read *et al.*, 1963) have been produced in some quantity and are probably the best known of the designs. Recently Hoffman and Rawlins, (1970) built some at the U.S. Salinity Laboratory and others are planned by G. N. Thorne and R. B. Austin of Rothamsted Experimental Station and Plant Breeding Institute respectively, and by L. G. Morris and his colleagues at the Volcani Institute of Agricultural Research, Israel,

The main advantage of daylit cabinets over artificially-lit cabinets is that they allow the plants to be grown in light of similar quality to that available to commercial growers. Some plant species grow abnormally under the fluorescent lamps commonly used in artificially-lit cabinets in the U.K. A list of such plants and their growth peculiarities has recently been compiled at Reading University (A. P. Hughes, private communication), and Thorne (1970) has published examples from barley and sugar beet. The use of daylight should overcome this problem of abnormal plant behaviour which presumably results from the spectral composition of the light from flourescent lamps.

Another feature of daylit cabinets is that the light flux density varies seasonally, diurnally and even minutely. This can be disadvantageous when making measurements which integrate changes in plant or environmental factors over periods of time, but it is advantageous in that plants in the cabinets experience natural diurnal and seasonal trends.

The disadvantages of daylit cabinets are that all the transparent parts above the plants must be easily accessible and frequently cleaned and that they are necessarily poorly insulated. Sheets of glass and transparent plastic have high thermal conductivities which result in high rates of heat exchange between the cabinet and its surroundings and hence heavy loads on the cabinet air-conditioning system. Double glazing results in too great a reduction in light flux density to be worth considering in most situations.

The prototype daylit cabinet at G.C.R.I. essentially consists of sides of 6 mm plate glass and a top of 10 mm armoured glass bedded on "non-hardening" mastic in a frame of 29 mm steel angle (Fig. 1). This transparent plant space is cubic with sides 2·15 m long. Within the space,

154 mm from the east side is suspended a 6 mm sheet of "Perspex" extending right across the cabinet, with a gap at the top, forming one side of the return air duct.

Glass was chosen as the material for the main shell of the cabinet, despite its brittleness, because "Perspex", the only other material seriously considered, has a much higher thermal coefficient of linear expansion than the steel of the frame, is inclined to craze as it ages, attracts and holds dust by static electrical charges generated at the surface and is

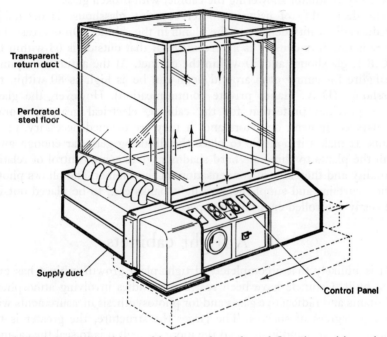

**Fig. 1.** The G.C.R.I. cabinet with the perforated steel floor in position, viewed from the south-east.

inflammable. The internal division between the plant space and the return air duct was nevertheless made of "Perspex" because it has to be moved frequently for cleaning and can readily be replaced.

This cubic shape of cabinet has far from ideal transmission properties and cylindrical and hemispherical shapes were considered at the design stage. However, we live in a "rectangular" society which produces glass, steel and other materials in flat rectangular sheets and it is cheaper and simpler to use these rather than to have curved parts specially formed. Also, more is known about airflow patterns in rectangular cabinets and there is therefore less development work with such cabinets.

The G.C.R.I. cabinet stands inside a glasshouse which has a mansard roof supported on a slender steel framework to maximize light transmission and is glazed with large sheets of diffusing glass. It has 3·7 m headroom throughout and a large door in the east gable to admit cabinets. The cabinet stands on the south side of the ridge and there are large ventilators on the south sill and the north ridge. This arrangement provides ventilation across the cabinet without there being too much obstruction of direct sunlight by ventilation gear and without running the risk of a faulty ventilator showering the cabinet with broken glass.

The desirability of using an outer covering glasshouse is debatable; it reduces light flux density to the plants in the cabinet. On overcast days the radiation flux density as a percentage of that outside is 68 within the G.C.R.I. glasshouse and 50 within the cabinet. At the autumnal equinox the figure for sunny days around noon can be as high as 80 within the glasshouse (D.W. Hand, private communication). However, the glasshouse provides protection for the cabinet, electrical gear, temporary ancillary equipment, operators and, if they are deemed necessary, guard plants. It makes it possible to place the diffusing glass far enough away from the plants to eliminate hard shadows, gives some control of relative humidity and therefore of condensation on the cabinet, and allows photoperiod curtains and supplementary light banks etc., to be placed outside the costly controlled environment space.

# III. Airtight cabinets

It is unlikely that a completely airtight plant growth cabinet has ever been built. Cabinets have been sealed for studies involving atmospheric pollutants and radioactive gases and for photosynthesis measurements with varying degrees of success. The larger the structure, the greater is the number of seams and joints, and the more difficult it is to seal the cabinet. A recent advance in airtight cabinets has been a 1 m³ cabinet with separate root and shoot compartments. This has been developed by Siemens for the Forestry Research Institute, Freiberg, West Germany.

The specification for the G.C.R.I. cabinet calls for less than 0·001 air changes per hour. This has yet to be achieved but if it is achieved there will be no need to measure cabinet leakage rate during photosynthesis experiments. Daunicht (1968), for instance, has used airtight cabinets in this way. By shutting off the carbon dioxide supply it will be possible to measure the carbon dioxide compensation point and by controlling the injection rate of carbon dioxide into the cabinet it will be possible to control photosynthesis rates at levels below the potential maximum for that light intensity. Also, it will be possible to study the effects on plants of abnormal concentrations of other gases, e.g. low oxygen concentration.

The problems of airtight cabinets are:

1. Actually making the cabinet airtight. All seams have to be carefully welded and flanges have to be machined, gasketted, coated with mastic and held together with closely spaced bolts.

2. Relieving changes in air pressure differential across the cabinet glazing caused by changes in temperature and barometric pressure and doing so without losing cabinet air. This necessitates the fitting of a "lung" delicately counterbalanced to respond to small pressure changes. If the "lung" is made of flexible material it may be another source of leakage in the system.

3. Fitting a pressure relief valve which, in the event of the "lung" malfunctioning, will operate at a pressure intermediate between that at which the "lung" normally functions and that at which the cabinet explodes. The valve must have a bore sufficiently large that, if the "lung" suddenly collapsed under its own weight, it could pass air at the rate necessary to prevent pressure building up in the cabinet. A large bore "S" bend with a shallow liquid trap would seem to be ideal.

4. Ensuring that the pressure in the cabinet is as near atmospheric as possible. The cabinet glass is likely to be the weakest part of the system and should be exposed to the least possible pressure. Also, having the cabinet pressure near atmospheric ensures that, if the cabinet door is opened when the main fan is running, no other part of the cabinet air conditioning system is unduly pressurized. To meet this condition the pressure drop across components in the flow duct between the main fan and the cabinet must equal that in the return duct between the same points.

In the G.C.R.I. cabinet the main fan develops a pressure differential of $1.49$ kN m$^{-2}$ (6 in. water) and the glass will just withstand a sustained pressure of $0.37$ kN m$^{-2}$ ($1.5$ in. water). The lowest leakage rate achieved so far is $0.02$ air changes per hour.

It is found in practice that when cabinets are operated continuously in the airtight mode there is an accumulation of phytotoxic gases (see Daunicht, 1968). Airtight cabinets must therefore be fitted with some means of taking in fresh air at a controlled rate when the operator so wishes and, if plants are to be grown in the cabinet for some part of their lives without carbon dioxide enrichment and without the carbon dioxide concentration falling more than $10\%$ below ambient, a fresh air exchange rate of up to $0.05$ m$^3$ sec$^{-1}$ for each square metre of cabinet floor area may be necessary.

# IV. Other features of the G.C.R.I. cabinet

The cabinet has a temperature range of 10–30°C and dewpoint control of relative humidity in the range 80–90% R.H. at 10°C and 45–90% R.H. at 30°C. The airflow rate past the plants is 0·4 m sec$^{-1}$ which is equivalent in this cabinet to one circuit of air every 12 seconds. This rate of airflow was chosen as a compromise between faster flows which cause a reduction in growth rate (Morse and Evans, 1962) and slower flows which increase the temperature gradient in the cabinet.

The air flows vertically upwards through the cabinet because:

1. The temperature and humidity gradients accompanying vertical airflow are vertical and affect plants equally. Horizontal airflow produces horizontal temperature and humidity gradients which affect plants unequally and are severe in that part of the canopy where the maximum amount of radiation is being intercepted, i.e. around the leaves that are photosynthesizing actively.

2. Plants spaced uniformly in a vertical airflow all experience a similar movement of air past their leaves. In a horizontal airflow the rows of plants on the input side deflect the air and, in the case of closely packed plants, may force the airstream up over the top of the canopy leaving pockets of hot, humid air within the canopy.

3. The baffles etc., necessary to ensure uniform airflow throughout the plant space, can be placed beneath the plant space floor where they can be as numerous and as opaque as desired.

As an alternative to the normal perforated steel floor on which potted plants can stand, two soil troughs on rails can be winched in through a removable panel to fill the cabinet base (Fig. 2). In this case, air is introduced to the cabinet through perforated polythene pipes attached to the upper air outlets and laid between the plants on the surface of the soil.

Air exits from the cabinet via a return air duct on the east wall and insulated ducts beneath the glasshouse floor lead the air to and from the air conditioning plant in a sunken room to the north (Fig. 3). Air from the cabinet first passes through the "lung", which is essentially an expanding part of the ductwork, to ensure that it is swept adequately and therefore contains a representative sample of the cabinet air. The air then passes through the pre-heater, spray washer, after-heater, and finally the main fan. The spray washer is supplied with chilled water, from a chiller unit, mixed in a four-way mixing valve with water from the washer sump. In the washer the air is virtually saturated at the required dewpoint. On those rare occasions when the required dewpoint is higher than the temperature of the water in the washer, the pre-heater is called into operation.

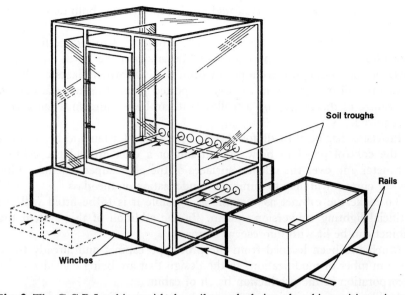

**Fig. 2.** The G.C.R.I. cabinet with the soil troughs being placed in position, viewed from the north-west.

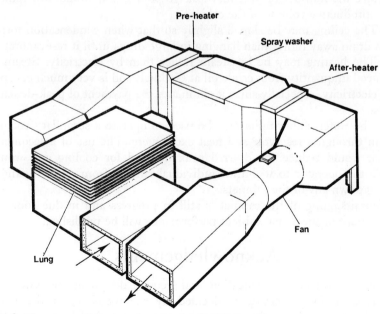

**Fig. 3.** The air conditioning plant for the G.C.R.I. cabinet.

The air leaving the washer is heated to the required dry bulb temperature in the after-heater.

To reduce the leakage of air from the cabinet and to reduce light obstruction, there is only one door and this is set in the north wall. It is therefore necessary to leave a path within the crop when plants are being grown in soil troughs or in the case of potted plants to stand the pots in the centre of the cabinet on a trolley that can be withdrawn when access is required.

Provision has been made for the incorporation of a fan and heater next to the control panel to blow hot air out of a duct around the cabinet perimeter and over the outside surfaces of the glass superstructure. This hot-air curtain will help to minimize condensation on the glass.

To make the cabinet as versatile as possible it is to be fitted with an artificial lighting conversion system. By the addition of this system the cabinet can be lit with fluorescent lamps.

Much has been learned from the prototype cabinet and already there are a number of modifications to the design that are being considered for incorporation in the production batch of cabinets:

1. The air conditioning equipment may be sited in a large basement immediately beneath each cabinet, and as far as possible with components welded together. This would reduce the number of flange joints and therefore the number of potential leakage points, and would also reduce the unproductive volume of the cabinet.

2. The ceiling may be sloped slightly so that when condensation forms it can drain away rather than hanging in large drops until it re-evaporates.

3. The heating may be by steam rather than by electricity. Steam is produced in quantity from crude oil at G.C.R.I. and is very much cheaper than electricity, especially since it eliminates the payment of peak-demand tariffs.

4. The water chiller units may be used to operate a secondary cooling system through a reservoir and heat exchangers. The use of a secondary system would reduce the diurnal peak demand for cooling and would enable the operator to withdraw individual chillers from service without closing down any of the cabinets.

Commissioning of the cabinet is still in progress and in due course a full account of the actual cabinet performance will be published.

# Acknowledgements

The performance, specification and general design of the G.C.R.I. prototype daylit cabinet were decided by the members of the Plant Physiology Department in consultation with staff of N.I.A.E. and the cabinet was developed and built by Environment and Air Conditioning Ltd., Blackpool, Lancashire.

## References

A.I.B.S. Bioinstrumentation Advisory Council (1971). Controlled environment enclosure guidelines. *Bioscience* **21**, 913–914.

DAUNICHT, H. (1968). Techniques of $CO_2$ experimentation. *Acta Hort.* **7**, 88–99.

HOFFMAN, G. J. and RAWLINS, S. L. (1970). Design and performance of sunlit climate chambers. *Trans. Am. Soc. agric. Engrs* **13**, 656–660.

MORSE, R. N. and EVANS, L. T. (1962). Design and development of CERES —an Australian phytotron. *J. agric. Engng Res.* **7**, 128–140.

READ, W. R., CUNLIFFE, D. W., CHAPMAN, H. L. and KOWALCZEWSKI, J. J. (1963). Naturally lit plant growth cabinets. *In* "Engineering Aspects of Environmental Control for Plant Growth", pp. 102–120. C.S.I.RO., Melbourne.

SCHWABE, W. W. (1957). Twelve miniature glasshouses with control of temperature and daylength. *In* "Control of the Plant Environment" (J. P. Hudson, ed.), p. 191. Butterworth, London.

THORNE, G. N. (1970). Use of controlled environments for studying the effects of climate factors on growth and yield. *In* "Prediction and Measurement of Photosynthetic Productivity". *Proc. IBP/PP Technical Meeting, Trebon 1969* (I. Setlik, ed.), pp. 399–404. Centre for Agricultural Publishing & Documentation, Wageningen.

# Appendix

## A. Comparison of standard plant growth cabinets available in the U.K. using data published by the manufacturers. June 1971

Where cabinet model numbers are given they have been chosen as typical of a range made by that manufacturer.

Many manufacturers are prepared to make cabinets to customers' specifications or at least to modify their standard cabinets in certain respects.

In addition to the manufacturers listed below the German firm of Weiss (U.K. agent unknown) makes a range of cabinets. Also, Climair Air Conditioning Limited is known to be interested in cabinet manufacture.

CPCE—H

Table I

| | R. K. Saxton (No longer made. Data for comparison only) | Prestcold | Environment and Air Conditioning | Controlled Environments | |
|---|---|---|---|---|---|
| Manufacturer | | | | | |
| U.K. Agent | — | — | — | R. W. Gunson Ltd. | |
| Model number | — | — | — | E8VH | PGW36 |
| Plant floor area (m²) | 1·9 | 1·9 | 1·9 | 0·7 | 3·3 |
| Height of plant space (m) | 1·2 | 1·2 | 1·2 | 1·2 | 2·0 |
| Temperature | | | | | |
| range with full lights (°C) | 5 to 33 | 5 to 30 | 5 to 48 | 10 to 45 | 10 to 45 |
| spatial variation (°C) | ±0·25 | — | — | ±0·5 | ±0·5 |
| temporal variation (°C) | ±0·25 | ±0·5 | ±0·25 | ±0·5 | ±0·5 |
| Relative humidity | | | | | |
| range at 30°C (% R.H.) | 53 to 93 | 50 to 95 | 20 to 95 | 30 to 90 | 30 to 90 |
| temporal variation (% R.H.) | — | ±2 | ±2 | ±2 | ±2 |
| Airflow rate (m sec$^{-1}$) | adjustable 0·061 to 0·178 | — | 0·076 | <0·45 | 0·25 to 0·36 |
| Light flux density | | | | | |
| maximum (klx) | 40 at 1·2 m | 36·5 at 1·2 m | 28 at 1·2 m | 53 at 0·5 m | 48 at 0·5 m |
| spatial variation (% of mean) | ±4 | ±4 | — | — | — |
| Overall cabinet l × b × h (m) | 2·4 × 1·8 × 2·8 | 1·8 × 1·5 × 2·5 | 2·1 × 1·6 × 2·6 | 1·8 × 0·8 × 2·0 | 3·4 × 1·5 × 2·5 |
| Overall refrigeration unit l × b × h (m) | 1·3 × 0·7 × 1·6 | 1·5 × 0·6 × 1·5 | — | — | — |
| Cabinet materials | sheet steel | sheet steel | within cabinet sheet steel and aluminium | within cabinet aluminium sheet on wood | within cabinet fibreglass and aluminium sheet on wood |
| Method of heating plant space | electricity | electricity | electricity | hot gas from condenser | hot gas from condenser |
| Method of cooling plant space | secondary coolant coils | secondary coolant coils | spray washer | primary refrigeration | primary refrigeration |
| Method of cooling lamps | vent to ambient | primary refrigeration | vent to ambient | (lamps in plant space) | (lamps in plant space) |
| Airflow direction in plant space | vertical up | vertical up | vertical up | vertical up | vertical up |
| Alarm system | comprehensive | comprehensive | comprehensive | high and low temperature | high and low temperature |

| Manufacturer | Fisons | | Sherer-Gillett | Vötsch | |
|---|---|---|---|---|---|
| U.K. Agent | — | | Lab. Equipment Consultants Ltd. | Tar Residuals Ltd. | |
| Model number | 140G2 | 1620G | CEL 37-14 | VEPH 01/1000 | VKZPH 005/158 |
| Plant floor area (m²) | 0·5 | 1·3 | 1·3 | 0·9 | 8·0 |
| Height of plant space (m) | 0·8 | 1·2 | 1·2 | 1·1 | 2·1 |
| Temperature | | | | | |
| range with full lights (°C) | 5 to 45 | 5 to 45 | 10 to 43 | −10 to +45 | −5 to +50 |
| spatial variation (°C) | — | ±0·6 | — | ±0·5 | ±1·0 |
| temporal variation (°C) | ±0·5 | ±0·25 | ±1·0 | ±0·5 | ±1·0 |
| Relative humidity | | | | | |
| range at 30°C (% R.H.) | (not controlled) | 40 to 90 | (control an optional extra) | 40 to 95 | 25 to 95 |
| temporal variation (% R.H.) | | ±3 | | ±5 | ±5 |
| Airflow rate (m sec⁻¹) | — | 0·075 to 0·21 | 0·38 | approx. 0·3 | — |
| Light flux density | | | | | |
| maximum (klx) | 20 at 0·25 m | 30 at 0·75 m | 54 | 27 at 0·9 m | 30 at 1·1 m |
| spatial variation (% of mean) | — | ±4 | — | — | — |
| Overall cabinet l × b × h (m) | 1·3 × 0·7 × 1·3 | 2·6 × 1·2 × 2·9 | 2·1 × 0·9 × 2·0 | 2·0 × 0·9 × 1·9 | 3·14 × 3·74 × 2·6 |
| Overall refrigeration unit l × b × h (m) | 0·7 × 0·4 × 0·4 | within cabinet | within cabinet | within cabinet | 1·5 × 0·9 × 1·2 |
| Cabinet materials | sheet steel | sheet steel and stainless steel | sheet steel | sheet steel and stainless steel | sheet steel and aluminium |
| Method of heating plant space | electricity | electricity | electricity | electricity | electricity |
| Method of cooling plant space | secondary coolant coils | primary refrigeration | primary refrigeration | primary refrigeration | secondary coolant coils |
| Method of cooling lamps | vent to ambient | primary refrigeration | (lamps in plant space) | vent to ambient | vent to ambient |
| Airflow direction in plant space | vertical up | horizontal | vertical up | horizontal | horizontal |
| Alarm system | high temperature | comprehensive | high and low temperature | comprehensive | comprehensive |

# B. *Notes on the acquisition of plant growth cabinets*

1. Growth cabinets consist essentially of a plant space, illuminated by lamps or daylight, through which air at a controlled temperature is passed. Relative humidity is sometimes also controlled. Naturally, the cost increases with the degree of sophistication.

The purchase of a cabinet implies that the purchaser has drawn up an outline experimental programme to cover the useful life of the cabinet, knows what environmental conditions are required and is satisfied that these can be obtained most economically with the cabinet purchased. Probably most purchasers err on the side of sophistication to cover all possible future requirements.

2. As well as considering those aspects of cabinets listed on the "comparison" table, intending purchasers should satisfy themselves that:

(a) there is not only room at the intended location to stand the cabinet and refrigeration unit, but also room to open all doors and access panels and withdraw the various components of the cabinets, e.g. fluorescent lamps,

(b) the cabinet can be dismantled sufficiently to gain entry to the intended location,

(c) the floor of the room where the cabinet will stand is strong enough to support its weight,

(d) the ventilation of the room is adequate to dissipate the heat from lamps, condensers, etc., and prevent the build-up of carbon dioxide,

(e) the lamps can be switched, individually, or in groups, or dimmed, or their distance from the plants varied, to give adequate control of light flux density at plant level,

(f) the cabinet fresh air intake rate is sufficient to prevent undue depletion of carbon dioxide when the plants are photosynthesizing actively,

(g) there are adequate supplies of single or triple phase electrical power for the cabinet and water of a suitable quality for humidifiers, water-cooled condensers and plant watering,

(h) spares are held in stock in the U.K. and will continue to be held for the expected life of the cabinet,

(i) the cabinet vendor can supply at reasonably short notice and at reasonable cost a qualified engineer to repair or maintain the cabinet (unless the purchasers retain a suitable engineer on their staff).

3. Intending purchasers should also, if possible, visit someone who already has a cabinet of their choice in order to:

(a) discuss the cabinet's defects and the differences between its actual and specified performance,

(b) see that there is reasonable access to the plants within the cabinet and all cabinet components requiring frequent attention,

(c) satisfy themselves that the noise made by the cabinet is tolerable or that the noisy components can be sited away from the main work area.

4. When a cabinet is to be custom built, a precise specification must be drawn up. Also subsequent amendments must be minuted to all parties concerned. The specification should include statements of:

(a) the required ranges and permissible tolerances on spatial and temporal variation for temperature, relative humidity, airflow rate and light flux density,

(b) whether the required conditions are to be met only with the cabinet empty or with a certain number, type and size of plants grown in a certain size of container present in the cabinet,

(c) the instruments and methods to be used to test that the cabinet meets the specification,

(d) the range of ambient conditions in which the cabinet will be expected to operate,

(e) the limitations on the overall physical size of the cabinet and associated equipment,

(f) any preferences as to the material from which the cabinet should be constructed. Also preferences for certain types of lighting, heating, refrigeration and control systems.

(g) a method of testing, for the manufacturer, plastics or other materials with volatile constituents likely to prove phytotoxic,

(h) the number, type and location of access doors, panels and pipes to the cabinet interior,

(i) the nature and extent of the alarm system required.

5. When a cabinet is to be custom built, the purchaser must draw up or have his financing authority draw up a contract stating:

(a) the method of paying for the work as it proceeds,

(b) the ownership of any patentable items or processes devised during the work,

(c) the legal liabilities of both parties for accidents to property or people in the employ of either of them,

(d) the penalties consequent upon the manufacturer failing to meet delivery dates, etc.,

(e) whether or not the manufacturer is expected to deliver, install and commission the cabinet,

(f) the period of time available to the purchaser for testing (and retesting after modification if necessary) the cabinet after it has been handed over by the manufacturer,

(g) the length of the guarantee period and the nature of the guarantee: including for both materials and labour.

6. When purchasing a cabinet, funds may be needed for:

(a) sensors and recorders for monitoring and for testing all parts of the cabinet specification,

(b) equipment for controlling the gaseous composition of the cabinet atmosphere (especially carbon dioxide),

(c) modifications to the building to allow for the entry of the cabinet, its safe accommodation within the building, supply of services to the cabinet and interconnection of the cabinet and refrigeration unit,

(d) hand tools and spares for the cabinet,

(e) extra manpower to help with experiments and the repair and maintenance of the cabinet. As a guide, one technician is desirable for the repair and maintenance of every six cabinets.

## Address list of plant growth cabinet manufacturers or their agents

CLIMAIR AIR CONDITIONING LTD.
60 George Street, Richmond, Surrey, England.
ENVIRONMENT AND AIR CONDITIONING LTD.
Mowbray Drive, Blackpool, Lancashire FY3 7UN, England.
FISONS SCIENTIFIC APPARATUS LTD.
Bishop Meadow Road, Loughborough, Leicestershire, England.
R. W. GUNSON LTD.
20–21 St Dunstan's Hill, London E.C.3, England.
LABORATORY EQUIPMENT CONSULTANTS LTD.
1 Shore Road, Ainsdale, Southport, Lancashire, England.
PRESTCOLD LTD.
Theale, Nr. Reading, Berkshire, England.
TAR RESIDUALS LTD.
Plantation House, Mincing Lane, London E.C.3, England.
K. WEISS.
Giessen, D6301 Lindenstruth, West Germany.

*Section II*

# Environment—crop relations

# II.1. Introduction: some partisan remarks on the virtues of field experiments and physical analogues

J. L. MONTEITH

*Dept. of Physiological and Environmental Studies, University of Nottingham, Loughborough, Leicestershire, England*

The second section of this symposium consists of five papers concerned with the response of field crops to the physical environment of plant roots and shoots. The presentation of these papers at a meeting primarily concerned with controlled environments is not hard to justify. Most of the concepts we use to describe and to analyse crop environment relations have emerged from experimental work in the field rather than in the glasshouse or the growth room. Except for crops such as lettuce which grow relatively close to the ground, the glasshouse is an awkward system for exploring crop–weather relationships because light, temperature and carbon dioxide concentrations are liable to change from point to point depending on the distribution of glazing bars, the control of ventilation and the arrangement of plants on the staging. At the other extreme, experiments in growth rooms or cabinets provide only limited information about plant–weather relations because the physical environment is unrealistically uniform both in time and in space. It is therefore dangerous to predict from growth room studies how a species will perform when it is grown either as a glasshouse crop or in the open.

The main advantages of the field as a laboratory for plant–weather studies are (a) the availability of extensive and horizontally homogeneous stands so that edge effects can be ignored and large numbers of plants can be sampled during the growing season without reducing the population significantly; (b) the existence of a microclimate within the canopy which can be measured, analysed and sometimes predicted from a knowledge of the relevant characteristics of the weather and the vegetation; (c) the ability to calculate the exchange of heat, water vapour and carbon dioxide between the crop and the atmosphere above it from corresponding vertical gradients of temperature and concentration. Details of the technique are considered in Lake's contribution to this Section (II.4).

There are obvious disadvantages in field experiments, in particular, the unpredictability of weather and of the incidence of disease, but I believe these have been over-emphasized by the exponents of controlled environments. To be even more provocative, I believe the enormous sums lavished on phytotrons in the last decade would have been more profitably deployed in well-designed field experiments linked to complementary programmes of physiological work in the laboratory. Progress in crop ecology may even be inhibited by the distractions which phytotrons, like computers, offer to the young research worker and the result is that research stations tend to acquire new hardware faster than they produce new ideas. I am sure that Littlehampton is immune from such criticism, however! The very powerful research team which Dr Warren Wilson has formed since his own appointment to the staff seems admirably matched to the fine growth room and laboratory facilities which will be opened officially at the end of this symposium.

Early attempts to describe the response of crop plants to their environment were based on statistical analyses of relatively crude biological and physical measurements. This approach is sometimes successful for one species growing at one site but it cannot lead to confident generalizations about crop–weather relationships. Current attempts to examine these relationships are often based on financial or electrical analogues. In financial analogues, a balance sheet is drawn up to show how the income of heat, water or carbon to a plant or to a stand of vegetation is related to the expenditure in terms of convection, evaporation, respiration, etc. This is the kind of exercise which Leafe and his colleagues have been attempting for a grass sward (II.5). Although it is instructive to follow changes in the financial fortunes of a crop as it matures, there is a limit to the amount of information that a balance sheet can convey even to the most experienced of auditors. Electrical analogues have helped ecologists to get a better understanding of cause and effect in plant–weather relations. Fluxes of heat, water vapour and carbon dioxide behave like currents and differences of temperature and concentration are the corresponding potential gradients. Resistances to molecular or turbulent diffusion are calculated by dividing a potential difference by the flux it produces in a simple circuit. One great merit of this approach is that the same terminology and formal relationships can be used to describe diffusion in the free atmosphere, in the aerodynamic boundary layer of leaves, and in leaf tissue.

Numerous financial statements showing the energy, water and carbon balance of a growing crop have been published in the last 20 years and estimates of diffusion resistances have been obtained for a wide range of species. On the basis of this information, the construction of crop–environment "models" has become a popular activity among mathematically-minded ecologists who seek to reach general conclusions about crop behaviour from a limited amount of experimental evidence. Some of this activity is premature because there is still great ignorance about the mechanisms by which plants respond to the environment of shoots and roots, a point which Scott Russell will emphasize (II.2). It is true that the production of dry matter by a healthy crop can be estimated with surprising accuracy from primitive models of photosynthesis provided the leaf area index is known, but we shall not be able to predict changes of leaf area in the field until we can unravel the interdependent effects of temperature, soil water availability and nutrient supply on plant growth in general and on the behaviour of meristematic tissue in particular. This exercise calls for much more active participation by biochemists in the study of crop–environment relations.

The value of integrating biochemical analyses with crop-environment studies is revealed by several contributions to this symposium. Whittingham (II.6) has focused attention on the influence of light quantity on the distribution of assimilated carbon between different organic compounds and light quality is known to have major morphogenetic effects which crop physiologists seem to take for granted in field studies. Rackham (II.3) examines some of the morphogenetic consequences of changing the water balance of a barley crop and considers the implications in terms of yield. Other speakers in later sessions will be talking about the ways in which biochemical control mechanisms interact with the physical state of the plant environment to determine the rate and pattern of growth.

Much of the current confusion about the relation between "sources" and "sinks" of carbohydrate stems from the difficulty of reconciling biochemical and physical aspects of plant growth. My dictionary defines "sink" as "a place where things are engulfed or where foul things gather". The first part of this definition approaches the physicist's idea of a sink. In a steady-state system, matter or energy which is produced at a given rate by a source is engulfed at exactly the same rate by a complementary sink. In mathematical terms, the source and sink have the same magnitude but opposite sign and it follows that in physical terms they must have the same dimensions. A familiar example is the positive and negative terminals of a battery which act as a sink and source for electrons when they are connected by an external circuit. Physiologists, on the other hand, seem to regard plant sinks as places where assimilate gathers in such a way that further movement to the sink is sometimes inhibited. Alternatively, the size of sink presented by an organ is vaguely defined in terms of the rate at which it grows, but saying that one part of a plant grows faster because it is a bigger sink is merely a tautologous concealment of ignorance about governing mechanisms. Further confusion is introduced when sink size is defined in terms of a relative growth rate whereas source size is related to a net assimilation rate. As the two rates are dimensionally different, this procedure is not consistent with a physical model of source–sink relationships.

To clarify ideas about the relationship between photosynthetic rates and the distribution of assimilates it may be necessary to abandon the terminology of sources and sinks and to adopt a more appropriate physical analogue. Introducing the concept of capacity, for example, would allow existing electrical analogues of photosynthesis and respiration to be extended by the addition of condensers representing either pools of mobile carbohydrate or meristematic tissue. Alternatively, the flow of metabolites to different plant organs could be represented by a triode valve circuit in which the flow of electrons from cathode to anode is controlled by the voltage of a grid between them. The anode and grid potentials could be derived from a single battery representing an external source of radiant energy or else grid potentials could be controlled separately to represent the action of a hormone.

"Depend on it, Sir," said Dr Johnson, "when a man knows he is to be hanged in a fortnight, it concentrates his mind wonderfully." Physical analogues of plant–environment relationships may be short-lived too but in our present imperfect state of understanding they help to prevent woolly thinking and provide a valuable framework for the kind of discussion and argument which is stimulated by a symposium like this.

# II.2. Transport of nutrients from soil to crops

R. SCOTT RUSSELL

*Letcombe Laboratory, Wantage, Berkshire, England*

## I. Introduction

No other aspect of the environment in which plants grow can be so readily modified as the supply of nutrients in the rooting medium. Modern fertilizer technology can usually provide the nutrients which plants require at an acceptable cost, so that the amount of solar radiation incident on foliage, temperature, water or disease usually imposes more intractable restraints on the productivity of crops. This generalization is likely to be in error only when root development is so restricted during at least part of the growing period that plants are unable to use the nutrients which can be provided. Such situations occur in the cultivation of field crops, but in the controlled environments, with which this symposium is concerned, the provision of an adequately favourable rooting medium should present no insuperable problems.

It does not, however, follow that the nutritional requirements of plants are supplied with the maximum efficiency. The following among other questions can be posed. Would it be possible by manipulating the rooting environment or by taking account of desirable root characteristics in breeding programmes to reduce the quantities of metabolites which are diverted to root growth without impairing their efficiency as absorbing organs? Could adequate nutrition be ensured with a reduced input of nutrients into the rooting medium?

The aim of this paper is to assist in the discussion of such questions. The information required is very different from that on which agricultural research on fertilizer use has hitherto mainly relied. The pioneers of soil chemistry recognized that the nutrient requirements of crops could be identified by soil analysis together with measurements of the nutrient content and yield of plants. Their successors adhered to this successful

111

course and plant physiology made but a minor contribution. However, for our present purpose, the paramount need is knowledge of the physiology and morphological characteristics of root systems which influence their ability to absorb nutrients and of the manner in which root function is influenced both by the nature of the rooting medium and by the requirements of the shoot.

# II. Factors which determine nutrient uptake by intact plants

The obvious starting point is to review some of the principal factors which influence nutrient uptake; for convenience relationships between root morphology and absorption will be considered separately in a later section of this paper.

The most commonly recognized factors which control nutrient uptake by plant roots—and indeed the only ones manifest in detached root systems which for simplicity have been the preferred experimental material in many physiological studies—are the external concentration and metabolic processes in roots. Relationships between external concentration and absorption are too familiar to require detailed discussion; when the external supply is low absorption is frequently approximately proportional to the external supply, though at higher concentrations each successive increment leads to a smaller enhancement of uptake. The radial transfer of nutrients to vascular tissues of roots is dependent on the expenditure of metabolic energy. The well-known effects of oxygen supply, temperature and respiratory inhibitors are evidence in this direction, as also is the fact that the ionic concentration in the transpiration stream can on occasions much exceed that in the outer medium. It does not, however, necessarily follow that all ions are actively transported in the strict sense of that term, that is to say that they are moved against an electrochemical potential gradient; the active transport of one ion can cause another ion of opposite charge to move from a compartment of lower to higher concentration, thus maintaining electroneutrality. The detailed study of this question in plant roots is considerably more difficult than in simpler tissue systems but the weight of the evidence, for example that of Higinbotham et al. (1967), suggests that, at the moderate or low external concentrations which plants normally experience, both potassium and phosphate are actively transported into the vascular tissue, in the strict sense of that term. The rate at which ions subsequently move to the shoots in the vascular sap can be much influenced by the rate of water movement. This explains why in some circumstances nutrient uptake varies closely with the rate of transpiration (Russell and Barber, 1960).

The physiological control of absorption does not, however, lie entirely in the root system and except when the external supply is grossly deficient the metabolic demand of the plant can exert an important influence. This is implicit in the familiar observation that nutrient uptake is greatest when other factors of the environment are most favourable for growth. Among the most detailed and laborious investigations which illustrate the influence of metabolic demand are those conducted at the Waite Research Institute over 25 years ago. Some of the evidence which led to the conclusion that "the rate of intake of phosphorus was seen to be more determined by internal factors of demand than by external factors of supply" is shown in

### Table I

Uptake of phosphorus by oat plants in sand culture between 46 and 82 days from germination—results per pot of 5 plants. Williams (1948)

| Initial external supply of phosphorus mg/pot | 8 | 90 |
|---|---|---|
| *Uptake* mg/pot | | |
| Leaves | 0·47 | 2·8 |
| Stems | 0·38 | 4·1 |
| Roots | 0·55 | 2·1 |
| *Uptake per* g *increment in plant weight* | | |
| Leaves | 0·6 | 0·5 |
| Stems | 1·0 | 0·9 |
| Roots | 0·9 | 0·7 |

Table I (Williams, 1948). A more than ten-fold increase in the supply of phosphate, within the range in which a response in growth occurred in oats, caused a marked increase in the phosphate content of plants but uptake per g increment in plant dry weight was little affected. Moreover, in young plants the increased growth resulting from the addition of phosphate led to a four-fold increase in the uptake, per g root weight, of nitrogen which was provided at a constant level (Fig. 1); nitrogen content per g dry weight of shoot tissue was, however, little affected.

Another, and perhaps more striking, illustration of the effect of plant demand on uptake is provided by the potassium nutrition of cereals. After mid season the uptake of potassium frequently ceases and sometimes a considerable loss of this mobile ion occurs despite the continuing uptake of nitrate and phosphate (Woodford and McCalla, 1936). This loss of potassium appears to be due to the fact that the metabolic demand of this nutrient reaches its peak at the time of maximum vegetative development and thereafter declines; Gregory and |Richards (1929) found that the physiological symptoms of potassium deficiency in cereals, which had been supplied with limited quantities of that nutrient, could be greatest at approximately the stage of growth when the highest plant content was observed by Woodford and McCalla.

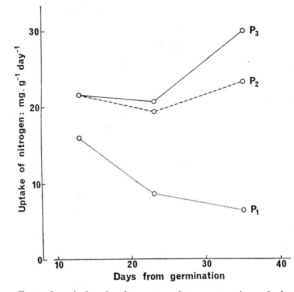

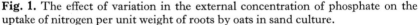

**Fig. 1.** The effect of variation in the external concentration of phosphate on the uptake of nitrogen per unit weight of roots by oats in sand culture.
Ratio of concentrations of phosphate—$P_1 : P_2 : P_3 : : 8 : 90 : 600$; all treatments receive the same level of nitrogen. (Williams, 1948.)

The effect of metabolic demand on uptake is also apparent from experiments in which the nutrient supply to different parts of the root system is varied. Thus Drew and Nye (1969) and Drew *et al.* (1969) showed that if only a small part of a root system is in contact with soil, the remainder being in nutrient-free sand, absorption per cm of root can be up to five times greater than that when the entire root system is in contact with the same soil. This effect, which occurred within a few days, is but the first stage in the response of roots to such conditions. Over a hundred years ago Nobbe (1862) realized that roots proliferate in zones of favourable nutrient supply; if only a small part of a root system receives ample nutrients it can give rise to more numerous and longer laterals than if the entire root system experienced similar conditions. This situation, which is illustrated by more recent work in Fig. 2 (Drew and Ashley, 1971) indicates that a feedback mechanism must exist between root and shoots; the extent of ion uptake by any one part of the root system can influence the supply of metabolites which subsequently reach it from the shoot, thus modifying the subsequent pattern of root growth. Discussion of the nature of these

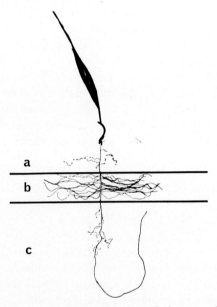

**Fig. 2.** The effect of the external concentration of nitrate on lateral root development.

A single seminal axis of barley (var. Proctor) was grown on filter paper through three separate compartments supplied with complete nutrient solution containing different nitrate concentrations: (a) 0·01mM, (b) 1·0mM, (c) 0·01mM. (Drew and Ashley, 1971)

feedback mechanisms lies beyond the scope of this paper; it involves perhaps some of the most complex aspects of the hormonal control of growth (Vaadia and Itai, 1969). From the viewpoint of the present discussion the important implication is that root systems should not be regarded merely as absorbing or supporting organs. Evidence that a root system exceeds the size which could provide adequate water and nutrients in a given set of circumstances thus would not prove that the extra root growth makes no contribution to the developmental process in the shoot.

# III. Relationships between the morphology of root systems and their ability to absorb nutrients

The environment to which root systems are exposed can cause wide variations, not only in their total size but also in the relative contributions of their component parts, for example axes and laterals (Hackett, 1968); marked intervarietal differences can also occur (Troughton and Whittington, 1969). The obvious starting point in considering the significance of these structural differences is a study of the extent to which different types of root member can contribute to the nutrition of the intact plant and how these contributions change as the root ages. The investigation of this subject is complicated by the fact that entry of ions into any one part of a root system, or translocation from it, can be much influenced by the activity of other parts of the root system; unequivocal information can thus be obtained only when nutrients which reach plant shoots from different parts of the root system can be distinguished from those contributed simultaneously from elsewhere. Despite the ingenuity of earlier workers, among whom Steward and his colleagues were outstanding (Prevot and Steward, 1936), this requirement could not be fully satisfied until it became possible to apply nutrients labelled with radioactive tracers to selected parts of the root systems, the remaining tissues being provided with similar but unlabelled nutrients. Solution culture provides the most convenient opportunity for detailed studies. Moreover, the general form of root systems grown in solution culture can be broadly similar to that in favourable and uniform soil (Hackett, 1969), apart from the sparse development of root hairs. Thus results obtained in solution culture should provide a useful general guide to the performance of different types of root member in soil, provided that account is taken both of morphological changes induced by the soil and of certain differences in the ionic environment which occur in soil and to which reference is made in a subsequent section.

## A. Observations in solution culture

The most detailed observations on the contribution of different parts of root systems to the nutrition of the intact plant have been made on barley (*Hordeum vulgare*) (Russell and Sanderson, 1967; Clarkson and Sanderson, 1971); however, some observations on *Cucurbita* (Murray *et al.*, 1972) suggest that the same general pattern of nutrient uptake occurs in the roots of dicotyledons before secondary thickening.

The ability to absorb ions is not, as was formerly often supposed, confined to the young white apical parts of roots where metabolic activity is high and the cells are thin walled. The fraction of the absorbed potassium and phosphate, but not calcium, which is translocated from the older parts of cereal root axes, for example some 40–50 cm from the apex, can be comparable to that provided by the younger tissues so long as part of the cortex remains intact (Table II and Fig. 3). The ability of ions to enter the

### Table II

Uptake and concentration of potassium by different parts of intact barley root axes (Russell and Clarkson, 1972).
*External concentration of* K : 0·1 mM

| Type of axis | Uptake n moles mm$^{-3}$ day$^{-1}$ | | Translocation % | |
|---|---|---|---|---|
| | Seminal | Nodal | Seminal | Nodal |
| Distance from root apex (mm) | | | | |
| 10 | 1·7 | 1·1 | 48 | 40 |
| 20–40 | 2·3 | 5·3 | 61 | 55 |
| 60–80 | — | 1·9 | — | 71 |
| 150 | 0·94 | 2·5 | 48 | 57 |
| >300 | 2·5 | 3·7 | 48 | 56 |

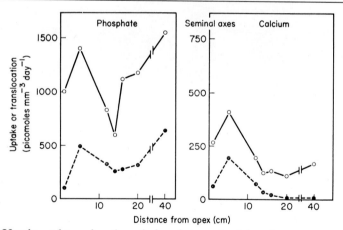

**Fig. 3.** Uptake and translocation of phosphate and calcium by segments of intact root from seminal axes of barley three weeks old.

Solid line, total uptake; broken line, translocation from treated segment.

Experimental conditions: Uptake was measured for 24 h at 20°C; relative humidity 65–70%; light intensity 2 × 10⁴ lux; day length 16 h; culture solution, pH 6·0, 3μM–KH₂PO₄, 1·25 μM CaCl₂ (Clarkson and Sanderson, 1971).

stele in zones where the tertiary endodermal wall is heavily developed appears to be due to the existence of numerous plasmodesmata at the base of pits which provide cytoplasmic continuity with the cells of the pericycle (Fig. 4) (Clarkson *et al.*, 1971). The pattern of absorption of all nutrients is not, however, identical throughout the root system; the most striking

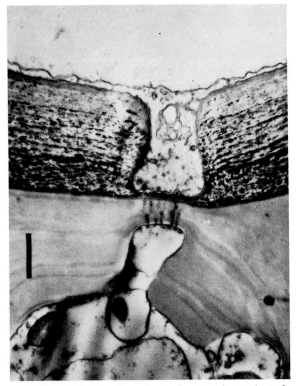

**Fig. 4.** Electron micrograph showing plasmodesmata (centre) at the base of pits linking cell of the endodermis (top) and pericycle (bottom). The tertiary endodermal wall shows dark bands of osmiophilic material. Scale bar = 1·0 μm (Russell, Clarkson and Newbould, 1971). (Photograph by courtesy of Dr A. W. Robards, University of York.)

contrast so far reported, though not the only one, is that little radial transfer of calcium occurs to the stele after the endodermis is well developed (Fig. 3).

The varying ratios in which nutrients are absorbed by different parts of root systems, even when a constant external concentration of each nutrient is provided, shows the complexity of relationships between the form of root systems and their capability as absorbing organs. Nonetheless, for the study of practical problems, it is important to consider what measurable parameter of root development is likely to give the best general guide. Is it the length, the surface area or the volume of the root system? On this subject again information is mainly confined to cereals. If all parts of the root system receive the same external supply, the relative contribution of different types of root members—for example axes and laterals—varies much more closely with their volume than with their surface area or length (Fig. 5).

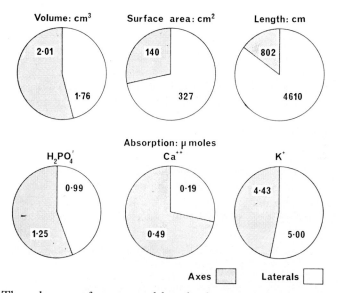

**Fig. 5.** The volume, surface area and length of root axes and laterals, and their contribution to the uptake of phosphate, calcium and potassium by barley plants c. 3 weeks old (Clarkson and Sanderson, 1971; Russell and Clarkson, 1972).

## B. Uncertainties in soil and other solid media

Under field conditions the most serious limitations to root development and function frequently arise from inadequate water supply in periods of drought, from anaerobic conditions, especially in waterlogged soil, or from the restriction of the root extension due to mechanical impedance. In controlled environments root systems should be exempt from these stresses and it is therefore unnecessary to consider them here. However, even in the most favourable and homogeneous soil the nutrient environment of plant roots is likely to contrast with that in aerated culture solution in at least one important respect; the supply of nutrients to all parts of the root system is unlikely to be uniform. Numerous studies of the movement of nutrients through soil towards plant roots (Barber, S.A., 1962; Passioura,

1963; Nye, 1966) show that the rate at which some ions, for example phosphate and potassium, enter plants can be limited by their rate of diffusion through the bulk soil, depletion occurring in the neighbourhood of roots. In contrast other ions, for example sulphate, can be moved towards roots by mass flow in water at a greater rate than into roots so that they can accumulate near them (Wray and Tinker, 1969).

The realization of the restraint which diffusion can impose on nutrient uptake from soil has stimulated theoretical studies of the effects of root form and distribution on absorption (e.g. Passioura, 1963; Nye and Tinker, 1969; Barley, 1970). In his recent review of this subject Barley concluded:

> Diffusion theory facilitates prediction of the hypothetical effects of the configuration of the root system on nutrient uptake. However, the processes operating are not nearly so simple as has to be assumed and the main use of theory is in the design of experiments of a kind which are amenable to analysis. Our present inability to interpret uptake patterns is limited chiefly by lack of knowledge of functional differences between roots of different age and form.

To assess the validity of this cautious judgement it is relevant to consider the nature of the assumptions which it is necessary to make both on the "absorbing power of roots" and on the nature of the contact which they maintain with the soil.

The sole plant physiological parameter of which account has usually been taken is the "root absorbing power" ($\alpha$) which relates the external concentration in the soil solution to the flux into roots as follows:

$$\alpha = \frac{\text{Flux (g.cm}^{-2}.\text{sec}^{-1})}{\text{Solution concentration (g cm}^{-3})}$$

This approach relates the absorbing power of roots to their surface area. The application of the model does not require $\alpha$ to be constant, but it is assumed to vary in a regular and predictable way. Nye and Tinker (1969) recognized that wide variations would cause the value of their approach to be very limited and expressed the reasonable opinion that the average value of $\alpha$ (or the product of $\alpha \times$ root radius) was likely to be sufficiently consistent "if each piece of root had approximately the same history". This situation, however, occurs only in simple root systems which consist of unbranched axes with a relatively constant diameter. The majority of well-developed root systems are much more complex. Axes and laterals normally vary widely in their diameter, their capacity for extension and sometimes also in their basic histological patterns; their "physiological histories" are not the same. The view that "$\alpha$" gives a realistic description of their absorbing power is contested by a number of facts referred to earlier in this discussion; the ability of different types of root members, for example axes and laterals to absorb nutrients, appears to be less related to their surface area than to their volume; contrasting relationships occur for different ions; depending on shoot demand, and nutrient uptake from elsewhere, absorption, from a constant external supply by any one part of the root system can vary widely.

The concept that the root absorbing power can, in the general case, be related solely to root area may thus be regarded as inadequate, and unfortunately this is not the only obstacle to the application of mathematical models. Of necessity they assume that the entire root system makes comparable contact with soil that displays diffusion characteristics which can be measured—that is to say those of the bulk soil. There is evidence that the situation is much more complex though at present it is only possible to enumerate the questions of which account must be taken—quantitative evaluation must await future research. Electronmicrographic studies

### Table III

Radioactivity of the foliage of mycorrhizal and non-mycorrhizal sweetgum seedlings 135 days old grown in a sterilized soil containing phosphorus-32. (Gray and Gerdemann 1967)

|  | Mean activity in foliage (cpm/mg fresh weight) |
| --- | --- |
| Mycorrhizal seedlings | 353 |
| Non-mycorrhizal seedlings | 24 |

encourage the view of Jenny and Grossenbacher (1963) that the intimate contact which mucilage can establish between the surfaces of young roots and the soil may significantly influence ion transfer. Moreover the soil adjacent to roots can be modified not only by the wide array of soluble plant exudates but by the abundant flora of the rhizosphere for which they provide the substrate. Few detailed studies of the effects of these organisms on the transfer of ions to plants have yet been carried out but in some circumstances their effect has been shown to be considerable. When the potential of phosphate in the soil is low, microbial competition can depress uptake by roots (Barber, D. A. and Benians, 1970) while vesicular-arbuscular mycorrhiza can enhance it (Table III) (Gray and Gerdemann, 1967), presumably because of the manner in which they explore the surrounding soil. Vesicular-arbuscular mycorrhiza are relatively widespread (Gerdemann, 1968) and if the results in Table III prove to be representative, microbiological effects on the transfer of phosphate to roots may deserve consideration equally with the diffusion of that ion through the bulk soil to the root cylinder.

Finally, it is necessary to take account of the fact that all types of root member may not make similar contact with the solid media. In soils of complex structure root axes may, for example, be confined to the larger pores, or voids between the structural units, these latter being penetrated only by the finer root members. It has been considered that in these circumstances root hairs may fulfil a major function by increasing the area of contact between roots and the solid media. The observation that phosphate can be rapidly depleted from soil in the root hair zone (Lewis and Quirk, 1967) is compatible with this view but does not prove it; the mobilization of phosphate by rhizosphere organisms which are abundant in the same region seems a possible alternative explanation.

The effect of many of the uncertainties to which attention has been directed should be least in studies of nutrient uptake by young unbranched root systems grown in soil. The most interesting theoretical assessments relate to such situations and suggest that the absorption of ions which diffuse slowly through the bulk soil should depend mainly on the total length of the root system (Nye and Tinker, 1969; Brewster and Tinker, 1970). However, model calculations cannot at present be confidently extended to more complex systems which in practice are more important. As Barley (1970) indicated, this is because of inadequate knowledge of functional differences between roots of different age and form; information is required both on their physiological characteristics and on the complex environments immediately external to root–soil interfaces. At present no better generalization seems possible than that suggested by solution culture studies—namely that, when no secondary thickening has occurred, the inherent ability of root systems to absorb nutrients can be approximately related to the volume of living tissue. Much more research—especially in plant physiology and microbiology—is necessary before the consequences of modifications imposed by the soil can be confidently predicted for the majority of circumstances. It may be hoped that the considerable progress which has lately been made in physico-chemical studies of ion diffusion will be a stimulus to this work.

# IV. Conclusions

Three principal reasons suggest that research on the transfer of nutrients from soil to plants is likely to make a minor contribution to future improvement in the productivity of crops in controlled environments. *Firstly*, existing fertilizer technology can ensure an adequate nutrient supply if roots are provided with a reasonably favourable environment. *Secondly*, the provision in controlled environments of a rooting medium which does not unduly restrict root growth presents few problems. *Thirdly*, when the nutrient supply does not seriously restrict root growth the rate at which nutrients are absorbed by roots is much influenced by the metabolic demand of the above ground parts. Under field conditions crop yields can be limited because unfavourable soil factors prevent sufficient root development for an adequate and continuing supply of water and nutrients but these problems should not occur in controlled environments.

This is not, however, to suggest that the performance of root systems should be ignored in work directed towards the enhancement of productivity in controlled environments. Some reference has been made to the complex interaction between root and shoot which influences plant growth and there are many other aspects of this subject which lie beyond the scope of plant nutrition. The effect of root temperature on shoot growth, for example, is considerable and complex (Davidson, 1969; Watts, 1971; Walker, 1970); especially as root temperature could be independently regulated in controlled environments, its influence on the productivity of crops seems particularly worthy of more detailed studies. Furthermore, even though we cannot at present reach definite conclusions on the manner in which the configuration of roots influences their ability to absorb ions which diffuse slowly in the soil, it is none the less evident that the rate of diffusion through the bulk soil is amongst the factors which can limit the uptake of some major nutrient ions. Rapid diffusion is thus one of the desirable characteristics of the rooting medium—though perhaps not in practice the most important one—and it would be of interest to know whether part of the advantage to culture systems which dispense with soil, for example straw bale culture of tomatoes and cucumbers (Anon., 1964), lies in this characteristic.

Finally it should be emphasized that information remains very meagre on relationships between the morphology of root systems and the uptake of nutrients in water, in those crops which are most profitably grown in controlled environments. The study of this question would be the first requirement if it were considered relevant to take detailed account of the configuration of their root systems in programmes for crop improvement.

# References

ANON. (1964). Tomato-culture on straw bales. First year progress report—1964. *Rep. Lee Valley exp. Hort. Stn 1964*, 18–23.

BARBER, D. A. and BENIANS, G. J. (1970). The uptake of phosphate by barley plants from soil under sterile and non-sterile conditions. *Rep. Agric. Res. Coun. Letcombe Lab. 1969*, 31–32.

BARBER, S. A. (1962). A diffusion and mass-flow concept of soil nutrient availability. *Soil Sci.* **93**, 39–49.

BARLEY, K. P. (1970). The configuration of the root system in relation to nutrient uptake. *Adv. Agron.* **22**, 159–201.

BREWSTER, J. L. and TINKER, P. B. (1970). Nutrient cation flows in soil around plant roots. *Proc. Soil Sci. Soc. Am.* **34**, 421–426.

CLARKSON, D. T., ROBARDS, A. W. and SANDERSON, J. (1971). The tertiary endodermis in barley roots: fine structure in relation to radial transport of ions and water. *Planta* **96**, 292–305.

CLARKSON, D. T. and SANDERSON, J. (1971). Relationship between the anatomy of cereal roots and the absorption of nutrients and water. *Rep. Agric. Res. Coun. Letcombe Lab. 1970*, 16–25.

DAVIDSON, R. L. (1969). Effect of root–leaf temperature differentials on root–shoot ratios in some pasture grasses and clover. *Ann. Bot.* **33**, 561–569.

DREW, M. C. and ASHLEY, T. W. (1971). Effect of variations in the supply of nitrate on root development. *Rep. Agric. Res. Coun. Letcombe Lab. 1970*, 7–8.

DREW, M. C. and NYE, P. H. (1969). The supply of nutrient ions by diffusion to plant roots in soil. II. The effect of root hairs on the uptake of potassium by roots of rye-grass (*Lolium multiflorum*). *Pl. Soil* **31**, 407–424.

DREW, M. C., NYE, P. H. and VAIDYANATHAN, L. V. (1969). The supply of nutrient ions by diffusion to plant roots in soil. I. Absorption of potassium by cylindrical roots of onion and leek. *Pl. Soil* **30**, 252–270.

GERDEMANN, J. W. (1968). Vesicular-arbuscular mycorrhiza and plant growth. *A. Rev. Phytopath.* **6**, 397–418.

GRAY, L. E. and GERDEMANN, J. W. (1967). Influence of vesicular-arbuscular mycorrhizas on the uptake of phosphorus-32 by *Liriodendron tulipifera* and *Liquidambar styraciflua*. *Nature, Lond.* **213**, 106–107.

GREGORY, F. G. and RICHARDS, F. J. (1929). Physiological studies in plant nutrition. 1. The effect of manurial deficiency on the respiration and assimilation rate in barley. *Ann. Bot. O.S.* **43**, 119–161.

HACKETT, C. (1968). A study of the root system of barley. I. Effects of nutrition on two varieties. *New Phytol.* **67**, 287–300.

HACKETT, C. (1969). Quantitative aspects of the growth of cereal root systems. *In* "Root Growth" (W. J. Whittington, ed.), pp. 134–147. Butterworths, London.

HIGINBOTHAM, N., ETHERTON, B. and FOSTER, R. J. (1967). Mineral ion contents and cell transmembrane electropotentials of pea and oat seedling tissue. *Pl. Physiol., Lancaster* **42**, 37–46.

JENNY, H. and GROSSENBACHER, K. (1963). Root-soil boundary zones as seen in the electron microscope. *Proc. Soil Sci. Soc. Am.* **27**, 273–277.

LEWIS, D. G. and QUIRK, J. P. (1967). Phosphate diffusion in soil and uptake by plants. III. P-31 movement and uptake by plants as indicated by P-32 autoradiography. *Pl. Soil* **26**, 445–453.

MURRAY, R. S. H., CLARKSON, D. T. and SANDERSON, J. (1972). The Absorption of ions by the root system of marrow seedlings. *Rep. Agric. Res. Coun. Letcombe Lab. 1971*, 3–4.

NOBBE, F. (1862). Über die feinere Verästelung der Pflanzenwurzeln. *Landw. VersSta.* **4**, 212–224.

NYE, P. H. (1966). The effect of nutrient intensity and buffering power of a soil, and the absorbing power, size and root hairs of a root, on nutrient absorption by diffusion. *Pl. Soil* **25**, 81–105.

NYE, P. H. and TINKER, P. B. (1969). The concept of a root demand coefficient. *J. appl. Ecol.* **6**, 293–300.

PASSIOURA, J. B. (1963). A mathematical model for the uptake of ions from the soil solution. *Pl. Soil* **18**, 225–238.

PREVOT, P. and STEWARD, F. C. (1936). Salient features of the root system relative to the problem of salt absorption. *Pl. Physiol., Lancaster* **11**, 509–534.

RUSSELL, R. S. and BARBER, D. A. (1960). The relationship between salt uptake and the absorption of water by intact plants. *A. Rev. Pl. Physiol.* **11**, 127–140.

RUSSELL, R. S. and CLARKSON, D. T. (1972). Uptake and distribution of nutrients in crop plants. *In* "Potassium in Biochemistry and Physiology". *8th Int. Congr. Potash Inst.* (in press).

RUSSELL, R. S., CLARKSON, D. T., and NEWBOULD, P. (1971). Tracer studies of the root systems of crop plants. *4th Int. Conf. peaceful Uses atom. Energy*, Paper 506.

RUSSELL, R. S. and SANDERSON, J. (1967). Nutrient uptake by different parts of the intact roots of plants. *J. exp. Bot.* **18**, 491–508.

TROUGHTON, A. and WHITTINGTON, W. J. (1969). The significance of genetic variation in root systems. *In* "Root Growth" (W. J. Whittington, ed.), pp. 296–314. Butterworths, London.

VAADIA, Y. and ITAI, C. (1969). Interrelationships of growth with reference to the distribution of growth substances. *In* "Root Growth" (W. J. Whittington, ed.), pp. 65–79. Butterworths, London.

WALKER, J. M. (1970). Effects of alternating versus constant soil temperature on maize seedling growth. *Proc. Soil Sci. Soc. Am.* **34**, 889–892.

WATTS, W. R. (1971). Role of temperature in the regulation of leaf extension in *Zea mays*. *Nature, Lond.* **229**, 46–47.

WILLIAMS, R. F. (1948). The effects of phosphorus supply on the rates of intake of phosphorus and nitrogen and upon certain aspects of phosphorus metabolism in gramineous plants. *Aust. J. sci. Res. Ser. B* **1**, 333–361.

WOODFORD, E. K. and MCCALLA, A. G. (1936). The absorption of nutrients by two varieties of wheat grown on the black and gray soils of Alberta. *Can. J. Res. C* **14**, 245–266.

WRAY, F. J. and TINKER, P. B. (1969). A scanning apparatus for detecting concentration gradients around single plant roots. *In* "Root Growth" (W. J. Whittington, ed.), pp. 418–422. Butterworths, London.

# Discussion

**Lake** asked if experiments had been done on effects of the flux of ions into the plant on plant growth rates. In principle an experiment could be conducted to determine the effect of a series of rates of nitrogen uptake on plant growth. **Scott Russell** thought that this approach could help little to solve outstanding problems. No constant relationship between the flux of ions into plant roots and growth could be expected because of the numerous other interacting factors which influence growth; moreover in any one species under a constant set of conditions, uptake per unit volume of root tissue and its influence on the dry matter increment could vary considerably with time depending on the changing pattern of growth. Relationships between the uptake of nitrogen and plant growth have, of course, been widely studied; the results relate to the specific conditions of the experiment only. When the external concentration is raised above the range in which a response in growth occurred "luxury uptake" could further complicate interpretation.

# II.3. Responses of the barley crop to soil water stress

O. RACKHAM

*Department of Applied Biology, University of Cambridge, England*

## I. The Nuffield Applied Plant Physiology Project

It has long been known to farmers that drought is a major factor limiting the production of spring cereals in eastern England. Until recently the phenomenon has not had the scientific attention which it deserves, although published data for Woburn show a substantial response to irrigation in barley and wheat in roughly half the years studied. Despite the large variations in timing of rainfall, in cereal genotype, and in cultivation history, most of the Woburn figures fit a linear relation (Fig. 1) between the response to irrigation in different years and the amount of irrigation needed.

The Nuffield Applied Plant Physiology Project, begun jointly in 1966 by the Plant Breeding Institute, Trumpington, the Departments of Agriculture and Botany, Cambridge University, and the Meteorological Office Research Unit (M.O.R.U.), Cambridge, was intended to develop means of producing controlled partial drought in the soil of experimental plots, and to study the responses of barley to such drought with a view to elucidating the physiological mechanisms bringing about reduction in yield.

This paper summarizes the work of the project up to 1970, and especially the full-scale experiments of 1969 and 1970. Space prevents any aspect from being presented in detail, and it has been necessary to leave out such important matters as the differences in behaviour of the main stem and the tillers, as well as the whole of the meteorological work (for some of which see Grant, 1970).

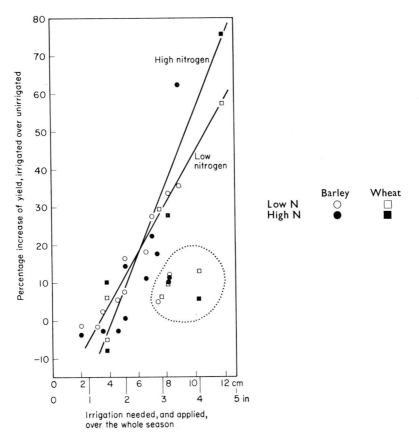

**Fig. 1.** Summary of 18 years of irrigation experiments at Woburn, computed from the published data of Penman (1962, 1970). In each year either barley (one of four varieties) or wheat (one of three varieties) was grown, usually at two levels of nitrogen. Both nitrogen treatments were irrigated or unirrigated, irrigation being applied as needed according to a standard policy. The points fall into two groups, of which the larger group (outside the dotted line) shows a clear relation at both levels of nitrogen between the irrigation needed in each season and the percentage increase of yield, with no distinction between wheat and barley.

# II. Soil moisture as a controllable environmental variable

Much of the literature on drought in cereals is concerned with pot experiments. These are difficult to relate to normal agriculture because (leaving out the complications of the aerial environment) it is very difficult to simulate in small volumes of soil the natural development of drought down a root profile. It was accordingly decided to develop methods of controlling soil moisture in a crop grown as far as possible under normal agricultural practice. This decision has been vindicated in the course of the project by a number of discoveries which suggest that the distributions of both moisture and roots in the subsoil depend critically on the presence of worm burrows and other permanent features which cannot be simulated in disturbed earth.

Preliminary experiments showed that a satisfactory method of producing partial drought was to lay gutters between the rows of a crop (sown with an ordinary 12-row seed drill) to intercept a proportion of the rainfall (varying between 30% and 60% according to the state of the crop). To allow for other effects of gutters on the crop a second treatment was introduced, consisting of "leaky gutters" with slots cut in them to return the intercepted water immediately to the soil.

Irrigation was applied with trickle nozzles at the soil surface. The practice was to maintain a soil moisture deficit close to 2 in. (50 mm) below field capacity for the whole or for part of the growing season. The M.O.R.U. provided the necessary information from weekly measurements of soil moisture profiles by the neutron scattering method, interpolated with the help of weighing lysimeters. Irrigation water was applied in quantities ranging from 13 to 52 mm at one time.

In most seasons, either gutters and leaky gutters or irrigation and control can be relied upon to produce a measurable drought comparison; the former pair will do so in rainy periods and the latter in natural drought.

The greatest control over the timing of drought is produced by equipping plots with both gutters and irrigation, but even this control is only partial. Not only does the drying of the soil depend on transpiration; at least on the experimental site (a gravel river terrace at Trumpington, Cambridge, modified by periglacial solefluxion) the rise in soil moisture content as measured after irrigation (or heavy rain) is often 10–20 mm short of the water applied. Although part of this discrepancy may be accounted for by increased transpiration, it is probable that considerable quantities of water are lost by percolation down near-vertical channels or burrows which penetrate the subsoil to at least 2 m (Kirby and Rackham, 1971). It is not known how widespread this phenomenon is, but it clearly limits the degree to which soil moisture can be controlled experimentally.

All the following experimental data were obtained on treatment plots of $6 \times 7\frac{1}{2}$ ft ($1 \cdot 8 \times 2 \cdot 3$ m), each containing 12 rows of crop and surrounded by a large area of untreated crop. The cultivar used was 'Proctor' except where otherwise stated.

In the rest of this paper the term "drought" is used in its ordinary

**Table I**

Grain yields in the Nuffield experiments, 1966–1970

| Year | Treatments | Water reaching ground during growing season, mm | | | Dry weight of grain, g m$^{-2}$ | | | Remarks |
|---|---|---|---|---|---|---|---|---|
| | | Drier treatment | Wetter treatment | Difference | Drier treatment | Wetter treatment | % difference $\dfrac{drier-wetter}{wetter}$ | |
| 1966 | Gutters and control | | | | 301 | 326 | −8 | Pilot experiments |
| 1967[1] | Gutters and leaky gutters | 131 | 189 | 58 | 225 | 289 | −22 | |
| 1968[1] | Gutters and control | 163 | 263 | 100 | 188 | 208 | (−10) | Severe differential mildew damage |
| 1969 | Gutters and leaky gutters | 104 | 201 | 97 | 298 | 376 | −21 | Sown on 25 March |
| 1969 | Control and irrigation | 201 | 353 | 152 | 393 | 421 | −7 | |
| 1970 | Gutters and leaky gutters | 71 | 110 | 39 | 191 | 187 | (+2) | Sown on 16 April |
| 1970 | Control and irrigation | 110 | 260 | 150 | 131 | 306 | −57 | |

(Differences in parentheses do not reach the 5 % level of significance)
[1] 'Maris Concord'.

environmental (rather than clinical) sense and refers principally to the effects of either gutters or the absence of irrigation.

# III. Effects of drought on grain yield and yield components

Table I* shows the differences of yield corresponding to differential drought treatments. The effects are of the same order of magnitude as those obtained in the drought experiments of Bingham (1966) with wheat, and the irrigation experiments of Penman (1962, 1970) and Kirby (1968); and some of the data are consistent with a response of the kind shown in Fig. 1. Nevertheless, the relation between the degree of drought and the response of the crop is not a simple one and depends on the timing of the drought as well as its magnitude. The very large irrigation response in 1970 may be attributed in part to the unirrigated crop, in this year of late sowing, being subjected to drought at an early stage of root development at which stage it was unable to extract moisture from deep in the ground.

In terms of yield components, the effects of the drier treatments in most seasons are attributable to an increased proportion of stems which fail to produce an ear, and to a lesser extent to an increased number of spikelets which become sterile at a relatively late stage of development. This is illustrated by some results for 1969 (Table II). This appears to be the commonest pattern of drought response in these experiments, although in some other instances drought has been observed to reduce the spikelets per ear. The mean weight of a grain may either be reduced by a drought treatment, as in Table II, or increased.

In 1970 there was a severe natural drought in June followed by rain in July. The experimental programme included gutters (producing drought both before and after ear emergence), irrigation (no drought at any time) and gutters + irrigation (drought before ear emergence, irrigation after). Comparison of these treatments tells us to what extent reduction in numbers of grains due to early drought can be compensated for by additional moisture at the time of grain filling. In this year (Table III) no such compensation took place. Although the total dry weight at final harvest was slightly greater with gutters + irrigation than with gutters, the increase was more than cancelled out by the much larger proportion which consisted of tillers stimulated into late growth and still green at the time of harvest, and there was no corresponding increase in the dry weight of ripe grain. Late tillers (see V below) are biologically important as a survival

---

* All figures in the tables are provisional. The grain weights in Tables I and III are based on different sets of subsamples.

## Table II

1969 gutters and leaky gutters: yields and yield components

| | Gutters G | Leaky gutters LG | % difference $\dfrac{LG - G}{LG}$ |
|---|---|---|---|
| Plants per m² | 260 | 265 | (+2) |
| Stems per m² (at final harvest) | 640 | 602 | (−6) |
| Ears per m² | 472 | 532 | +11 |
| Spikelets per m² (at final harvest, fertile + sterile) | $1 \cdot 115 \times 10^4$ | $1 \cdot 250 \times 10^4$ | +11 |
| Grains per m² | $0 \cdot 860 \times 10^4$ | $1 \cdot 039 \times 10^4$ | +17 |
| Grain dry wt, g per m² | 298 | 376 | +21 |
| Proportion of stems producing ears | 0·737 | 0·884 | +17 |
| Spikelets per ear | 24·34 | 24·35 | (+0·05) |
| Proportion of spikelets producing grain | 0·805 | 0·849 | +5 |
| Mean weight of a grain, mg | 34·7 | 36·3 | +5 |

## Table III

1970 irrigation and gutters: yields and yield components

| | Gutters G | Gutters + irrigation GI | Irri- gation I | % differences $\dfrac{G - I}{I}$ | $\dfrac{GI - I}{I}$ |
|---|---|---|---|---|---|
| Plants per m² | 260 | 270 | 262 | (−1) | (+3) |
| Stems per m² (at final harvest) | 661 | 681 | 648 | (+2) | (+5) |
| Ears per m² | 321 | 302 | 512 | −37 | −41 |
| Spikelets per m² | 7004 | 6384 | 11,142 | −37 | −43 |
| Grains per m² | 4977 | 4291 | 8711 | −43 | −51 |
| Grain dry wt, g per m² | 180 | 152 | 300 | −40 | −50 |
| Total above-ground dry wt, g per m² (including green tillers) | 390 | 428 | 623 | | |
| Dry wt of green tillers, g per m² | 7 | 85 | 2 | | |

"Gutters + irrigation" is a crop subject to gutters throughout its life and irrigated to within about 5 cm of field capacity in July only. The figures (except where stated) exclude material that was still green at time of final harvest.

mechanism, but agriculturally counter-productive; there are strong indications that they withdraw dry matter that would otherwise have been added to ears already formed.

# IV. Effects of drought on photosynthetic area and assimilation

Variables recorded during growth analysis were "total" dry weight (excluding roots which are the subject of a separate study) and its division into "stems" (including leaf sheaths and dead leaves), "leaves" (i.e. green laminae), and ears, and the green areas of "leaves" and "stems". Measurements of awn and ear areas were thought to be too inaccurate to be justified.

Values of net assimilation rate were worked out for the period up to ear emergence. Expressed as "unit (leaf $+ \frac{1}{2}$ stem) rate", (i.e. treating each cm$^2$ of "stem" as equivalent to $\frac{1}{2}$ cm$^2$ of "leaf" because it has one photosynthetic surface instead of two), they range from 1·6 to 4·4 mg cm$^{-2}$ week$^{-1}$. No clear evidence was found of any treatment effects on net assimilation rate. The economics of drought-induced differences in dry weight must therefore be interpreted in terms of the duration of photosynthetic area and of the distribution of dry matter within the plant.

Results for 1970 serve as an illustration (Fig. 2). Irrigation began on June 4. Throughout June the unirrigated plots showed severe drought symptoms, associated with a rapidly-developing soil moisture deficit which reached 100 mm by June 22. But the differences in total dry weight during this period were modest and attributable to delayed "stem" expansion and accelerated "leaf" senescence in the drought plots. Large differences in total dry weight did not develop until after ear emergence. Under irrigation, emergence took place normally, the ears being carried aloft on a terminal internode which accounts for part of the comparatively large "stem" area index at this time. With the other treatments, the terminal internode failed to elongate and ear emergence was delayed by some weeks and was never completed. The differences in total dry weight during July were therefore attributable in part to the much higher "stem" area index of irrigated plots, and in part to the effect of drought in reducing the exposed area of awns and ears available for photosynthesis. Under irrigation, not only was the total dry weight of the crop much greater than in unirrigated plots, but an appreciably higher proportion of this weight appeared as grain.

It is noteworthy, however, that the mean weight of an ear is much less sensitive to treatment than is the weight of ears per plot: the greater weight

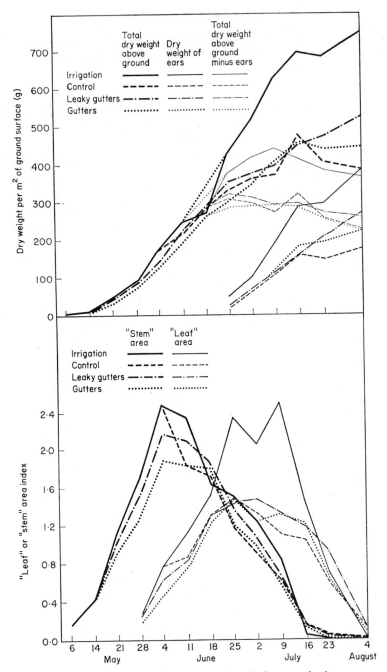

**Fig. 2.** Progress of dry weight (excluding roots) and photosynthetic area at weekly intervals during 1970.

per plot of the irrigated ears is largely due to there being more of them. This is associated with the fact that the dry weight of stems + leaves reaches a maximum, in the case of control and "leaky gutters" plots, soon after the ears appear, but goes on increasing much longer under irrigation. There may thus be a compensatory mechanism involved in determining the mean weight of an ear at any stage. In the case of irrigation, much of the ear's dry matter must come from its own photosynthesis. With the drought treatments, the ear's photosynthesis is restricted by incomplete emergence and consequent shading, but the ear draws its dry matter instead from the vegetative parts of the plant.

We may note finally that rain in July intermittently alleviated the drought in the grain-filling stage for leaky gutters but not for gutters. The total dry weight of "leaky gutters" plots went on increasing, and some of this increase went into the grain, although most of it went into late tillers (cf the yield-component analysis of "gutters + irrigation" above).

# V. Effects of drought on the life-histories of tillers, ears, spikelets and grains

The yield-component study suggests that the reduction of ears per unit ground area, which is one of the main effects of drought, is chiefly due to the death of a larger proportion of those that are produced, and not to a reduced production of tillers. Detailed records of tillers were kept in 1970 (Fig. 3) and in 1969.

In the first few weeks after seedling emergence, the plant produces ten or more tiller buds in the axils of the lower leaves on the main stem and lower-order tillers. Most of these never exceed 1 mm in length, but provide a reserve of buds from which new tillers can be formed later. If conditions are suitable, tiller buds elongate into tillers in sequence in a hierarchical order. The term "tiller" will be restricted to those tillers which have elongated far enough to emerge from the leaf-sheath to which they are axillary.

The main tillering period has not so far proved to be markedly susceptible to drought. This is partly because a drought does not easily develop until the leaves of the crop have covered the ground for a sufficient period of time for soil moisture to be seriously depleted by transpiration. It is probable that drought can delay temporarily the development of the later tillers, but this effect is difficult to disentangle from the effect on tillering of the shade produced by gutters. After the main tillering period is over, there is a gap of some weeks in which the tiller population does not change appreciably.

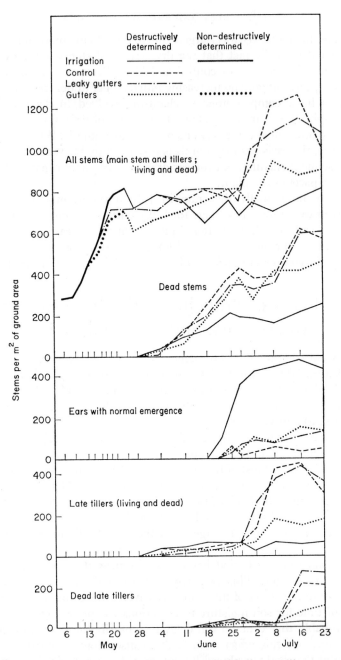

**Fig. 3.** Numbers of total stems, dead stems, ears with "normal" emergence (see section IV above), and living and dead late tillers at weekly or shorter intervals during 1970. Non-destructive determinations, made repeatedly on the same batch of plants, are less variable than destructive determinations.

The death of tillers is a separate phase occupying the first three weeks of June. The early stages have not been affected by drought treatments hitherto, but a marked divergence arises in the later stages; either the rate (Fig. 3), or the time at which tiller death ends, being affected. This phase overlaps with the emergence of ears, a process which, as we have seen, may be delayed and be very incomplete under drought.

The next process is the production of late tillers. This took place to an appreciable extent only in 1970 in these experiments, although it frequently occurs in farming practice. Field observation suggests that it follows water stress in June relieved by rain in July. In the 1970 experiments, late tillering was marked in "control" and "leaky gutters" (dry June, rain in early July), was less frequent in "gutters" (dry June, dry July), and was completely suppressed in "irrigation" (wet June, wet July). Late tillering is followed (Fig. 3) by the death of some of the late tillers.

The death of tillers is one of the numerous adjustments which the plant makes in the course of its development. A large stock of tiller buds is made, most of which remain dormant. Some of these develop to produce a population of tillers rather larger than the population of ears which would be formed under optimum conditions. This population is reduced by the death of excess tillers to an extent determined, *inter alia*, by the soil moisture status prevailing later in the season. Late tillering is a further biological compensation in which the plant reacts to improved soil moisture status later in the season by the stimulation of its dormant buds.

More limited records were kept of the production and fate of spikelets in the treatments. Each ear differentiates up to 40 potential spikelets, of which about 15 at the tip of the ear degenerate before ear emergence. They are then sufficiently small not to be recorded at final harvest: the yield component "spikelets per ear" includes only those spikelets which survive till the end of June. In 1970 the production and loss of potential spikelets were both unaffected by treatment, so that spikelets per ear did not depend on drought. There are, however, indications that this may not always be the case.

The difference between "spikelets per ear" and "grains per ear" is due mainly to the failure of spikelets at the base of the ear to produce a grain. In 1970, in the drought treatments, the number of spikelets failing in the middle of the ear was almost equal to the number failing at the base, but this is probably an unusual result of a very severe drought. Similar failure at the tip of the ear is comparatively infrequent. This type of failure occurs, or at least is predetermined, around or before the time of ear emergence; it was not prevented in 1970 by July irrigation (Table III). It has been suggested that it is caused by drought interfering with pollination (cf. Bingham, 1966), but evidence for this is lacking in barley as yet.

# Acknowledgements

The work was financed by the Nuffield Foundation. The general strategy of the project and the conduct of the pilot experiments (Table I) were in the hands of a committee consisting of Mr M. J. Blackwell (succeeded by Mr D. R. Grant), Dr G. C. Evans, Dr E. J. M. Kirby, Mr D. Morgan and the author. The sponsors of the project were Dr G. D. H. Bell, Professor Sir Frank Engledow, Professor Sir Joseph Hutchinson and Professor Sir Harry Godwin. I am indebted to all those named for frequent valuable discussion. Mr R. Dawkins, Mr P. Orchard and Mrs M. Williams gave technical help.

## References

BINGHAM, J. (1966). Varietal response in wheat to water supply in the field, and male sterility caused by a period of drought in a glasshouse experiment. *Ann. appl. Biol.* **57,** 365–377.

GRANT, D. R. (1970). Some measurements of evaporation in a field of barley. *J. agric. Sci., Camb.* **75,** 433–443.

KIRBY, E. J. M. (1968). The response of some barley varieties to irrigation and nitrogen fertilizer. *J. agric. Sci., Camb.* **71,** 47–52.

KIRBY, E. J. M. and RACKHAM, O. (1971). A note on the root growth of barley. *J. appl. Ecol.* **8,** 919–924.

PENMAN, H. L. (1962). Woburn irrigation, 1951–59. III. Results for rotation crops. *J. agric. Sci., Camb.* **58,** 365–379.

PENMAN, H. L. (1970). Woburn irrigation, 1960–8. VI. Results for rotation crops. *J. agric. Sci., Camb.* **75,** 89–102.

# Discussion

In reply to **Monteith's** question, whether leaf water potential or stomatal behaviour had been measured to define plant water status, **Rackham** stated that pilot measurements of leaf water potential indicated that if large water stresses do develop they only do so for comparatively short periods of time. **Jarvis** asked for a definition of "drought", which to him was a very quantitative concept. Within the context of his paper, Rackham meant a comparison between either irrigation and control plots, or gutters and leaky gutters.

# II.4. Gas exchange of field crops

J. V. LAKE

*Rothamsted Experimental Station, Harpenden, Hertfordshire, England*

## I. Introduction

The methods to be described provide estimates of the net rates of exchange of carbon dioxide ($F$ mg m$^{-2}$ s$^{-1}$) and water vapour ($E$ mg m$^{-2}$ s$^{-1}$) between the foliage and the air. If these flux densities are expressed on the basis of ground area and integrated with respect to time, they give the crop growth and the evaporation. The water-use efficiency, $F/E$ is of obvious practical importance to agriculture in semi-arid regions and it now seems that it may be of more general interest, especially in glasshouses. As Bowman has mentioned, Dutch horticulturists attempt to control the vapour-pressure deficit, $\Delta e$, of the air in glasshouses, claiming that this has an optimum value for a given crop. Now for a crop with given surface properties, the main effect of varying $\Delta e$ is to change the ratio $F/E$ (Bierhuizen and Slatyer, 1965), so that the existence of an optimum $\Delta e$ may be explicable in terms of a corresponding optimum water-use efficiency for the crop.

Studies of crop gas exchange have improved our understanding of how meteorological processes affect the "microweather" of the foliage and how physiological and meteorological processes interact to produce photosynthesis and transpiration. Such understanding makes it possible to predict and compare the rates of growth and water use of various genotypes in a given environment and such predictions may be used in deciding land use, plant breeding programmes and crop management.

Implicit in much of the effort expended on research on crop photosynthesis is the notion that, for a given genotype, photosynthetic rate and the yield of useful plant material are positively correlated, i.e. $\int F\mathrm{d}t \propto Y$(mg m$^{-2}$ or £m$^{-2}$), the yield per unit ground area. This proposition has not yet been the subject of direct experimental test, although most published measurements of total and useful dry matter production seem

139

to support it. In principle, there could be lack of correlation between ∫Fdt and Y for two reasons, both to do with the distribution of assimilates. First, as Warren Wilson has mentioned, conditions causing rapid photosynthesis may not also cause rapid expansion of leaf area and there is evidence that whether $F$ is increased by the use of bright light (Hughes and Evans, 1962), carbon dioxide enrichment (Hurd, 1968) or oxygen depletion (Bjorkman et al., 1967) the result is always to increase leaf thickness. However, although the increase in crop growth rate is thus less than might be expected from short-term measurements of the effect of the treatments on $F$, the positive correlation between $F$ and growth is sustained. The second possible cause of failure of the correlation is that conditions favouring rapid photosynthesis may not also favour the production of economically useful plant parts; they may even prevent it, e.g. by causing failure of pollination. The allometric relations of leaf area and economically useful plant parts to total dry matter production are often influenced by plant water relations, possibly via the ratio $F/E$ discussed earlier.

Understanding of the relation between photosynthesis and crop yield would be greatly increased if measurements of gas exchange, as well as the more usual measurements of growth analysis and crop yield, could be made in ordinary experiments where treatments such as irrigation, transpiration suppression, fertilizer, spacing, sowing date and pathogen control are being compared. If the experimental plots are very large, micrometeorological methods, to be described in the next section, can be used, but for plots of more usual size leaf canopy enclosures have to be used and the part of this paper describing these might well be entitled "Gas exchange of field crops in controlled environments", giving it a tenuous relevance to the title of the symposium.

# II. Estimates from micrometeorology

## A. Above crops

Micrometeorological methods of estimating crop gas exchange are all essentially one-dimensional and are valid only when the air flow is in equilibrium with the crop surface in respect of the velocity and stress distributions (Bradley, 1968). In other words, they apply to a part of the crop well away from the windward edge, and for measurements in the air above the foliage Bradley's observations indicate that the height–fetch ratio should be about 1–200. Monteith (1968) notes the further condition that the fetch should be at least 50 times the height of upwind trees or buildings.

Given sufficient fetch, the steady-state vertical flux densities of carbon dioxide, water vapour, sensible heat ($Q$) and momentum ($\tau$) are given by the equations for turbulent diffusion:

$$F = -K_C \frac{d\phi}{dz} \text{g m}^{-2} \text{sec}^{-1} \tag{1}$$

$$E = -K_V \frac{d\chi}{dz} \text{g m}^{-2} \text{sec}^{-1} \tag{2}$$

$$Q = -K_Q \rho c_p \frac{dT}{dz} \text{W m}^{-2} \tag{3}$$

and
$$\tau = K_M \rho \frac{du}{dz} \text{g m}^{-1} \text{sec}^{-2} \tag{4}$$

where $K$ is the turbulent diffusivity (m$^2$ sec$^{-1}$), the subscripts $C$, $V$, $Q$ and $M$ refer respectively to carbon dioxide, water vapour, sensible heat and momentum, $\phi$ and $\chi$ are the concentrations (g m$^{-3}$) of carbon dioxide and water vapour in the air, $T$ and $u$ are the air temperature and horizontal windspeed, $\rho$ and $c_p$ are the density and specific heat of the air and $z$ is the height. Note that $\tau$, the drag exerted on the wind by the crop, is a force per unit area and so has the same units as pressure.

An alternative set of flux density equations can be written based on the correlation, at any point above the crop, between the fluctuations in the vertical component of wind ($w$) and those in the concentration of the entity under consideration; thus,

$$F = \overline{\phi' w'} \tag{5}$$
$$E = \overline{\chi' w'} \tag{6}$$
$$Q = \overline{c_p \rho T' w'} \tag{7}$$
$$\tau = \overline{\rho u' w'} \tag{8}$$

where the bars represent time averages and the primes represent deviations from the mean values. To use these eddy correlation equations requires sensors with very fast ($<1$ sec) response times. It is possible to measure $w'$ and $\chi'$ (Dyer *et al.*, 1967), so $E$ can be found directly from (6). Unfortunately accurate measurement of $\phi'$ has not yet been achieved, so direct use of (5) is not possible.

Most methods for estimating $F$ and $E$ exploit the likelihood that some of the turbulent diffusivities in equations (1) to (4) are equal in size. They can be classified into energy balance and momentum balance (or aerodynamic) techniques.

The energy balance technique assumes equality of $K_C$, $K_V$ and $K_Q$. The measured flux density of heat transport into the ground is subtracted from the net radiation measured above the crop and the remaining energy is taken to be dissipated as sensible $(Q)$ and latent $(LE)$ heat ($L$ is the latent heat of vaporization of water). Measurements are made of $\phi$, $\chi$ and $T$ at two heights above the crop and equations (1), (2) and (3) can then be integrated and re-arranged to yield estimates of $F$ and $E$. The main practical difficulty is that in strong wind the vertical gradients of $\phi$, $\chi$ and $T$ are too small to be easily measured with good accuracy.

The momentum balance technique requires measurements of fewer variables, but it depends on an accurate estimate of the wind profile. Having deduced $\tau$, the downward transfer of momentum, from the measured wind profile, measurements of $\phi$, $\chi$ and $u$ at two heights above the crop allow $F$ and $E$ to be found from equations (1), (2) and (4), assuming equality of $K_C$, $K_V$ and $K_M$. Strong winds make it easier to measure and interpret the wind profile but more difficult to measure the concentration differences. Note that Monteith's (1963) method of deducing the value of an aerodynamic resistance for the crop is identical in principle to the momentum balance technique for estimating $K_M$.

An indirect eddy correlation technique has been used for the measurement of $F$ by Japanese workers (Uchijima, 1970). On windy days, when mechanical turbulence predominates, $\tau$ is estimated from (8), using sonic anemometry to measure $u'$ and $w'$. Measurements of $\phi$ and $u$ at two heights above the crop are then used in (1) and (4) to give estimates of $F$. On calm, clear days with thermal turbulence dominant, $Q$ is estimated from (7), using sonic anemometers and thermometers to measure $w'$ and $T'$. Measurements of $\phi$ and $T$ at two heights above the crop then give $F$ from (1) and (3). This use of eddy correlation still assumes the equality of the various turbulent diffusivities, whereas the direct use of equation (5), were it possible, would not do so.

Equality of the turbulent diffusivities has been checked experimentally by Denmead (1969), who found good agreement between all the diffusivities in the air layers close to the surface under conditions of near-neutral stability. Denmead (1970) doubted whether the agreement would necessarily hold under other conditions.

Estimates of $F$ from measurements made above the crop can be compared directly with crop dry weight gain, provided that the micrometeorological equipment can be kept working for long enough (about a week) for the gain to become accurately measurable. Micrometeorological estimates of $E$ can be checked against crop evaporation over a similar time interval by measuring changes in soil moisture, or over much shorter time intervals (one hour or less) by the use of weighing lysimeters.

# B. Amongst foliage

Measurements within a crop canopy make it possible to estimate the contribution to $F$ and $E$ from each horizon of foliage, but large inaccuracies can be expected for three reasons.

First, as there are sources and sinks within the profile, the fluxes are not constant with height, so that it is not permissible to integrate equations (1) to (4), and the gradients, $d\phi/dz$ etc. must be measured directly. The contribution from a given foliage layer (i.e. its source or sink strength) is then found from the change in flux density between top and bottom of the layer e.g. from $dF/dz$ which depends on $d^2\phi/dz^2$. As the concentration differences are usually small, measurements of the profile accurate enough to obtain a good estimate of this second differential would be difficult, even were there no sampling problem. In practice, the sampling problem provides the second potential source of inaccuracy, for whereas good horizontal homogeneity can reasonably be hoped for above the crop, it is plainly less probable within the crop. The third source of inaccuracy is that the assumption of equality of the turbulent diffusivities for mass, heat and momentum is more questionable in the air among foliage. Denmead (1970) suggested that the momentum balance approach was likely to be especially unreliable within crop canopies and this view is supported by Millington and Peters' (1969) observation that the coefficient of variation of measured windspeed at a height of 40 cm in a soybean crop was twice as great as at the top of the foliage (110 cm).

Millington and Peters (1969) avoided using the energy- or momentumbalance techniques and instead measured the turbulent diffusivity for mass directly, using propane gas liberated at point sources placed in and above a crop. Each source was at the centre of two concentric, horizontal, perforated gas sampling rings, 8 cm and 12 cm in diameter. Thus the radial gradient in volumetric gas concentration, $d\overline{C}/dx$ could be measured and to a good approximation

$$K_C = K_V = \frac{q}{4\pi x^2 d\overline{C}/dx} \text{ cm}^2 \text{ sec}^{-1} \qquad (9)$$

where $q(\text{cm}^3 \text{ sec}^{-1})$ is the propane source strength.

Legg and Long (in press) also used a tracer gas. They measured the profile of concentration near the centre of a wheat field in which nitrous oxide was supplied at a uniform flux density at ground level. As there were no sources or sinks for the gas within the foliage, an equation of the same form as (1) could be used to estimate the diffusivity at any height, from the measured concentration gradient at that height. There was no substantial difference between daytime profiles of the diffusivities for nitrous oxide and for sensible heat estimated by the energy balance method. However, the diffusivity always decreased monotonically with depth below the upper surface of the crop, and it is doubtful whether the energy balance approach would be so satisfactory under conditions when the gradient of diffusivity with height changes sign. Millington and Peters (1969) showed that such a change of sign can occur; in a leafy soybean crop, alleyways between the rows were said to have provided a path for air movement beneath the bulk of the foliage, so that the diffusivity at 40 cm was greater than in the relatively undisturbed air amongst the foliage at 60 cm.

As the products of photosynthesis may move from one foliage horizon to another, the dry weight gain in a particular horizon will not necessarily be equivalent to the micrometeorological estimate of the net rate of carbon dioxide uptake, so there is no fully independent test of the accuracy of this estimate. Similarly, there is no independent way of testing the accuracy of the estimate of evaporation from each layer. Laboratory measurements of the effects of light, temperature, water vapour pressure and (in some circumstances) carbon dioxide concentration on the photosynthesis and transpiration of individual leaves can be used in conjunction with measured or estimated leaf microclimate to calculate the gas exchange in each foliage layer (see section IV below), but this procedure makes use of some of the measurements required in the micrometeorological estimate of the gas exchange and so cannot provide an independent check of its validity.

# III. The use of enclosures

## A. History

Musgrave and Moss (1961) were among the first to place a transparent enclosure around several whole plants in the field to measure their gas exchange. Others include Jeffers and Shibles (1969), Puckridge (1969), Egli et al. (1970), Connor and Cartledge (1970) and Leafe, who describes his method in this volume (II.5).

An enclosure provides the opportunity to measure the photosynthetic response curves of the foliage to light, temperature and carbon dioxide concentration, varied independently, but few investigators have done this. Jeffers and Shibles were concerned with the relation between crop photosynthesis, leaf area index and solar radiation, but they did not go on to use their results to deduce any basic photosynthetic attributes of the foliage, such as the maximum rate of light-saturated carbon dioxide uptake or the apparent photosynthetic efficiency. Puckridge and Ratkowsky (1971) made a detailed study of the light response curves of a wheat crop and made useful deductions about the relations between leaf area index, light interception and the photosynthetic attributes of the foliage (see section IV below). However, they did not vary the composition of the enclosure air. Nor did Connor and Cartledge (1970), who were also principally concerned with the photosynthetic use of intercepted light.

Musgrave and Moss (1961) tested the effect of carbon dioxide concentration on photosynthesis and Egli *et al.* (1970) measured the effect on transpiration rate, but in neither of these investigations was the shape of the response curves studied critically.

## B. *Aims*

Before describing some of the potentially fruitful aims, it is worthwhile mentioning one that is probably futile, although often pursued, namely the attempt to imitate within the enclosure the conditions occurring outside, so that the enclosure is used to measure the "natural" rates of crop gas exchange. This seems to be merely a very poor substitute for the micro-meteorological techniques, and is doomed to relative failure by the impossibility of maintaining within the enclosure either the radiation environment or the wind shear occurring outdoors.

As already indicated, one of the more fruitful aims is to measure the separate effects of the various environmental factors on foliage gas exchange, using the control systems of the enclosure to overcome the correlations between factors (e.g. leaf temperature and solar radiation) that often occur in nature and hamper the interpretation of micrometeorological studies.

In nature, too, the ambient carbon dioxide concentration is such that crop photosynthesis is limited by both light and carbon dioxide for much of the day, so that the observations lie on part of a complex response surface and it is difficult to deduce from them the fundamental attributes of the photosynthetic mechanism. An enclosure makes it possible to vary the factors beyond the naturally occurring range, so that photosynthesis is limited by only one of them at a time. For example at large carbon dioxide concentrations and in dim light, light is the limiting factor and an apparent photosynthetic efficiency for the canopy can be calculated from the initial slope of the photosynthesis/intercepted light response curve; at small carbon dioxide concentrations and in bright light, diffusion of carbon dioxide from the enclosure air to the chloroplasts becomes the limiting factor, so that an apparent resistance to this diffusion can be calculated for the canopy from the initial slope of the photosynthesis/ carbon dioxide response curve. This resistance can then be compared with the corresponding resistance to the transport of water vapour between leaves and air, deduced from the measured evaporation rate, leaf temperature and air vapour pressure; the comparison must be made with caution as the main sinks for carbon dioxide in the canopy may not be coincident with the main sources of water vapour, but in principle the enclosure can be used in much the same way as Gaastra (1959) used a leaf chamber in the laboratory. In more recent leaf-chamber studies, oxygen concentration has often been included as a variable and this is also possible in a leaf-canopy enclosure. By this means, fundamental information can be obtained about the rate of respiratory processes during photosynthesis (see, e.g. Lake, 1971).

The contributions to gas exchange by the separate foliage horizons in an enclosure can be measured only by damaging the plants by defoliating successive layers (Puckridge, 1969). This compares unfavourably with the micrometeorological technique, which is non-destructive.

## C. Technical considerations

The aims described have some bearing on enclosure design. In particular, they affect ways of considering the exchange of gases between the enclosure air and the soil or the outside air, and the method of temperature control.

### 1. Soil gas exchange

Ideally, the soil and root gas exchange would be measured separately from the shoot gas exchange, but this has yet to be attempted.

The enclosure air can be separated from the soil air by covering the ground with a layer of plastic through which the plants' stems project (Musgrave and Moss, 1961; Egli et al., 1970). Leafe will be describing a technique whereby the enclosure air is kept at a pressure that blows it into the soil, so that soil air cannot enter the enclosure. Instead of separating the enclosure air from the soil air by the above methods, the rate at which soil produces carbon dioxide can be measured by covering a patch of soil between the plant rows with a small sub-enclosure (Puckridge, 1969) or by using the main enclosure to measure it after the plant shoots have been harvested (Connor and Cartledge, 1970). Jeffers and Shibles (1969) simply report that, before using the main enclosure, they removed organic debris from the surface layers of soil, when the soil produced so little carbon dioxide that there was no need to measure it.

It is not necessary to seal off the soil air or measure the rate at which soil produces carbon dioxide if this production remains nearly constant while the enclosure is in use, and if the principal aim is to find the slope of the response curve of photosynthesis to light or carbon dioxide. This is so in much of the current work at Rothamsted.

Evaporation from the soil is trivial compared with transpiration when the plant cover intercepts all the solar radiation, or when the soil surface is very dry. If the soil surface is wet and there is not a complete cover of foliage, evaporation of soil water is not negligible. It can be made so by covering the soil with a reflecting material (which need not be sealed around the stems). This will affect the amount of light intercepted by the foliage, but a measurement of this intercepted light is in any case one of the fundamental experimental observations.

## 2. Leakage

It is difficult to make a large enclosure airtight, but some leakage is acceptable and need not be measured when carbon dioxide is injected into the enclosure to maintain the concentration similar to that in the air outside, as was done by Puckridge (1969) and by Connor and Cartledge (1970), and when the water vapour concentrations in the inside and outside air are also nearly equal. Alternatively, the rate of leakage can be controlled by blowing air into the enclosure at a measured rate and fast enough to ensure that all the leakage is outwards, as has been done with small enclosures for plants (Koller and Samish, 1964) with leaf chambers (Wolf et al., 1969) and with leaf-canopy enclosures, as Leafe will describe. However, ordinary outside air is usually used for the supply as it is difficult to provide any other gas mixture fast enough.

When using gas mixtures of different composition from ordinary air, e.g. to measure the slope of the photosynthesis/carbon dioxide response curve, the leakage rate of the enclosure must be measured. This is conveniently done by injecting a tracer gas (nitrous oxide is used at Rothamsted) at a measured rate and measuring the resulting concentration in the enclosure air (Lake et al., 1968). It remains necessary to keep the leakage rate small enough to ensure that, when carbon dioxide is not injected into the enclosure, the balance between uptake by photosynthesis and supply by leakage from outside air can result in a volumetric concentration of less than $100 \times 10^{-6}$, so that the initial slope of the response curve can be established accurately. When the leakage rate is of this order (usually around 0·1 enclosure volumes per hour) there is no difficulty in supplying oxygen from a cylinder fast enough to maintain constant concentrations in the range 0·2 to 0·5. As the response of photosynthesis to oxygen concentration is linear at small carbon dioxide concentrations (Lake, 1971), there is no need to aim at oxygen concentrations smaller than 0·2.

### 3. Leaf temperature control

If the enclosure is to be used in the same way as a laboratory leaf chamber, it is desirable to measure and control leaf temperature rather than air temperature. The two will differ and vary with position in the foliage canopy, but both the difference and the variation are diminished by stirring vigorously. Because one aim is to measure transpiration rate, the enclosure air must be passed over a cool surface on which the transpired water can condense and be collected and measured. The temperature of this sets the dew point of the air and its surface must be cooler than any other surface within the enclosure. After passing over the cooled surface, the air can be heated to maintain the average leaf temperature at the desired value. The cooling load can be minimized by making the transparent covering of the enclosure of thin polyethylene or polypropylene film, transparent to terrestrial radiation, but thin films tend to flap in the wind and thereby increase the enclosure leakage rate, so at Rothamsted the use of semi-rigid acrylic sheet is preferred.

# IV. Estimates from plant attributes and weather

Rates of crop photosynthesis and transpiration in given weather can be calculated from the environmental response curves of individual leaves measured in the laboratory, or of the foliage canopy measured *in situ* with the use of micrometeorological techniques or enclosures. With either method, the principal problem is to find simple yet accurate ways of defining the response curves and the foliage geometry.

## A. Estimates from leaf physiology

Photosynthesis of single leaves is often described approximately by an equation of the form

$$F_l + B_l = \frac{\varepsilon_l I \phi / r_l}{\varepsilon_l I + \phi / r_l} \tag{10}$$

where the subscript $l$ indicates that the basis of measurement is unit leaf area, $B_l$ is the rate of release of respiratory carbon dioxide, $I$ (Wm$^{-2}$) is the flux density of the photosynthetically active radiation absorbed in the leaf and $\varepsilon_l$ (g sec$^{-1}$ W$^{-1}$) is the apparent photosynthetic efficiency, differing from the efficiency at individual chloroplasts because of inhomogeneity of illumination within the tissue (Monteith, 1963). If $\phi$ is the concentration of carbon dioxide at the chloroplasts, the resistance $r_l$ (sec cm$^{-1}$) represents the inverse of the rate constant of the carboxylation process. More usefully, for our purpose, $\phi$ can be taken as the ambient concentration, when $r_l$ contains both diffusive and biochemical components. On one view (Gaastra, 1959; Chartier, 1970), the biochemical component is negligible, on another (Wareing et al., 1968) it predominates, so that at present equation (10) is essentially empirical.

The rate of respiration during photosynthesis cannot be measured directly, but it is possible to measure the light compensation point, $I_c$, and the carbon dioxide compensation point, $\Gamma$, both of which presumably depend on $B_l$. Acock et al. (1971) have therefore proposed replacing equation (10) by one of the form

$$F_l = \frac{\varepsilon_l(I - I_c)(\phi - \Gamma)/r_l}{\varepsilon_l(I - I_c) + (\phi - \Gamma)/r_l} \qquad (11)$$

This equation is probably sufficiently accurate for the present purpose, although the problem of writing one that exactly defines $F_l$ over the whole range of values of $\phi$ and $I$ with the minimum of empiricism has yet to be solved.

The leaf boundary-layer resistance is usually trivial compared with the other components of $r_l$ in equation (11), so that an equation based on measurements with an adequately stirred laboratory leaf chamber requires no modification when used to calculate photosynthesis in the field. However, several of the terms in the equation depend on leaf temperature, $T_l$, and estimation of this requires a knowledge of the boundary-layer resistance, $r_a$, which can be calculated from leaf dimensions and windspeed (Thom, 1968).

The net radiation absorbed in the leaf (flux density $H_l \, \mathrm{Wm^{-2}}$) is dissipated as latent and sensible heat which diffuse through the boundary layer, so that

$$H_l = LE_l + \rho c_p(T_l - T)/r_a \qquad (12)$$

and the evaporation rate is given by

$$E_l = \frac{\chi_{\mathrm{sat}}.(T_l) - \chi}{r_a + r_s} \qquad (13)$$

where $\chi_{\mathrm{sat}}.(T_l)$ is the saturated water vapour content of the air at leaf temperature, $\chi$ and $T$ are the ambient water vapour content and temperature and $r_s$ is the stomatal resistance to water vapour diffusion. If $r_s$ is known for given environmental conditions from laboratory measurements, $T_l$ and $E$ can be found from (12) and (13), although if the leaves are anisotropic in surface roughness and stomatal frequency then strictly allowance should be made for the differences between the value of $r_a$ for momentum, sensible heat and water vapour.

In principle, the foliage elements (leaves or parts of leaves and if necessary stems etc.) above unit ground area can be assigned to classes, each containing elements with similar physiological parameters and similar microclimate, so that the gas exchange of each class can be calculated from equations (11) to (13) and the contributions from the classes can be summed to give the total leaf canopy gas exchange.

The adequacy of the classification depends on the description of foliage geometry, the meteorological methods used to calculate foliage microclimate from given above-crop weather and the degree of understanding of the effects of age and history on the photosynthetic attributes of the leaves.

Some simplification is inevitable; for example, Begg and Jarvis (1968) disregarded variations in temperature, carbon dioxide concentration and leaf physiology within the foliage of *Stylosanthes humilis*. They also disregarded the variation in illumination between sunlit and shaded leaves within each of the 10 cm layers into which they divided the foliage. Despite these simplifications, they were able to draw from their calculations a seemingly useful conclusion about the agricultural management of the crop.

Waggoner (1969), in a much more complex analysis, calculated from the above-crop weather the profiles of wind-speed, leaf temperature and carbon dioxide concentration and the interactions between these and the gas exchange of each foliage layer, but he nevertheless disregarded the possible variations in leaf physiology with age and the known variations in leaf illumination within a foliage layer.

The potential complexity of these calculations is almost unlimited and there probably remains room for an inherently simpler analysis which treats the leaf canopy as a whole, as outlined below.

## B. Estimates from crop physiology

Evaporation from crops is well understood and there is no need to describe the various methods of calculation here, so attention will be confined to carbon dioxide exchange.

When deriving equations for leaf carbon dioxide exchange, it is usual to ignore the inhomogeneity of chloroplast illumination within the tissues and it seems reasonable to consider accepting, with caution, the probably greater inhomogeneities that occur within a foliage canopy. The obvious starting-point is to consider whether equations of the form of (10) or (11) can be used to fit experimental measurements of canopy gas exchange, measured not on the basis of unit leaf area, but on either unit plan area of foliage of unit area of ground.

Once the leaf area per unit plan area of foliage has exceeded some limit there probably can be no further increase in the area of leaves that have enough light to contribute significantly to photosynthesis. If so, equation (11) can be written to give the rate of carbon dioxide uptake of unit plan area of foliage, $F_f$ and the rate per unit plan area of ground, $F$ is simply $\alpha F_f$, i.e.

$$F = \alpha \frac{\varepsilon_f(I - I_{c,f})(\phi - \Gamma_f)/r_f}{\varepsilon_f(I - I_{c,f}) + (\phi - \Gamma_f)/r_f} \qquad (14)$$

where $\alpha$ is the fraction of ground covered by foliage.

This reasoning gains strong support from the measurements of Puckridge and Ratkowsky (1971) who found that, for wheat during the six weeks before anthesis, $F$ measured under standard conditions in a leaf-canopy enclosure increased linearly with increase in the light interception of the foliage canopy, i.e. the intercepted light expressed as a fraction of that measured above the foliage. This fraction was measured at noon at Adelaide, Australia, i.e. with the sun high in the sky, and would thus be closely similar to our fraction $\alpha$. All the results from two wheat cultivars at three densities of sowing and for leaf area indices ranging from 1 to 6 fitted closely on the same straight line.

Puckridge and Ratkowsky fitted their measurements of $F$ at various light intensities to equation (10), using the measured rate of dark respiration as an estimate of $B$. As they did not include the fraction $\alpha$ in the right-hand side of the equation, it is not surprising that they found that both $\phi/r$ and $\phi/\varepsilon r$ ($P'_{max}$ and $K$ in their equation) seemed to increase with leaf area index.

The parameters $\varepsilon_f$, $I_{c,f}$, $\Gamma_f$ and $r_f$ in equation (14) can all be found by using a leaf-canopy enclosure to measure the slopes and intercepts of the $F/I$ and $F/\phi$ curves near their origins. Thus we can put $\alpha \varepsilon_f = dF/dI$ ($I \to 0$), $I_{c,f} = I(F = 0)$, $\Gamma_f = \phi(F = 0)$ and $r_f = \alpha \, d\phi/dF(\phi \to 0)$. The values of the parameters in equation (14) will vary with mean leaf temperature and the appropriate coefficients can be found by using an enclosure. When using equation (14) to calculate photosynthesis in given weather, equations of the form of (12) and (13) could presumably then be used to deduce an approximate mean leaf temperature, but in view of the uncertainties it is probably more satisfactory to assume that leaf temperature is the same as the above-crop air temperature.

# V. Conclusion

This review has inevitably emphasized aspects of the subject I consider merit further attention. Firstly the relation between net rate of carbon dioxide uptake and economic yield and the possible existence of an optimum water-use efficiency for some crops could both usefully be the subject of direct experiment. Secondly, there is scope for progress in estimating crop gas exchange in given weather from physiological attributes of the foliage canopy as a whole, measured with the use of a transparent enclosure, and from a measurement of the proportion of ground covered by the foliage.

# References

ACOCK, B., THORNLEY, J. H. M. and WARREN WILSON, J. (1971). Photosynthesis and energy conversion. *In* "Potential Crop Production" (P. F. Wareing and J. P. Cooper, eds), pp. 43–75. Heinemann, London.

BEGG, J. E. and JARVIS, P. G. (1968). Photosynthesis in Townsville Lucerne (*Stylosanthes humilis*). *Agric. Met.* **5,** 91–109.

BIERHUIZEN, J. F. and SLATYER, R. O. (1965). Effect of atmospheric concentration of water vapour and $CO_2$ in determining transpiration-photosynthesis relationships of cotton leaves. *Agric. Met.* **2,** 259–270.

BJORKMAN, O., HIESEY, W. M., NOBS, M., NICHOLSON, F. and HART, R. W. (1967). Effect of oxygen concentration on dry matter production in higher plants. *Yb. Carnegie Instn Wash.* **66,** 228–232.

BRADLEY, E. F. (1968). A micrometeorological study of velocity profiles and surface drag in the region modified by a change in surface roughness. *Q. Jl R. met. Soc.* **94,** 361–379.

CHARTIER, P. (1970). A model of $CO_2$ assimilation in the leaf. *In* "Prediction and measurement of photosynthetic productivity". *Proc. IBP/PP technical meeting, Trebon, 1969* (I. Setlik, ed.), pp. 307–315. Centre for Agricultural Publishing & Documentation, Wageningen.

CONNOR, D. J. and CARTLEDGE, O. (1970). Observed and calculated photosynthetic rates of *Chloris gayana* communities. *J. appl. Ecol.* **7,** 353–362.

DENMEAD, O. T. (1969). *In* "Physiological aspects of crop yield" (J. D. Eastin, F. A. Gaskins, C. Y. Sullivan and C. H. M. van Bavel, eds) Discussion, pp. 137–140, American Society of Agronomy and Crop Science Society of America, Madison, Wisconsin.

DENMEAD, O. T. (1970). Transfer processes between vegetation and air: measurement, interpretation and modelling. *In* "Prediction and measurement of photosynthetic productivity". *Proc. IBP/PP technical meeting, Trebon, 1969* (I. Setlik, ed.), pp. 149–164. Centre for Agricultural Publication & Documentation, Wageningen.

DYER, A. J., HICKS, B. B. and KING, K. M. (1967). The Fluxatron. A revised approach to the measurement of eddy fluxes in the lower atmosphere. *J. appl. Met.* **6,** 408–413.

EGLI, D. B., PENDLETON, J. W. and PETERS, D. B. (1970). Photosynthetic rate of three soybean communities as related to carbon dioxide levels and solar radiation. *Agron. J.* **62,** 411–414.

GAASTRA, P. (1959). Photosynthesis of crop plants as influenced by light, carbon dioxide, temperature and stomatal diffusion resistance. *Meded. LandbHoogesch. Wageningen* **59** (13), 1–68.

HUGHES, A. P. and EVANS, G. C. (1962). Plant growth and the aerial environment. II. Effects of light intensity on *Impatiens parviflora*. *New Phytol.* **61**, 154–174.

HURD, R. G. (1968). Effects of $CO_2$—enrichment on the growth of young tomato plants in low light. *Ann. Bot.* **32**, 531–542.

JEFFERS, D. L. and SHIBLES, R. M. (1969). Some effects of leaf area, solar radiation, air temperature and variety on net photosynthesis in field-grown soybeans. *Crop Sci.* **9**, 762–764.

KOLLER, D. and SAMISH, Y. (1964). A null-point compensating system for simultaneous and continuous measurement of net photosynthesis and transpiration by controlled gas-stream analysis. *Bot. Gaz.* **125**, 81–88.

LAKE, J. V. (1971). The behaviour of plants in various gas mixtures. *Proc. R. Soc. B.* **179**, 177–188.

LAKE, J. V., BROWNE, D. A. and BOWMAN, G. E. (1968). A glasshouse as a cuvette. *In* "Functioning of Terrestrial Ecosystems at the Primary Production Level" (F. E. Eckardt, ed.), pp. 329–333. *Nat. Resour. Res.* **5**, UNESCO, Paris.

LEGG, B. J. and LONG, I. F. (in press). Microclimate factors affecting evaporation and transpiration. *In* Proc. Symp. on soil water physics and technology (M. Fuchs, ed.). International Soil Science Society.

MILLINGTON, R. J. and PETERS, D. B. (1969). Exchange (mass transfer) coefficients in crop canopies. *Agron. J.* **61**, 815–819.

MONTEITH, J. L. (1963). Gas exchange in plant communities. *In* "Environmental Control of Plant Growth" (L. T. Evans, ed.), pp. 95–112. Academic Press, New York.

MONTEITH, J. L. (1968). Analysis of the photosynthesis and respiration of field crops from vertical fluxes of carbon dioxide. *In* "Functioning of Terrestrial Ecosystems at the Primary Production Level" (F. E. Eckardt, ed.), pp. 349–358. *Nat. Resour. Res.* **5**, UNESCO, Paris.

MUSGRAVE, R. B. and MOSS, D. N. (1961). Photosynthesis under field conditions. I. A portable, closed system for determining net assimilation and respiration of corn. *Crop Sci.* **1**, 37–41.

PUCKRIDGE, D. W. (1969). Photosynthesis of wheat under field conditions. II. Effect of defoliation on the carbon dioxide uptake of the community. *Aust. J. agric. Res.* **20**, 623–34.

PUCKRIDGE, D. and RATKOWSKY, D. A. (1971). Photosynthesis of wheat under field conditions. IV. The influence of density and leaf area index on the response to radiation. *Aust. J. agric. Res.* **22**, 11–20.

THOM, A. S. (1968). The exchange of momentum, mass and heat between an artificial leaf and the airflow in a wind tunnel. *Quart. Jl R. met. Soc.* **94**, 44–55.

UCHIJIMA, Z. (1970). Carbon dioxide environment and flux within a corn crop canopy. *In* "Prediction and measurement of photosynthetic productivity",

*Proc. IBP/PP technical meeting, Trebon, 1969.* (I. Setlik, ed.), pp. 179–196. Centre for Agricultural Publication & Documentation, Wageningen.

WAGGONER, P. E. (1969). Environmental manipulation for higher yields. *In* "Physiological Aspects of Crop Yield" (J. D. Eastin, F. A. Haskins, C. Y. Sullivan and C. H. M. van Bavel, eds), pp. 343–373. American Society of Agronomy and Crop Science Society of America, Madison, Wisconsin.

WAREING, P. F., KHALIFA, M. M. and TREHARNE, K. J. (1968). Rate limiting processes in photosynthesis at saturating light intensities. *Nature, Lond.* **220,** 453–457.

WOLF, D. D., PEARCE, R. B., CARLSON, G. E. and LEE, D. R. (1969). Measuring photosynthesis of attached leaves with air sealed chambers. *Crop Sci.* **9,** 24–27.

# Discussion

**James** queried the assumption that the transfer coefficients were the same. **Lake** replied that there had been only two rigorous tests, one by Denmead (1969) where he compared the carbon dioxide transfer coefficient with the others in a layer quite close to the ground under conditions of neutral stability, and the other by Legg and Long (in press) using nitrous oxide as a tracer gas in a wheat crop. In both tests agreement was quite good. Variation in $K_{mass}$ (for propane) had been measured by Millington and Peters (1969) at different heights at three stages in the life of a soybean crop. Only at the second stage did $K_{mass}$ vary in a monotonic way with height; in the other two stages it varied with height in an extraordinary way which would make meaningless any attempt to measure gas exchange down the profile. **Monteith** added that over a very extensive horizontal plane there was no reason to suppose that the diffusion coefficients of heat, water vapour and carbon dioxide would be different. In practical situations, however, the failure to achieve horizontal uniformity was likely to be much more serious than differences in the coefficients. **Lake** stated that in the range of stabilities occurring in a long-term experiment there was unlikely to be any problem in estimating $K_{mass}$ above the crop except in very stable conditions. At night under stable conditions there were anomalies suggesting that there could be huge convection cells above the field. **Rappaport** asked whether there was an optimum value of $F/E$; agronomists in the past have sought large values. Lake replied that until hearing Bowman's paper he had not realized that the Dutch glasshouse control system ($\Delta x$) operated on the air vapour pressure deficit, nor that it was thought that there was an optimum for this. The existence of such an optimum would imply an optimum value of water use efficiency, $F/E$. **Rackham** referred to Rothamsted work where response to irrigation was curvilinearly related to the seasonal amount of water required, with a minimum value below which there was a negative response to additional water in wet seasons. **Jarvis** supported the concept of an optimum $F/E$; assimilation chamber experiments show reduced rates of photosynthesis with some stomatal closure at vapour pressure deficits for most plants of about 12 mb. Work at both Nottingham and Aberdeen indicated inhibition of plant growth at very small vapour pressure deficits, with an optimum at about 5–6 mb.

# II.5. Micro-environment, carbon dioxide exchange and growth in grass swards

E. L. LEAFE

*The Grassland Research Institute, Hurley, Berkshire, England*

## I. Introduction

However much information we have from controlled environments, we shall never completely understand growth in the field until we measure crop processes in the natural environment. The aim of the work described here is to apply measurement techniques typical of work in controlled environments to the grass crop growing under natural conditions, and to translate laboratory and growth room findings to the field situation. By so doing we hope to understand the reasons for the pattern of productivity of grass swards in the field and to discover what factors limit productivity.

The intensively managed grass crop has a characteristic dry-weight production curve (Alberda and Sibma, 1968; Alberda, 1968). In the spring, or following recovery from cutting, there is an initial phase of increasing growth rate. This is succeeded by a phase in which growth remains fairly constant and whose duration becomes progressively shorter in successive growth periods. Finally, towards the end of each growth period, the growth rate declines, sometimes abruptly; yield reaches a ceiling and may even decline unless the crop is harvested. Alberda used the de Wit model of photosynthesis of leaf canopies (de Wit, 1965) to calculate theoretical yields from grass swards and compared them with actual yields. He concluded that variations in leaf area, leaf geometry, the rate of respiration and the environment partially explain the pattern of growth but the phase of declining growth rate and ceiling yield require further explanation.

Clearly we need to know more about the processes which lead to dry weight change if we are to understand the pattern of growth of the sward.

157

Because dry weight increase is predominantly an accumulation of carbon compounds, we are especially concerned with the process of carbon dioxide exchange and its relation to the physical environment and the changing structure of the crop canopy. The way in which the distribution of the assimilated carbon is affected by the environment is equally important, but is not the main concern in this paper.

An enclosure method employing infrared gas analysis was chosen to measure carbon dioxide exchange because of its relative simplicity and convenience. The apparatus and technique at an early stage of development have been described (Stiles and Leafe, 1970); the present apparatus is described briefly in this paper.

# II. Materials and methods

## A. The crop

The investigations described were carried out during 1970 in an S.24 perennial ryegrass sward sown in 1968. The sward received liberal mineral nutrients and was irrigated whenever the nominal soil water deficit reached 0·5 in. (12·5 mm). Measurements were made in the first growth period (between the time when growth began in the spring and the first cut on June 17), and in the third growth period (between the second defoliation on June 30 and the third defoliation on August 27). Thus, in order to examine the declining phase of growth, the sward was allowed to remain uncut for longer than in normal agricultural practice, but the area in which the third growth period was measured was harvested normally beforehand. 130 kg ha$^{-1}$ of nitrogen were applied as calcium nitrate at the beginning of each growth period.

## B. Measurement of carbon dioxide exchange

An enclosure method of carbon dioxide exchange measurement was chosen for these studies because of its relative simplicity and particularly because of its adaptability to mobile equipment, which allows measurements to be made at several locations within a field. This provides for replication and comparison of treatments and genotypes which is the wider objective of the programme of our research. Jarvis (1970) and Eckardt (1970) have recently discussed the advantages and disadvantages of enclosure methods, and their relationship to micrometeorological methods and these will not be discussed further here.

Figure 1 shows a general view of the apparatus, and Fig. 2 the functional relationships. The size of the enclosed plot, a square with a 50 cm side, was chosen on grounds of the acceptable bulk, weight and power requirements of a mobile apparatus. The plot enclosure is in two parts: a square metal rim, grooved on the top edge to receive a cover, and perforated on

**Fig. 1.** Field enclosure apparatus for carbon dioxide exchange measurement.

the two sides which are connected to the trolley by air ducts: and a cover
of either thin plastics film (Melinex 0·001 in.—0·025 mm) or sheet metal. A
fan at the left of the trolley draws air from the enclosure and blows it,
according to the action of a thermostat, either over or by-passing a cooling
heat exchanger, and thence back to the enclosure. This provides for
turbulence, air temperature control (set, in this experiment, to follow
ambient) and for removal of excess water vapour from the circulating air.
Water vapour content, however, is not controlled. The measuring air-
stream is drawn from a mast 4·5 m high and metered into the circulating

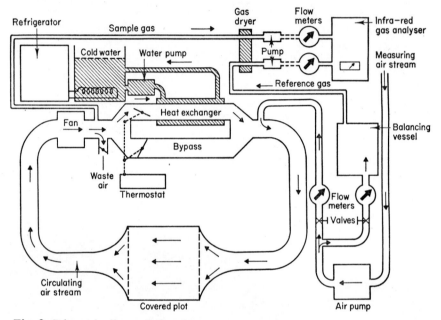

**Fig. 2.** Schematic diagram of enclosure apparatus.

air-stream, the flow rate being chosen according to the rate of photosynthesis to ensure that carbon dioxide depletion in the system does not
exceed 10%. In the present experiment a flow rate of 400 litres min$^{-1}$ was
used throughout. The introduced air is entrained in the circulating air
stream; the pressure created is released through an adjustable port which
enables the internal pressure to be regulated at about 3 mm water gauge.
An important feature of the system is the use of the internal air pressure as
a seal to exclude carbon dioxide arising from soil and root respiration.
Samples of air, taken before and after passing through the enclosure, are
dried and passed through 3 mm bore nylon tube to a differential infrared gas analyser housed in a field laboratory. To eliminate errors arising

from fluctuations in ambient carbon dioxide concentrations, the reference and sample flows are balanced, and the transit times through the nylon tubes to the analyser are synchronized. Since it is necessary to make an air seal between the enclosure and the ground, fixed sampling points are established before the crop is sown. Sheet metal rims are embedded so that their grooved upper edges are at ground level: these rims have little apparent effect on the crop once the sward is established. When gas exchange measurements are made, the base rim of the enclosure is inserted into the rim in the field, and the transparent or opaque metal cover is placed on top; air seals are then formed by filling the grooves with water.

Measurements were made twice weekly and, on each occasion, three plots were used for a period of 30 min for photosynthesis followed by 15 min for dark respiration. Incoming radiation, measured with a Kipp solarimeter, was recorded simultaneously, and the photosynthesis–radiation response was determined by comparison of the two records after allowing for the radiation absorption by the cover. At this early stage in the development of the method, values could only be determined when radiation was substantially constant for long enough for carbon dioxide equilibrium conditions to be attained within the enclosure (about 2 min at the flow rate used). The experimental area was arranged in three blocks each 10 m × 30 m. Each block contained 8 plots for carbon dioxide exchange measurement and these were sampled in turn.

## C. Radiation and temperature measurement

Hourly integrals of total incoming short-wave radiation were used in the estimation of cumulative carbon dioxide exchange over the two growth periods. These data were collected, using a Kipp solarimeter, as part of the Institute meteorological record.

To measure the distribution of radiation in the crop canopy, miniature tube solarimeters 360 × 8 mm (Szeicz, 1964), were placed in the crop at the beginning of each growth period. They were placed at ground level and at vertical intervals of 5 cm, and the crop was allowed to develop around them. Their output was scanned hourly and light interception profiles calculated. No attempt was made to discriminate between the photosynthetically active and non-active part of the spectrum.

Air and soil temperature profiles were measured hourly using an array of small thermistor probes.

## D. Dry weight and leaf area estimation

The crop was sampled weekly to determine above- and below-ground dry weight. Six 30 × 30 cm quadrats were selected randomly, two from each block, and the above-ground material removed. From each sample, a sub-sample was removed and its leaf area determined using an electronic planimeter (Paton Industries T2). After leaf area measurement, both sample and sub-sample were oven dried and weighed. Leaf area index ($L$) was obtained by comparison of dry weights in the sample and sub-sample.

Below ground parts were sampled by taking four 30 cm × 5 cm diam. soil cores in each area from which the above-ground material had been removed. After removal of soil by washing, material from the four cores was combined, oven dried, and the dry weight calculated after ashing.

## E. Stratified leaf area estimation

At weekly intervals in the third growth period, material was removed from 30 cm² quadrats in 5 cm strata; leaf area in each stratum was determined with the planimeter. The method was laborious and only two replicates were measured.

Earlier work (Grassland Research Institute annual report for 1969) had indicated that the rapid decline in growth rate at the end of a growth period was due to a decline in the rate of canopy photosynthesis. In perennial ryegrass, the photosynthetic efficiency of a leaf falls markedly with age (Woledge, J., personal communication). The change in canopy structure from erectophile to planophile, which occurs as growth proceeds, may increase the average age of foliage intercepting full sunlight. To investigate this, leaf material in each stratum was assigned to three age categories: (a) expanding and youngest fully expanded leaf, (b) second leaf and (c) third and older leaves on the tiller. Tillers in the sward seldom retain more than 3 or 4 leaves. Because the samples contained a large number of leaf pieces, categorization was visual. Whole tillers were sampled at the time of the stratified clip to aid categorization. From a knowledge of the radiation profiles existing within the canopy, changes in the percentage of light intercepted by leaves in each age category were then calculated.

# III. Results

## A. Canopy net photosynthesis ($P_{n,c}$) and shoot dark respiration ($R_{s,d,c}$)

Figure 3 shows traces for $P_{n,c}$ and radiation (uncorrected for absorption by the enclosure), during a whole day in April 1971. This continuous record illustrates better the character of the primary data than the short-term measurements made on replicate plots in 1970. Measurement began in the

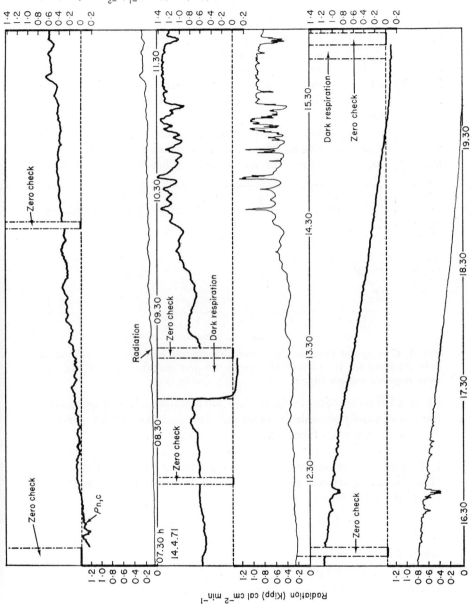

**Fig. 3.** Canopy net photosynthesis per unit ground area ($P_{n,c}$) and incoming short-wave radiation (Kipp solarimeter), 14 April, 1971. S.24 perennial ryegrass. L 3·0, 90 % radiation intercepted.

CPCE—M

early morning at light levels below compensation point; the morning was overcast and radiation levels rose slowly. At 13.00 h a dark respiration measurement was made and the plot was changed. Intermittent bright periods occurred in the afternoon, followed by mainly clear sky, with a few isolated clouds until darkness fell. Light compensation point was reached at 19.30 h. The pattern of response of $P_{n,c}$ to these changes in radiation intensity is readily seen. The gaseous volume of the apparatus imposes a smoothing effect on the $P_{n,c}$ trace and the transient responses are faster than recorded.

The processing of these data presents difficulties. In 1970, $P_{n,c}$ values were taken during periods when radiation remained constant, or substantially so, long enough for equilibrium values to be reached. This

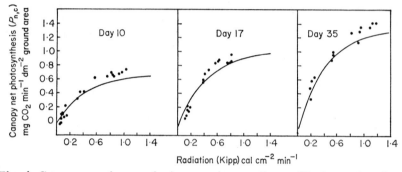

**Fig. 4.** Canopy net photosynthesis per unit ground area ($P_{n,c}$) as a function of light intensity for 10, 17 and 35 days in the first growth period. Fitted curves from response surface Fig. 5.

method has serious drawbacks on days when radiation is fluctuating rapidly but it was usually possible to obtain sufficient data to construct an approximate photosynthesis function. Figure 4 shows photosynthesis functions for three days in the first growth period. To utilize the data more effectively, response surfaces were constructed relating $P_{n,c}$, radiation and time (Fig. 5). The surfaces which were fitted by least squares method had equations of the form:

$$P_{n,c} = a_0 + a_1 t + a_2 t^2 + a_3 t^3 + a_4 t^4$$
$$+ (b + b_1 t^1 + b_2 t^2 + b_3 t^3 + b_4 t^4) \times \log_{10}(r)$$

where $t$ = time in days,

$r$ = radiation (cal cm$^{-2}$ min$^{-1}$) [1 cal cm$^{-2}$min$^{-1}$ = 697·8 W m$^{-2}$]

Coefficient of multiple determination ($R$) First growth period 0·88,

Second growth period 0·93

These surfaces summarize the change of $P_{n,c}$ during the growth period and provide a ready means of integrating $P_{n,c}$ over time. Earlier work had shown that shoot respiration of the canopy in the dark $(R_{s,d,c})$ responds to temperature changes within a few minutes and this caused considerable scatter in the measurements made at different times of the day and on different days. In Fig. 6, the measurements for both growth periods are

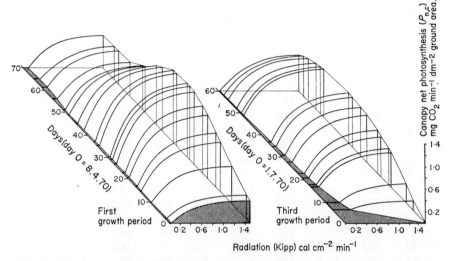

**Fig. 5.** Response surfaces showing the dependence of canopy net photosynthesis per unit ground area $(P_{n,c})$ on radiation and time from the beginning of the growth period. First and third growth periods.

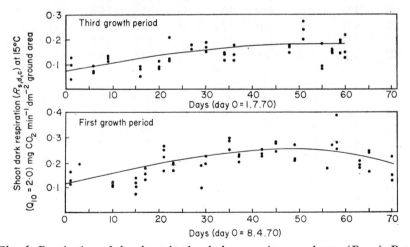

**Fig. 6.** Respiration of the shoot in the dark per unit ground area $(R_{s,d,c})$. Rate adjusted to 15 °C assuming that $Q_{10}$ for dark respiration is 2·0. First and third growth periods.

## Table I

Daily values of incoming radiation (Kipp solarimeter) cal cm$^{-2}$ day$^{-1}$, and mean air temperatures °C at 5 cm. First and third growth periods.

| | First | | Third | | | First | | Third | |
| Day | Radn. | Temp. | Radn. | Temp. | Day | Radn. | Temp. | Radn. | Temp. |
|---|---|---|---|---|---|---|---|---|---|
| 0 | 258 | 0·6 | 377 | 13·8 | 35 | 481 | 12·2 | 274 | 17·5 |
| 1 | 193 | 1·6 | 295 | 13·1 | 36 | 267 | 11·8 | 206 | 17·9 |
| 2 | 176 | 4·1 | 248 | 12·4 | 37 | 228 | 11·0 | 273 | 17·6 |
| 3 | 372 | 4·2 | 203 | 15·5 | 38 | 351 | 9·8 | 292 | 15·8 |
| 4 | 67 | 3·8 | 215 | 17·7 | 39 | 337 | 8·6 | 410 | 16·0 |
| 5 | 145 | 3·2 | 486 | 20·6 | 40 | 448 | 13·0 | 207 | 16·4 |
| 6 | 304 | 6·9 | 632 | 24·6 | 41 | 339 | 14·3 | 614 | 14·7 |
| 7 | 165 | 10·7 | 330 | 19·3 | 42 | 562 | 12·2 | 309 | — |
| 8 | 180 | 10·8 | 415 | 16·1 | 43 | 434 | 9·6 | 326 | — |
| 9 | 174 | 10·4 | 398 | 15·2 | 44 | 439 | 10·3 | 481 | — |
| 10 | 304 | — | 579 | 17·0 | 45 | 334 | 13·6 | 329 | — |
| 11 | 384 | 2·5 | 622 | 18·6 | 46 | 658 | 17·5 | 294 | — |
| 12 | 384 | 6·0 | 636 | 19·5 | 47 | 553 | 14·0 | 338 | — |
| 13 | 133 | 11·2 | 257 | 14·3 | 48 | 649 | 14·4 | 322 | — |
| 14 | 162 | 10·0 | 258 | 12·5 | 49 | 479 | 16·4 | 37 | — |
| 15 | 201 | 10·4 | 290 | 12·7 | 50 | 402 | 17·2 | 160 | — |
| 16 | 257 | 8·0 | 304 | 17·0 | 51 | 498 | 13·6 | 139 | — |
| 17 | 303 | 7·4 | 346 | 17·7 | 52 | 499 | 16·0 | 216 | — |
| 18 | 187 | 5·2 | 189 | 15·0 | 53 | 313 | 16·0 | 317 | — |
| 19 | 423 | 4·8 | 429 | 10·9 | 54 | 375 | 16·8 | 312 | — |
| 20 | 421 | 6·6 | 410 | 12·2 | 55 | 539 | 20·0 | 294 | 17·6 |
| 21 | 435 | 7·1 | 449 | 13·4 | 56 | 677 | 17·1 | 387 | 18·9 |
| 22 | 312 | 8·0 | 389 | 16·2 | 57 | 714 | 16·0 | 430 | 19·0 |
| 23 | 395 | 11·4 | 217 | 15·6 | 58 | 705 | 17·2 | 446 | 16·7 |
| 24 | 489 | 11·5 | 346 | 12·4 | 59 | 508 | 17·1 | 487 | 17·7 |
| 25 | 539 | 11·7 | 164 | 13·6 | 60 | 520 | 19·2 | 387 | 19·2 |
| 26 | 573 | 12·7 | 202 | 16·3 | 61 | 587 | 20·8 | 307 | 16·8 |
| 27 | 540 | 14·0 | 166 | 16·1 | 62 | 633 | 22·8 | 411 | 15·4 |
| 28 | 471 | 13·4 | 463 | 14·4 | 63 | 465 | 22·6 | | |
| 29 | 356 | 13·0 | 595 | 15·6 | 64 | 389 | 20·9 | | |
| 30 | 399 | 13·7 | 569 | 15·3 | 65 | 418 | 20·4 | | |
| 31 | 214 | 11·2 | 490 | 16·8 | 66 | 514 | 20·1 | | |
| 32 | 101 | 11·1 | 492 | 17·4 | 67 | 546 | 17·4 | | |
| 33 | 93 | 10·4 | 417 | 17·9 | 68 | 615 | 18·4 | | |
| 34 | 373 | 11·4 | 295 | 18·3 | | | | | |

Daily mean. First growth period 391 cal. cm$^{-2}$
Third growth period 352 cal. cm$^{-2}$

shown after adjustment to the value at 15 °C on the assumption that
$Q_{10} = 2.0$. The pattern of $R_{s,d,c}$ was consistent in the two growth periods;
after an initial rise in the rate there was little change except for a tendency
to decline towards the end of the first growth period.

## B. Radiation and temperature

Hourly integrals of incoming radiation were used in calculating cumulative $P_{n,c}$ over the growth periods, but, because of the volume of these
data, only daily totals of radiation are shown in Table I.

The percentage of radiation intercepted by the crop canopy during the
two growth periods is shown in Fig. 7(c). Because of an instrument failure
in 1970, part of the data for the first growth period is taken from 1969.

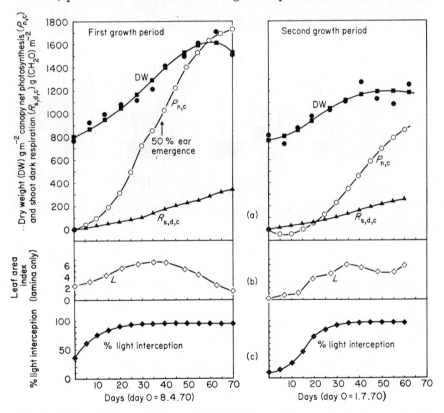

**Fig. 7.** (a) Cumulative total dry weight (DW) (g m$^{-2}$), canopy net photosynthesis
($P_{n,c}$) and respiration of the shoot in the dark ($R_{s,d,c}$) per unit ground area (g
hexose equivalent m$^{-2}$). (b) Leaf area index ($L$), lamina area only. (c) % light
interception by the canopy ($c$. 0·4–2·0 $\mu$m). First and third growth period.

The crops in 1969 and 1970 were almost identical. Radiation interception profiles for the third growth period are shown in Fig. 8.

A detailed description of the thermal climate will be published elsewhere: in this paper we are concerned primarily with the effect of temperature upon carbon exchange, but so far it has not been possible to use the data to take account of the effect of temperature variation upon $P_{n,c}$. The hourly

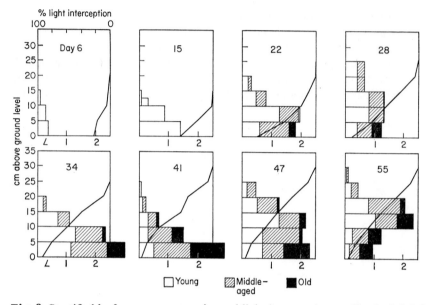

**Fig. 8.** Stratified leaf area, age categories and light interception profiles ($c.$ 0·4–2·0 $\mu$m). Third growth period.

mean temperature at the mid-point in the canopy was used in the calculation of the cumulative values of $R_{s,d,c}$, but because of the volume of these data, only the daily mean temperatures 5 cm above ground are given (Table I).

## C. Dry weight and leaf area

The means of the total dry weight at each harvest and a fitted regression of the form:

$$DW = a_0 + a_1t + a_2t^2 + a_3t^3 + a_4t^4 + a_5t^5$$

are shown in Fig. 6(a). In the third growth period the last term gave no significant improvement and was omitted. For the first growth period $F = 74\cdot0\,(P\,0\cdot01)$ and $R = 0\cdot90$, and for the third growth period $F = 13\cdot76$

and $R = 0.64$. Sample variability was a serious problem in estimating total dry weight changes, especially in the third growth period. In part this was due to the difficulty of below-ground sampling but also to lack of homogeneity in the above-ground samples.

Leaf area indices (lamina area only) during the two growth periods are shown in Fig. 6(b). In the first growth period, leaf area declined after ear emergence but there was a compensating increase in the area of stem and inflorescence: at late stages these constitute major light intercepting structures.

## D. Stratified leaf area

Figure 8 shows the stratified leaf area in the third growth period, and the division of leaf area into age categories from the third week onwards. Light extinction curves are superimposed on these diagrams. The efficiency of the canopy depends upon the amount of light intercepted and on the

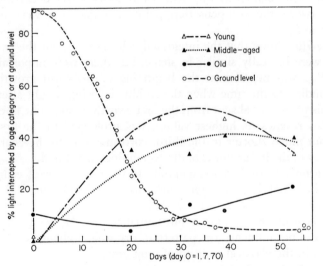

**Fig. 9.** Percentage light interception (*c.* 0·4–2·0 μm) by leaves in three age categories and at ground level. Third growth period.

efficiency of the leaves by which it is intercepted. Figure 9 shows the percentage of light intercepted by leaves in each of the three categories and by the ground. After cutting, only "old" leaves remained. As they senesced after cutting and became shaded by newly emerging leaves, interception by these leaves fell. Light interception reached 95% after 30 days; interception by "young" leaves reached a maximum about this time, and thereafter fell. Maximum interception by "middle aged" leaves reached a plateau somewhat later. After the initial decline, interception by "old" leaves began to rise and continued to do so through the growth period.

## E. Integration with time of $P_{n,c}$ and $R_{s,d,c}$

The $P_{n,c}$ response surfaces summarize the effect of time on the changing efficiency of the canopy. Crop performance, however, depends on both the efficiency of the canopy and the actual radiation it receives, and it was important to test whether the predicted values for $P_{n,c}$ and $R_{s,d,c}$ were in reasonable accord with the dry weight changes taking place. $P_{n,c}$ was integrated over time for both growth periods using the surfaces in Fig. 4 and hourly integrals of radiation. The results, expressed in g hexose m$^{-2}$ are shown in Fig. 7 (a). $R_{s,d,c}$ was computed by assuming a linear change in the intervals between measurements and integrating over the dark period using hourly mean temperatures ($Q_{10} = 2 \cdot 0$). The results expressed in g hexose m$^{-2}$ are shown in Fig. 7(a). Respiratory losses occurring at light levels between the compensation point and darkness were arbitrarily assigned to $P_{n,c}$.

Figure 7(a) shows that the integrated values of $P_{n,c}$ for the two growth periods were basically similar in shape, but there were important differences. $P_{n,c}$ was negative at the beginning of the third growth period, corresponding to the time when the stubble is losing weight after defoliation. This phase was absent from the first growth period. The linear phase, when $P_{n,c}$ reaches its highest values, was prolonged in the first growth period but much shorter in the third, corresponding to the characteristic differences in the linear phase of dry weight increase. Finally, $P_{n,c}$ declined in both growth periods, corresponding to the attainment of ceiling yield.

After the initial rise, $R_{s,d,c}$ remained substantially unchanged throughout both growth periods except for a slight tendency to decline towards the end. Thus while $R_{s,d,c}$ took a substantial toll of the net photosynthesis input, it did not influence the pattern of dry weight change in the manner envisaged in the classical concept of crop growth.

# IV. Discussion

To understand the reasons for the pattern of productivity of the perennial ryegrass sward, more information was needed about the primary process of carbon dioxide exchange and its relation to canopy structure and the environment. The development of an enclosure method for carbon dioxide exchange measurements was a subsidiary objective in this work; we have continued to develop and improve the method and believe that it has a valuable role in exploring crop behaviour in the field, and will prove of special value in comparative studies.

Checking the results of carbon dioxide flux measurements is difficult with both enclosure and micrometeorological methods. There is no absolute method with which to compare results, and comparison with growth analyses is of limited value. The credibility of results can be assessed by constructing a total carbon budget, but this is bedevilled in the field by the problem of measuring root respiration and the loss of material by death and detachment. Robson (1971) has shown that in simulated swards in a growth room, root and shoot respiration in the dark are roughly proportional to their respective dry weights, and we have used this relationship to estimate root respiration in the field. However, this gives a figure approximately 25% of gross photosynthesis $(P_{n,c} + R_{s,a,c})$ which is higher than the 15–20% quoted by Osman (1971). Osman has also confirmed earlier evidence that root respiration may be up to 50% higher after shoot illumination than after a period in the dark, and Robson's measurements, which were made following a period of illumination, may be too high for this reason. In the third growth period root respiration may be overestimated in view of the finding by Woodford and Gregory (1948) and Davidson and Milthorpe (1966) that defoliation markedly depresses root respiration.

At present we have no satisfactory way of estimating the loss of carbon by death and detachment of tissue.

Table II shows the increasing, linear and decreasing phases of dry weight change in the two growth periods. Ash-free dry weight ($DW_a$) was calculated using Hunt's figure for ash content (Hunt, 1966), and carbon fluxes are expressed as g hexose equivalent. In the third growth period the negative residual balance in the first two phases, and in the overall budget, implies an underestimate of $P_{n,c}$ or an overestimate of losses: the latter seems more probable but the errors associated with dry weight estimation in this growth period lead to uncertainty.

In neither growth period was there a sharply defined maximum growth rate or rate of $P_{n,c}$ corresponding to a critical $L$. $P_{n,c}$ rose quickly up to about 85% light interception during the exponential phase of dry weight change, remained fairly constant in the linear phase, and finally declined as ceiling yield was approached. There was no evidence that the declining growth rate was due to an increasing respiratory burden; on the contrary, the respiration rate fell as growth rate declined. This is in keeping with the recent views on crop growth reviewed by Brown and Blaser (1968) and with the suggestion by de Wit et al. (1971) that respiration should be linked with growth rather than with leaf area or dry weight.

A low growth rate in the linear phase, coupled with the progressively

E. L. LEAFE

earlier attainment of a ceiling, appears to be a major factor restricting yield in growth periods later in the season. Decreasing radiation is a partial explanation; but in the third growth period in this experiment, mean daily radiation was only 10% less than in the first (Table I). A more important factor appears to be the lower photosynthetic efficiency of the canopy (Figs 5 and 7). This may be due partly to the unfavourable spatial

### Table II

Total carbon budget g m$^{-1}$, first and third growth periods. $DW_a$ = ash-free dry weight $P_{n,c}$, $R_{s,d,c}$, $R_r$ = canopy net photosynthesis, shoot dark respiration, root respiration as hexose equivalent. $D_{r,s}$ = death and detachment of root and shoot.

| | $\Delta DW_a =$ | $P_{n,c} -$ | $R_{s,d,c} -$ | $R_r -$ (assumed) | $D_{r,s}$ (by difference) |
|---|---|---|---|---|---|
| *First growth period* | | | | | |
| Days | | | | | |
| 0–28 | 324 | 645 | 92 | 178 | 51 |
| 29–49 | 326 | 735 | 131 | 177 | 101 |
| 50–70 | 2 | 355 | 120 | 122 | 111 |
| 0–70 | 652 | 1735 | 343 | 477 | 263 |
| *Third growth period* | | | | | |
| 0–19 | 152 | 36 | 53 | 80 | −248 |
| 20–41 | 203 | 451 | 116 | 142 | −10 |
| 42–62 | 14 | 350 | 101 | 114 | 121 |
| 0–62 | 368 | 837 | 270 | 336 | −137 |

distribution of leaves in relation to radiation, although Alberda (1968) from a consideration of the de Wit model, discounts an important effect of leaf angle at this stage. However, a factor which appears largely to have been ignored is the effect of canopy structure upon light interception by leaves of different ages, although the effect of leaf age on photosynthetic efficiency is well documented. Figure 9 shows that towards the end of the third growth period, the proportion of radiation intercepted by "young" leaves was falling whereas interception by "old" leaves was rising.

In perennial ryegrass, the canopy changes from erectophile to planophile progressively earlier in successive growth periods (Alberda and Sibma, 1968). As a result of the prostrate habit there is a progressive tendency for older leaves to form a "thatch", and for new leaves produced near the ground to emerge into shade rather than sunlight. This adverse situation is aggravated by the seasonal decline in the rate of leaf production. Anslow's results (1968) are of interest in this connection. He found that when all but the expanding leaf was removed from swards of S.24 perennial ryegrass, thus reducing leaf area by 80%, the sward nevertheless yielded 75% of the undefoliated sward. Anslow attributed this to the better illumination of the expanding leaf when older leaves were removed.

In conclusion, a word of caution is needed. We have shown that declining growth rates and lowered ceiling yields in the grass sward appear to be related to the lowered photosynthetic efficiency of the crop canopy. It would be tempting to conclude that growth rate declines *because* photosynthesis declines. However, the converse explanation is possible: photosynthesis may decline because growth rate declines or, indeed, a feed-back situation may exist in which both effects operate. The relation between sink and source is by no means clear.

# Acknowledgements

I should like to thank the Director of the Grassland Research Institute for his encouragement, and my colleagues in the Botany Division, particularly Mr W. Stiles, Mr L. Jones, Miss S. Mallett and members of the Biometrics Department.

# References

ALBERDA, TH. (1968). Dry matter production and light interception of crop surfaces: IV. Maximum herbage production as compared with predicted values. *Neth. J. agric. Sci.* **16,** 142–153.

ALBERDA, TH. and SIBMA, L. (1968). Dry matter production and light interception of crop surfaces: III. Actual herbage production in different years, as compared with potential values. *J. Br. Grassld Soc.* **23,** 206–215.

ANSLOW, R. C. (1968). The production of dry matter by swards of perennial ryegrass, differing in average age of foliage. *J. Br. Grassld Soc.* **23,** 195–201.

BROWN, R. H. and BLASER, R. E. (1968). Leaf area index in pasture growth. *Herbage Abstracts* **38,** 1–9.

DAVIDSON, J. L. and MILTHORPE, F. L. (1966). The effect of defoliation on the carbon balance in *Dactylis glomerata. Ann. Bot.* **30,** 185–198.

ECKARDT, F. E. (1970). Research on the structure and function of the photosynthetic apparatus under field conditions: aims and methods. *In* "Prediction and measurement of photosynthetic productivity". *Proc. IBP/PP technical meeting, Trebon, 1969* (I. Setlik, ed.), pp. 379–384. Centre for Agricultural Publishing and Documentation, Wageningen.

HUNT, L. A. (1966). Ash and energy content of material from seven forage grasses. *Crop Sci.* **6**, 507–509.

JARVIS, P. G. (1970). Characteristics of the photosynthetic apparatus derived from its response to natural complexes of environmental factors. *In* "Prediction and measurement of photosynthetic productivity". *Proc. IBP/PP technical meeting, Trebon, 1969* (I. Setlik, ed.), pp. 353–367. Centre for Agricultural Publishing & Documentation, Wageningen.

OSMAN, A. M. (1971). Root respiration of wheat plants as influenced by age temperature and irradiation of shoots. *Photosynthetica* **5**, 107–112.

ROBSON, M. J. (1971). *Rep. Grassld Res. Inst. 1970*, 58.

STILES, W, and LEAFE, E. L. (1970). Measurement of photosynthesis and respiration in the field. *Rep. Grassld Res. Inst. 1969*, 127–135.

SZEICZ, G. (1964). A miniature tube solarimeter. *J. appl. Ecol.* **2**, 145–147.

WIT, C. T. DE (1965). Photosynthesis of leaf canopies. *Landbouwk. Onderz.* **663**, 1–57.

WIT, C. T. DE, BROUWER, R. and PENNING DE VRIES, F. W. T. (1971). A dynamic model of plant and crop growth. *In* "Potential Crop Production" (P. F. Wareing and J. P. Cooper, eds), pp. 116–142. Heinemann, London.

WOODFORD, E. K. and GREGORY, F. G. (1948). Preliminary results obtained with an apparatus for the study of salt uptake and root respiration of whole plants. *Ann. Bot.* **12**, 335–370.

# Discussion

**Wareing** asked whether **Leafe** had data on photosynthesis at different temperatures. Leafe replied that, up till now, his chief concern had been with seasonal differences in the photosynthetic efficiency of the grass canopy and its relation to dry weight change; the effect of temperature had not been investigated systematically. **Ludwig** asked whether Leafe's data provided any information on a correlation between daily integrated radiation and the rate of respiration at night. Only in the present season had respiration been measured overnight; correlation between photosynthesis during the day and respiration overnight had not yet been made. In the period following cutting, the relation between photosynthesis and respiration is changed. Initially the crop loses weight as substrates in the stubble and roots are utilized; only as leaf area is re-established is a positive carbon balance restored.

# II.6. The relationship between crop physiology and analytical plant physiology

C. P. WHITTINGHAM

*Rothamsted Experimental Station, Harpenden, Hertfordshire, England*

## I. Field measurement of crop production

Plant physiologists have been concerned in measuring crop yields and those factors that are likely to determine the yield under a range of environmental and cultural conditions. In the earlier studies attempts were made to correlate final yields and climatic factors but by the early 1920s it was realized that measurements of final yield alone were inadequate. In 1925 the Rothamsted report stated "It is now however recognized that more useful information has been obtained from field observations during the growth of the crops than from the final weighings. The field laboratory has therefore been built and equipped for making measurements on the growing plant."

There followed a period when growth analysis became the foremost tool of the crop physiologist. Because all the organic substances in the plant are the product of photosynthesis it follows that the analysis of yield is primarily an analysis of the activity of crops as photosynthetic systems. The increase in dry weight of plants in a given period was taken as a measure of net photosynthesis and the total leaf area was considered the best measure of photosynthetic machinery. Thus, by dividing one by the other, an assessment of photosynthetic efficiency, the net assimilation rate, could be obtained.

From the middle 1930s through to the early 1940s measurements of leaf area index and net assimilation rate were made on many field crops at Rothamsted. D. J. Watson concluded that, although net assimilation rate differed widely between species, it differed little between varieties and was not much affected by nutrient supply. Differences in yield of dry matter between crops resulted mainly from differences in leaf area, or better leaf area duration, and the problem of increasing crop yields was seen at that time as the problem of increasing leaf area index, particularly during early spring and summer before mutual shading of leaves began to be significant. Thus, Watson and Baptiste (1938) proposed that the sowing of sugar beet should take place as early as possible to increase leaf area early in the season; increasing plant density (over quite wide limits) to increase the leaf area index without change of sowing date had a much smaller effect (Watson, 1958).

# II. Meteorological methods

Recently the gas exchange of field crops has been determined from quantitative studies of the microclimate surrounding the crop (Monteith and Szeicz, 1960). With this technique the immediate response to a change in conditions can be determined without disturbing the natural environment. The profile of carbon dioxide concentration, of light intensity, and of wind speed is determined above and within the crop canopy. By reference to an electrical analogue, the flux is taken as proportional to the difference in concentration in the atmosphere and that at the photosynthetic centre within the plant and inversely proportional to a resistance term. The resistance may be broken down into several individual components and the effect of the environment on each of them determined.

# III. Gasometric methods and the use of radioactive tracers

The photosynthetic activity of plants, even in the field, may be measured more directly than from observations of dry weight gain. The crop may be enclosed in a transparent cover (e.g. Musgrave and Moss, 1961) and the change with time in concentration of carbon dioxide within it determined. Alternatively, part of a plant or individual leaves attached to or detached from the plant may be placed in a closed assimilation chamber. Less sophisticated equipment is required if radioactive carbon dioxide is used. The levels of radioactivity required are in no way dangerous and, provided certain simple precautions are followed, rates of photosynthesis and respiration under a wide range of conditions can be measured.

At the Plant Breeding Institute in Cambridge, the rate of photosynthesis of leaves of different varieties of wheat was measured by determining the rate at which labelled carbon dioxide was taken up by attached leaves placed in chambers in the field (Lupton, 1969); also the proportion of carbon translocated to the grain was estimated. From such measurements during the period when the grain was developing, good predictions of the ultimate grain yield were made. Similar experiments by others had shown the relative contribution of the flag and other leaves to the growth of the grain, and the difference between wheat and barley in this respect (Thorne, 1965).

Determinations of the photosynthetic activity of leaves, either attached or detached from the plant, placed in an assimilation chamber, have been severely criticized. Enclosing the leaf within a chamber results in rapid changes in the environment of the leaf. The light intensity to which the leaf is exposed is decreased, the temperature of the leaf raised (sometimes by a considerable amount) and the partial pressure of oxygen, of carbon dioxide, and of water vapour surrounding the leaf are all changed. In addition, handling of some leaves changes both rates of metabolism and stomatal aperture. In spite of this, some observations of the rate of photosynthesis of wheat plants, determined both using a chamber and from meteorological observations, were in reasonable agreement. More data are needed to establish the conditions that minimize the errors which may be introduced by the use of a chamber. The method has the advantage that the rate of photosynthesis of a given leaf can be determined in a wide range of conditions including different light intensities and different concentrations of carbon dioxide and of oxygen. Such observations are planned for future work at Rothamsted in conditions approximating as closely as possible to those in the field. The observations will include also determinations of the relative proportions of different products of photosynthesis under a wide range of conditions.

Miss Bishop and I made some preliminary observations with tomato plants grown and measured in a controlled environment (Bishop and Whittingham, 1968). The plants were treated with radioactive carbon dioxide and the products of photosynthesis determined using paper chromatography. Plants exposed at an intermediate light intensity to three times the normal concentration of carbon dioxide in air produced more sucrose relative to amino acids than plants exposed to a normal concentration of carbon dioxide. In other experiments (Lea and Whittingham, unpublished) similar differences were observed even when the total fixation of carbon was made the same under the two conditions. The ratio of radioactive sucrose to radioactive glycine and serine was greater the greater the concentration of carbon dioxide (Fig. 1), (Bishop and Whittingham, 1968). The glycine and serine appear outside the chloroplast of the photosynthetic cell sooner than does sucrose (Roberts et al., 1970). In most plants sucrose is the metabolite translocated from the leaves to other parts, so different conditions may change the proportion of carbon translocated from a leaf even when the rate of photosynthesis is unaltered.

Until recently, it was assumed that the respiratory activity of plants, as measured in the dark, continued unchanged in the light. On that basis the net assimilation rate approximates to the rate of photosynthesis because the latter is often at least ten times the former. Recent experiments have

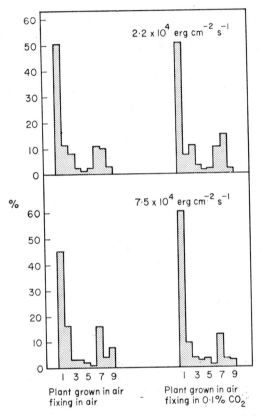

**Fig. 1.** Distribution of radioactivity in various compounds of the ethanol-soluble fraction for tomato leaves photosynthesizing at two different light intensities. 1, sucrose; 2, glycine and serine; 3, aspartate; 4, alanine; 5, unknown; 6, glutamate; 7, organic acids; 8, sugar phosphates; 9, remainder. (Bishop and Whittingham, 1968.)

shown that, under certain conditions, carbon dioxide may be produced three to five times as fast in the light as in the dark (Decker, 1957; Zelitch, 1968), and that the process responsible, photorespiration, is biochemically distinct from the process of dark respiration. Until now, most measurements of photorespiration have of necessity been made in conditions very different from those in the field, so that the practical importance of photorespiration for crop plants and the conditions that increase it have still to be defined. A better understanding will come when the relationship between the biochemistry of photosynthesis and environmental factors has been further studied.

# IV. Source–sink effects

In the previous section it has been pointed out that only some of the products of photosynthesis are immediately available for translocation. Translocation may in turn influence photosynthesis. For example in both potato and sugar beet, the photosynthetic activity of the leaves has been shown to be related to the size of the root or tuber to which the leaves are attached. Such effects are most easily studied in a controlled environment when different parts of the plant can be exposed to different treatments, e.g. the aerial parts of potato kept at a different temperature from that of the tubers in the soil. Such experiments have indicated that there is an excess of foliage in the normal potato plant. Moreover the growth rate of the tuber has been shown to be independent of changes in the leaf area of the crop, suggesting that the tubers may be unable to accept all the potential products of photosynthesis. Probably similar considerations apply to the sugar-beet plant (Thorne and Evans, 1964). Experiments on wheat at Rothamsted, at the Plant Breeding Institute in Cambridge, in Sweden and in Australia, have shown that both the capacity of the ears and the size and longevity of the photosynthetic system after anthesis can influence grain yield. Removing some of the grains from wheat plants in the field decreased yield; and removing ears from plants in a closed canopy decreased the photosynthetic activity of the leaves for two to six days following, although this effect has not been confirmed by some workers.

When the sink capacity or rate of translocation is inadequate for the rate of photosynthesis, there must be a period during which photosynthetic products accumulate in the leaves. It has been frequently claimed that this then slows the rate of photosynthesis. But relatively few investigators have both determined the rate of photosynthesis and at the same time made chemical analyses of the leaf. The general hypothesis must be considered unproven. However, Habeshaw (1970) showed that in the sugar-beet plant there was a simple relationship between the decline in rate of photosynthesis during the day and the accumulation of starch in the leaves. Earlier Hartt (1963) had shown a related effect in sugar-cane leaves.

In most studies of growth of cereals in the field, the roots have been neglected because of their inaccessibility. Methods are being developed at Rothamsted to measure the amount and distribution of roots in the soil at different stages of growth and in different conditions. Elsewhere information is being obtained about the ability of roots to absorb water and nutrients, but most of these studies are in the laboratory. At the present time, we do not know from field studies which part of the root absorbs water fastest and whether the same portion absorbs nutrients.

The interaction between the growth of roots and the photosynthetic activity of the leaves has been investigated only in general terms. Information concerning the distribution of dry matter between the different parts of a plant has come from growth analysis measurements. But how far growth depends on the amount of photosynthate available for distribution, and how far the rate of photosynthesis is determined by the capacity of different parts of the plant to accept photosynthate, is not yet clear.

# V. The influence of hormones on rate of photosynthesis

Differentiation in plants is controlled by the presence or relative abundance of growth-promoting and retarding chemicals. It follows from the previous section that there may be an indirect effect of hormone activity in one part of the plant on the photosynthetic activity of another part. But direct effects have also been achieved. Turner and Bidwell (1965) showed that spraying bean leaves with indol-3yl-acetic acid increased the rate of photosynthesis at saturating light intensities. Sprays of gibberellic acid had a similar effect on tomato leaves (Coulombe and Paquin, 1959) and red clover plants (Treharne and Stoddart, 1968).

# VI. The development of models of plant growth

The photosynthesis of a crop can be related to the incident light falling on it, provided both the relationship between absorbed light energy and the rate of photosynthesis and that between the incident light intensity and the energy absorbed by the photosynthetic pigments, are known. Unless it is assumed, probably unwisely, that the concentration of carbon dioxide is appreciably constant, the relationship between rate and light intensity will be a function also of the concentration of carbon dioxide. In addition, the loss from respiration must be allowed for before photosynthesis can be related to crop yield, and further factors to allow for the distribution of total photosynthate to different portions of the plant. The formulation of a mathematical model of plant growth will help to make it apparent where our present knowledge is inadequate. In addition it may be possible to predict the relative contribution of the various terms in the general yield equation and hence the relative importance of different unknowns.

De Wit has emphasized the need for further knowledge concerning respiration in the intact plant. To produce a satisfactory model it is generally postulated that only a part of respiratory metabolism is related to plant growth, called "coupled" or useful respiration, the remaining part (the "basal" respiration) being assumed to be unrelated to growth. In a preceding section of this paper, I have suggested that photosynthesis could equally well be considered as composed of at least two components; one closely correlated to the rate of translocation from the leaf, the other showing little or no correlation. Further, there is evidence that the process responsible for producing carbon dioxide in the light (photorespiration) is biochemically separate from normal direct respiration. In some plants internal factors ranging from starch to sugar phosphates, from hormones to nucleic acids, regulate the rate of photosynthesis. My view is that on most of these aspects more information is required before even preliminary models can be usefully formulated.

# VII. Results of enrichment with carbon dioxide

The beneficial effect on yield by tomatoes of carbon dioxide enrichment discovered by the practical horticulturist raises problems for the plant physiologist. Methods of growth analysis have been applied at the Glasshouse Crops Research Institute to study this effect (Hurd, 1968). Plants grown in controlled environment chambers were measured during a period of seven to eight weeks. The photosynthetic rate, i.e. dry weight increase, was very significantly increased by enrichment but the effect slowly diminished with time. Less of the products of photosynthesis were used to form new leaf area, so that the leaves on enriched plants increased relatively more in thickness than in area. At the end of a six-week period, the enriched plants had 40% more dry weight, but only 20% more leaf area. There was some indication that the dry weight of the root had been increased relatively more as a result of enrichment with carbon dioxide. Unfortunately, in these experiments the possibility that root restriction may have influenced the growth of the larger plants, especially under the enriched conditions, could not be discounted, although there were indications that the change in distribution of photosynthesis began early in the experiment before roots were probably much restricted. Enrichment also modifies the relative rate at which other parts of the plant develop, for example the flower primordium number is increased and more fruits are set in the first truss. Enrichment may also hasten flowering.

Similar experiments have been concerned with the growth of China Asters in controlled environments (Hughes and Cockshull, 1969). Enrichment to 600 ppm produced a significant increase of 30% in total dry weight at the onset of flowering and 20% at flowering maturity. The effects on leaf area were much smaller than in tomato although it was clear that the effect of the enhanced photosynthetic rate would have been greater in the long term were it not for the concomitant decrease in leaf area ratio. At 900 ppm the effects of enrichment were more variable.

The factors that control the relationship between growth and increase in leaf area on the one hand, and leaf thickness on the other, are probably complex. They could be related to a difference in balance of the different types of photosynthetic product. One practical finding contrary to earlier theories was the observation that enrichment was effective in winter when the light was dim. This can only be explained if enhancement results in a difference in metabolism as well as a change of rate. At the Lee Valley and Stockbridge House Experimental Horticulture Stations, a prototype light modulated master control system has been introduced into glasshouses, so that temperatures fluctuate in a manner determined by light intensity. This was compared with "blue-print" management using arbitrary changes in temperature based on practical experience. All compartments were enriched with $CO_2$. The light modulated system gave no beneficial effect on the growth of either tomatoes or lettuce compared with the "blue-print" system although there was some advantage in the growth of cucumbers. In future experiments light modulated control of the concentration of carbon dioxide will be attempted. But at the present time we cannot say how light, temperature and concentration of carbon dioxide mutually interact even considering rate relationships alone. If we accept the complexity introduced by changes in the biochemistry of photosynthesis as well as changes in rate, we certainly are not yet able to programme environmental control in the glasshouse. An understanding of the effect of environmental change on the growth of field crops presents an even greater challenge.

# References

BISHOP, P. M. and WHITTINGHAM, C. P. (1968). The photosynthesis of tomato plants in a carbon dioxide enriched atmosphere. *Photosynthetica* **2**, 31–38.

COULOMBE, L-J and PAQUIN, R. (1959). Effets de l'acide gibberellique sur le metabolisme des plantes. *Can. J. Bot.* **37**, 897–901.

DECKER, J. P. (1957). Further evidence of increased carbon dioxide production accompanying photosynthesis. *J. sol. Energy Sci. Engng* **1**, 30–41.

HABESHAW, D. (1970). Unpublished report to S.B.R.E.C.

HARTT, C. (1963). Translocation as a factor in photosynthesis. *Naturwiss.* **21**, 666–667.

HURD, R. G. (1968). Effects of $CO_2$ enrichment on the growth of young tomato plants in low light. *Ann. Bot.* **32**, 531–542.

HUGHES, A. P. and COCKSHULL, K. E. (1969). Effects of carbon dioxide concentration on the growth of *Callistephus chinensis* cultivar Johannistag. *Ann. Bot.* **33**, 351–365.

LUPTON, F. G. H. (1969). Estimation of yield in wheat from measurements of photosynthesis and translocation in the field. *Ann. appl. Biol.* **64**, 363–374.

MONTEITH, J. L. and SZEICZ, G. (1960). The carbon dioxide flux over a field of sugar beet. *Q. Jl R. met. Soc.* **86**, 205–214.

MUSGRAVE, R. B. and MOSS, D. N. (1961). Photosynthesis under field conditions. I. A portable, closed system for determining net assimilation and respiration of corn. *Crop Sci.* **1**, 37–41.

ROBERTS, G. R., KEYS, A. J. and WHITTINGHAM, C. P. (1970). The transport of photosynthetic products from the chloroplasts of tobacco leaves. *J. exp. Bot.* **21**, 683–692.

THORNE, G. N. (1965). Photosynthesis of ears and flag leaves of wheat and barley. *Ann. Bot.* **29**, 317–329.

THORNE, G. N. and EVANS, A. F. (1964). Influence of tops and roots on net assimilation rate of sugar-beet and spinach beet and grafts between them. *Ann. Bot.* **28**, 499–508.

TREHARNE, K. J. and STODDART, J. L. (1968). Effects of gibberellin on photosynthesis in red clover (*Trifolium pratense* L.). *Nature, Lond.* **220**, 457–458.

TURNER, W. B. and BIDWELL, R. G. S. (1965). Rates of photosynthesis in attached and detached bean leaves, and the effect of spraying with indoleacetic acid solution. *Pl. Physiol., Lancaster* **40**, 446–451.

WATSON, D. J. and BAPTISTE, E. C. D. (1938). A comparative physiological study of sugar-beet and mangold with respect to growth and sugar accumulation. 1. Growth analysis of the crop in the field. *Ann. Bot. O.S.* **6**, 437–480.

WATSON, D. J. (1958). The dependence of net assimilation rate on leaf-area index. *Ann. Bot.* **22**, 37–54.

ZELITCH, I. (1968). Investigations on photorespiration with a sensitive $C^{14}$ assay. *Pl. Physiol., Lancaster* **43**, 1829–1837.

# Discussion

**Lake** suggested that the chemical products did not change over the concentration of carbon dioxide normally encountered, but **Whittingham** stated that the three-fold enrichment used in the Lee Valley is above the optimum for glycolic acid. **Incoll** wondered whether the concentrations used in glasshouses were relevant to the field situation; $\Delta CO^2$ through the crop is very small so that there should be little difference in the type of photosynthesis through the canopy. Whittingham, however, was referring to the $\Delta CO_2$ of the chloroplasts which show difference between parts of leaves as well as between leaves. **Scott Russell** thought that Whittingham's statement that just measuring $CO_2$ gave inadequate information was a dangerous one, but this was defended on the grounds that with very little change in technique more information could be obtained.

# II.7. Crop processes and physics

P. D. JARMAN

*Glasshouse Crops Research Institute, Littlehampton, Sussex, England*

## I. Introduction

This paper depicts crop processes in controlled environments against a broad perspective that includes all the physical phenomena that are thought to occur in our universe. The intention of this exercise is to define the class of physical problems to which crop processes belong, the class of low-energy physics which includes the complex carbon chemistry known as biology, and to indicate some of the inadequacies of the language of physics to describe these processes.

The life forms that exist in our biosphere are particular kinds of bound matter which are synthesized and temporarily maintained in a constant stream of energy flowing from a hot source, the sun, through our biosphere to a cold sink, colder parts of the universe. These life forms can exist only because the sun is very slowly burning up its hydrogen so that the energy flowing through our biosphere lies in a very restricted range of intensities and qualities: our biosphere is a quiet, but not too quiet, controlled environment in the proximity of this larger than average middle-aged star. Compared to the major activities in the universe, the natural fluctuations in the physical conditions of our biosphere are very small but they are still not small enough for adequate control of crop processes, and the conditions themselves may not be optimum for these processes since plants appear to have an obstinate nostalgia for the climates of long ago: plants, particularly those with C3 biochemical pathways, thrive better in artificial environments having low oxygen or high carbon dioxide concentrations.

## II. Our biosphere and the sun

The volume of our biosphere is roughly a thousandth of that of the earth around which it exists in the form of a shell. During the $4.5 \times 10^9$ year history of the earth, its atmosphere has changed from a probably hydrogen-

185

rich reducing one to one that is now rich in oxygen, and life has evolved probably from chemosynthetic anaerobic bacteria to the present photo-synthetic plants and man. This evolution resulted from the early synthesis of a trap for the sun's radiation: chlorophyll. The sun is a star of absolute magnitude $+ 5$ and of spectroscopic type GO; in its present state it emits electromagnetic radiation at a rate of $4 \times 10^{26}$ W ($6 \times 10^7$ W m$^{-2}$) with maximum intensity at a wavelength of 540 nm from its 6300°C surface, the photosphere; $2 \times 10^{17}$ W of this radiation, 1 part in $10^9$, is intercepted by the earth. The gravitational collapse of the sun is being held up by a thermonuclear reaction in which protons, the nuclei of hydrogen atoms, fuse together at its $2 \times 10^7$ °C centre. This fusion process is controlled by the very slow weak interaction, proton + proton $\rightarrow$ deuteron + positron + neutrino, since there is no bound state of the helium isotope of atomic weight 2. If such a bound state did exist, and the proton–proton interaction would only need to be a few per cent stronger for such a state to occur, then the hydrogen of the sun would burn up $10^{18}$ times faster. The dura-tion of this fusion process—the burn-up time of the sun's hydrogen—is estimated to be $10\cdot3 \times 10^9$ years of which $4\cdot5 \times 10^9$ years have passed. The initial gravitational conglomeration or birth of the sun took about $140 \times 10^6$ years, at the end of which its centre was hot enough for the proton–proton fusion reaction to begin. When the hydrogen is exhausted in about $5\cdot8 \times 10^6$ years' time, the gravitational collapse will probably be resumed and possibly after about $500 \times 10^6$ years, there will be a very energetic flare up of its helium and carbon nuclei before its final gravitational collapse into a cold dense stellar corpse known as a white dwarf (Dyson, 1971).

# III. Plants and the electromagnetic interaction

Plants and processes going on within them are manifestations almost exclusively of the electromagnetic interaction between charged particles and of the lowest in energy requirements of the three kinds of excited states of bound matter, the atomic, as shown in Table I which also includes the other universal interactions and their bound states and spectroscopies.

For further details see, for example, Weisskopf (1968). An interaction is a coupling, attractive or repulsive, between two or more simple entities or particles that have well-defined positions, energies and momenta. Almost the whole of biology and chemistry is contained within the framework of the electromagnetic interaction and atomic or molecular spectroscopy; the life forms or biomass of our biosphere are temporary traps for the low-energy quanta that are associated with the weak binding between electrons and atomic nuclei. For the binding of electrons to positively-charged nuclei of atoms, and of atoms with atoms to produce molecules and plants,

## Table I

Universal interactions, bound states and spectroscopies

(*The electromagnetic interaction and its associated atomic and molecular spectroscopies account for nearly all biology and chemistry*)

### A. INTERACTIONS

| Type | Electromagnetic | Gravitational | Strong | Weak |
|---|---|---|---|---|
| Source | Charge | Mass | Baryons | Leptons |
| Range | Very large | Very large | $1/10^{15}$ metres (= size of atomic nucleus) | $1/10^{15}$ metres |
| Relative strength | $10^{-2}$ | $10^{-40}$ | 1 | $10^{-13}$ |
| Coupling by | Photons | Gravitons | Pi and K mesons | W meson |

### B. BOUND STATES AND SPECTROSCOPIES RESULTING FROM ATTRACTIVE INTERACTIONS

| Bound state | Binding | Bound parts | Spectroscopy | Typical excitation energy in eV | Particles/quanta emitted/absorbed when excitation level is lowered/raised |
|---|---|---|---|---|---|
| Nucleon (proton or neutron) | ? | (Quarks?) | Baryonic | $10^9$ | Photons, electrons, muons, pions and kaons (mesons), and neutrinos |
| Nucleus | Strong | Nucleons | Nuclear | $10^5$ | Photons, electrons and neutrinos |
| Atom | Electromagnetic | Electrons and protons | Atomic | 1 | Photons |
| Molecule | Electromagnetic | Electrons and protons | Molecular | 1 | Photons |
| Plant | Electromagnetic | Molecules and ions | Molecular | 1 | Photons |
| Solar system | Gravitational | The sun, planets and their moons | — | — | — |

and for the existence of the discrete energy levels of atomic and molecular spectroscopy, the coupling must be long-range and its overall effect must be attractive so that the bound system has negative potential energy; it needs this energy to separate its constituent particles. Examples of bound states appear in Table I. The electromagnetic interaction occurs between charged particles; it is attractive between particles having unlike charges and repulsive between those with like charges. Molecules and plants are examples of bound matter in which the attractive electromagnetic forces dominate the repulsive forces. The binding strength and energy levels of bound matter are determined by certain universal laws of nature which are incorporated into the fundamental physical theory known as quantum mechanics. For bound and condensed matter, the two most significant of these laws are that there exist only a finite number of discrete energy levels and that there are restrictions on the number of Fermi particles that can be in a certain energy level (Fermi particles have half-integral spin and anti-symmetric wave functions; only one such particle can occupy a given quantum state. Electrons, protons and neutrons are all Fermi particles). The average density of the atomic matter of molecules and plants is determined by the electron distributions associated with the lowest energy levels, and these depend on the strength of the electromagnetic interaction binding the system together. It is only about $10^{-16}$ of the density of nuclear matter such as that of an atomic nucleus or a white dwarf, a very dense terminal phase of a star. These are bound together by the strong interaction which has a range of only about $10^{-15}$ m, about the size of a nucleus. The nuclear energy levels associated with this interaction are about $10^5$ larger than those of atomic spectroscopy; the radiation environment of the biosphere will cause inappreciable changes to these nuclei since the quanta of solar radiation have far too little energy. I am, of course, neglecting the use of radioactive isotopes in certain experiments on plants. The gravitational interaction between the plant and the earth is generally of secondary interest. I should point out that the electromagnetic interaction is often disguised as, for example, an elastic, a friction or a collision effect—diffusion is a collision-dominated transport process in which particles flow down concentration gradients under the influence of electromagnetic forces which act when the particles collide with one another.

Table I shows that the energy activity within our biosphere is many orders of magnitude less than that at the centre of the sun or in nuclear reactors where changes to nuclear processes dominate the scene, and even these hotter environments are many orders of magnitude less active energetically than the hot spots of the universe such as the quasars, pulsars or neutron stars, and black holes associated with the birth and death of stars; environments in which the complex changes to energy and matter associated with excited baryons occur. The table indicates that as the environment becomes hotter, these changes increase in complexity and we can comfort ourselves that in our relatively cold biosphere, only the simplest of changes can occur and only those in which the number of material particles, those with non-zero rest mass, remain constant, and in which antiparticles do not occur. Nevertheless, life forms are probably the most complex kind of bound matter that exists in the universe since hot environments dissociate all weakly bound matter; in the hottest environments, only simple unbound particles and anti-particles exist.

# IV. The energy enrichment of plants

So far our biosphere has been depicted merely as an environment in which low energy physics takes place: biology, a complex form of carbon chemistry, in particular. A conceptual framework can now be used that belongs to the animate rather than the inanimate by introducing the ideas of complexity and organization that distinguish the one form of bound matter from the other. A small bacterial cell can be regarded as the least complex form of life but we shall for convenience follow Morowitz's (1968) analysis of the relatively large cell of *Escherichia coli*. Its non-aqueous fraction contains $2 \times 10^{10}$ atoms (47% are H, 30% C, 14% O, 8% N, 1% other atoms of low atomic number). The bonds between these atoms have strengths between 2 and 7 eV and the total bond energy of the non-aqueous fraction is $6 \cdot 9 \times 10^{10}$ eV: it requires this energy to separate all these atoms from one another. If an identical set of atoms to those in this cell are allowed to interact at a temperature of 300°K—corresponding to an English summer day—the equilibrium distribution of bonds would correspond to simple molecules having a total bond strength of about $7 \cdot 48 \times 10^{10}$ eV; the equilibrium state of these atoms is at an energy level of $(7 \cdot 48 - 6 \cdot 94) \times 10^{10} = 5 \cdot 4 \times 10^9$ eV lower than that level corresponding to the bacterial cell as shown in Fig. 1.

This cell can be said to have an energy enrichment of $5 \cdot 4 \times 10^9$ eV per $2 \times 10^{10}$ atoms $= 0 \cdot 27$ eV per atom over that of the equilibrium state which would have existed if the sun had not shone upon the earth. (If the aqueous fraction of the cell is included, the energy enrichment is only $0 \cdot 07$ eV per atom.) This energy enrichment is so large that the probability that it could have occurred by a spontaneous fluctuation in an equilibrium ensemble of these atoms maintained at 300°K is only $10^{-10^{11}}$: this probability is so extremely small that even if we were to sample a larger 300°K ensemble containing all the atoms of the universe as frequently as $10^{16}$ times per second throughout the universe's history of about $10^{18}$ seconds, the probability of finding an *Escherichia coli* cell is not significantly higher than $10^{-10^{11}}$. The energy enrichment of plant cells will probably be slightly lower than that of this bacterial cell since they contain less protein, but this is scarcely amenable to calculation.

All forms of life in our biosphere are so energy-rich that a continual flow of energy must pass through them to create and sustain them against degradation to lower energy states. Nevertheless, degradation or death occurs and life forms are only temporary traps to the flow of energy from

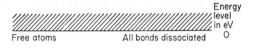

Free atoms                    All bonds dissociated

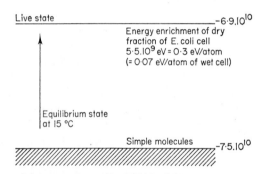

**Fig. 1.** Energy enrichment of a cell of *Escherichia coli* containing $2.10^{10}$ atoms (30 % C, 47 % H, 14 % O, 8 % N, 1 % other atoms of low atomic number).

the sun. It is therefore emphasized that the set of life forms or biomass within our biosphere is an example of steady state non-equilibrium thermodynamics; the life forms are far from being equilibrium states, but, taking an annual-global average, the quantity of energy received from the sun by the earth at the top of its atmosphere, 350 W m$^{-2}$ (Sellers, 1965), equals that which is emitted as infrared radiation to colder parts of the universe. An average crop temporarily traps about 0·5% of this energy. The annual yield of dry biomass in our biosphere is about $1 \times 10^{41}$ atoms, and the total energy trapped per year is about $3 \times 10^{40}$ eV, about 0·18% of the total energy incident on the earth's surface. Therefore, the annual-global average energy enrichment is about 0·3 eV per atom of biomass, which is rather closer to the order of magnitude agreement with the energy enrichment of the bacterial cell than I was expecting!

In seeking to fathom out the physical processes occurring within plants, we can temper our sense of wonder about plants with one of incredulity! To a physicist it is odd that only certain forms of biomass should have appeared in our biosphere and, although there are at present at least $10^6$ species of this selected biomass (Altman and Dittmer, 1964), it is most odd that nearly all of them are dependent on various types of specialized arrangements of chlorophyll molecules. In seeking to rationalize the peculiar paths favoured in evolution, I would anticipate that organizations of such a ubiquitous molecule should be relatively very efficient in their

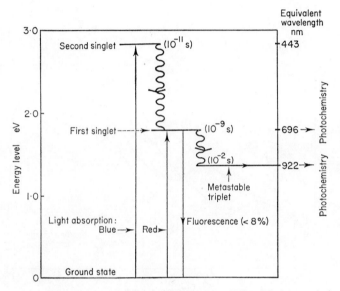

**Fig. 2.** The excitation of a chlorophyll molecule. (The lifetimes of the excited states are given in brackets), (after Gaffron, 1960).

light-trapping, exciton-transmitting and electron-releasing ability. However, although the conversion of light-energy to the energy enrichment of matter or chemical energy is never very efficient, there would appear to be nothing particularly outstanding about chlorophyll. It absorbs blue and red light by excitation of the first and second singlet levels as shown in Fig. 2 but these levels are short-lived and the excitation energies are degraded by radiationless transitions to the metastable triplet level which is sufficiently long-lived to transfer energy to the electron-releasing sites of photosynthesis. In the case of blue light of 430 nm, 52% of the absorbed energy is lost by such degradation into heat. Furthermore, of all colours green light is least absorbed by accessory pigments; the unabsorbed green

light merely but beautifully adorns the plant kingdom! This basic in-
efficiency in the use of light is clearly shown in Fig. 3 which shows the
action spectra of an intact bean leaf (Balegh and Biddulph, 1970). The
experimental data are the carbon dioxide assimilation rates for a given flux
of quanta or photons incident on the leaf; the action spectra have been
normalized to give 1·00 at a wavelength of 670 nm at which the highest
photosynthetic efficiency per quantum is achieved. The normalization
value of 1·00 corresponds to about 0·115 molecules of carbon dioxide being

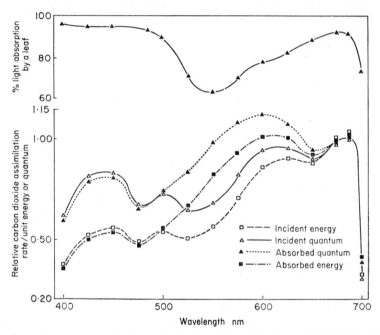

**Fig. 3.** Action spectra of an intact bean leaf (after Balegh and Biddulph, 1970),
and light absorption by a leaf (after Moss and Loomis, 1952).

fixed for one incident quantum, which is equivalent to a maximum photosynthetic efficiency of 8·8 photons per assimilated carbon dioxide molecule.
The figure also shows the absorption as measured by Moss and Loomis
(1952). We can see that even after allowance is made for the low absorption
in the green, the chlorophyll and other pigments do not even achieve a
uniform photosynthetic efficiency on a per absorbed quantum basis as the
unbroken lines indicate: blue light then appears to be 15% less efficient
than red light.

Considerably less than half of the energy of blue light is used by the bean
leaf in photosynthesis; however, blue light is effective in phototropism and

in the high energy photomorphogenetic effect. It is possible that under low light conditions the plant could advantageously have black leaves containing a range of light trapping pigments having several long-lived metastable levels.

The peculiarity of the ubiquity of chlorophyll is partly mitigated by the favourable circumstances for its early appearance during the first third of the earth's history: Granick (1967) points out that not merely is its low molecular weight precursor, protoporphyrin, readily synthesized from the simple molecules, glycine, pyridoxal-P and succinyl-CoA, but this molecule is also the precursor of haem, a constituent of the cytochromes which occur in chloroplasts, ribosomes and mitochondria: protoporphyrin could have been selected because of its importance in biosynthetic pathways to both photosynthetic and respiratory pigments. Chlorophyll $a$ occurs in both photo-systems of blue green algae and cytochrome $b_3$ exists in its ribosome granules; the fossil remains of these algae have been found in the two billion year old Gunflint formation in Canada, and Olson (1970) places the emergence of chlorophyll in an ancestral heterotrophic prokaryote in the early Precambrian $3 \cdot 8 \times 10^9$ years ago.

# V. The organization of plants

"The really distinctive thing about living processes is that they manifest programmed activities" (Longuet-Higgins, 1970). There exist instructions of the form IF, THEN which control a plant's response to environmental changes, but there also exist instructions whereby a plant is organized temporally and spatially from its germination to its reproductive phase. These self-realization instructions act also through cell differentiation, and the description of this in terms of the present ill-defined concepts of polarity, gradient, morphogenetic functions and dominance is likely to be one unlike any description of inanimate matter. At present it appears that the mathematical analysis of plant development is rather lagging behind that of the development of simple animate life (see, for example, Webster, 1971; Goodwin and Cohen, 1969): this may be due to difficulties in experimental plant embryology and to the availability of chemicals that can control plant development. Chemical manipulation of plants has possibly diverted interest from formulating theories of phytomorphology.

Controlled environments assist in the proper study of crop physics, which is concerned essentially with the distribution, flow and transformations of energy and of matter in plants and their environments, our biosphere. We can expect to apply the existing conceptual framework of physics to account for some of these processes, but this framework is inadequate to describe the function of each organ of a plant in relation to the whole plant, and to describe the set of such functions: the organization of the plant. Models of angiosperms have tended to be descriptions of their vegetative phases; let us hope that they will some day flower as these plants do!

# References

ALTMAN, P. L. and DITTMER, D. S. (1964). "Biological Data Book", p. 561. Federation of American Societies for Experimental Biology, Washington.

BALEGH, S. E. and BIDDULPH, O. (1970). The photosynthetic action spectrum of the bean plant. *Pl. Physiol. Lancaster* **46**, 1–5.

DYSON, F. J. (1971). Energy in the universe. *Scient. Am.* **224**, 50–59.

GAFFRON, H. (1960). *In* "Plant Physiology" (F. C. Steward, ed.), Vol. 1b, p. 50. Academic Press, New York.

GOODWIN, B. S. and COHEN, M. H. (1969). A phase shift model for the spatial and temporal organisation of developing systems. *J. theor. Biol.* **25**, 49–107.

GRANICK, S. (1967). *In* "Biochemistry of Chloroplasts" (T. W. Goodwin, ed.), Vol. 2, pp. 373–410. Academic Press, New York.

LONGUET-HIGGINS, C. (1970). *In* "Towards a Theoretical Biology" (C. H. Waddington, ed.). Vol. 3, "Drafts", p. 240. Edinburgh University Press.

MOROWITZ, H. J. (1968). "Energy Flow in Biology". Academic Press, New York.

MOSS, R. A. and LOOMIS, W. E. (1952). Absorption spectra of leaves. I. The visible spectrum. *Pl. Physiol., Lancaster* **27**, 370–391.

OLSON, J. M. (1970). The evolution of photosynthesis. *Science, N.Y.* **168**, 438–446.

SELLERS, W. D. (1965). "Physical Climatology", p. 32. University of Chicago Press.

WEBSTER, G. (1971). Morphogenesis and pattern formation in hydroids. *Biol. Rev.* **46**, 1–46.

WEISSKOPF, V. F. (1968). The three spectroscopies. *Scient. Am.* **218**, 15–29.

*Section III*

# Environment–Plant Relations

# III.1. Environment–plant relations: Introduction

W. W. SCHWABE

*Department of Horticulture, Wye College, University of London, Wye, Ashford, Kent, England*

The papers in this third section cover a wide range of topics. They represent a progression from the more detailed study of the functioning of the leaf in relation to light and carbon dioxide and the subsequent translocation of photosynthate within the plant, to morphogenetic studies of environmental effects on tuberization, flowering and hormonal changes in the plant. The common factor in these papers is the fact that all are concerned with the effect of the environment on the *individual plant*.

However, I do not think that this contrasts too strongly with the second section of this symposium, and I feel that the importance of distinguishing between the growth of a *crop* and that of the *individual* plant is sometimes exaggerated. This difference in emphasis probably derives too much from the problem of how to reach optimum productivity per unit area of ground in the minimum amount of time, which often leads to equating maximum photosynthesis with optimum yield. Clearly there are instances, especially in horticultural plants, when crop yield is not limited by photosynthate production, and other factors, often internal, are critical. The plant breeder selecting exclusively on the basis of yield has always taken this into account, even if unconsciously. However, it is essential to improve on this portmanteau approach. In order to enable the plant breeder to select on a more rational basis, the physiologist needs to define those aspects of the physiology of the plant which contribute principally to the yield of fruit, seed, leaf or whichever organ represents the product ultimately required. Once these characteristics have been identified it becomes possible to select for them, as well as taking into account such other considerations as will make for ease of industrial production, harvesting, packing, and last but not least consumer preference.

In this respect the growth responses of the crops to the environment are perhaps the most important; and an enormous amount of research has gone into the elucidation of environmental effects. Among these, two classes of effects may be distinguished; in one the environmental effect is itself related quantitatively to the response, e.g. in terms of carbohydrate production, largely the subject of Section 2; in the other the environmental conditions act rather in a trigger fashion and this is commonly so when morphogenetic responses are induced.

In both these aspects, there is often a high degree of adaptability within the individual plant, which is capable of compensating for adverse environmental conditions to a marked extent. One might, perhaps, describe this kind of behaviour as the biological equivalent of Le Chatelier's Principle, and I would like to mention some examples to illustrate this

### Table I

Net assimilation rates $(E)$ in *Xanthium strumarium* grown in different daylengths consisting of full daylight

| Daylength (h) | E as mg cm$^{-2}$ week$^{-1}$ | Per cent of short-day treatment | E as mg CO$_2$ dm$^{-2}$ daylight h$^{-1}$ | Per cent of short-day treatment |
|---|---|---|---|---|
| 24 | 5·49 | 177 | 4·79 | 59 |
| 14 | 3·75 | 121 | 5·06 | 62 |
| 8 | 3·10 | 100 | 8·11 | 100 |

point. In experiments on net assimilation rates of several species in Swedish Lapland with continuous daylight, the values obtained with *Xanthium strumarium* (*pennsylvanicum*) gave (as one would expect) a maximum with the longest period of illumination when expressed in the usual manner as mg cm$^{-2}$ week$^{-1}$. However, if note is taken of the actual hours of light a different picture emerges. Those plants with the shortest light periods are the most efficient (Table I).

Expressed as a percentage of the photosynthetic time lost, the 8 h day plants made up 35% by greater efficiency.

This kind of effect is much enhanced by light quality and intensity, etc., periods of relatively low intensity light with high red and far red content being the most efficient (Schwabe, 1956). For instance in the chrysanthemum cultivar 'Sunbeam' a period of some hours of low light below the compensation point increases dry matter accumulation substantially at all temperatures used, largely, it seems, owing to increased leaf area which then functions more efficiently during the high light periods (Fig. 1).

A similar story may be cited for mineral nutrition of plants. Richards and Coleman (1952), and Smith and Richards (1962) found that under conditions of severe potassium deficiency, many species including cereals and legumes produce the amine putrescine. Accumulation of this intrinsically toxic substance to as much as 10% of the total nitrogen, serves to maintain the ionic balance in the deficient plant and thus stabilizes its

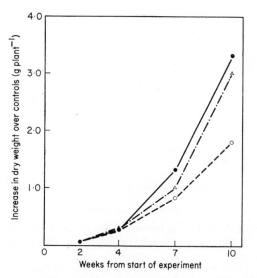

**Fig. 1.** The increase in dry weight produced by 8 h supplementary low light per day at constant day and night temperatures of 17°C (closed circles), 22°C (open circles), 27°C (triangles). Main light period was 8 h daylight. Controls received main light period only. Fully vernalized plants of *Chrysanthemum morifolium* cv. 'Sunbeam' were used.

metabolism. The conclusion I would draw from this, is that in the breeding of new cultivars one should perhaps look specifically for genotypes with such adaptability, which would put up more readily with the vagaries of *un*controlled environments.

In the case of those conditions which have after-effects triggering off morphogenetic or other physiological responses one might cite examples such as vernalization, which, quite apart from the ultimate effect on flowering, leads to a profound change in rates of growth, etc., e.g. Fig. 2 shows the effect of only two weeks' chilling on stem elongation rates in the chrysanthemum grown in short-day at 22°C. The after-effects on transpiration rates of temporary wilting, or of merely detaching a leaf, fall into the same category (Fig. 3). Frost hardening of plants is another well-known example, though in this case the changes are reversible. Daylength effects on leaf senescence in *Kleinia* are a further example where long-day conditions during the early stages of leaf development cause a permanent

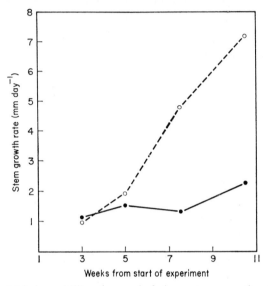

**Fig. 2.** Effect of 14 days chilling (open circles) on stem growth rate (mm day$^{-1}$ of chrysanthemum compared with unvernalized controls (closed circles).

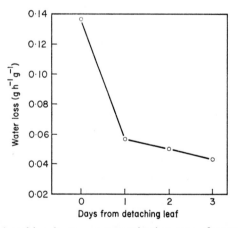

**Fig. 3.** Effect of detaching leaves on transpiration rate of young mature tomato leaves in weighed potometers. Water loss is expressed in terms of fresh weight. Leaves compared had been detached immediately and one, two or three days prior to testing. They were kept fully turgid at all times before and during testing.

change leading to accelerated leaf death, weeks later (Table II). Effects of this nature resemble nothing so much as a *memory* and the analogy may even be extended to the suggested association of memory in the flat worm or vertebrate with the production of specific DNAs.

However, in spite of this, I harbour some doubts whether the assumption that *all* these responses, especially all those associated with phytochrome and morphogenesis are operated via a gene-activating mechanism. The sequence normally postulated is the classic one of gene activation leading to the production of new RNAs and new proteins. The initial triggering is often regarded as being due to hormonal effects, whose action is so important in the integration of the activities of the plant as a coordinated organism (cf. Osborne's paper III.5). These doubts are reinforced by the kind of evidence produced by Nissl and Zenk (1969) in relation to the extreme rapidity of auxin action, which could hardly be explained

**Table II**

Survival of detached leaves of
*Kleinia articulata* after 156 days

| Treatment | % survival |
|---|---|
| SD leaves in SD | 94 |
| SD leaves in LD | 65 |
| LD leaves in SD | 56 |
| LD leaves in LD | 0 |

by a gene-activation mechanism; much the same applies to phytochrome responses such as those of *Mimosa pudica* (Fondeville *et al.*, 1967).

Environmental effects on morphogenesis in the plant usually, though not always (Schwabe, 1958), affect meristematic and relatively *un*differentiated cells. The production of new organs, therefore, seems to be due to cells which are relatively similar and any new structure such as a floral meristem could arise simply as the result of relatively non-specific activation of cell division and expansion, but especially the *reorientation* of the plane of cell division. It would indeed be a big step forward if we knew what mechanism determines changes in the orientation of the metaphase plate in such tissue.

Only subsequently when the organs begin to assume their more mature function need there be a specialization of metabolism. In looking for evidence for such a view, it might be interesting for example to see at what stage in the development of floral organs, differences in metabolism first appear.

As regards the morphogenetic control exerted by the environment, this seems to operate in a variety of ways, it may be simply via substrate as in some forms of apical dominance which can operate through nitrogen level (Gregory and Veale, 1957) or leaf differentiation in ferns by carbohydrate supply, as in the young bracken sporeling in which the degree of differentiation of the first leaf appears to be determined by the size of the mother prothallus. Examples of effects through hormonal control are, of course, legion and no examples are needed. By contrast the more long-lasting effects of vernalization may well operate more directly at the gene level.

# References

FONDEVILLE, J. C., SCHNEIDER, M. J., BORTHWICK, H. A. and HENDRICKS, S. B. (1967). Photocontrol of *Mimosa pudica* leaf movement. *Planta* **75**, 228–238.

GREGORY, F. G. and VEALE, J. A. (1957). A reassessment of the problem of apical dominance. *Symp. Soc. exp. Biol.* **11**, 1–20.

NISSL, D. and ZENK, M. H. (1969). Evidence against induction of protein synthesis during auxin-induced initial elongation of avena coleoptiles. *Planta* **89**, 323–341.

RICHARDS, F. J. and COLEMAN, R. G. (1952). Occurrence of putrescine in potassium-deficient barley. *Nature, Lond.* **170**, 460–461.

SMITH, T. A. and RICHARDS, F. J. (1962). The biosynthesis of putrescine in higher plants and its relation to potassium nutrition. *Biochem. J.* **84**, 292–294.

SCHWABE, W. W. (1956). Effects of natural and artificial light in arctic latitudes on long- and short-day plants as revealed by growth analysis. *Ann. Bot.* **20**, 588–622.

SCHWABE, W. W. (1958). Effects of photoperiod and hormone treatment on isolated rooted leaves of *Kalanchoe blossfeldiana*. *Physiologia Pl.* **11**, 225–239.

# III.2. Net assimilation of plants as influenced by light and carbon dioxide

P. CHARTIER

*Station de Bioclimatologie, Versailles, France*

## I. Introduction

This paper will be concerned only with light and carbon dioxide as factors affecting the net assimilation of leaves and canopies, and although both factors can have important effects on the utilization of the photosynthetic products in growth and development, these aspects will not be treated here.

The two main features of the net assimilation of leaves which have been studied recently are photorespiration and comparisons between $C_3$ and $C_4$ plants. Some of these features have been introduced into a model of the total process of carbon dioxide fixation by the leaf (Chartier, 1970) and a further analysis of the intracellular resistances of bean and maize leaves will be made here in terms of their transfer and chemical components. The partition of solar energy between the leaves of a canopy will also be considered from the point of view of the effect of irradiance upon crop photosynthesis.

## II. A model of the net assimilation of the leaf

Several models have been developed to estimate the different elementary processes of net assimilation in the leaf, (Rabinowitch, 1951; Monteith, 1963; Chartier, 1969, 1970; Lake, 1967a, b; Laisk, 1968; Acock *et al.*, 1971; Lommen *et al.*, 1971) and each tries to gather the diffusion of carbon dioxide and the various biochemical, photochemical and respiratory processes into one coherent arrangement. The main features of the model presented by Chartier (1970) are given below.

From Rabinowitch (1951), a formula was constructed for photosynthetic rate at the level of the biochemical and photochemical reactions.

$$F + R = \frac{\alpha E \frac{C_2}{r_x}}{\alpha E + \frac{C_2}{r_x}} \tag{1}$$

[handwritten: $\alpha = $ initial slope (b), $C_2 = P_{max}$ (a)]

Here $F$ is the net assimilation per unit area of leaf (kg of $CO_2$ m$^{-2}$ sec$^{-1}$)

$R$ is the photorespiration expressed per unit area of leaf (kg of $CO_2$ m$^{-2}$ sec$^{-1}$)

$\alpha$, the maximum efficiency of light energy conversion (kg of $CO_2$ J$^{-1}$)

$E$, the incident radiation per unit area of leaf (W m$^{-2}$)

$C_2$, the concentration of carbon dioxide at the carboxylation sites (kg of $CO_2$ m$^{-3}$)

$r_x$, the resistance to carboxylation (m$^{-1}$ sec)

A Michaelis-Menten equation (Lommen et al., 1971) can be used instead of equation (1):

$$F + R = \frac{P_M}{1 + \frac{K}{C_2}} \tag{2}$$

where $P_M$ is the maximal value of $(F + R)$ obtained from the carbon dioxide response curve and $K$ is a constant.

Equations (1) and (2) are identical if:

$$P_M = \alpha E \tag{3}$$ [handwritten: units of flux]

$$K = \alpha E \, r_x \tag{4}$$ [handwritten: units of conc.]

Under steady state conditions, the quantity of carbon dioxide which disappears in chemical reactions is equal to the quantity which arrives by diffusion from the air and from the respiratory sites (Fig. 1). From this figure, net assimilation can be written according to Gaastra's method (Gaastra, 1959).

$$F = \frac{C_0 - C_1}{r_a + r_s + (1 - n)r_m} \tag{5}$$

$$F + R = \frac{C_1 - C_2}{n r_m} \tag{6}$$

where $C_0$ is the concentration of carbon dioxide in the air (kg of $CO_2$ m$^{-3}$),

$C_1$, the concentration of carbon dioxide at the sites where the respiratory carbon dioxide is evolved (kg of $CO_2$ m$^{-3}$),

$r_a$, the diffusion resistance for carbon dioxide transfer in the boundary layer (m$^{-1}$ sec),

$r_s$, the diffusion resistance for carbon dioxide transfer through the stomata and cuticle (m$^{-1}$ sec),

$r_m$, the intracellular transfer resistance for carbon dioxide from the intercellular spaces to the sites of carboxylation—also called the mesophyll resistance (m$^{-1}$ sec),

$n$, that fraction of $r_m$ which is between the sites where the respiratory carbon dioxide is evolved and the sites of carboxylation (0 < n < 1).

In the present model, the concentration of carbon dioxide at the carboxylation sites ($C_2$) is not fixed. It has sometimes been proposed that $C_2$

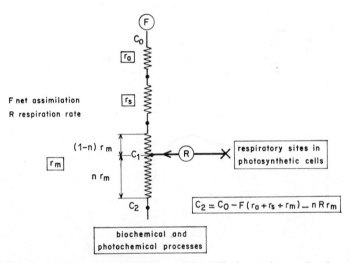

**Fig. 1.** Photorespiratory carbon dioxide and the diffusion pathway of carbon dioxide from the air to the sites of carboxylation.

The expression placed on the right-hand side of the scheme gives the relationship between the concentration of carbon dioxide at the carboxylation sites ($C_2$) and the different terms of the diffusion pathway, the carbon dioxide concentration in the air ($C_0$), the photorespiratory intensity ($R$) and the net assimilation rate ($F$).

is either equal to zero or it is equal to the carbon dioxide compensation point ($\Gamma$). Here, $C_2$ varies with all the terms introduced in equations (5) and (6), and therefore:

$$C_2 = C_0 - F(r_a + r_s + r_m) - nRr_m \qquad (7)$$

Replacing $C_2$ by this expression in equation (1) yields:

$$F + R = \frac{\alpha E \dfrac{(C_0 - F(r_a + r_s + r_m) - nRr_m)}{r_x}}{\alpha E + \dfrac{(C_0 - F(r_a + r_s + r_m) - nRr_m)}{r_x}} \qquad (8)$$

*measured* $F \propto E$

*unknown* $R$. $r_m + r_x$

*assumed* $n$ .

$\Big)$ solved by simultaneous eqs.

$\Big)$ in $E$.

The relation between $F$ and $E$ is a non-rectangular hyperbola (Fig. 2) and comments about this relation can be found elsewhere (Chartier, 1969, 1970).

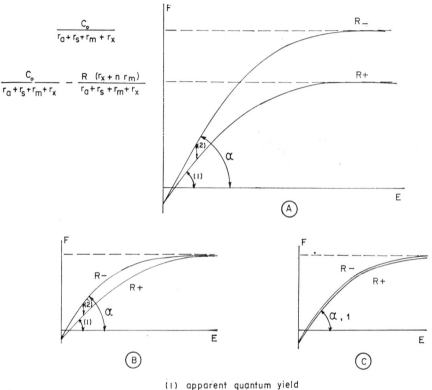

(1) apparent quantum yield
(2) photorespiration

**Fig. 2.** Possible effects of removing photorespiration upon the relationship between incident radiation $(E)$ and the net assimilation of a leaf $(F)$
A. Plant with photorespiration and low recycling
B. Plant with photorespiration and high recycling
C. Plant without photorespiration.

# III. Net assimilation as affected by photorespiration

The net assimilation of the leaf depends upon its photorespiration (Jackson and Volk, 1970) and the effect of removing it can be predicted from equation (8), (see Fig. 2) and can be considered either under limiting light or under saturating light conditions.

## A. Light-saturated conditions

Under saturating light, equation (8) or direct calculation yield:

$$F = \frac{C_0}{r_a + r_s + r_m + r_x} - \frac{R(nr_m + r_x)}{r_a + r_s + r_m + r_x} \tag{9}$$

It can be demonstrated from equation (9) that, at saturating light, the carbon dioxide compensation point $(\Gamma)$ can be expressed as follows, *i.e* $F = 0$

$$\Gamma = R(nr_m + r_x) \tag{10}$$

Equation (9) can now be rearranged assuming that $R$ does not change with the carbon dioxide concentration in the air: *an apparat: not likely*

$$F = \frac{C_0 - \Gamma}{r_a + r_s + r_m + r_x} \tag{11}$$

This is the expression used by several authors (e.g. Lake, 1967b).

If photorespiration is suppressed, then:

$$F' = \frac{C_0}{r_a + r_s + r_m + r_x} \tag{12}$$

where $F'$ is the assimilation rate in the absence of photorespiration.

Under saturating light, the difference observed may be important (Fig. 2A) or it may not (Fig. 2B and C). In the first case, the increase in net assimilation is:

$$F' - F = \frac{R(r_x + nr_m)}{r_a + r_s + r_m + r_x} \tag{13}$$

For $C_3$ plants (Fig. 2A), it appears that the intensity of photorespiration is high, and that $(r_x + nr_m)$ is relatively high compared with

$$(r_a + r_s + (1 - n)r_m).$$

At this point, two different conclusions can be drawn, but the experiments under saturating light do not indicate which is the correct choice.

*a.* The chemical component of the intracellular resistance $(r_x)$ is more important than the resistance to diffusion.

*b.* The transfer resistance $(r_m)$ is high and the greatest part of the transfer resistance lies between the sites of release of the photorespiratory carbon dioxide in the cytoplasm and the sites of carboxylation inside the chloroplasts (i.e. there is a high value of $n$).

On the basis of this last assumption, it would be worth looking for correlations between maximal net assimilation and characteristics of chloroplast structure.

For $C_4$ plants, it is also possible to draw two different conclusions, namely:

a. photorespiration is very low or does not exist or

b. recycling is fast, i.e. $(r_x + nr_m)$ is low compared with

$$(r_a + r_s + (1 - n)r_m).$$

## B. Light-limiting Conditions

Under limiting light, the difference observed when photorespiration is removed can be obtained either from equation (8) or by direct calculation:

$$F' - F = R \qquad (14)$$

For $C_3$ plants (Fig. 2A), it appears that $R$ is high and increases with irradiance and, therefore, the quantum yield or the maximum efficiency of light energy conversion measured at low light intensity is greatly underestimated for the leaf of $C_3$ plants (Björkman, 1966; Björkman and Gauhl, 1969; Bull, 1969). Thus, it is necessary to measure photorespiration under steady-state conditions, in order to study leaf photosynthesis.

For $C_4$ plants, the absence of any effect (Fig. 2C) means that photorespiration is very low and it is possible, therefore, to separate the two conclusions arrived at earlier, i.e. there is either no photorespiration or the level of recycling is high.

# IV. Intracellular resistance of $C_3$ and $C_4$ plants

The intracellular resistance of the leaf can be separated into transfer $(r_m)$ and chemical $(r_x)$ components (Chartier, 1970; Chartier et al., 1970) and comparison between $C_3$ and $C_4$ plants is made from this point of view.

For bean leaves (Bull, 1969; Jackson and Volk, 1970) the intensity of photorespiration $(R)$ seems to be high ($0\cdot3$–$0\cdot7$ times the net assimilation). When $R$ is equal to one third of the net assimilation plus dark respiration, and $n$ is equal to one, equation (8) yields the following at near optimum leaf temperatures (Chartier, 1970):

$$\alpha = 6\cdot60 \; \mu g \; CO_2 \; J^{-1}$$

and between 150 and 220 W m$^{-2}$, at normal carbon dioxide concentrations

$$r_m = 440 \; m^{-1} \; sec$$
$$r_x = 35 \; m^{-1} \; sec$$

A relatively low value of $r_x$ in comparison with $r_m$ indicates that the chemical machinery is operating more effectively than the diffusion process, and even if one adopts different hypothetical values for photo-respiration ($R$) and $n$, the ratio of $r_x$ to $r_m$ is always lower than 0·08. When $R$ decreases, the values of the maximal efficiency of light energy conversion ($\alpha$) are lower and the values of $r_m$ higher. When $n$ decreases, it modifies only $r_m$, which increases.

As far as maize leaves are concerned (e.g. Bull, 1969), the photo-respiration ($R$) is equal to zero and from our experiments:

$$\alpha = 6 \cdot 10 \; \mu g \; CO_2 \; J^{-1}$$

and between 400 and 700 W m$^{-2}$, at a $CO_2$ concentration of about 120 vpm,

$$r_m = 45 \; m^{-1} \; sec$$
$$r_x = 15 \; m^{-1} \; sec$$

### Table I

Transfer and chemical components of the intracellular resistance of a legume (*Calopogonium mucunoides*) and, the average value for three grasses (*Pennisetum purpureum, Panicum maximum, Cenchrus ciliaris*)

|         | $r_m$(m$^{-1}$ sec) | $r_x$(m$^{-1}$ sec) | $r_x \div r_m$ |
|---------|---------------------|---------------------|----------------|
| Legume  | 221                 | 24                  | 0·11           |
| Grasses | 34                  | 27                  | 0·75           |

(From Ludlow, 1971)

In our experiments with maize leaves, the accuracy with which $r_m$ and $r_x$ can be partitioned is low, compared with bean leaves. One reason may be the large effect of a light gradient inside these leaves, which have a transfer resistance ($r_m$) low as compared to $r_x$. A small error in the determination of stomatal resistance would also produce inaccuracies as it is the highest resistance in these plants.

The main difference between the two kinds of plants concerns the intracellular resistance (Bull, 1969; Ludlow, 1970) and these calculations show that the intracellular transfer resistance $r_m$ is lower in $C_4$ than in $C_3$ plants. Ludlow (1971) used the technique outlined above and obtained similar results by introducing photorespiration into the calculations (Table I). The assumptions made in these calculations are shown in Table II.

The differences in photorespiration do not account for all the differences in net assimilation of $C_3$ and $C_4$ plants, for diffusion resistances are also different and the plateau of the light response curve of $C_3$ plants in which photorespiration has been suppressed, is not as high as that for $C_4$ plants as far as no compensation appears in stomatal resistance. These differences in the intracellular transfer resistance between $C_3$ and $C_4$ plants may be caused by different locations of carbon dioxide acceptors and corresponding enzymes, and their different affinities for carbon dioxide molecules. The presence of PEP carboxylase in the reticulum of the mesophyll chloroplasts is an important fact from this point of view. Among $C_3$ plants the structure of the chloroplast itself can offer some restraints to carbon dioxide diffusion towards the carboxylation sites. It can be assumed from low recycling of photorespiratory carbon dioxide

## Table II

*List of assumptions introduced in the calculation of $r_m$ and $r_x$*

1. Steady state conditions are obtained at all stages of the assimilation process when constant exchange of $CO_2$ is observed at the leaf surface.

2. The intracellular transfer resistance ($r_m$) and the carboxylation resistance ($r_x$) are constant within the range of irradiances and $CO_2$ concentrations in air used in the experiments.

3. The stomatal resistance ($r_s$) for $CO_2$ can be obtained by measuring the transpiration rate.

4. There are no significant influences of either a $CO_2$ gradient inside the intercellular spaces or a light gradient inside the mesophyll, and no errors are introduced in determining photorespiration ($R$) and the sites where photorespiratory $CO_2$ is evolved ($n$).

5. There is no significant influence of uncertainties in equation (1).

and the values of $r_m$ and $r_x$ for bean leaf that the main part of $r_m$ is in the chloroplast structures.

Experimental evidence of an important chemical resistance based on correlations between the activity of photosynthetic enzymes and the net photosynthetic rate seem to be contrary to the above results. The transfer component of the intracellular resistance, however, is not a pure diffusion process and chemical transport mechanisms are involved. The variations in enzyme activity, as expressed by the variations of $r_x$, may be insufficient to explain the differences observed in the assimilation rate. According to Björkman (1968), the activity of RuDP carboxylase is not the same in sun and shade leaves. Prioul (1971), using the above method for the partition of $r_m$ and $r_x$, noted, for *Lolium multiflorum*, a simultaneous decrease of $r_x$ and $r_m$ with an increased irradiance during the growing period

(Table III). The resistance to carboxylation ($r_x$) is four times greater at 16 W m$^{-2}$ than at 110 W m$^{-2}$, but the ability of $r_m$ to determine the plateau of the light curve is much more important. The list of assumptions corresponding to the above model (Table II) gives the limits of its usefulness.

One can conclude from this apparent discrepancy that the connections between enzymes and chloroplast structures may be as important as the nature of these enzymes.

**Table III**

Variations of $r_m$ and $r_x$ in the third leaf of *Lolium multiflorum* at the end of a growing period of three weeks at 17°C (day) and 13°C (night) and different light intensities.

| Light intensity (W m$^{-2}$) | 16 | 45 | 85 | 110 |
|---|---|---|---|---|
| $r_m$(m$^{-1}$ sec) | 1964 | 1101 | 768 | 627 |
| $r_x$(m$^{-1}$ sec) | 167 | 123 | 69 | 41 |

(From Prioul, 1971)

# V. Solar irradiances of the leaves of the canopy as factors affecting crop photosynthesis

To study crop photosynthesis one needs to introduce additional parameters because of the variation in environmental conditions from leaf to leaf. Although the gradient of carbon dioxide concentration in the air within a canopy in the field is relatively small, the solar irradiances of the different leaves are much more variable, and the influence of leaf age, and the presence of other organs, cannot be ignored.

The variation in irradiance is due not only to the height of a leaf within the canopy, but sunflecks may also introduce heterogeneity in each layer. The sunlit leaves are lighted by an irradiance which varies according to the angle made by the sun's rays and the plane of the leaf (de Wit, 1965; Chartier, 1969). The main question is what is the leaf area ($f_{vj}$) of the $v$ th canopy layer which is lighted by a given value of irradiance ($E_{vj}$).

If the net assimilation ($F_{vj}$) of the leaves of the layer which are lighted by a certain irradiance ($E_{vj}$) is known, it follows that

$$P_v = \Sigma_j (F_{vj} f_{vj}) \tag{15}$$

where $P_v$ is the net assimilation of the whole leaf area of the layer $v$.

Crop photosynthesis, or more precisely, the net assimilation of the whole leaf area of the canopy is the sum of the different $P_v$ values, and these depend on the partition of light within the canopy. This has been observed for a maize canopy and the leaf area indices corresponding to each class of irradiance and to each layer within the canopy are shown in Fig. 3.

To obtain useful data for computing the photosynthesis of a homogeneous canopy, a definition of a coherent set of measurements has to be made. A methodological study (Chartier, 1969) yielded the following factors which should be measured:

  *a.* direct solar irradiance
  *b.* solar elevation
  *c.* profile of downward diffuse radiation
  *d.* profile of upward diffuse radiation
  *e.* profile of relative sunfleck area
  *f.* profile of leaf area index
  *g.* leaf inclination frequencies.

Provision for spectral modification of the light within the canopy must also be made if the sensors used respond to near infrared wavelengths.

It has been suggested that changes in the partition of light between the leaves, as influenced by crop geometry for example, may only induce a slight change in crop photosynthesis. Two comments can be made concerning this suggestion.

First, as long as the solar radiation above the canopy is low compared with the saturating irradiance obtained from light curves for the different leaves, the partition of light will have no effect and only a change in the proportion of solar energy reflected towards the sky or transmitted to the soil surface will affect crop photosynthesis.

Secondly, the position of the sun moves during the day and consequently the pattern of light partition changes also, but it is possible to compensate for the diurnal variation in net assimilation in different kinds of crop geometry. From a purely geometric point of view, therefore, crop geometry may appear as a minor factor, but as the physiological response of the leaf changes during the day it cannot be ignored. A favourable leaf arrangement in the early morning may be more beneficial than a favourable arrangement at noon and the converse could be true if either the plant's responses or the climate changed.

Only crops in the field have been considered in this section and for horticultural crops, the role of partition of solar energy between the leaves may be more important. Measurements must be made to determine the area of leaves lit by the different irradiances that can be obtained in the

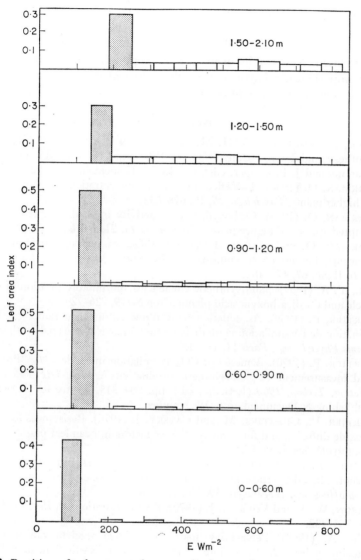

**Fig. 3.** Partition of solar energy between the leaves of a canopy of a $F_1$ hybrid maize (I.N.R.A. F7 × E.P.1).

The leaf area index of the whole crop was 3·1. The sun's elevation was 55° (at noon, local time, Versailles—La Miniere, 1 August). Each layer of the canopy was divided into shaded leaves (one class of irradiance per layer) and sunlit leaves (ten classes of irradiance, divided according to the angles made by the planes of the leaves and the sun's rays). The thickness of each layer is indicated, and only total radiation was considered (300–3000 nm), i.e. no provision was made for spectral modification of the light within the canopy.

canopy (similar to the results presented in Fig. 3) and their physiological characteristics.

In agricultural sciences, the chapter of crop photosynthesis is far from being closed. New results in plant physiology have to be considered and their importance, relative to the other elementary processes of carbon dioxide assimilation, has to be assessed.

## References

ACOCK, B., THORNLEY, J. H. M. and WARREN WILSON, J. (1971). Photosynthesis and Energy Conversion. *In* "Potential Crop Production" (P. F. Wareing and J. P. Cooper, eds), pp. 43–75. Heinemann, London.

BJÖRKMAN, O. (1966). The effect of oxygen concentration on photosynthesis in higher plants. *Physiologia Pl.* **19**, 618–633.

BJÖRKMAN, O. (1968). Carboxydismutase activity in shade-adapted and sun-adapted species of higher plants. *Physiologia Pl.* **21**, 1–10.

BJÖRKMAN, O. and GAUHL, E. (1969). Effect of temperature and oxygen concentration on photosynthesis in *Marchantia polymorpha*. *Yb. Carnegie Instn Wash.* **67**, 479–482.

BULL, T. A. (1969). photoxynthetic efficiencies and photorespiration in Calvin cycle and $C_4$-dicarboxylic acid plants. *Crop Sci.* **9**, 726–729.

CHARTIER, P. (1969). Assimilation nette d'une culture couvrante. I.—Détermination de l'assimilation nette de la culture à partir d'une analyse théorique. *Annls Physiol. vég., Paris* **11**, 123–159.

CHARTIER, P. (1970). A model of $CO_2$ assimilation in the leaf. *In* "Prediction and measurement of photosynthetic productivity". *Proc. IBP/PP technical meeting, Trebon, 1969* (I. Setlik, ed.), pp. 307–315. Centre for Agricultural Publishing & Documentation, Wageningen.

CHARTIER, P., CHARTIER, M. and ČATSKÝ, J. (1970). Resistances for carbon dioxide diffusion and for carboxylation as factors in bean leaf photosynthesis. *Photosynthetica* **4**, 48–57.

GAASTRA, P. (1959). Photosynthesis of crop plants as influenced by light, carbon dioxide, temperature and stomatal diffusion resistance. *Meded. LandbHoogesch. Wageningen* **59**, No. 13, 1–68.

JACKSON, W. A. and VOLK, R. J. (1970). Photorespiration. *A. Rev. Pl. Physiol.* **21**, 385–432.

LAISK, A. (1968). Perspektivy matematicheskogo modelirovaniya funktsii fotosinteza lista. *In* "Fotosintez i Produktivnost 'Rastitel' nogo pokrava", pp. 5–45. Akad. Nauk. Est. S.S.R. Tartu.

LAKE, J. V. (1967a). Respiration of leaves during photosynthesis. I.—Estimates from an electrical analogue. *Aust. J. biol. Sci.* **20**, 487–493.

LAKE, J. V. (1967b). Respiration of leaves during photosynthesis. II.—Effects on the estimation of mesophyll resistance. *Aust. J. biol. Sci.* **20**, 495–499.

LOMMEN, P. W., SCHWINTZER, C. R., YOCUM, C. S. and GATES, D. M. (1971). A model describing photosynthesis in terms of gas diffusion and enzyme kinetics. *Planta* **98**, 195–220.

LUDLOW, M. M. (1970). Effect of oxygen concentration on leaf photosynthesis and resistances to carbon dioxide diffusion. *Planta* **91,** 285–290.

LUDLOW, M. M. (1971). Analysis of the difference between maximum leaf photosynthetic rates of $C_4$ grasses and $C_3$ legumes. *In* "Photosynthesis and Photorespiration" (M. D. Hatch, C. B. Osmond and R. O. Slatyer, eds), pp. 63–67. Wiley Interscience, New York.

MONTEITH, J. L. (1963). Gas exchange in plant communities. *In* "Environmental control of plant growth" (L. T. Evans, ed.), pp. 95–112. Academic Press, New York and London.

PRIOUL, J. L. (1971). Réactions des feuilles de *Lolium multiflorum* à l'éclairement pendant la croissance et variation des résistances aux échanges gazeux photosynthétiques. *Photosynthetica* **5,** 364–75.

RABINOWITCH, E. I. (1951). "Photosynthesis and related processes" **2** (1), Interscience, New York.

WIT, C. T. DE (1965). Photosynthesis of leaf canopies. *Versl. landbouwk. Onderz.* **663,** 1–57.

# Discussion

At the end of this paper, **Monteith** emphasized that two important assumptions had been made in these calculations, namely (a) all chloroplasts were equally illuminated, and (b) there was no variation in $r_m$ and that, therefore, the carbon dioxide concentration at each chloroplast was the same. He maintained that if this were true and if $r_x = 0$, then the light response curve should consist of two straight lines and that it would become curved if there were a range of light intensities within the leaf or a range of stomatal diffusive resistances. If heterogeneity existed, then $r_x$ would be overestimated and as Chartier had already calculated that it was small in relation to $r_m$, it was likely to be even smaller in a real situation. There followed some discussion of the significance of membrane permeability and of the role that bicarbonate and carbonate ions might play in calculations of diffusion resistances. **Chartier** maintained that his calculations demonstrated that the main component of the mesophyll resistance ($r_m$) lay between the sites where photorespiratory carbon dioxide was evolved and the sites of carboxylation (i.e. $nr_m$), and that for $C_3$ plants this resistance was in the liquid phase in the chloroplast structures.

**Jarvis** pointed out that the response to low oxygen levels was not necessarily an accurate measure of photorespiration as it was possible that photorespiration itself might be affected by the oxygen level. Even if photorespiration were inhibited by the removal of oxygen it was not to be expected that there would be an exactly equivalent increase in carbon dioxide flux into the leaf, because the sources of carbon dioxide would be different and the carbon dioxide concentrations at the various points of the resistance network would be changed depending upon whether the rate of photosynthesis was limited by the carbon dioxide concentration at the chloroplast, the rate of supply of carbon dioxide or by the activity of the carboxylating enzymes.

# III.3. The response of the potato plant and tuber to temperature

W. G. BURTON

*A.R.C. Food Research Institute, Norwich, England*

## I. Introduction: phases in the development of the seed tuber during storage

The seed tuber is as logical a point as any at which to start considering the effects of temperature in a repeated tuber ⇌ plant cycle. It has the advantage in the present context that, while the potato crop is not grown in a controlled environment, the seed tuber may often be subjected to a fairly rigid temperature regime before planting.

The life history of a seed potato tuber is illustrated diagrammatically in Fig. 1 from the more or less gradual cessation of elongation of the stolon on the parent plant. The abscissa represents the lapse of time and the

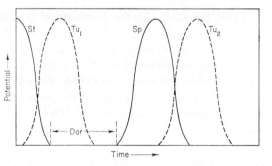

**Fig. 1.** Phases in the life of an unplanted seed potato tuber.
St: Stolon elongation on parent plant.
Sp: Sprout growth.
Tu₁: Formation of the tuber.
Tu₂: Formation of next-generation tubers in the absence of foliage.
Dor: Bud dormancy.

217

ordinate the physiological or biochemical *potential* of the organ for the two types of activity we are considering—extension growth and radial expansion. The former is manifested either as stolon elongation (St in the diagram) or as sprout growth (Sp); the latter as tuber formation (Tu). The different phases of development are represented, for convenience, by identical curves, although the time scale, shape and magnitude of each phase could in fact differ.

From the end of the curve St to the beginning of the curve Sp the buds are dormant (Dor in Fig. 1). The figure assumes the onset of bud dormancy to be fairly gradual as the main centre of cell division moves from the growing point of the stolon to the pith, peripheral cortex and pericycle (Artschwager, 1924) before becoming so slight as to be negligible. Typically, though not necessarily, there is some lapse of time between the end of tuber growth—which in its later phases consists mainly of cell enlargement—and the potential resumption of extension growth.

Dormancy or otherwise is a property of each individual bud and there is a gradation in the depth of dormancy from the oldest, most deeply dormant, to the youngest, least dormant bud. As a background to discussing the effect of temperature upon these phases in the life of a seed tuber we could make some suggestions which are neither proved to be true nor universally accepted, but are consistent with observation (e.g. Burton, 1957, 1963, 1966). The first is that tuber initiation and the onset of bud dormancy are one and the same phenomenon, resulting from a swing in the biochemical balance, not instantaneous but extending over a period of weeks, from a state in which extension growth can occur, through a phase of radial expansion, to a state in which cell division has virtually ceased.

The second is that this swing in the biochemical balance results normally from the translocation from the foliage, or in other cases mobilization in the seed tuber, of labile substances in excess of the requirements for the growth which can be sustained on other grounds. This leads to the increased diversion of labile reactants into cycles of reactions which result in the accumulation of a product, or group of products, which inhibit cell division. A major component of the resultant inhibitory balance can be postulated to be not readily diffusible, giving the possibility of very local differences in bud dormancy.

The third suggestion is that the temperature coefficients of the various reactions in which the above labile reactants are involved are such that their diversion into cycles resulting in growth inhibition is favoured by low temperature, while at high temperatures there can be a partial or complete reversal.

Continual replenishment of the postulated labile reactants may keep the balance inhibitory to cell division, but when the supply dwindles the further metabolism, or the reverse reactions, cause a swing back to a state permissive of growth. As indicated above, a high temperature would appear to favour this reversal.

# II. Effects of storage temperature on the seed tuber

## A. Dormancy

In general, an increase in temperature results in a shortening of the dormant period (Table I). The results of Schippers (1956) on the behaviour of 40 cultivars stored at temperatures from 3 to 20°C showed the

### Table I

Bud dormancy of some British cultivars (1957 crop, lifted third week September), stored at various temperatures

| | Period of bud dormancy (weeks) | | | | | |
|---|---|---|---|---|---|---|
| | | | Stored at | | | |
| | 4·4°C | | 10°C | | 22·5°C | |
| Cultivar | After tuber initiation | After harvest | After tuber initiation | After harvest | After tuber initiation | After harvest |
| 'Arran Consul' | >42 | >28 | 26 | 12 | 22 | 8 |
| 'Arran Pilot' | 30 | 12 | 23 | 5 | 23 | 5 |
| 'Arran Victory' | 28 | 12 | 21 | 5 | 19 | 3 |
| 'Arran Viking' | 31 | 16 | 20 | 5 | 23 | 8 |
| 'Craig's Defiance' | 25 | 8 | 23 | 6 | 20 | 3 |
| 'Golden Wonder' | 41 | 26 | 27 | 12 | 23 | 8 |
| 'Home Guard' | 31 | 12 | 24 | 5 | 22 | 3 |
| 'King Edward' | 31 | 16 | 21 | 6 | 20 | 5 |
| 'Majestic' | >44 | >28 | 28 | 12 | 24 | 8 |
| 'Ulster Chieftain' | 34 | 16 | 23 | 5 | 23 | 5 |
| 'Ulster Prince' | 33 | 14 | 33 | 14 | 27 | 8 |

(From Burton, 1963)

average comparative lengths in arbitrary units, of that part of the dormant period remaining after harvest, to be as follows:

| 3°C | 5°C | 10°C | 20°C | |
|-----|-----|------|------|-----------------|
| 100 | 67  | 40   | 33   | (3°C $\equiv$ 100) |
| 300 | 200 | 120  | 100  | (20°C $\equiv$ 100) |

Tubers in the ground would be in the range 10–20°C in Schipper's experiments and the dormant period remaining during storage at such temperatures would be the time necessary for biochemical changes already in progress to reach a state permissive of growth. These changes could be expected to be slower at lower temperatures and the period of dormancy longer; but this scarcely explains the marked effect of temperature below 10°C, and particularly below 5°C, compared with that above 10°C. It seems reasonable to postulate a possible link between this increased effect of low temperature and other changes in the tuber which show a parallelism. These include a marked increase in sugars, which must be associated with increased turnover of labile intermediates of carbohydrate metabolism—and, we could suggest, renewed synthesis, for a time, of growth inhibiting components of the biochemical balance.

## B. Apical dominance

If tubers are stored at a temperature at which vigorous growth is possible (10°C or above) a shoot grows first from the distal bud, the dormancy of which ends first, the products from the growth of which prevent the growth of the other buds. This establishment of apical dominance is prevented by storing at a temperature too low for growth (5°C or below) or by rubbing off the shoots as they are formed, in which case the biochemical balance in successively older buds completes in turn the swing to a biochemical state permissive of growth. When environmental conditions permit, all the buds then grow simultaneously and with roughly equal vigour (Appleman, 1918, 1924; Bushnell, 1928, 1929; Kawakami, 1952; Toosey, 1959). Suppression of growth by the products of the growth of other buds implies a readily diffusible influence, unlike the postulated component in the growth–dormancy balance which, we suggested above, is not readily diffusible and remains local until metabolized.

## C. Sprout growth

### 1. Rate of growth

When a bud is no longer dormant growth is very slow, and in slow-growing varieties may not be noticeable over a long period, at 5°C and below. In cultivars which grow rapidly, however, some growth may be noticed after prolonged storage even at a temperature as low as 2°C (Krijthe, 1946). Above 5°C an increased temperature leads to increased growth up to an optimum at about 20°C, above which there is usually a decrease again:

| | | | | |
|---|---|---|---|---|
| Storage temperature °C | 10 | 15 | 20 | 25 |
| Sprout growth (16 Dec–8 Apr g/tuber) | 1·17 | 3·07 | 4·70 | 2·45 |
| Sprout growth (% total weight) | 1·18 | 2·74 | 4·45 | 2·50 |

(Data from Burton, 1958. cv. 'Majestic').

## 2. Duration of the phase of potential shoot growth

Krijthe (1962) determined changes in the potential for shoot growth at 2–7°C by transferring stored samples at regular intervals to 20°C and measuring the growth after four weeks. She found that tubers of cv. 'Libertas' reached their maximum potential for growth by May at 7°C, while at 5 and 2°C it was not reached until August, consistent with an increased temperature reducing the time-scale of development. The fall in potential did not follow this pattern, however, being sooner and greater at 2 than at 5°C. Here we may be concerned with re-synthesis of inhibiting substances as a result of the increased metabolic turnover at 2, as compared with 5°C and above, with no drain upon the products. If seed tubers are stored at a high temperature (e.g. 20°C) emergence after planting can be retarded or reduced consistent with the potential for shoot growth having passed its maximum.

## D. Tuber formation in the absence of foliage

Tuber formation in the absence of foliage is noticed frequently if seed tubers have been stored at 20°C or above, particularly if this is followed by a drop in temperature. Davidson (1958) gave a good illustration of a typical example of this, induced by storing cv. 'Dr. McIntosh' at 27°C before planting in cold ground. In such a case a plant may never emerge and farmers refer to the misses in the field as being due to "little potato". In less extreme cases a plant emerges. This may be exemplified by some unpublished results of Burton and Wilson, who stored seed tubers of cv. 'Record' at 20°C before planting field trials at ten centres. Emergence was normal but tuber formation was, on average, 4 days before emergence, ranging from 15 days before to 7 days after.

Tuber formation in the absence of foliage does not necessarily require that the seed tubers should have been stored at a high temperature. The pre-requisite may be that there should be a considerable mobilization of the tuber reserves prior to there being any drain to an established plant, in which case we would expect it eventually to occur at lower temperatures, taking senescent sweetening (see below) as the index of mobilization; or even to follow low-temperature sweetening. In the experiments of Burton and Wilson, referred to above, seed tubers were also stored at 2 °C. At three of the ten centres this resulted in tuber formation before or coincident with emergence.

# III. Effects of temperature on the growing plant

In broad terms we may regard the material for the growth of tubers as being surplus to the requirements of the haulm, and we might expect tuber growth to be very sensitive to conditions which influence the net production of dry matter and its allocation. Temperature provides a good example because of its effects on the net assimilation rate of functional leaves, on the pattern of foliage growth, and on the functional life span of the leaves. Underlying these direct effects, however, may be effects carried over from the storage of the seed tubers.

## A. Continuing effects of seed storage

The continuing effects of seed storage are consistent with an increased temperature of storage reducing the time scale of the phases illustrated in Fig. 1. Thus over the range 2–12 °C, Fischnich and Krug (1963) found more rapid emergence and earlier tuber initiation the higher the temperature, although at 12 °C the final haulm growth and yield tended to be reduced. This tendency is aggravated by yet higher temperatures of storage at which the seed tubers may well have passed still further from the stage of maximum potential shoot growth to the stage of tuber formation. Burton and Wilson (unpublished) found emergence to be no earlier from seed stored at 20 than from that stored at 2 °C and growth to be more rapid in plants from the latter. Final weights of haulm and tubers averaged over ten centres (cv. 'Record') were, respectively, 723 and 1264 g from seed stored at 2 °C and 430 and 845 g from seed stored at 20 °C. In general, Fischnich and Krug suggested that seed storage at 4 °C might be optimal provided the plants had time to mature, but stressed the importance of taking local growing conditions into account in assessing their results.

Temperatures of seed storage which either permit or prevent apical dominance may obviously have an influence upon the subsequent pattern of growth. Each bud which grows from a potato tuber produces a main stem which, after the disintegration of the tuber, is a separate plant;

## Table II

Effect of seed storage conditions on numbers of plants (i.e. main stems) and on yield

| Treatment of seed tubers:— | Sprouted in warm glasshouse (12–18°C) 16 Oct.–7 Dec. to induce apical dominance. Then unheated store (6–10°C) to planting[1] | 2°C 16 Oct.–2 Feb. Sprouted in warm glasshouse (12–18°C) 2 Feb.–7 Mar. Then unheated store (7–10°C) to planting[1] | 2°C 16 Oct. to planting[1] |
|---|---|---|---|
| Av. no. of sprouts/tuber at planting (estimated) | 1·5 | 3·7 | 0·0 |
| Av. no. plants (i.e. main stems) per "root" | 1·60 | 3·89 | 3·63 |
| 1000s per ha | 42·5 | 104·3 | 97·1 |
| Av. no. tubers per "root" | 19·1 | 24·0 | 15·8 |
| per main stem | 11·9 | 6·2 | 4·4 |
| 1000s per ha | 506 | 647 | 427 |
| Av. wt. (g) tubers per "root" Total | 1848 | 1774 | 1702 |
| >45 mm | 1523 | 1302 | 1472 |
| Av. wt. (g) tubers per main stem Total | 1155 | 456 | 469 |
| >45 mm | 952 | 335 | 406 |
| Av. wt. (g) of single tuber | 97 | 74 | 107 |
| Yield Total t ha$^{-1}$ | 48·9 | 47·4 | 45·3 |
| >45 mm | 40·3 (82·4%) | 34·8 (73·4%) | 39·2 (86·5%) |

[1] Results are the mean of those from two planting dates: 1–4 April and 20–22 April. Temperatures given for glasshouse and unheated store are ranges of monthly max.–min. mean.

(From the results of Toosey, 1962)

and a "root" of potatoes is an intermingled group of competing plants. Under any given growing conditions the yield per unit area could be expected to be influenced by the number of such plants. The effect, however, is not as great as might be expected because of the more-or-less compensating variation in the number of tubers per plant (Table II, based on the results of Toosey, 1962) and the advantage to be gained from encouraging apical dominance may be problematical.

## B. Net assimilation rate

Some of the extensive results of Winkler (1961, 1971) are given in Table III and illustrate the general conclusion that for every 10°C rise in

### Table III

Net assimilation and respiration (in mg $CO_2$ per g dry matter per hour) of mature potato leaves and stems

| Leaf or stem temp. °C | Net assimilation | | | | Respiration | |
|---|---|---|---|---|---|---|
| | Leaves | | | Stems | | |
| | 10,000 lux | 30,000 lux | 50,000 lux | 30,000 lux | Leaves | Stems |
| 10 | 23·0 | 29·7 | 37·1 | | | |
| 12 | 25·4 | 34·0 | 40·6 | −0·07 | 1·4 | 0·61 |
| 15 | 29·2 | 38·4 | 45·8 | +0·09 | 1·8 | 0·75 |
| 18 | 31·0 | 41·6 | 48·0 | +0·08 | | 0·87 |
| 20 | 30·8 | 41·8 | 48·1 | −0·11 | 2·7 | 0·97 |
| 23 | 27·1 | 37·9 | 44·4 | | 3·2 | |
| 25 | 23·8 | 33·2 | 40·5 | −0·23 | 3·6 | 1·26 |
| 27 | 18·6 | 26·6 | 36·0 | | | |
| 30 | 14·5 | 19·8 | 26·4 | −0·40 | 5·8 | 1·78 |
| 32 | 9·7 | 14·6 | 19·8 | | 6·5 | |
| 34 | 3·0 | 9·0 | 12·0 | | | |
| Temp. at which net assimilation fell to zero | 36·5–37°C | 37°C | 38°C | | | |

Cultivar, 'Cosima' (From Winkler, 1971)

temperature, respiration is roughly doubled—rather less in the case of stems; that the assimilation and respiration of the stems are practically in balance in average light; that both gross and net assimilation by the leaves reach a maximum at about 20 °C; and that net assimilation by the leaves falls to zero at about 36–38 °C.

When we come to apply such results to plants growing in the field, a

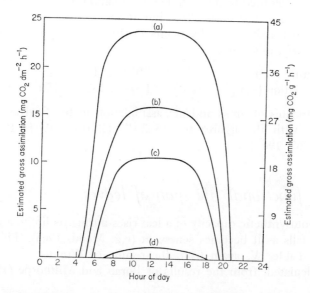

**Fig. 2.** Estimated photosynthesis in a fully developed potato plant in the field (N. Europe, July–August), allowing for shading and diurnal change in light intensity. Rates expressed on a dry matter basis (from Burton, 1966).
(a) Leaf in full sunlight and at right angles to incident light (for comparison).
(b) Plant in field (cloudless day).
(c) Plant in field ("average" weather conditions—55 % light intensity; see Burton, 1966).
(d) Plant in field (very dull cloudy weather).

major point to be considered is the light incident on the leaves. Space does not allow a full treatment here, but Burton (1966) discussed this in some detail. His conclusions are illustrated in Fig. 2 and show that the gross assimilation at 30,000 lux and 20 °C might be about 19 mg $CO_2$ per g dry weight averaged over the whole plant, compared with the corresponding value for leaves, in Table III, of 44 mg. The reduction is due to three factors—the most photosynthetically active leaves are exposed on average to a light intensity of only about 9000 lux; about one quarter to one third of the dry matter in the haulm is in unproductive stems and petioles; and the photosynthetic capacity of young and old leaves is less than given in Table III (see p. 224).

Gross assimilation averaged over 24 h is much less. Curve c in Fig. 2 corresponds to the gross assimilation of about 200 mg $CO_2$ per g dry weight in 24 h, an average of about 8·3 mg h$^{-1}$ at 20°C. If we apply to this figure Winkler's results on the effect of temperature on assimilation and proportionately weighted respiration, net assimilation by a whole plant in the field falls to zero, not at 36–38°C, but at about 30°C. Very approximate figures for net assimilation by plants in the field in mg $CO_2$ per g dry weight per day, might be:

| Temperature (°C) | 10 | 15 | 20 | 25 | 30 |
|---|---|---|---|---|---|
| Net assimilation (mg g$^{-1}$ day$^{-1}$) | 120 | 150 | 150 | 100 | 7 |

Actual estimates of gross and net assimilation in the field are in broad agreement with the figures for 15–20°C (Burton, 1964; Burton and Wilson, 1967, 1968).

# C. The functional life span of leaves

The photosynthetic capacity of a leaf rises during its life to a maximum and then falls as it becomes senescent (e.g. Meinl, 1965). This is illustrated in Table IV, again from the results of Winkler (1971). Burton (1964) calculated, from the results of Borah and Milthorpe (1962), that

**Table IV**

Net assimilation and respiration of young, adult and senescent leaves. Light intensity, 10,000 lux. Results expressed as mg $Co_2$ (g dry weight)$^{-1}$ h$^{-1}$.

| Temperature of leaf, °C | Net assimilation | | | | Respiration | | |
|---|---|---|---|---|---|---|---|
| | Young leaves 25 Jul. | Adult leaves 3 Aug. | Leaves $\frac{1}{4}$yellow-green 2–3 Sept. | Leaves $\frac{3}{4}$yellow-green 2–3 Sept. | Young leaves 25 Aug. | Adult leaves 27 Jul. | Leaves $\frac{3}{4}$yellow-green 3 Sept. |
| 12 | 22·4 | 25·4 | 15·8 | 9·6 | 1·9 | 1·4 | 1·1 |
| 15 | 24·5 | 29·2 | 18·8 | 11·6 | 2·5 | 1·8 | 1·4 |
| 18 | 25·3 | 31·0 | 19·1 | 12·1 | — | — | 2·0 |
| 20 | 24·2 | 30·8 | 17·4 | 11·2 | 4·2 | 2·7 | 2·3 |
| 25 | 16·7 | 23·8 | 12·4 | 8·6 | 6·6 | 3·6 | 3·6 |
| 30 | 7·4 | 14·5 | 6·8 | 5·0 | 10·2 | 5·8 | 5·6 |

Cultivar 'Cosima' (From Winkler, 1971)

the decrease in photosynthetic capacity with age was more rapid the higher the temperature. From the end of the third to the end of the seventh week of their experiments the rate of gross synthesis of dry matter per unit leaf area fell by 24, 67 and 83% at 15, 20 and 25°C, respectively. The respective weighted average ages of the leaves were 5·4, 4·8 and 5·1 weeks. There are certain reservations to be made in that this effect of temperature was observed on plants in growth chambers in which growth was much less than that to be expected in the field; while decrease in activity was observed at an age when, according to Winkler, it would normally still be maximal.

## D. The pattern of foliage growth

Borah and Milthorpe (1962) found that the number of leaves on a stem increased linearly with time, the rate of increase being maximal at 20°C— 1·6, 3·1 and 2·1 new leaves per week being produced at 15, 20 and 25°C respectively. During the first few weeks the increase in leaf area was greater the higher the temperature, but thereafter was greatest at 20°C. The rate of stem elongation, and, with adequate light, the degree of branching, were greater the higher the temperature. The net result was that haulm growth increased with temperature over the range 15–25°C, but that, after the first few weeks, the absolute leaf area, the proportion of the weight or dry weight present as leaves, and the leaf area per unit weight or dry weight, were all maximal at 20°C.

Again, as mentioned above, the observations were on plants in which growth was much less than would be expected in the field, but the general findings are in agreement with those of other workers (e.g. Bodlaender, 1961).

## E. Tuber growth and second growth

The results in the foregoing sections suggest that at a constant temperature the maximum surplus of carbohydrate to participate in tuber initiation and growth would occur at 18–20°C and that an even greater surplus might result if a temperature optimal for net assimilation during the daylight hours (18–20°C) were coupled with a lower temperature during the night to stimulate tuber initiation and reduce respiratory loss. Average temperatures as high as 30°C would leave no surplus for tuber growth, and in fact the increased demands of greater haulm growth coupled with a smaller leaf area might leave no surplus at 25°C.

The above expectations are borne out in practice. There is general agreement that the optimum average temperature for tuber formation and

CPCE—Q

growth lies in the range 15–20 °C (Bushnell, 1925; Werner, 1934; Went, 1959; Bodlaender, 1960, 1963; Engel and Raeuber, 1961; Borah and Milthorpe, 1962). The highest yields are obtained with differing day and night temperatures, the optima being 20 °C (day) and 10–14 °C (night) with a diurnal mean of about 17 °C (Engel and Raeuber, 1961; Borah and Milthorpe, 1962; Engel *et al.*, 1964; Raeuber and Engel, 1966). At a constant temperature of 25 °C the yield is very small (Borah and Milthorpe, 1962) while at 29 °C Bushnell (1925) found no tubers to be formed.

After the tubers have formed and are growing, an increase in temperature can reduce growth by affecting the carbohydrate supply and can also reverse the biochemical changes which led to the replacement of extension growth by, successively, radial expansion and cell enlargement (Bodlaender *et al.*, 1964). In extreme cases the buds on the young tubers grow and produce foliage which, if conditions later permit, will produce tubers again, the first formed tubers being depleted. More commonly, there is a temporary reversion to a state which permits radial expansion and some extension at the distal end at the expense of the rest of the tuber, supplemented by supplies from the foliage. Average figures obtained by Bodlaender *et al.*, for the incidence of this "second growth" in seven varieties were (expressed as a percentage of number of tubers) 2·6 (ascribed to high level of fertilizer N) at 16 °C, 9·5 at 22 °C and 46·1 at 27 °C.

# IV. Effects of temperature upon the biochemistry of the tuber

A stored tuber is in a state of drifting biochemical dynamic equilibrium, the constituent reactions of which are temperature sensitive, and temperature changes can thus cause changes in composition. These have been followed in detail for a few of the important constituents.

Figure 3 illustrates the marked sweetening which occurs at low temperatures, an effect first studied by Müller-Thurgau (1882), the mechanism of which is even now not understood. Sugars also accumulate after prolonged storage at higher temperatures, the onset of this senescent sweetening being earlier the higher the temperature (Fig. 4).

The immediate response of tuber respiration to temperature, as given by Müller-Thurgau (1882) shows a doubling for a rise of 10 °C

| Temperature °C | 0 | 3 | 6 | 10 | 20 |
|---|---|---|---|---|---|
| Sugars respired (mg h$^{-1}$). | 2·3 | 2·8 | 3·5 | 4·5 | 9·5 |

Superimposed upon this are changes positively correlated with temperature-induced changes in sugar content, the net result being that respiration may be as great at 0 as at 20 °C (Fig. 5). An increase also accompanies senescent sweetening. Observed rates of oxygen uptake or carbon dioxide output are activated by partial pressure differences between the intercellular and ambient atmospheres, the rate of diffusion of oxygen being $c$. $4 \times 10^{-3}$ cc per $cm^2$ of periderm $min^{-1}$ $atm^{-1}$ (Burton, 1965a).

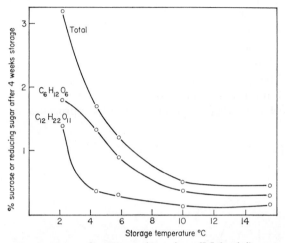

**Fig. 3.** The sugar content of potato tubers (cv. 'Majestic') stored at various temperatures (from Burton, 1965b).

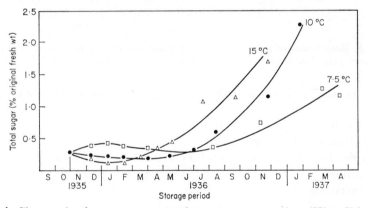

**Fig. 4.** Changes in the sugar content of mature potatoes (cv. 'King Edward') during prolonged storage at 15°, 10° and 7·5°C (from Barker, 1938).

The corresponding value for carbon dioxide would be $3·4 \times 10^{-3}$ cc. Observed changes in uptake or output thus indicate changed concentrations of oxygen or carbon dioxide in the tuber with possible effects on reactions in which they participate. Temperature can thus have an indirect as well as a direct effect upon such reactions.

Of the free amino acids, proline, of interest in connection with sprout growth, has shown most change during storage. Very little is found in the freshly harvested tuber. Thereafter there is an increase leading to accumulation at low temperatures but at higher temperatures this does not occur because of translocation to growing sprouts (Heilinger and Breyhan, 1959; Breyhan et al., 1959; Heilinger, 1961; Talley et al., 1964).

At temperatures above 25 °C softening of the tissues has been observed, ascribed to an increase in free soluble pectin and a decrease in protopectin and middle lamella pectin, these pectic changes being accelerated by increased temperature (Dastur and Agnihotri, 1934).

There is a marked loss of ascorbic acid during the first month or two after harvest but thereafter synthesis and loss approach a state of balance.

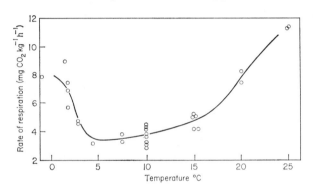

**Fig. 5.** Respiration of potato tubers at various storage temperatures. The points relate to a number of varieties and investigations (from Burton, 1966).

This is usually tilted towards loss by lowering the temperature, and a negative correlation between ascorbic acid content and storage temperature has been observed over the range from − 1 to 15 °C (Karikka et al., 1944; Barker and Mapson, 1950).

In the Introduction I referred to a tuber ⇌ plant cycle. It would be fitting if this section could be concluded in a way exemplifying this cycle, by correlating its contents with the observations in the other sections. Precise chemical information giving unequivocal links with phases of development is however, to say the least, scanty. It is in this field that further progress must be made. Nor have possible permanent effects of temperature been discussed above. A successful commercial cultivar can well have a life of upwards of a century during which period any influence to which it is exposed could conceivably have a permanent, though dwindling, effect (e.g. Scaramella-Petri, 1965). Again, this is a subject on which evidence is scanty.

# References

APPLEMAN, C. O. (1918). Physiological basis for the preparation of potatoes for seed. *Bull. Md agric. Exp. Stn* **212**, 79–102.

APPLEMAN, C. O. (1924). Potato sprouts as an index of seed value. *Bull. Md agric. Exp. Stn.* **265**, 237–258.

ARTSCHWAGER, E. F. (1924). Studies on the potato tuber. *J. agric. Res.* **27**, 809–836.

BARKER, J. (1938). Changes of sugar-content and respiration in potatoes stored at different temperatures. *Rep. Fd Invest. Bd 1937*, 175–177.

BARKER, J. and MAPSON, L. W. (1950). The ascorbic acid content of potato tubers. II. The influence of the temperature of storage. *New Phytol.* **49**, 283–303.

BODLAENDER, K. B. A. (1960). De invloed van temperatuur op de ontwikkeling van de aardappel. *Jaarb. Inst. biol. scheik. Onderz. LandbGewass.* (1960), 69–83.

BODLAENDER, K. B. A. (1961). The influence of temperature on the growth of potatoes. *Proc. 1st trienn. Conf. Eur. Ass. Potato Res. 1960*, 238–239.

BODLAENDER, K. B. A. (1963). Influence of temperature, radiation and photo-period on development and yield. *In* "The Growth of the Potato" (J. D. Ivins and F. L. Milthorpe, eds), pp. 199–210. Butterworths, London.

BODLAENDER, K. B. A., LUGT, C. and MARINUS, J. (1964). The induction of second growth in potato tubers. *Eur. Potato J.* **7**, 57–71.

BORAH, M. N. and MILTHORPE, F. L. (1962). Growth of the potato as influenced by temperature. *Indian J. Pl. Physiol.* **5**, 53–72.

BREYHAN, TH., HEILINGER, F. and FISCHNICH, O. (1959). Über das Vorkommen und die Bedeutung des Prolins in der Kartoffel. *Landw. Forsch.* **12**, 293–295.

BURTON, W. G. (1957). The dormancy and sprouting of potatoes. *Fd Sci. Abstr.* **29**, 1–12.

BURTON, W. G. (1958). The effect of the concentrations of carbon dioxide and oxygen in the storage atmosphere upon the sprouting of potatoes at 10°C. *Eur. Potato J.* **1**, 47–57.

BURTON, W. G. (1963). Concepts and mechanism of dormancy. *In* "The Growth of the Potato" (J. D. Ivins and F. L. Milthorpe, eds), pp. 17–41. Butterworths, London.

BURTON, W. G. (1964). The respiration of developing potato tubers. *Eur. Potato J.* **7**, 90–101.

BURTON, W. G. (1965a). The permeability to oxygen of the periderm of the potato tuber. *J. exp. Bot.* **16**, 16–23.

BURTON, W. G. (1965b). The sugar balance in some British potato varieties during storage. I. Preliminary observations. *Eur. Potato J.* **8**, 80–91.

BURTON, W. G. (1966). "The Potato. A survey of its history and of factors influencing its yield, nutritive value, quality and storage". 2nd edn. Veenman, Wageningen.

BURTON, W. G. and WILSON, A. R. (1967). The production, translocation and accumulation of carbohydrates and content of sugars, as affected by locality. *Eur. Potato J.* **10**, 330–331.

BURTON, W. G. and WILSON, A. R. (1968). Synthesis of dry matter in the variety Record and the proportion incorporated in the tubers. *Eur. Potato J.* **11**, 291.

BUSHNELL, J. (1925). The relation of temperature to growth and respiration in the potato plant. *Tech. Bull. Minn. agric. Exp. Stn* **34**, 1–29.

BUSHNELL, J. (1928). The effect of length of storage on the type of sprouting of potatoes. *Proc. Potato Ass. Am.* **15**, 15–18.

BUSHNELL, J. (1929). The normal multiple sprouting of seed potatoes. *Bull. Ohio agric. Exp. Stn* **430**.

DASTUR, R. H. and AGNIHOTRI, S. D. (1934). Study of the pectic changes in the potato tuber at different stages of growth and in storage. *Indian J. agric. Sci.* **4**, 430–450.

DAVIDSON, T. M. W. (1958). Dormancy in the potato tuber and the effects of storage conditions on initial sprouting and on subsequent sprout growth. *Am. Potato J.* **35**, 451–465.

ENGEL, K.-H. and RAEUBER, A. (1961). Beiträge zur Phänometrie der Kartoffel. *Eur. Potato J.* **4**, 152–164.

ENGEL, K.-H., MEINL, G. and RAEUBER, A. (1964). Das tagesperiodische Wachstum der Kartoffelknollen und der Verlauf der Temperatur. *Z. angew. Met.* **4**, 364–369.

FISCHNICH, O. and KRUG, H. (1963). Environmental factors influencing sprout growth and subsequent plant development in the field. *In* "The Growth of the Potato" (J. D. Ivins and F. L. Milthorpe, eds), pp. 72–78. Butterworths, London.

HEILINGER, F. (1961). Stoffliche Veränderung in der Kartoffelknolle während der Lagerung. *Proc. 1st trienn. Conf. Eur. Ass. Potato Res. 1960*, 241–242.

HEILINGER, F. and BREYHAN, TH. (1959). Zur Kenntnis der Aminosäuren in Kartoffelknollen. *LandbForsch-Völkenrode* **9**, 17–18.

KARIKKA, K. J., DUDGEON, L. T. and HAUCK, H. M. (1944). Influence of variety, location, fertilizer and storage on the ascorbic acid content of potatoes grown in New York State. *J. agric. Res.* **68**, 49–63.

KAWAKAMI, K. (1952). Physiological aspects of potato seed tubers. *Mem. Hyogo Univ. Agric.*, 1–114.

KRIJTHE, N. (1946). De invloed van de bewaring var aardappelknollen op den bouw van de knoppen en op de ontwikkeling tot volwassen plant. *Meded. LandbHoogesch. Wageningen* **47** (6), 1–36.

KRIJTHE, N. (1962). Observations on the sprouting of seed potatoes. *Eur. Potato J.* **5**, 316–333.

MEINL, G. (1965). Ein Beitrag zur Photosynthesemessung bei Kartoffeln. *Eur. Potato J.* **8**, 133–144.

MÜLLER-THURGAU, H. (1882). Ueber Zuckeranhäufung in Pflanzentheilen in Folge niederer Temperatur. *Landw. Jbr.* **11**, 751–828.

RAEUBER, A. and ENGEL, K.-H. (1966). Untersuchungen über den Verlauf der Massenzunahme bei Kartoffeln (*Solanum tuberosum* L.) in Abhängigkeit von Umwelt- und Erbguteinflüssen. *Abh. met. Diensts dt. demok. Rep.*, *Berlin* **76** (10), 1–117.

SCARAMELLA-PETRI, P. (1965). Caractéristiques morphologiques des tubercules de pommes de terre développées en des endroits écologiquement différents de l'Italie. *Eur. Potato J.* **8**, 247.

SCHIPPERS, P. A. (1956). De invloed van de temperatuur op de duur van de rustperiode. *Publ. Aardappelbew., Wageningen, Ser. A.* No. **108**, 1–13.

TALLEY, E. A., FITZPATRICK, T. J. and PORTER, W. L. (1964). Chemical composition of potatoes. IV. Relationship of the free amino acid concentrations to specific gravity and storage time. *Am. Potato J.* **41**, 357–366.

TOOSEY, R. D. (1959). Control of sprout numbers in maincrop potatoes. *Agriculture, Lond.* **66**, 346–350.

TOOSEY, R. D. (1962). Influence of pre-sprouting on tuber number, size and yield of King Edward potatoes. *Eur. Potato J.* **5**, 23–27.

WENT, F. W. (1959). Effects of environment of parent and grandparent generations on tuber production by potatoes. *Am. J. Bot.* **46**, 277–282.

WERNER, H. O. (1934). The effect of a controlled nitrogen supply with different temperatures and photoperiods upon the development of the potato plant. *Res. Bull. Neb. agric. Exp. Stn* **75**, 1–132.

WINKLER, E. (1961). Assimilations vermögen, Atmung und Erträge der Kartoffelsorten Oberarnbacher Frühe, Planet, Lori und Agnes im Tal (610 m) und an der Waldgrenze bei Innsbruck und Vent (1880 m bzw. 2014 m). *Flora, Jena* **151**, 621–662.

WINKLER, E. (1971). Kartoffelbau in Tirol. II. Photosynthese vermögen und Respiration von verschiedenen Kartoffelsorten. *Potato Res.* **14**, 1–18.

# Discussion

From the discussion that followed this paper, it appeared that the optimum storage temperature for seed tubers could vary with the cultivar, with spacing in the field, and with growing conditions. In general, for most cultivars, about 10 °C would be a good temperature provided growth before planting was not excessive (say <5 cm). **Burton** agreed that in many experiments in controlled environments the whole plant was exposed to different day and night temperature combinations, although the underground parts would normally be exposed to a more uniform environment in the field. Some work took account of this. A point of interest which emerged during the discussion of the biochemical changes which occurred during the storage was that, although the increase in proline was thought to be due to protein hydrolysis, there was no accompanying increase in level of the other constituent amino acids of the protein. No explanation could be offered for this.

# III.4. Photoperiodic control of flowering in the chrysanthemum

K. E. COCKSHULL

Plant Physiology Department, Glasshouse Crops Research Institute, Littlehampton, Sussex, England

## I. Introduction

The discovery that flowering could be regulated by the lengths of the light and dark periods in each daily cycle (Garner and Allard, 1920) was quickly followed by the realization that it was possible to modify the natural photoperiod within the protected environment of the glasshouse, and to use this technique to extend the natural flowering season of responsive species such as the chrysanthemum (Laurie, 1930). Post (1947) subsequently demonstrated that by careful selection of cultivars and by accurate control of night temperature, it was possible to produce chrysanthemum flowers at any time of the year if the daylength was restricted to 12 h or less per day, and his observations have formed the basis for the commercial, year-round production of chrysanthemum flowers and flowering pot plants. In order to make further improvements in what is already one of the most intensive crop-production systems in modern horticulture, it is necessary to obtain an even greater understanding of the nature of the response.

## A. The nature of the response

The control of photoperiodic responses is commonly pictured as a simple "on–off" switch, particularly in a species such as *Xanthium strumarium* L., which responds to a single favourable light–dark cycle. This view of the mechanism is apparent in the concept of a critical night length for short-day plants and was reinforced by the discovery of a photoreceptor pigment (phytochrome) which could be switched repeatedly between its two forms according to the wavelength of the incident radiation (Butler et al., 1959). Hamner (1940), however, was careful to point out that his observations on the flowering responses of *Xanthium* and of soybean indicated that the response was quantitative rather than a strict "all-or-none" reaction, for he and his co-workers showed that the degree of flowering obtained was affected by the duration and intensity of the light period, the duration of the dark period, and the number of successive inductive cycles given (Mann, 1940; Snyder, 1940).

Quantitative aspects can also be demonstrated in species which require a number of successive inductive cycles for flower initiation; exposure to fewer cycles results in the production of incomplete flowers, or "vegetative inflorescences", as in *Rudbeckia* (Murneek, 1940) and *Kalanchoe* (illustrated in Lang, 1965). It seems, therefore, that the switch is not an appropriate analogy and Butler et al. (1964) have demonstrated that even phytochrome cannot be switched entirely into one form or another by irradiation, for equilibrium mixtures of both forms are created over the range of physiologically-important wavelengths. Recently, anatomical and histochemical investigations of the development of apical meristems of quantitative short-day plants have indicated that they are continually progressing towards the flowering condition, even in long-days (Nougarède et al., 1965; Heslop-Harrison and Heslop-Harrison, 1970). The Heslop-Harrisons have suggested that, in these cases, photoperiod is acting by regulating the rate of progress along a predetermined developmental pathway rather than by activating new pathways. *Chrysanthemum morifolium* Ramat is probably a plant of this type for although flowering is accelerated by short-days, flower buds are eventually formed in long-days (Chan, 1950; Schwabe, 1950). These buds grow very slowly and often contain no florets. Vegetative growth is normally continued by shoots which grow out from leaf axils below the terminal "flower", but these too eventually form terminal flower buds and the process can be repeated many times (Schwabe, 1951). The repetitiveness of this sequence would seem to support the view that the apical meristems of chrysanthemum are always progressing towards the flowering condition.

# II. Experiments with chrysanthemum

## A. *Quantitative estimates of flowering*

In order to quantify the responses to photoperiod and to gain some insight into the mechanisms involved it is essential that the treatments are given in artificially-lit controlled environments, for they alone can provide light and dark periods of independent durations together with control of the flux density and spectral composition of the light period.

It is also necessary to measure the responses in some suitable way. Cockshull and Hughes (1967, 1972) have described a series of flower stages based upon the macroscopic development of the complete chrysanthemum inflorescence, and this scale has been used to measure the rates of flower *development* in different treatments (Cockshull and Hughes, 1971a, 1971b; Hughes and Cockshull, 1971a, 1971b). Such a system does not necessarily yield any information on the time of flower initiation, as the requirements for initiation and development may differ. To overcome this, microscopic examination of apical meristems has been used to detect the earliest anatomical changes associated with flowering, which in chrysanthemum are an increase in the height and diameter of the apical meristem. This change is followed by the formation of a flattened receptacle with involucral bracts at its base and florets on its surface. (Popham and Chan, 1952). Cathey and Borthwick (1957) divided this developmental sequence into ten discrete stages and used the resulting scale to assess the effectiveness of different treatments in promoting flower *initiation*.

The formation of a receptacle terminates leaf production by that apical meristem; the number of leaves and bracts formed below the flower can be used as a measure of the vegetative development that occurred before flower initiation began and constitutes a measure of the speed of flowering. Finally, the number of flowers formed can also be used to assess the effectiveness of a given treatment. Most of these methods have been used in the experiments described here.

## B. *General methods*

Rooted stem cuttings of *Chrysanthemum morifolium* Ramat cv. 'Bright Golden Anne', obtained from Messrs. Framptons Nurseries Limited, were used in these experiments. This cultivar is widely grown in commercial practice; it does not require a vernalization treatment, and the cuttings are produced in long-day conditions. The light source for the main light period of 8 h (18·3 °C) was "warm-white" fluorescent lamps; incandescent lamps were only used to interrupt the normal 16 h dark period (15·6 °C)—a night-break treatment—for the first week of growth. For convenience, the night-break treatment will be called a "long-day" while treatment with uninterrupted, 16 h dark periods will be called a "short-day".

## C. Effects of number of inductive cycles

The simplest quantitative approach is to expose intact plants to different numbers of inductive short-days given in succession. In some preliminary experiments at the Glasshouse Crops Research Institute, plants were grown at a light flux density of 44 W m$^{-2}$ for 8 h per day, and short-days were begun after a week of night-break treatment in the artificially-lit controlled environments. Samples of ten plants were removed after 0, 4, 8, 12, 16 and 20 short-days and transferred to a glasshouse where they received a long-day treatment (November 1970 to January 1971). Records were taken about 10 weeks after the start of the glasshouse treatments when flower buds were visible, although none had developed very far in these long-day conditions. The data for leaf number (Table I) confirmed that a terminal flower bud was formed without exposure to short-days (0 short-days), as suggested by both Chan (1950) and Schwabe (1950). In this experiment the bud was formed after the initiation of 30 leaves and it consisted of a receptacle surrounded by bracts. No florets were formed on this occasion although they have been observed on other occasions and were formed in all the short-day treatments. Four short-days led to receptacle initiation at a lower leaf number, and a still lower leaf number was obtained with eight short-days. Increasing the number of short-days appeared to hasten flower initiation and leaf number could be regarded, therefore, as a measure of the intensity of the stimulus produced by short-days. The anatomical changes which led both to receptacle initiation and the cessation of leaf production at the terminal meristem, normally began after about seven short-days (Fig. 1) under these conditions, and no further reductions in leaf number could thus be obtained by further exposure to short-days.

All axillary apical meristems were examined and their stage of development was also assessed against the scale of Cathey and Borthwick (1957). The data for flower number (Table I) show the number of apices per plant which had reached at least stage 2 (receptacle initiation). When no short-days were given, a single terminal flower formed after 10 weeks while two flowers were formed after exposure to four short-days and the number increased rapidly as more short-day cycles were given. The data suggested that the endogenous stimulus was not produced for long once the plant was returned to long-days, for it was not permanently switched to flower production. The data also suggested that the effect of successive short-days on flower number was more than additive.

The pattern of distribution of the flowers produced is shown in Fig. 2. The terminal apical meristem was the first to respond and then, as more short-days were given, the axillaries followed in a basipetal progression.

These observations could be interpreted as indicating that there was preferential transport of stimulus to the terminal apical meristem where it was utilized in receptacle initiation, for it appeared that almost no stimulus was available to the axillary meristems until a terminal receptacle had been formed after eight short-days. The operation of such a scheme would require the presence of an accurate transport system but few vascular

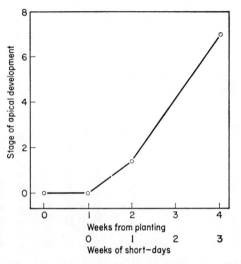

**Fig. 1.** Development of the terminal apical meristem at a light flux density of 44 W m$^{-2}$ (125 J cm$^{-2}$ in 8 h).
stage 2 = receptacle initiation, stage 5 = floret initiation.

## Table I

Effects of number of successive inductive cycles on flowering of chrysanthemum

| Number of cycles | Leaf number below the flower | Apical stage of terminal bud | Flower number |
|:---:|:---:|:---:|:---:|
| 0 | 30·0 | 3·6 | 1·0 |
| 4 | 24·8 | 6·4 | 2·2 |
| 8 | 23·4 | 6·6 | 3·8 |
| 12 | 22·6 | 7·2 | 15·4 |
| 16 | 22·8 | 8·0 | 21·2 |
| 20 | 22·6 | 8·2 | 27·4 |

Each inductive cycle consisted of 8 h light at a flux density of 44 W m$^{-2}$ followed by 16 h darkness. Means of 5 plants per treatment.

elements exist in the area of the growing point and the system would have to discriminate between axillary and apical meristems which might be less than 0·5 mm apart.

The problem might be simplified if the pattern were determined by the *competence* of a tissue to respond to the stimulus, possibly through the action of another endogenous regulator. If the terminal apical meristem was, at least initially, the only tissue competent to respond, then there would be no need for a very accurate transport system and the stimulus could be more generally distributed within the plant. The phenomenon of apical dominance could act as the regulator of competence, for the

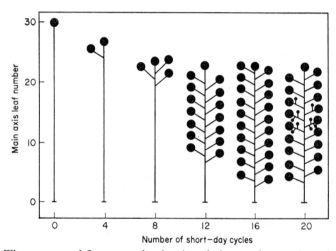

**Fig. 2.** The pattern of flower production in relation to the number of inductive short-days received. Each "flower bud" is represented by a closed circle.

growth of axillary meristems is inhibited by the presence of an active, *vegetative*, terminal meristem (Phillips, 1969). Release from dominance normally proceeds basipetally after surgical removal of a terminal apex, and apical dominance is removed by receptacle initiation in chrysanthemum (Schwabe, 1951, 1953). In order to complete the hypothesis it would also have to be assumed that the endogenous, translocatable change produced by short-day treatment was rapidly lost on return to long-days.

A hypothesis of this type could explain the flowering pattern observed in the present experiments, for receptacle initiation began at the terminal meristem about seven days after the start of continuous short-day treatment (Fig. 1), and in the four and eight short-day treatments, therefore, the axillary meristems would not have been released from apical dominance until after the plants had been returned to long-days, i.e. they became competent in the absence of the short-day stimulus and remained vegetative. A few of the upper axillary meristems were either not subjected to apical dominance or became competent while the stimulus was still present for a few axillary flowers were formed in addition to the terminal one. Where twelve short-days were given, a number of primary axillary meristems became competent while the stimulus was present and many flowers were formed. With longer exposures to short-days the secondary axillary meristems, which had been dominated by the primaries, also became competent and formed flowers, e.g. in the twenty short-day treatment (Fig. 2). If this hypothesis is correct, flower number in chrysanthemum is an estimate both of the intensity of the stimulus produced and of its duration.

Reece *et al.* (1946, 1949) suggested that a similar mechanism might regulate flower production in the Haden mango (*Mangifera indica* L.) in which inflorescences were normally formed only from terminal buds. The growth of axillary buds was inhibited until the fruits were picked at the end of the flowering season and they then developed as vegetative shoots. Axillary flowers could be initiated, however, if the terminal bud was removed at the start of the flowering period. The stimulus to form flowers apparently arose in the leaves as a response to the photoperiod. Further experiments showed that the stimulus did not persist in the plant, because axillary flowers were not formed if, after a developing terminal flower was removed, the branch was immediately ringed and defoliated above the ring. Reece *et al.* concluded that a bud had to contain dividing cells before the stimulus created in the leaves could evoke a response and Carr (1953) and Salisbury (1955), also concluded that active buds were required to stabilize the flowering stimulus.

There are a few other reports in which it has been proposed that internal correlative inhibitions can regulate flower initiation (Laibach and Kribben, 1953; Nasr and Wareing, 1961; Chouard and Tran Thanh Van, 1970); of these Laibach and Kribben suggested that the degree of apical dominance exerted by a terminal bud could regulate both the distribution of flowers and the time at which buds became "ripe" to respond to a flowering stimulus.

## D. Effects of the light period

Lang (1965) identified three qualities of the light period which could be studied, namely its duration (independent of the duration of darkness), its spectral composition, and its intensity. The chrysanthemum is relatively insensitive to the duration of the light period (Cockshull and Hughes, unpublished data) and the effects of the spectral composition of the light period have not been investigated in this plant. The effects of light intensity were studied in a series of experiments at the A.R.C. Unit of Flower Crop Physiology and these are summarized here. They were mainly concerned with the responses of chrysanthemum when grown as a flowering pot-plant. To produce the more bushy habit required in this form of culture, the terminal growing point and its surrounding young leaves were removed. This operation was usually performed one week after the start of short-days and its effect was to release the lower axillary meristems from apical dominance; they then grew out and rapidly formed inflorescences

### Table II

Effects of light level on flowering of chrysanthemum

| light level | | | flowering characteristics | | |
|---|---|---|---|---|---|
| integral J cm$^{-2}$ day$^{-1}$ | flux density W m$^{-2}$ | Equivalent time of year[1] | short-days to anthesis | leaf no. per lateral | floret number |
| 250 | 86·6 | Aug.–Sept.; April–May | 65 | 7·3 | 282 |
| 125 | 43·3 | October; February | 73 | 8·4 | 252 |
| 63 | 21·7 | December; January | 93 | 10·5 | 245 |
| 31 | 10·9 | Some winter days | 112 | 15·9 | — |

[1] The time of year when a similar daily total of visible radiation would be received inside a glasshouse in the South of England.

on short lateral branches. The flowering data on the following pages all refer to the performance of the meristems which terminated these lateral axes.

In two early experiments (Hughes and Cockshull, 1971a) chrysanthemum plants were grown at four different, constant light flux densities. The radiation total supplied in 8 h at these flux densities is shown in Table II together with the time of year when similar daily totals of visible radiation would be received inside glasshouses in the South of England. The cultivar 'Bright Golden Anne' normally flowers after 10 weeks of short-day treatment and the number of days to anthesis (flower stage 8) is also shown in Table II for one of the experiments. Flowering was seriously delayed at the two lower flux densities and similar delays are normally experienced in natural light when radiation levels are low, as in winter (Schwabe, 1953), or if they are deliberately reduced by shading (Vince, 1960). The number of leaves formed below the flower (Table II) was increased at the lower flux densities, indicating that receptacle initiation was delayed, and this was confirmed when development of the apical meristems was assessed (Fig. 3). An additional quantitative aspect was the relationship between floret number and light (Table II).

These relationships were investigated further by transfer of plants at

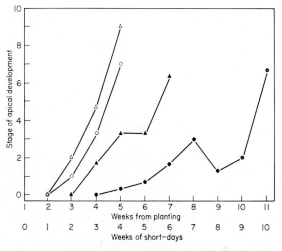

**Fig. 3.** Effect of light level on apical development (lateral meristems). Stages as in Fig. 1.

△ 250 J cm$^{-2}$ day$^{-1}$   ▲ 63 J cm$^{-2}$ day$^{-1}$
○ 125 J cm$^{-2}$ day$^{-1}$   ● 31 J cm$^{-2}$ day$^{-1}$

weekly intervals, from a standard regime receiving 125 J cm$^{-2}$ to either a lower (31 J cm$^{-2}$ in an 8 h day) or a higher light level (375 J cm$^{-2}$ in an 8 h day) (Cockshull and Hughes, 1971a). Plants remained in the new conditions for two weeks before they were returned to the standard one, and successive transfers had one week in common. The stages of flower development reached after 11 weeks of growth (10 weeks of short-days) showed that low light in the first weeks of short-days delayed development although it had relatively little effect when given in the later stages of growth (Fig. 4a). Transfer to the higher light level had almost no effect on development and it could be concluded that the standard treatment was an adequate one for studying developmental processes in chrysanthemum. The data for leaf number (Fig. 4b) indicated that transfer to low light in the first two weeks of short-days delayed receptacle initiation. The two treatments which produced this effect (week 1 and week 2) had the second week of short-days in common and microscopic examination revealed that receptacle initiation had normally occurred in the apices of the lateral branches by the end of the second week of short-days in the standard regime. Low light delayed this process and also delayed the rate of floret initiation in the third and fourth week of short-days, although the number

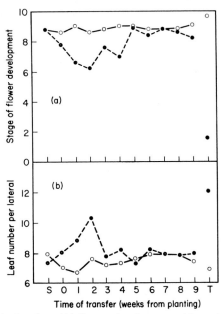

**Fig. 4.** Effect of light level on (A) flower development 11 weeks after planting, (B) leaf number per lateral branch.
   ○ Transfers to 375 J cm$^{-2}$ day$^{-1}$ for 2 weeks.
   ● Transfers to 31 cm$^{-2}$ day$^{-1}$ for 2 weeks.
   S Standard condition of 125 J cm$^{-2}$ day$^{-1}$ throughout.
   T Transfer condition of 31 (●) or 375 (○) J cm$^{-2}$ day$^{-1}$ throughout.

of florets formed was significantly reduced only when low light was given at the start of floret initiation (week 3) (Cockshull and Hughes, 1971a).

   The investigations showed that two stages in the initiation and development of a complete inflorescence were affected by the light level. There appeared to be little carry-over of any beneficial effects from previous high-light periods and once development had proceeded beyond these critical stages, the further development of the flower was relatively unaffected by the light level (Cockshull and Hughes, 1971a, 1972). Of these two processes, receptacle initiation appeared to be the more important, for delay at this stage produced the greater delay in flowering (Fig. 4a).

The facts presented so far, suggested that transfer from a low light level (31 or 63 J cm$^{-2}$ day$^{-1}$) to a higher, adequate level (125 J cm$^{-2}$ day$^{-1}$) for short periods at the start of short-days should cause early initiation, and allow further flower development to proceed more or less normally even if the plants were returned to a low light level for the remainder of their growth. Experiments in artificially-lit controlled environments (Cockshull and Hughes, 1972) showed that the expected response

### Table III

Effect of transfer on stage of flower development after 10 weeks of short-days

| Transfer treatment | Length of transfer period | | | |
|---|---|---|---|---|
| | 1 week | | 2 weeks | |
| | Exp. 1 | Exp. 2 | Exp. 1 | Exp. 2 |
| 63 J cm$^{-2}$ day$^{-1}$ throughout | 4·28 | 6·38 | 4·28 | 6·38 |
| To 125 J cm$^{-2}$ day$^{-1}$ at start of SD | 5·70[1] | 6·60 | 7·13[1] | 7·83[1] |
| To 125 J cm$^{-2}$ day$^{-1}$ after 1 week of SD | 5·67[1] | 7·19[1] | 6·26[1] | 7·30[1] |
| To 125 J cm$^{-2}$ day$^{-1}$ after 2 weeks of SD | 4·47 | 7·80[1] | 6·20[1] | 8·30[1] |
| 125 J cm$^{-2}$ day$^{-1}$ throughout | 8·84[1] | 8·68[1] | 8·84[1] | 8·68[1] |

SD = short-days.
Least significant difference at $P = 0.05$ for comparison between any pair of means in Experiment 1 = 1·16 and for Experiment 2 = 0·81.

[1] Indicates significantly different from the mean for 63 J cm$^{-2}$ day$^{-1}$ throughout.
(after Cockshull and Hughes, 1972)

did occur (Table III) and that transfer to higher light for two weeks at the start of the inductive short-day treatment, gave earlier flowering than in low light throughout. It was even possible to flower plants in 12 weeks with an input of only 47 J cm$^{-2}$ day$^{-1}$, averaged over the whole growing period, provided that the first two weeks of short-days were spent at 125 J cm$^{-2}$ day$^{-1}$.

At this stage it was necessary to determine whether the responses were directly related to the light flux density or to the quantity of visible radiation received per day. To do this, plants were grown either at constant light flux densities of 43·3 W m$^{-2}$, and 21·7 W m$^{-2}$, which gave daily totals of 125 J cm$^{-2}$ and 63 J cm$^{-2}$ in 8 h respectively, or the same totals were achieved by the use of three different light flux densities to provide stepped intervals through each day, namely 21·7, 43·3 and 86·6 W m$^{-2}$, and 10·9, 21·7 and 43·3 W m$^{-2}$ respectively. The results (Table IV) showed that the flowering response was determined by the daily light total and that there were no effects of giving higher flux densities at mid-day and lower ones at the ends of the day (Hughes and Cockshull, 1971b). Unpublished experiments at the Glasshouse Crops Research Institute compared the effects of giving 125 J cm$^{-2}$ day$^{-1}$ either as 43·3 W m$^{-2}$ for 8 h per day or 28·9 W m$^{-2}$ for 12 h per day and showed that under the standard conditions of different day and night temperatures, no major differences in response could be detected. Cockshull and Hughes (1972) also demonstrated that it was not necessary to give 125 J cm$^{-2}$ every day,

### Table IV

Comparison of the effects of stepped and constant light flux densities on flower development in chrysanthemum

| Daily total | Light flux density | Flower score after 72 days | Floret number |
|---|---|---|---|
| 63 J cm$^{-2}$ day$^{-1}$ | constant | 5·7 | 220 |
| 63 J cm$^{-2}$ day$^{-1}$ | stepped | 6·0 | 217 |
| 125 J cm$^{-2}$ day$^{-1}$ | constant | 9·0 | 259 |
| 125 J cm$^{-2}$ day$^{-1}$ | stepped | 8·7 | 264 |

(after Hughes and Cockshull, 1971b)

since no differences in flowering were observed when plants were given lower (31 J cm$^{-2}$) and higher (219 J cm$^{-2}$) levels on alternate days such that the average remained at 125 J cm$^{-2}$ day$^{-1}$. The plants responded to the light level integrated over the two days indicating that the products of the light reaction could probably be stored for at least 24 h, although the response to a lower average level was not examined.

As a result of these experiments it was concluded that delayed flowering in winter could be overcome by supplementing the low levels of natural light with light from artificial sources for the first two weeks of short-days (Cockshull and Hughes, 1971b; 1972). The details of the techniques have been published (Canham et al., 1969) and up to 12 days' advance in flowering has been obtained in commercial or semi-commercial trials (Canham 1970; Cockshull and Hughes 1971b).

Other workers have also shown that floral induction in short-day plants is related to the light level preceding an inductive dark period and this evidence and the various hypotheses proposed have been reviewed by Gregory (1948) and by Lang (1965). They concluded that the photosynthetic assimilation of carbon dioxide must be involved in the response, although the products of this process could be used in various ways. They could be required in the dark period as substrates for the synthesis of a flowering stimulus or they could combine with a product of the dark period, which was formed independently of the level of assimilate, to form a more light-stable compound or one which could be translocated out of the leaf. The concentration of assimilates at the apical meristems could also be involved in the responses of chrysanthemum. It is also possible that low light levels change the growth regulator status of the plant; application of indol-3yl-acetic acid in chrysanthemum can delay flowering (Lindstrom and Asen, 1967) and inhibit flower development and growth (Schwabe, 1951).

# III. Conclusions

Flowering in *Chrysanthemum morifolium* is a quantitative response to the environment and even in favourable conditions, internal factors can regulate the evocation of the response. The data indicate that there are steps in the developmental pathway which are traversed rapidly only if the level of radiation received at the time is adequate. These steps are probably sensitive to the level of new assimilates available within the leaves or at the meristems. The identification of these steps can only be made in transfer experiments and the effective levels can only be determined in artificially-lit environments. As yet relatively few examples exist from other plants, but light-sensitive steps have been identified in the development of wheat ears (Walpole and Morgan, 1971) and in lily flowers (Kamerbeek et al., 1969). In chrysanthemums which have a cold requirement, Schwabe (1956) has shown that high light levels are required immediately after vernalization to stabilize the vernalization stimulus, and Cooper (1964) has indicated that tomato fruit development is sensitive to light level. Such responses are particularly important in the production of glasshouse crops for it is economically feasible to supplement the low levels of natural light for short periods within this protected environment.

## References

BUTLER, W. L., HENDRICKS, S. B. and SIEGELMAN, H. W. (1964). Action spectra of phytochrome *in vitro*. *Photochem. Photobiol.* **3**, 521–528.
BUTLER, W. L., NORRIS, K. H., SIEGELMAN, H. W. and HENDRICKS, S. B.

(1959). Detection, assay, and preliminary purification of the pigment controlling photoresponsive development of plants. *Proc. natn. Acad. Sci. U.S.A.* **45**, 1703–1708.

CANHAM, A. E. (1970). Supplementary light for pot chrysanthemums, 1969/70. *Shinfield Prog.* **16**, 31–42.

CANHAM, A. E., COCKSHULL, K. E. and HUGHES, A. P. (1969). Supplementary illumination of chrysanthemums. *Comm. Grower* No. **3850**, 334.

CARR, D. J. (1953). On the nature of photoperiodic induction II. Photoperiodic treatments of de-budded plants. *Physiologia Pl.* **6**, 680–684.

CATHEY, H. M. and BORTHWICK, H. A. (1957). Photoreversibility of floral initiation in chrysanthemum. *Bot. Gaz.* **119**, 71–76.

CHAN, A. P. (1950). The development of crown and terminal flower buds of *Chrysanthemum morifolium*. *Proc. Am. Soc. hort. Sci.* **55**, 461–466.

CHOUARD, P. and TRAN THANH VAN, M. (1970). L'induction florale et la mise à fleurs en rapport avec la méréstematisation et en rapport avec la levée de la dominance apicale. *In* "Cellular and molecular aspects of floral induction" (G. Bernier, ed.), pp. 449–461. Longman, London.

COCKSHULL, K. E. and HUGHES, A. P. (1967). Distribution of dry matter to flowers in *Chrysanthemum morifolium*. *Nature, Lond.* **215**, 780–781.

COCKSHULL, K. E. and HUGHES, A. P. (1971a). The effects of light intensity at different stages in flower initiation and development of *Chrysanthemum morifolium*. *Ann. Bot.* **35**, 915–926.

COCKSHULL, K. E. and HUGHES, A. P. (1971b). Supplementary lighting of chrysanthemum. *Acta Hort.* **22**, 211–220.

COCKSHULL, K. E. and HUGHES, A. P. (1972). Flower formation in *Chrysanthemum morifolium*: the influence of light level. *J. hort. Sci.* **47**, 113–127.

COOPER, A. J. (1964). The seasonal pattern of flowering of glasshouse tomatoes. *J. hort. Sci.* **39**, 111–119.

GARNER, W. W. and ALLARD, H. A. (1920). Effect of the relative length of day and night and other factors of the environment on growth and reproduction in plants. *J. agric. Res.* **18**, 553–606.

GREGORY, F. G. (1948). The control of flowering in plants. *Symp. Soc. exp. Biol.* **2**, 75–103.

HAMNER, K. C. (1940). Interrelations of light and darkness in photoperiodic induction. *Bot. Gaz.* **101**, 658–687.

HESLOP-HARRISON, J. and HESLOP-HARRISON, Y. (1970). The state of the apex and the response to induction in *Cannabis sativa*. *In* "Cellular and molecular aspects of floral induction" (G. Bernier, ed.), pp. 3–26. Longman, London.

HUGHES, A. P. and COCKSHULL, K. E. (1971a). The effects of light intensity and carbon dioxide concentration on the growth of *Chrysanthemum morifolium* cv. Bright Golden Anne. *Ann. Bot.* **35**, 899–914.

HUGHES, A. P. and COCKSHULL, K. E. (1971b). A comparison of the effects of diurnal variation in light intensity with constant light intensity on growth of *Chrysanthemum morifolium* cv. Bright Golden Anne. *Ann. Bot.* **35**, 927–932.

KAMERBEEK, G. A., BOONTJES, J. and DURIEUX, A. J. B. (1969). Ontwikkeling en bloei van lelies. *Jversl. Lab. BloembOnderz., Lisse 1968–1969*, 25–28.

LAIBACH, F. and KRIBBEN, F. J. (1963). Apikaldominanz und Bluhreife. *Beitr. Biol. Pfl.* **30**, 127–158.

LANG, A. (1965). Physiology of flower initiation. *In* "Encyclopedia of Plant Physiology" (W. Ruhland, ed.), pp. 1380–1536. Springer-Verlag, Berlin.

LAURIE, A. (1930). Photoperiodism—practical application to greenhouse culture. *Proc. Am. Soc. hort. Sci.* **27**, 319–322.

LINDSTROM, R. S. and ASEN, S. (1967). Chemical control of flowering of *Chrysanthemum morifolium*, Ram. I. Auxin and flowering. *Proc. Am. Soc. hort. Sci.* **90**, 403–408.

MANN, L. K. (1940). Effect of some environmental factors on floral initiation in *Xanthium*. *Bot. Gaz.* **102**, 339–356.

MURNEEK, A. E. (1940). Length of day and temperature effects in *Rudbeckia*. *Bot. Gaz.* **102**, 269–279.

NASR, T. A. A. and WAREING, P. F. (1961). Studies on flower initiation in black currant I. Some internal factors affecting flowering. *J. hort. Sci.* **36**, 1–10.

NOUGARÈDE, A., GIFFORD, E. M., Jr. and RONDET, P. (1965). Cytohistological studies of the apical meristem of *Amaranthus retroflexus* under various photoperiodic regimes. *Bot. Gaz.* **126**, 281–298.

PHILLIPS, I. D. J. (1969). Apical dominance. *In* "Physiology of Plant Growth and Development" (M. B. Wilkins, ed.), pp. 165–202. McGraw-Hill, London.

POPHAM, R. A. and CHAN, A. P. (1952). Origin and development of the receptacle of *Chrysanthemum morifolium*. *Am. J. Bot.* **39**, 329–339.

POST, K. (1947). Year round chrysanthemum production. *Proc. Am. Soc. hort. Sci.* **49**, 417–419.

REECE, P. C., FURR, J. R. and COOPER, W. C. (1946). The inhibiting effect of the terminal bud on flower formation in the axillary buds of the Haden Mango (*Mangifera indica* L.). *Am. J. Bot.* **33**, 209–210.

REECE, P. C., FURR, J. R. and COOPER, W. C. (1949). Further studies of floral induction in the Haden Mango (*Mangifera indica* L.). *Am. J. Bot.* **36**, 734–740.

SALISBURY, F. B. (1955). The dual role of auxin in flowering. *Pl. Physiol., Lancaster* **30**, 327–334.

SCHWABE, W. W. (1950). Factors controlling flowering of the chrysanthemum I. The effects of photoperiod and temporary chilling. *J. exp. Bot.* **1**, 329–343.

SCHWABE, W. W. (1951). Factors controlling flowering of the chrysanthemum II. Day-length effects on the further development of inflorescence buds and their experimental reversion and modification. *J. exp. Bot.* **2**, 223–237.

SCHWABE, W. W. (1953). Effects of temperature, daylength and light intensity in the control of flowering in the chrysanthemum. *Rep. 13th int. hort. Congr., 1952*, **2**, 952–960.

SCHWABE, W. W. (1956). Factors controlling flowering in the chrysanthemum VI. Devernalization by low light intensity in relation to temperature and carbohydrate supply. *J. exp. Bot.* **8**, 220–234.

SNYDER, W. E. (1940). Effect of light and temperature on floral initiation in cocklebur and Biloxi soybean. *Bot. Gaz.* **102,** 302–322.

WALPOLE, P. R. and MORGAN, D. G. (1971). Acceleration of senescence induced in wheat by light. *Nature (New Biol.)* **230,** 191–192.

VINCE, D. (1960). Low temperature effects on the flowering of *Chrysanthemum morifolium* Ramat. *J. hort. Sci.* **35,** 161–175.

# Discussion

The discussion was mainly concerned with whether the responses to light level were mediated by hormonal changes or whether they arose from changes in the level of substrates. **Schwabe** pointed out that in some short-day plants (e.g. *Kalanchoe*), a reduction in the light intensity for part of the daily light period had the same effect as lengthening the day, which would suggest that hormonal changes were as important as substrate levels. It was suggested that low temperatures, carbon dioxide enrichment and sucrose applications could each be used to attempt to replace the requirement for high light levels, if the level of substrate was limiting. Of these, only carbon dioxide enrichment had been used on chrysanthemum and it gave some slight improvement in flowering at low light. **Wareing** emphasized that there could be both direct and indirect effects of substrate levels acting, for example, in the leaves and meristems respectively, and that it was necessary to separate these two effects.

The production of incomplete and "vegetative flowers" was discussed and it was agreed that whilst these were seldom produced in natural conditions they were readily induced in controlled environments if plants were given inadequate conditions for the formation of complete flowers. **Cockshull** stated that the exact nature of the regulator of competence was unknown but it was likely to involve the normal hormonal balance required for the maintenance of apical dominance. Schwabe questioned whether a regulator of competence was required, for phyllotaxis could be explained in terms of "fields of inhibition" which implied the presence of a transport system in the growing point. It was agreed that transport within the growing point must occur for even a regulator of competence must be translocated from the apical meristem, but it was not known how accurate this sytem had to be.

# III.5. Hormonal mediation of plant responses to the environment

DAPHNE J. OSBORNE

*A.R.C. Unit of Developmental Botany,*
*University of Cambridge, England*

## I. Introduction

It is a central dogma of modern biology that the genetic constitution of an organism determines the basic form and pattern of its development and determines that the individual shall be a recognizable member of its species. Within this framework, the expression of a genome is subject to considerable diversity and during the growth and development of an individual the extent and diversity of this expression results from the many and varying environmental changes to which the organism is exposed. Hormones play a central role in translating changes in the environment into a control of the biochemical pathways within the cell. Changes in the environment are reflected in the alteration in levels of plant hormones, auxin, gibberellins, cytokinins, abscisic acid and ethylene. In turn, we infer that these changes in hormonal levels in different parts of the plant regulate the type of growth and differentiation that occurs there as well as co-ordinating the different plant parts in the growth of the whole organism. In order for such a control system to be operable, the changes in hormone levels must be highly sensitive to environmental conditions and take place relatively quickly, i.e., at most within a few hours. Furthermore, growth responses similar to those that are evoked following the hormone change should be elicited by artificially modifying the endogenous hormone levels from an external source. In this short review I propose to describe some of the results that show how hormones can mediate the expression of both genome and environment in the regulation of plant growth.

# II. Environmental control of hormone levels

Some of the changes in hormone levels occurring in plants in the space of a few hours, and the kinds of environments that can bring them about are listed in Tables I and II.

Eighteen hours of darkness, for example, can reduce the diffusible auxin levels (Table I) in the apical bud of a tobacco plant to half; re-illumination for the same time can restore the original level, but the degree of restoration is related to the total light energy received. The content of carbon dioxide in the atmosphere can also be important and

### Table I

Environmental control of auxin levels in apical buds of tobacco plants

|  | Avena *units* | |
|---|---|---|
|  | Before | After |
| Light → dark (18 h) | 9·4 | 7·1 |
| 5 days dark → light (18 h) | 0 | 14·6 |
| 4 days dark → light (18 h) of different flux densities | | |
| 94 ergs cm⁻² sec⁻¹ | 0 | 1·0 |
| 200 ergs cm⁻² sec⁻¹ | 0 | 3·1 |
| 630 ergs cm⁻² sec⁻¹ | 0 | 8·2 |
| 1260 ergs cm⁻² sec⁻¹ | 0 | 10·4 |
| Reduced $CO_2$ in ambient air } 4·5 days | 9·0 | 5·3 |

(after Avery *et al.*, 1937)

the results suggest that auxin production parallels photosynthetic activity (Avery *et al.*, 1937).

Large changes in gibberellin levels have been reported when plants transfer from dark to light (Table II). Radley (1963) found a three-fold increase in total gibberellin level in the leaves of spinach when short-day plants were exposed to 7 h light.

Cytokinins and abscisic acid (Table II) are remarkably sensitive reflectors of the water status of the plant. Thirty minutes of transpirational stress, induced by an air stream blown over tobacco plants, will effect a two-fold or more decrease in kinin content in root exudate subsequently collected from the cut stump of a detopped plant, and the concomitant measurement of kinins in the leaves also shows a decrease from the original value (Itai and Vaadia, 1971). Even more dramatic is the change in abscisic acid levels in wheat leaves reported for a 9% loss in fresh weight following a transpirational stress of 4 h; the abscisic acid level rises forty-fold (Wright and Hiron, 1969).

The production of ethylene gas by pea seedlings is highly sensitive to light and on exposure of dark-grown seedlings a decrease is detectable within $2\frac{1}{2}$ h (Burg and Burg, 1968). That reduced ethylene production in light could be a phytochrome-mediated response is suggested by the

### Table II

Environmental control of hormone levels

|  | | | *Before* | *After* |
|---|---|---|---|---|
| GIBBERELLIN | $\mu$g kg$^{-1}$ fresh weight | | | |
| | Spinach—short-day plants | | | |
| | Leaves dark → light (7 h) | | 0·73 | 2·22 |
| | Radley, 1963 | | | |
| CYTOKININ | $\mu$g kg$^{-1}$ fresh weight | | | |
| | Tobacco—30 min water stress | | | |
| | Leaves | | 44 | 26 |
| | Root exudate | | 140 | 55 |
| | Itai and Vaadia, 1971 | | | |
| ABSCISIC ACID | $\mu$g kg$^{-1}$ fresh weight | | | |
| | Wheat—4 h transpiration stress | | | |
| | Leaves (9% water loss) | | 3·3 | 128 |
| | Wright and Hiron, 1969 | | | |
| ETHYLENE | nl g$^{-1}$ fresh weight $^{-}$h$^{1}$ | | | |
| | Etiolated pea shoots | | | |
| | Dark → light (4 h) | | 0·4 | 0·1 |
| | Burg and Burg, 1968 | | | |
| ETHYLENE | Units plant$^{-1}$ h$^{-1}$ | | | |
| | Etiolated pea shoots | | | |
| | Dark → Red (20s) | | 52 | 10 |
| | Dark → Red → Far Red (20s) | | | |
| | (After 9·5 h) | | 10 | 19 |
| | Goeschl *et al.*, 1967 | | | |
| ETHYLENE | nl g$^{-1}$ fresh weight h$^{-1}$ | | | |
| | Xanthium | | | |
| | Stroking leaf surface | | | |
| | (After 3·5 h) | Ex I | 0·02 | 0·23 |
| | | Ex II | 0·06 | 0·56 |
| | Osborne (unpublished) | | | |

changes that result from a red or far-red exposure of 20 sec on the subsequent level of gas produced (Goeschl *et al.*, 1967). Since these light regimes also regulate the enhanced growth in plumular hook opening in both bean (*Phaseolus*) and pea, and applied ethylene will overcome the effects of a red-light exposure, the results are suggestive that phytochrome is involved in both processes. However, not all ethylene production is controlled through the phytochrome system, for ethylene production can be greatly and rapidly (within 30 min) stimulated by slight wounding (stroking a leaf with a camel-hair brush) quite independently of any change in light (Table II), and the rise in ethylene production on fruit ripening in complete darkness cannot be phytochrome-mediated.

# III. Role of hormones in plants

Although it is on record that almost every aspect of plant growth can be modified by applying one or other of the plant hormones, only a few aspects of growth modification will be selected to illustrate the hormone-mediated response of plants to their environment.

## A. Growth

An auxin was defined as a substance that stimulated the extension growth of shoot cells, and long ago Went and Bonner (1943) showed that detopping a tomato plant and removing the source of auxin reduced the growth of the stem below; by replacing the tip with auxin, growth could be restored to the original rate.

We know now that auxin is not the only hormone that controls the growth of cells of the shoot, and all the known hormones have a part to play.

Cell enlargement in the presence of auxin is always associated with an enhanced plasticity, and hence extensibility, of the cell wall. The greater cellulase and cellobiase activity that results from an auxin treatment may well be involved in the process (Ridge and Osborne, 1969; Fan and Maclachlan, 1966). But increases of cell size that occur in response to gibberellin are not necessarily associated with increases in wall plasticity and Cleland *et al.* (1968) propose that an increase in osmotic concentration of the cell will also lead to enhanced uptake of water. Certainly, hydrolases such as invertase and amylase which might cause higher levels of soluble sugars within the cell, show increased activity following a gibberellin treatment (Edelman and Hall, 1964; Chrispeels and Varner, 1967). Therefore, although auxin and gibberellin can each cause cell enlargement the mechanism of such growth can be different.

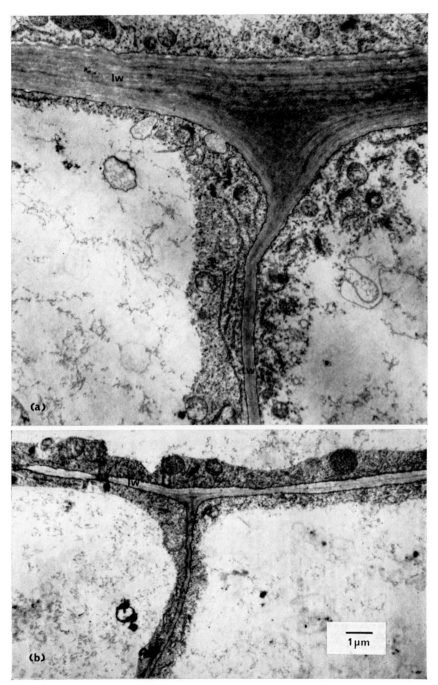

**Fig. 1.** Electron micrographs of cell walls from the cortex of extending stems of etiolated pea plants.

    a. From plants exposed to 100 ppm ethylene for 4 days (days 6–10).

    b. From control plants grown in air.

    lw = longitudinal wall.

    tw = transverse wall.

From Sargent, J. A. and Osborne, D. J., unpublished.

Ethylene too, plays a major role in the growth of cells, in most instances by reducing cell extension, although we become increasingly aware of examples in which cell enlargement is enhanced by the gas (Ku et al., 1970). Ethylene becomes particularly important in enclosed or poorly ventilated environments in which the plant's own production of the gas can build up to growth-regulating concentrations (>0·01 ppm). In these circumstances, extension growth of shoot cells is generally reduced and lateral growth is enhanced although total cell volume remains unaltered (Ridge and Osborne, 1969). If etiolated pea plants growing at 24°C are enclosed with 100 ppm of ethylene in the air for 2 days they will only extend a few millimetres compared with 6 cm or so in the controls. Although a lateral expansion of the immature cells occurs in ethylene, causing a swollen region below the stem apex, this lateral growth by no means compensates for the reduced stem elongation. Although no figures are yet available, it seems implicit that ethylene must cause an inhibition of mitotic activity at the meristem. The meristem is not, however, permanently impaired, for on removal of the ethylene, new growth appears quite normal.

Associated with the inhibition of growth in ethylene is a reduction in wall plasticity (Ridge, unpublished) and a marked increase in the deposition of hydroxyproline-rich proteins and cell wall material especially in the longitudinal as compared with the transverse walls (Fig. 1) (Osborne et al., 1972). Most of these effects of ethylene are reduced if the plants also receive additional auxin or carbon dioxide (Ridge and Osborne, 1970). It is apparent therefore, that the balance of ethylene and carbon dioxide in an enclosed atmosphere as well as the level of auxin produced by the apex must have a regulatory influence on the kind of cell expansion that occurs in a shoot.

Abscisic acid is a general inhibitor of cell elongation and this may be linked to the more general effect upon protein synthesis (Osborne, 1967, 1968; Mullins and Osborne, 1970). The onset of dormancy in buds and the cessation of shoot growth in response to decreasing day lengths has already been related (Eagles and Wareing, 1964) to the measured increase in levels of abscisic acid in short days.

## B. Senescence of leaves

From the considerable information in the literature it seems clear that at senescence, one or other of the hormones in a leaf falls below a critical level for the maintenance of the homeostatic control of cell metabolism and as soon as one hormone becomes limiting the balance is progressively disturbed. It seems that which hormone becomes in short supply depends upon the environmental conditions; under low light and short days, for example, both auxin and gibberellin levels decrease. In our common European deciduous trees the addition of either auxin (Osborne and Hallaway, 1964) or gibberellin (Brian *et al.*, 1959) will temporarily restore homeostasis, and senescence and subsequent leaf fall are retarded. In herbaceous plants, senescence of the old leaves is associated with a reduced cytokinin level in the leaf blades resulting, one believes, from an unequal competition for root cytokinins with the more vigorously metabolizing younger leaves above them. Addition of cytokinins again temporarily restores the homeostatic control and retards senescence (Osborne, 1967). Environmental stress such as wilting (Itai and Vaadia, 1971) or heat treatment (Mothes, 1964) which lowers endogenous kinin levels also enhances leaf senescence, and here too the application of a cytokinin will retard the degenerative processes. In wilting leaves, where lowered cytokinin levels are accompanied by large increases in the content of abscisic acid, subsequent senescence can be attributed to the combined effects of both of these hormones.

Fletcher *et al.* (1969) have shown how the seasonal changes in levels of a hormone can relate to the changing hormonal requirement by a leaf to prevent the onset of senescence. Gibberellin is much more effective than a cytokinin in retarding senescence in dandelion leaves growing in short days, but in long days, when gibberellin levels are relatively high, a cytokinin will retard senescence almost as readily as gibberellin.

The hormonal imbalance leading to an earlier senescence can also be manipulated by providing an *excess* of one or other substance. This occurs in young brussels sprouts on addition of the cytokinin benzyladenine (Dennis *et al.*, 1967) and in mature *Xanthium* leaves when auxin is added (Osborne, 1967).

The endogenous levels of hormones are not solely under the control of the environment for clearly the genetic constitution of the plant determines the potential extent of the response to any environmental situation. For example, the vase life of two varieties of roses can be related to the cytokinin levels that occur in the petals. Mayak and Halevy (1970) showed that not only did the levels of cytokinin fall from young to senescent petals in both varieties, but in the rose with a vase life of 8–12 days the cytokinin level in the buds was from two to ten times higher than that in the variety with a vase life of only 3–5 days. The vase life of the short-lived 3–5 day variety could be extended by applying a cytokinin to the buds.

It would seem, therefore, that the duration of leaf life and its period of usefulness to a plant as a photosynthetic organ must depend both on the genetic contribution of the individual and very greatly upon the environment to which the plant is subjected.

# IV. Sex, hormones and the environment

One of the best examples of the relationship between the genome, the environment, the levels of hormones and plant growth and differentiation is found in the sexual expression of the cucumber, *Cucumis sativus*. This plant produces male and female flowers on the same plant, the early nodes generally producing only male flowers, followed by nodes bearing flowers of both sexes. In experiments carried out in the first Phytotron at the California Institute of Technology the expression of sexuality was shown by Nitsch *et al.* (1952) to be closely controlled by the environment (Table III); short days and intermediate night temperatures favour female flower production. From more recent work on this subject it seems that the sex

## Table III

Sex expression in monoecious plants of *Cucumis sativus*

|  | *Day length* (h) | *% pistillate nodes* |
|---|---|---|
|  | 16 | 0 |
| Day temperature 26°C | 12 | 5 |
| Night temperature 17°C | 8 | 10 |
|  | Night temperature °C |  |
|  | 26 | 0·5 |
| Day temperature 20°C | 14 | 25 |
| Daylength 8 h | 10 | 10 |

(after Nitsch *et al.*, 1952)

of the flowers produced is determined by the levels of auxin and gibberellin in the plants; female flowers are produced when auxin levels are high and male flowers with high gibberellin levels.

In commercial cucumber production varieties producing large numbers of female flowers are favoured, and because the saleable fruit is parthenocarpic, male flowers are required only for seed production. This has led to the breeding of gynoecious mutants that produce only female flowers unless they are supplied with additional gibberellin externally.

Hayashi *et al.* (1971) have compared the endogenous gibberellin levels of the normal bisexual variety (M.S.U. 736) with those of the homozygous gynoecious line M.S.U. 713—715. As seen in Table IVa plants of the normal monoecious line, which produced both male and female flowers, had a higher gibberellin level than those of the gynoecious mutant. Galun *et al.* (1965) made a similar analysis of the auxin levels in comparable nodes of hermaphrodite and andromonoecious cucumber mutants; auxin levels in the hermaphrodite plants were much higher than those in the andromonoecious, staminate, mutant whether comparisons were made at nodes at equal stages of leaf or floral-bud development (Table IVb).

A convincing demonstration of the hormonal control of sexual expression

## Table IV

Total auxin and gibberellin levels in *Cucumis sativus* plants

a. Gibberellin. $\mu$g kg$^{-1}$ fresh weight in dark grown seedlings.

|  | *Monoecious* MSU 736 | *Gynoecious* MSU 713-5 |
|---|---|---|
| 6 day old | 727 | 219 |
| 18 day old | 724 | 533 |

Hayashi *et al.*, 1971

b. Auxin. $\mu$g IAA 100 g$^{-1}$ dry weight in comparable nodes bearing equally developed leaves.

|  | *Hermaphrodite* m/m  st/st | *Andromonoecious* m/m  st$^+$/st$^+$ |
|---|---|---|
| Upper nodes | 67·6[1] | 8·71 |
| Middle nodes | 36·3[2] | 7·08[1] |
| Lower nodes | 7·9 | 7·08[2] |

Converted from Table IV. (Galun *et al.*, 1965)

[1] nodes with equally developed floral buds.
[2] nodes with equally developed floral buds.

is seen in the experiments of Galun *et al.* (1962). Using buds from monoecious cucumbers removed at nodes that produced both pistillate and staminate flowers they could elicit all-female flower expression on the addition of auxin and totally suppress female expression by supplying gibberellin together with the auxin (Table V). However, as McMurray and Miller (1968) have indicated from their induction of female flowers with "Ethrel" (2-chloroethylphosphonic acid), (Fig. VI), it may well be that it is not auxin itself which controls the sexual expression of the bud, but rather the ethylene that is produced by the tissue in response to the auxin it contains. Morgan and Hall (1964) have clearly shown that applying auxin to a plant increases the ethylene production of that plant. We know that the apical bud of the shoot is not only the part that is richest in auxin; it is also the part that produces most ethylene (Goeschl *et al.*, 1967; Burg and Burg, 1968), so that the level of auxin and the production of

**Table V**

Sex expression in cultured buds of monoecious plants of *Cucumis sativus*

| | % pistillate buds | | |
|---|---|---|---|
| Control | GA | IAA | IAA + GA |
| | $(1 \text{ mg litre}^{-1})$ | $(0 \cdot 1 \text{ mg litre}^{-1})$ | |
| 0 | 0 | 92 | 0 |

Buds from node 8

(after Galun *et al.*, 1962)

**Table VI**

Sex expression at the first 20 nodes of plants of *Cucumis sativus* sprayed four times at the two leaf stage with "Ethrel"

| | % nodes staminate | % nodes pistillate |
|---|---|---|
| Control | 82·5 | 17·5 |
| "Ethrel" 120 ppm | 0 | 95 |

(after McMurray and Miller, 1968)

ethylene must be intimately related in the control of sexual differentiation in the meristem of the cucumber.

A similar hormonal control appears to exist in *Cannabis sativa* which has both male and female plants and in which sexual expression is modified by daylength and temperature (Cooke and Randall, 1968). Female plants contain some thirty times more auxin than the males (Conrad and Mothes, 1961) and female flowers can be induced on the staminate plants by treating them with auxin (Cooke and Randall, 1968) or "Ethrel" (Ram and Jaiswal, 1970).

In the control of sexual expression in these particular plants the implication is clear. The genome contains all the information for full development of both sexual characteristics, the genetic control lies in the regulation of the levels of hormone production that dictate the genic expression. This is borne out by some of the dwarf maize mutants (Phinney, 1956) in which the single gene mutations concern the failure of particular steps in the bio-synthesis of gibberellins and dwarfing may be overcome by the addition of gibberellin.

In the cucumber, any modification of the environment that results in the change in the relative levels of auxin and gibberellin within the appropriate limits should permit the whole range of male and female sexual expression to occur. In practice, the required expression can probably be obtained more easily by supplying the hormone that is deficient.

Such regulation of the genome is of considerable importance in breeding programmes for certain seedless fruit, such as the commercial cucumber, where seed can be routinely obtained from wholly pistillate plants by supplying gibberellin to produce male flowers at will. Induction of anthers and viable pollen in male sterile mutants of tomato has also been accomplished by gibberellin treatments (Phatak *et al.*, 1965; Kasembe, 1967).

Although examples of environmental control of hormone levels and the genetic limitations of hormone production are still few in the plant world, an increased knowledge of these close relationships should lead us to a better understanding of the control of plant growth.

# References

AVERY, G. S., BURKHOLDER, P. R. and CREIGHTON, H. B. (1937). Growth hormones in terminal shoots of *Nicotiana* in relation to light. *Am. J. Bot.* **24**, 666–673.

BRIAN, P. W., PETTY, J. H. P. and RICHMOND, P. T. (1959). Effect of gibberellic acid on the development of autumn colour and leaf fall of deciduous woody plants. *Nature, Lond.* **183**, 58–59.

BURG, S. P. and BURG, E. A. (1968). Auxin stimulated ethylene formation: Its relationship to auxin inhibited growth, root geotropism and other plant processes. *In* "Biochemistry and Physiology of Plant Growth Substances" (F. Wightman and G. Setterfield, eds), pp. 1275–1294. Runge Press, Ottawa.

CHRISPEELS, M. J. and VARNER, J. E. (1967). Hormonal control of enzyme synthesis: on the mode of action of gibberellic acid and abscisin in aleurone layers of barley. *Pl. Physiol., Lancaster* **42**, 1008–1016.

CLELAND, R., THOMPSON, M. L., RAYLE, D. L. and PURVES, W. K. (1968). Difference in effects of gibberellins and auxins on wall extensibility of cucumber hypocotyls. *Nature, Lond.* **219**, 510–511.

CONRAD, K. and MOTHES, K. (1961). Über geschlechtsgebundene Unterscheide in Auxin-Gehalt dioezischer Hanfpflanzen. *Naturwiss.* **48**, 26–27.

COOKE, H. R. and RANDALL, D. I. (1968). 2-haloethane phosphonic acids as ethylene releasing agents for the induction of flowering in pineapples. *Nature, Lond.* **218**, 979.

DENNIS, D. T., STUBBS, M. and COULTATE, T. P. (1967). The inhibition of brussels sprout leaf senescence by kinins. *Can. J. Bot.* **45**, 1019–1024.

EAGLES, C. F. and WAREING, P. F. (1964). The role of growth substances in the regulation of bud dormancy. *Physiologia. Pl.* **17**, 697–709.

EDELMAN, J. and HALL, M. A. (1964). The effect of growth hormones on the development of invertase associated with cell walls. *Nature, Lond.* **201**, 296–297.

FAN, D. F. and MACLACHLAN, G. A. (1966). Control of cellulase activity by indole-acetic acid. *Can. J. Bot.* **44**, 1025–1034.

FLETCHER, R. A., OEGEMA, T. and HORTON, R. F. (1969). Endogenous gibberellin levels and senescence in *Taraxacum officinale*. *Planta* **86**, 98–102.

GALUN, E., JUNG, Y. and LANG, A. (1962). Culture and sex modification of male cucumber buds *in vitro*. *Nature, Lond.* **194**, 596–598.

GALUN, E., IZHAR, S. and ATSMON, D. (1965). Determination of relative auxin content in hermaphrodite and andromonoecious *Cucumis sativus* L. *Pl. Physiol., Lancaster* **40**, 321–326.

GOESCHL, J. D., PRATT, H. K. and BONNER, B. A. (1967). An effect of light on the production of ethylene and the growth of the plumular portion of etiolated pea seedlings. *Pl. Physiol., Lancaster* **42**, 1077–1080.

HAYASHI, F., BOERNER, D. R., PETERSON, C. E. and SELL, H. M. (1971). The relative content of gibberellin in seedlings of gynoecious and monoecious cucumber (*Cucumis sativus*). *Phytochemistry* **10**, 57–62.

ITAI, C. and VAADIA, Y. (1971). Cytokinin activity in water-stressed shoots. *Pl. Physiol., Lancaster* **47**, 87–90.

KASEMBE, J. N. R. (1967). Phenotypic restoration of fertility in a male-sterile mutant by treatment with gibberellic acid. *Nature, Lond.* **215**, 668.

KU, H. S., SUGE, H., RAPPAPORT, L. and PRATT, H. K. (1970). Stimulation of rice coleoptile growth by ethylene. *Planta* **90**, 333–339.

MAYAK, S. and HALEVY, A. H. (1970). Cytokinin activity in rose petals and its relation to senescence. *Pl. Physiol., Lancaster* **46**, 497–499.

McMURRAY, A. L. and MILLER, C. H. (1968). Cucumber sex expression modified by 2-chloroethanephosphonic acid. *Science, N.Y.* **162**, 1397–1398.

MORGAN, P. W. and HALL, W. C. (1964). Accelerated release of ethylene by cotton following application of indole-3-acetic acid. *Nature, Lond.* **201**, 99.

MOTHES, K. (1964). The role of kinetin in plant regulation. *In* "Regulateurs naturels de la Croissance Végétale" (*Colloq. int. Cent. natn. Rech. scient.* 123), pp. 131–140. C.N.R.S., Paris.

MULLINS, M. J. and OSBORNE, D. J. (1970). Effect of abscisic acid on growth correlation in *Vitis vinifera* L. *Aust. J. biol. Sci.* **23**, 479–483.

NITSCH, J. P., KURTZ, E. B., LIVERMAN, J. L. and WENT, F. W. (1952). The development of sex expression in cucurbit flowers. *Am. J. Bot.* **39**, 32–43.

OSBORNE, D. J. (1967). Hormonal regulation of leaf senescence. *Symp. Soc. exp. Biol.* **21**, 305–321.

OSBORNE, D. J. (1968). Hormonal mechanisms regulating senescence and abscission. *In* "Biochemistry and Physiology of Plant Growth Substances" (F. Wightman and G. Setterfield, eds), pp. 815–840. Runge Press, Ottawa.

OSBORNE, D. J. and HALLAWAY, H. M. (1964). The auxin, 2,4-dichlorophenoxyacetic acid as a regulator of protein synthesis and senescence in detached leaves of *Prunus. New Phytol.* **63**, 334–347.

OSBORNE, D. J., RIDGE, I. and SARGENT, J. A. (1972). Ethylene and the growth of plant cells: role of peroxidase and hydroxyproline rich proteins. *Proc. 7th int. Conf. Plant Growth Regulation 1970* (D. J. Carr, ed.).

PHATAK, S. C., WITTWER, S. H., HONMA, S. and BUKOVAC, M. J. (1966). Gibberellin induced anther and pollen development in a stamenless tomato mutant. *Nature, Lond.* **209**, 635–636.

PHINNEY, B. O. (1956). Growth response of single-gene dwarf mutants in maize to gibberellic acid. *Proc. natn. Acad. Sci. U.S.A.* **42**, 185–189.

RADLEY, M. (1963). Gibberellin content of spinach in relation to photoperiod. *Ann. Bot.* **27**, 373–377.

RAM, H. Y. M. and JAISWAL, V. S. (1970). Induction of female flowers on male plants of *Cannabis sativa* L. by 2-chloroethanephosphonic acid. *Experientia* **26**, 214–216.

RIDGE, I. and OSBORNE, D. J. (1969). Cell growth and cellulases: regulation by ethylene and indole-3-acetic acid in shoots of *Pisum sativum. Nature, Lond.* **223**, 318–319.

RIDGE, I. and OSBORNE, D. J. (1970). Hydroxyproline and peroxidases in cell walls of *Pisum sativum:* regulation by ethylene. *J. exp. Bot.* **21**, 843–856.

WENT, F. W. and BONNER, D. M. (1943). Growth factors controlling tomato stem growth in darkness. *Archs Biochem.* **1**, 439–452.

WRIGHT, S. T. C. and HIRON, R. W. P. (1969). (+)—abscisic acid, the growth inhibitor induced in detached wheat leaves by a period of wilting. *Nature, Lond.* **224**, 719–720.

# Discussion

The discussion was mainly concerned with the effects of ethylene on plant growth. In connection with cell wall thickening, **Osborne** explained that existing protein in the cell wall did not become hydroxylated and although new hydroxyproline-rich protein was added, the increase in thickness of the wall was largely due to addition of carbohydrates, thus the weight of protein per unit weight of wall declined following ethylene treatment. It was agreed that ethylene could be produced under conditions of stress and that carbon dioxide could suppress the effects of ethylene in some situations. **Scott Russell** pointed out that carbon dioxide does not compete with ethylene in influencing root extension of cereals, and ethylene can *stimulate* root extension in rice. Osborne agreed that there were examples in which ethylene promoted growth; in aquatic plants, when oxygen concentrations were reduced, and in many fruits, where oxygen concentrations were normal. In her view, ethylene inhibited normal auxin-mediated cell extension, but some kinds of cell, which had reached their mature size, could be stimulated to a second phase of enlargement e.g. cells in separating abscission zones, and those in fruits (e.g. fig or peach) just prior to ripening.

# III.6. The control of the rate and direction of phloem transport

A. J. PEEL

*Botany Department, University of Hull, England*

## I. Introduction

As an introduction to the subject, it seems desirable to define the terms I shall be using in this brief review of a large, and as yet little understood, topic. The term "rate of translocation" is one which has been the object of abuse in phloem transport studies, since attempts to measure this have in fact generally been concerned with the measurement of the velocity of transport. It has been common practice to measure the time taken for a pulse of radioactivity to move through the phloem from point A to point B, express the data in terms of distance moved per unit time and to call this a "rate of translocation". In fact this would be a velocity, and the measurement of velocity has been attempted since data on this might enable us to gain information on the mechanism of longitudinal sieve tube transport. Velocity is, however, extremely difficult to measure for a number of reasons, and it is probable that the values quoted in the literature (Zimmermann, 1960) are minimum velocities.

In an excellent review (Canny, 1960) some of the confusion surrounding the terms velocity and rate has been removed. Canny has defined rate as mass transfer of solutes, measured in the units, mass transported per unit time, or specific mass transfer, mass per unit area of conducting tissue per unit time. Although mass transfer is difficult to measure, a number of measurements have been made on tubers and fruits, the values obtained lying within the range of 3–5 g carbohydrate per cm² phloem per hour. The relative mass transfer of a solute under different sets of conditions is however reasonably easy to measure, and I shall be primarily concerned with this.

Little need be said concerning the other terms to be used. A source may

265

be defined as a tissue or organ in which the export of a given solute exceeds its import, whilst the converse is true of a sink. The point must be made however that an organ could be a source of one solute, whilst it is a sink for a different solute, though whether these two states could exist concurrently is not known. It may be that they have to be separated in time, albeit by only minutes. The sieve tubes are the transport conduits.

# II. The control of the rate of mass transfer and direction of movement by sources and sinks

## A. Solute loading at the source

Since a solute cannot be translocated until it has been loaded into the sieve tubes, possibly the main effect of the source in determining the rate of longitudinal transport will lie in the control of the rate of solute movement into the transport conduits. This will be the case whether the source is assimilating leaf tissue, or storage tissue.

Weatherley et al. (1959) have suggested that the rate of loading of a solute from the storage cells of willow stems into the sieve tubes is governed by differences in the "potential" of the solute between these cells. The term potential was chosen since the process is probably active, and therefore potential may not be directly equated with concentration. Certainly evidence is available from the literature for this suggestion. As long ago as 1928 Mason and Maskell found that the mass of sugars in the bark of cotton changed in parallel with the concentration, and hence potential, of sugars in the leaves. Darkening of sugar cane leaves after the administration of $^{14}CO_2$ was found by Hartt et al. (1964) to reduce the movement of radioactivity out of the leaf.

The effect of a change in solute potential gradient on the rate of movement of sugars into the sieve elements may be seen by reference to Fig. 1. Here the xylem of a stem segment of willow was initially perfused with distilled water, this subsequently being replaced with a 4 atm. mannitol solution, sieve tube exudate being collected via severed aphid stylets. As the concentration of sugars within the sieve tube rose, and hence the potential gradient between these cells and the storage cells of the stem decreased, the sucrose flux into the sieve elements dropped.

The flux of solutes into the sieve elements is not controlled only by gradients of solute concentration. In work using potassium (Peel, 1963) it was demonstrated that although the potassium flux could be enhanced by increasing the potassium concentration in stem segments of willow, a point was reached where any further increase did not increase the flux into the sieve tubes. It seems possible therefore that an upper limit is reached to the rate at which the solute loading process can proceed.

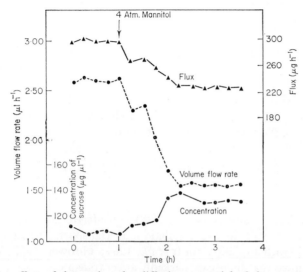

**Fig. 1.** The effect of decreasing the diffusion potential of the water bathing the sieve elements on volume flow rate, sucrose concentration and flux from an aphid stylet.

## Table I

The effect of $10^{-5}$M IAA upon the flux of sucrose into the sieve elements of bark strips of willow

| Experiment | Rate of stylet exudation ($\mu$l h$^{-1}$) | | Sucrose concentration ($\mu$g $\mu$l$^{-1}$) | | Sugar flux ($\mu$g h$^{-1}$) | |
|---|---|---|---|---|---|---|
| | A | B | A | B | A | B |
| 1 | 0·71 | 0·79 | 9 | 28 | 6 | 22 |
| 2 | 0·78 | 0·91 | 23 | 24 | 18 | 22 |
| 3 | 0·93 | 1·06 | 15 | 17 | 14 | 18 |
| 4 | 0·85 | 0·92 | 13 | 32 | 11 | 29 |
| 5 | 0·35 | 0·37 | 9 | 26 | 3 | 10 |
| 6 | 0·57 | 0·58 | 12 | 20 | 7 | 12 |

A—cambial surface of strip bathed with distilled water.
B—cambial surface of strip bathed with $10^{-5}$M IAA.

There is evidence that indol-3yl-acetic acid (IAA) can increase the rate of loading of sugars from the storage cells of willow stems (Lepp and Peel, 1970). Table I presents the data from a number of experiments in which the sucrose flux from an exuding aphid stylet, sited on a bark strip of willow, was measured when the strip was irrigated with distilled water, then with $10^{-5}$M IAA.

The source not only controls the rate of loading of a given solute, it also discriminates between chemically related species. Trip *et al.* (1965) applied a variety of labelled sugars to leaves, and found marked differences in the rate at which each was translocated; non-reducing sugars were translocated while reducing sugars were not. A similar situation has been found by Peel and Ford (1968) in willow. Here sucrose is loaded into the sieve elements, glucose and fructose are not.

## B. *Effects of source and sink on rate and direction of transport*

Although Mason and Maskell (1928) considered that sinks played a relatively minor role in the regulation of transport, subsequent work (Nelson and Gorham, 1957; Hartt *et al.*, 1964; Thrower, 1965; Wardlaw, 1967) has shown that sinks can markedly affect transport.

It is possible to use colonies of the aphid *Tuberolachnus salignus* Gmelin to illustrate the effect of sink size on the relative mass transfer of solutes.

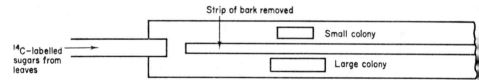

**Fig. 2.** The experimental system employed to investigate the effect of aphid colony sink size on the relative mass transfer of $^{14}$C-labelled assimilates exported by the leaves of willow cuttings.

The magnitude of an aphid colony sink is readily changed, merely by altering the number of feeding individuals. Figure 2 shows the system employed by Peel and Ho (1970) in a preliminary study of the effect of sink size on the relative mass transfer of $^{14}$C-labelled assimilates, exported from leaves allowed to photosynthesize in $^{14}$CO$_2$. Table II presents the results from a number of these experiments. Here the specific activity of the honeydew, collected over a period of 15 h from the application of $^{14}$CO$_2$ to the leaves, is a measure of the relative mass transfer of the $^{14}$C-label.

Both sources and sinks can influence the direction of transport. Removal of the first leaf of wheat plants increases the transport of assimilates to the developing grain from the second leaf (Wardlaw, 1967). Removal of the mature leaves between the growing apex and a source leaf in soybean, increased the movement of $^{14}$C-labelled assimilates from this leaf to the apex (Thaine et al., 1959). The position of sink areas can markedly affect the direction of transport. Actively growing suckers of sugar cane increase the amount of assimilates which are transported down the stem from mature leaves (Hartt et al., 1964). Competition occurs between sinks. Peel (1964) showed that tangential movement in the bark of willow cuttings would occur only if the root sink was excised.

### Table II

The effect of aphid colony size on the specific activity of honeydew (relative mass transfer of $^{14}$C-label)

| Experiment | Rate of honeydew production (mg dry wt h$^{-1}$) | | Specific activity of honeydew (cpm (mg dry wt)$^{-1}$) | |
|---|---|---|---|---|
| | Large colony | Small colony | Large colony | Small colony |
| 1 | 1·27 | 0·40 | 46,200 | 24,200 |
| 2 | 0·61 | 0·29 | 24,900 | 13,100 |
| 3 | 0·86 | 0·18 | 449,500 | 285,000 |
| 4 | 0·62 | 0·19 | 69,000 | 4,000 |
| 5 | 0·32 | 0·18 | 26,400 | 8 |
| 6 | 0·37 | 0·17 | 124,000 | 700 |

In connection with the phenomenon of competition between sinks, an aspect should be mentioned concerning measurements of the rate of translocation. If it is desired to measure the rate of translocation of a solute from the leaves to a sink area some distance away, then the rate of transport will depend not only upon the size of the sink, but also upon the size of sinks lying adjacent to the transport pathway. Tissues such as the xylem can act as considerable sinks in this connection. Hoad and Peel (1965) showed that it was possible to change the rate of translocation of $^{14}$C-assimilates and $^{32}$P-phosphates, exported from the leaves of willow cuttings towards an aphid colony, by altering the extent to which radial movement into the xylem occurred. As shown diagrammatically in Fig. 3, the greater the degree of radial movement of the tracer, the lower the rate of longitudinal transport of the tracer, and vice versa.

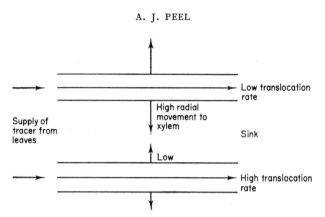

**Fig. 3.** Diagrammatic representation of the effect of radial movement from the sieve tubes on the longitudinal mass transfer of solutes.

# III. The control of the rate and direction of movement by the transport conduits

Whereas the literature contains a reasonable amount of data on the source–sink relationships in phloem transport from which certain undisputed conclusions can be drawn, this cannot be said of the work on the effects of the transport conduits on the rate and direction of movement. The reason for this is clear; since the mechanism of longitudinal sieve tube transport is still a matter of some considerable controversy, the results of experiments on sieve tube transport are subject to a variety of interpretations.

## A. *Polarity of sieve tube transport*

A problem which has not yet been conclusively solved is that concerned with whether a given solute is transported more readily in one direction, i.e. basipetally, than in the other, i.e. acropetally, or vice versa. An attempt to solve this was made by Weatherley *et al.* (1959). Using isolated segments of willow stem 40 cm in length, they took a number of readings from the morphological base and apex of the volume flow rate and sucrose concentration of exudate obtained from severed aphid stylets. No significant differences were found between the base and the apex of the segments (Table III).

Although no polarity would appear to exist in the case of sucrose transport, there is some evidence that IAA may show polarity of movement in the sieve tubes of stem segments of willow, at all events when these are maintained in a vertical position, morphological apex uppermost (Lepp and Peel, 1971a). These workers have presented evidence that [14]C-labelled IAA will move into the sieve tubes of willow. What has not been conclusively established is that the polar movement occurs within the sieve tubes.

**Table III**

The volume flow rate and sucrose concentrations of stylet exudate obtained from the morphological apex and base of stem segments of willow

| Segment | Mean volume flow rate ($\mu l\ h^{-1}$) | | L.S.D. | Mean sucrose conc. ($\mu g\ \mu l^{-1}$) | | L.S.D. |
|---|---|---|---|---|---|---|
| | base | apex | | base | apex | |
| 1 | 1·19 | 1·21 | 0·82 | 126 | 130 | 33 |
| 2 | 1·99 | 1·74 | 0·77 | 133 | 135 | 41 |

# B. Can different solutes move at different rates in the sieve tubes?

The short answer to this question is yes, if only for the reason that different rates of radial movement of two solutes out of the sieve tube will produce different rates of longitudinal mass transfer (Fig. 3). However, to the author's knowledge it has never been shown whether, in the absence of radial movement (if such a situation could ever be produced), two solutes could move with different rates of mass transfer (of course in the absence of radial transport, velocities would be readily measured). The data of Swanson and Whitney (1953) in which the simultaneous movement of a pair of foliar-applied isotopes was measured, takes no account of radial movement and therefore their conclusions that different solutes can move with different velocities, are invalid. Biddulph and Cory (1957) attempted to measure radial movement into the xylem of foliar-applied [14]C-sugars, [32]P-phosphates and tritiated water, during the movement of these tracers through the phloem. Once again however, their "velocity" data which appeared to show that the [14]C-label moved faster than the [32]P or [3]H-label must be suspect for they did not determine the extent to which radial movement took place into phloem cells adjacent to the sieve tubes.

## C. *Simultaneous bidirectional movement in sieve tubes*

As with attempts to determine whether different solutes can move at different rates, the problem of simultaneous bidirectional movement of two solutes has received the attention of a number of workers (Phillit and Mason, 1936; Palmquist, 1938; Chen, 1951).

Before considering this problem further it is necessary to define exactly what we mean by simultaneous bidirectional movement. Reference to Fig. 4 should clarify the situation. The essential point to notice is that the movements shown in Fig. 4(a) must occur in the same sieve tube.

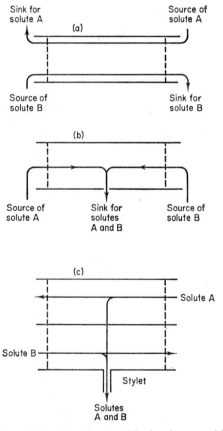

**Fig. 4.** (a) Pattern of possible solute fluxes with simultaneous bidirectional movement.

(b) Movement in opposite directions of two solutes towards a common sink.

(c) Possible effect of aphid stylet puncture on the stimulation of lateral movement between adjacent sieve tubes, each transporting a different solute.

In recent years aphids have been used to investigate whether simultaneous bidirectional movement can occur (Eschrich, 1967; Ho and Peel, 1969). The reasoning behind these experiments is that if two tracers are applied to a plant at a distance from each other, an aphid colony being allowed to feed between the two application sites, then if both tracers appear in the honeydew at the same time it would appear possible that simultaneous bidirectional movement is taking place. However, it is also possible that the transport processes shown in Fig. 4(b) are proceeding, i.e. not simultaneous bidirectional movement. In certain of the experiments performed by Ho and Peel (1969), aphids were sited some hours after tracer application, and it was found that the first drop of honeydew produced contained both tracers. Though these experiments would seem to provide good evidence for simultaneous bidirectional movement, the results could just as easily be explained by assuming that lateral movement of one tracer occurred from a sieve tube into an adjacent sieve tube which was transporting the other tracer (Fig. 4(c)).

The situation is by no means resolved. Probably the best evidence for simultaneous bidirectional movement is that gained by autoradiography (Trip and Gorham, 1968).

## D. Control of the rate and direction of sieve tube transport by growth substances

Since the work of Booth *et al.* (1962), it has become firmly established that growth substances can affect the distribution pattern of nutrients (Moorby, 1968; Milthorpe and Moorby, 1969). In a previous section of the present paper it was shown that IAA can influence the loading rate of sugars into the sieve elements. There would seem to be little, if any, incontrovertible evidence that growth substances can directly affect the transport processes within the sieve tubes, since much of the data which has been obtained could be interpreted in terms of an effect of growth substances on the rate or solute unloading at sinks (Davies and Wareing, 1965; Seth and Wareing, 1967). However, Davies and Wareing (1965) have produced some evidence that IAA may have a direct effect upon the longitudinal transport system.

The possibility that IAA can affect longitudinal sieve tube transport has been strengthened by the work of Lepp and Peel (1971b). Using isolated segments of willow, in which the bark was divided longitudinally into two halves by means of slits cut on diametrically opposite sides of the stem (Fig. 5(a)), $^3$H-glucose was applied to an abrasion on one half of the bark, $^{14}$C-IAA and $^3$H-glucose to an abrasion on the other half

(Fig. 5b). After 6 h, during which the segments were orientated vertically, morphological apex uppermost, the pieces of bark above and below the abrasions were assayed for tracer distribution.

The data presented in Table IV show that when ³H-glucose only was applied to the bark, the upward and downward distribution was very similar. When IAA was also applied, more than two-thirds of the tritium activity moved basipetally, as did the ¹⁴C-label from the IAA.

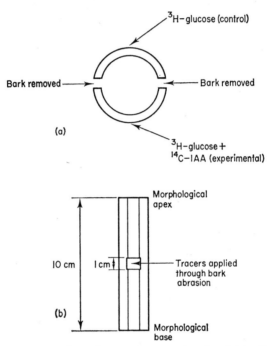

Fig. 5. (a) Transverse section of stem segment showing bark divided into two halves by means of longitudinal slits.

(b) Stem segments employed to investigate the effect of IAA on the movement of ³H-labelled glucose.

# IV. Conclusions

It is clear from this brief review that the mechanisms which control the rate and direction of phloem transport are complex, many aspects of them being poorly understood. In view of the state of knowledge of the mechanism of longitudinal sieve tube transport, it is not surprising that we know very little about the control by the transport conduits. Source and sink effects should be more amenable to analysis however, and there

## Table IV

Movement of $^{14}C$ and $^{3}H$-labels from $^{14}C$-IAA and $^{3}H$-glucose when these substances were applied through a bark abrasion on vertically orientated segments of willow stem

| Segment | Experimental half ($^{14}C$-IAA + $^{3}H$-glucose) | | | | Control half ($^{3}H$-glucose) | |
| | $^{14}C$ | | $^{3}H$ | | $^{3}H$ | |
| | apex | base | apex | base | apex | base |
|---|---|---|---|---|---|---|
| 1 | 236 | 573 | 426 | 1030 | 307 | 298 |
| 2 | 202 | 288 | 373 | 516 | 417 | 176 |
| 3 | 477 | 884 | 869 | 1612 | 451 | 486 |
| 4 | 70 | 463 | 129 | 838 | 242 | 61 |
| 5 | 310 | 800 | 569 | 1473 | 204 | 330 |
| 6 | 90 | 172 | 167 | 309 | 233 | 466 |
| 7 | 455 | 804 | 848 | 1493 | 302 | 432 |
| 8 | 226 | 415 | 404 | 741 | 211 | 268 |
| 9 | 384 | 587 | 698 | 1061 | 460 | 308 |
| 10 | 147 | 271 | 523 | 956 | 368 | 257 |
| Mean | 260 | 551 | 475 | 999 | 320 | 307 |
| ± | 101 | 162 | 189 | 303 | 83 | 104 |
| | | | | | | (P = 0·05) |

Mean % distribution of total activity recovered

| | | | | | | |
|---|---|---|---|---|---|---|
| | 30·0 | 70·0 | 30·0 | 70·0 | 52·5 | 47·5 |

Data given in cpm. Samples counted to same efficiency.

appears to be no reason why, with our present techniques, they should not be much better understood.

In this paper I have dealt exclusively with the physiological aspects of the control of rate and direction of transport. It must not be forgotten however that the vascular anatomy plays a very important role, certainly in the control of the direction of transport. It cannot be too strongly emphasized that before a study is made on any particular species, the vascular anatomy of this species should be thoroughly worked out.

## References

BIDDULPH, O. and CORY, R. (1957). An analysis of translocation in the phloem of the bean plant using THO, $P^{32}$ and $C^{14}$. *Pl. Physiol., Lancaster* **32**, 608–614.

BOOTH, A., MOORBY, J., DAVIES, C. R., JONES, H. and WAREING, P. F. (1962). Effects of indolyl-3-acetic acid on the movement of nutrients within plants. *Nature, Lond.* **194**, 204–205.

CANNY, M. J. (1960). The rate of translocation. *Biol. Rev.* **35**, 507–532.

CHEN, S. L. (1951). Simultaneous movement of $^{32}$P and $^{14}$C in opposite directions in phloem tissue. *Am. J. Bot.* **88**, 203–211.

DAVIES, C. R. and WAREING, P. F. (1965). Auxin-directed transport of radiophosphorus in plant stems. *Planta* **65**, 139–156.

ESCHRICH, W. (1967). Bidirectionelle translokation in Siebröhren. *Planta* **73**, 37–49.

HARTT, C. E., KORTSCHAK, H. P. and BURR, G. O. (1964). Effects of defoliation, deradication and darkening the blade upon translocation of $C^{14}$ in sugar cane. *Pl. Physiol., Lancaster* **39**, 15–22.

HO, L. C. and PEEL, A. J. (1969). Investigation of bidirectional movement of tracers in sieve tubes of *Salix viminalis* L. *Ann. Bot.* **33**, 833–844.

HOAD, G. V. and PEEL, A. J. (1965). Studies on the movement of solutes between the sieve tubes and surrounding tissues in willow. I. Interference between solutes and rate of translocation measurements. *J. exp. Bot.* **16**, 433–451.

LEPP, N. W. and PEEL, A. J. (1970). Some effects of IAA and kinetin upon the movement of sugars in the phloem of willow. *Planta* **90**, 230–235.

LEPP, N. W. and PEEL, A. J. (1971a). Patterns of translocation and metabolism of $^{14}$C-labelled IAA in the phloem of willow. *Planta* **96**, 62–73.

LEPP, N. W. and PEEL, A. J. (1971b). Influence of I.A.A. upon the longitudinal and tangential movement of labelled sugars in the phloem of willow. *Planta* **97**, 50–61.

MASON, T. G. and MASKELL, E. J. (1928). Studies on the transport of carbohydrates in the cotton plant. II. The factors determining the rate and direction of movement of sugars. *Ann. Bot. O.S.* **42**, 571–636.

MILTHORPE, F. L. and MOORBY, J. (1969). Vascular transport and its significance in plant growth. *A. Rev. Pl. Physiol.* **20**, 117–138.

MOORBY, J. (1968). The effects of growth substances on transport in plants. *In* "The Transport of Plant Hormones" (Y. Vardar, ed.), pp. 192–206. New Holland Publishing Co., Amsterdam.

NELSON, C. D. and GORHAM, P. G. (1957). Translocation of radioactive sugars in stems of soybean seedlings. *Can. J. Bot.* **35**, 703–713.

PALMQUIST, E. H. (1938). The simultaneous movement of carbohydrate and fluorescein in opposite directions in the phloem. *Am. J. Bot.* **24**, 97–105.

PEEL, A. J. (1963). The movement of ions from the xylem solution into the sieve tubes of willow. *J. exp. Bot.* **14**, 438–447.

PEEL, A. J. (1964). Tangential movement of $^{14}$C-labelled assimilates in stems of willow. *J. exp. Bot.* **15**, 104–113.

PEEL, A. J. and FORD, J. (1968). The movement of sugars into the sieve elements of bark strips of willow. II. Evidence for two pathways from the bathing solution. *J. exp. Bot.* **19**, 370–380.

PEEL, A. J. and HO, L. C. (1970). Colony size of *Tuberolachnus salignus* Gmelin in relation to mass transport of $^{14}$C-labelled assimilates from the leaves in willow. *Physiologia Pl.* **23,** 1033–1038.

PHILLIS, E. and MASON, T. G. (1936). Further studies on transport in the cotton plant. IV. On the simultaneous movement of solutes in opposite directions through the phloem. *Ann. Bot. O.S.* **50,** 161–174.

SETH, A. and WAREING, P. F. (1967). Hormone directed transport of metabolites and their possible role in plant senescence. *J. exp. Bot.* **18,** 67–77.

SWANSON, C. A. and WHITNEY, J. B. (1953). The translocation of foliar applied phosphorus-32 and other radioisotopes in bean plants. *Am. J. Bot.* **40,** 816–823.

THAINE, R., OVENDEN, S. L. and TURNER, J. S. (1959). Translocation of labelled assimilates in the soybean. *Aust. J. biol. Sci.* **12,** 349–372.

THROWER, S. L. (1965). Translocation of labelled assimilates in the soybean. IV. The effect of temperature on transport. *Aust. J. biol. Sci.* **18,** 449–461.

TRIP, P. and GORHAM, P. G. (1968). Bidirectional translocation of sugars in sieve tubes of squash plants. *Pl. Physiol., Lancaster* **43,** 877–882.

TRIP, P., NELSON, C. D. and KROTKOV, G. (1965). Selective and preferential translocation of $^{14}$C-labelled sugars in white ash and lilac. *Pl. Physiol., Lancaster* **40,** 740–747.

WARDLAW, I. F. (1967). The effect of water stress on translocation in relation to photosynthesis and growth. I. Effect during grain development in wheat. *Aust. J. biol. Sci.* **20,** 25–39.

WEATHERLEY, P. E., PEEL, A. J. and HILL, G. P. (1959). The physiology of the sieve tube. Preliminary experiments using aphid mouth parts. *J. exp. Bot.* **10,** 1–16.

ZIMMERMANN, M. H. (1960). Transport in the phloem. *A. Rev. Pl. Physiol.* **11,** 167–190.

# Discussion

The discussion was mainly concerned with whether the aphid stylet technique gave results which were relevant to the normal translocation processes occurring within intact plants. Some contributors to the discussion felt that artefacts could be introduced as a result of the reduction in hydrostatic pressure which would follow puncture of a sieve tube, the injection of chemicals from the aphid stylet, and the bark stripping techniques employed, which might produce wound reactions. Others felt that the system was too far removed from the natural situation in which a plant organ was the sink for the translocated materials, particularly if transport was not by mass flow within the sieve tubes. In **Peel's** view the sieve tubes were not damaged by insertion of an aphid stylet and the stylet would act in a similar way to a passive sink on the plant. The possibility that chemicals were exuded from the aphid stylets was being investigated. **Sexton** questioned whether colony size was a measure of sink strength as there would normally only be one stylet in each sieve tube. Peel pointed out, however, that there was interference between sieve tubes and, moreover, material could be drawn into the sieve tubes from the surrounding storage cells. Thus when the *density* of aphids was increased (i.e. a large colony had more aphids per unit area) the storage capacity could not meet this added requirement and the source of carbon was shifted towards the leaves.

# Section IV

# Internal Control Mechanisms

# IV.1. Internal control mechanisms: Introduction

J. F. SUTCLIFFE

*School of Biological Sciences, University of Sussex, England*

A plant is an intricate self-regulating system which responds rapidly and effectively to changes in its environment. The effects of unfavourable conditions such as extremes of temperature, low light intensity or water stress on the structure and function of plants and on their life-histories, have been studied extensively, but the underlying mechanisms which control these responses are still far from clear.

Control of metabolism is exerted by enzyme systems which regulate specific pathways, such as the Krebs cycle, glycolysis and the pentose phosphate pathway. The activity of individual enzymes may in turn be controlled by the rates of synthesis and breakdown of the enzyme molecules, or by changes in their configuration induced, for example, by changes of pH or redox potential or by accumulation of reaction products. Alternatively, enzyme activity may be regulated by alteration in position of the enzyme within a cell which may affect the availability of substrate or of essential co-factors. Although there is evidence from biochemical studies— some of it from plant materials—that such controlling influences operate in cells, it has rarely been possible yet to relate the activity of a specific enzyme, and still less the intensity of a metabolic process, to a particular controlling factor. The clearest case is perhaps that of nitrate reductase activity during the induction phase in young seedlings which appears to be controlled by the quantity of enzyme present. In certain circumstances photosynthesis seems to be regulated by the activity of a single enzyme, ribulose 1.5 diphosphate carboxylase, but the mechanism whereby this activity is controlled is still obscure. In my laboratory, a close correlation has been observed between the amounts of certain key enzymes of the Krebs cycle, glycolytic and pentose phosphate pathways in different regions of young pea roots, and the relative importance of these pathways in respiratory metabolism in each region. On the other hand, Varner (1965) has shown that the NADP requiring isocitrate dehydrogenase activity of the cotyledons of germinating *Vigna sesquipedalis* seedlings appears to be limited by the low concentration of NADP in the cells. The level of the co-enzyme is determined by another enzyme NAD kinase. Varner suggested that the cells may control isocitrate dehydrogenase activity by regulating the levels of both enzyme and co-enzyme. Sartirana and Bianchetti (1967) have proposed a mechanism for the control of phytic acid hydrolysis in wheat embryos through regulation of phytase activity by the level of inorganic phosphate, and we have shown recently (Guardiola and Sutcliffe, 1971) that the same regulatory process may also operate in pea cotyledons.

One of the outstanding achievements of plant physiologists during the past half century has been the identification of specific hormonal substances which regulate growth. Environmental stimuli such as light, gravity and water stress appear to exert their characteristic effects through an influence on the concentrations of various growth stimulants and inhibitors including auxins, gibberellins, kinins and abscisins. Besides controlling growth, these substances may regulate other physiological processes—either indirectly, as when stimulation of growth facilitates absorption of water and mineral salts, or directly as Wright will explain later in this programme.

Although we now have a great deal of information about the effects of growth regulators on plants, the basis of their action is still unknown. Early in the study of auxins it was conceived that these substances might activate a key enzyme or enzymes controlling the metabolic processes that lead to growth. Attempts to demonstrate effects of auxins and other growth regulators on enzyme systems *in vitro* have been unsuccessful, while some *in vivo* effects e.g. on cellulase can be interpreted to be a consequence of growth stimulation or inhibition rather than the reverse. The level of activity of several of the hydrolytic enzymes of the aleurone cells of germinating grass seedlings is under the control of gibberellic acid produced by the embryo. Activation of $\beta$ amylase in germinating wheat and barley grains by gibberellic acid involves reduction of disulphide bonds by means of which the inactive enzyme is bound to storage proteins in the endosperm cells. In the case of $\alpha$ amylase *de novo* synthesis of enzyme is involved.

As a result of such studies the idea is now gaining ground that growth regulators exert their primary effect by controlling enzyme synthesis or activation—probably through the intermediacy of messenger RNA. It is evident that the course of plant development is regulated continually, on the one hand by genetic information emanating from cell nuclei, and on the other by the balance of growth regulating substances, and that the two control systems are closely linked. The picture emerges of a sensitive control mechanism in which the synthesis of specific molecules of messenger RNA controlled by both genetic and hormonal factors leads to development of particular enzyme activities which in turn determine metabolic patterns and growth. Environmental factors may exert their effects on this system either directly e.g. through the provision of respiratory substrates, or indirectly through regulation of growth substance levels.

## References

GUARDIOLA, J. L. and SUTCLIFFE, J. F. (1971). Mobilization of Phosphorus in the cotyledons of young seedlings of the garden pea (*Pisum sativum*, L.). *Ann. Bot.* **35**, 809–823.

SARTIRANA, M. L. and BIANCHETTI, R. (1967). The effects of phosphate on the development of phytase in the wheat embryo. *Physiologia Pl.* **20**, 1066–1075.

VARNER, J. E. (1965). Enzymes. *In* "Plant Biochemistry" (J., Bonnre and J. E. Varner, eds), pp, 14–20. Academic Press, New York.

# IV.2. Biochemical limitations to photosynthetic rates

K. J. TREHARNE

*Welsh Plant Breeding Station, Aberystwyth, Wales*

## I. Introduction

The photosynthetic process involves many stages between the diffusion of atmospheric carbon dioxide into a leaf and its ultimate fixation into organic carbon in the chloroplast, and a complicated problem exists in attempting to evaluate the relative importance of any single component in this multi-step sequence. The rate of assimilation of carbon dioxide that a leaf may attain in a given environment is a function of a number of basic characteristics of the system. Gaseous carbon dioxide diffuses from the boundary layer through the stomata into the intercellular spaces and then dissolves and moves through the mesophyll aqueous films across cell membranes and cytoplasm to the carboxylation site in the chloroplast. The relative significance of the resistances to the flow of carbon dioxide through stomatal pores and through the leaf intercellular spaces, the "mesophyll resistance" (Penman, 1942), has been the subject of a number of reports (Gaastra, 1959, 1962; Slatyer and Bierhuizen, 1964; Holmgren *et al.*, 1965; Meidner, 1967). The passage of carbon dioxide through the liquid phase is not entirely a diffusion process, being aided by streaming (Meidner and Mansfield, 1968; Heath, 1969) and by chemical action (Barrs, 1968). The final stages, at the molecular level, include the efficiency of the photochemical reactions and the activity of a number of enzymatically catalysed reactions. Although the various components which affect the rate of carbon dioxide diffusion through the leaf may be regarded in terms of resistance, by analogy to Ohm's Law of electrical resistance, this approach is clearly inadequate when dealing with enzyme-catalysed chemical reactions, which can only be defined in kinetic terms. However, for the sake of convenience, the component processes which may act as rate-controlling steps in carbon assimilation will be referred to as resistances in the ensuing discussion.

A great deal of information is now available on leaf physical properties and photosynthetic rate and, without question, stomatal, mesophyll and liquid-phase "resistances" may each be significant rate-controlling steps in the overall sequence of carbon assimilation. A number of mathematical models have been put forward to attempt to evaluate these factors (Koller and Samish, 1964; Laisk, 1968; Chartier, 1969) but the relative importance of any component can vary with genotype and environmental conditions. As Laisk (1969) points out, since the conclusions of Gaastra (1959, 1962) concerning the concentration of carbon dioxide at the chloroplast carboxylating site, the significance of the role of the carboxylation step as a rate-determining process tends to have been underestimated.

I intend to confine subsequent discussion to the significance of the chemical processes as rate-determining steps in photosynthesis. The following sections cite evidence derived from a series of separate investigations, largely on forage crops, which deal, in the main, with the role of the photochemical and carboxylation reactions as possible determinants of photosynthetic rate of leaves.

# II. Genetic variation in photosynthesis and chloroplast activity

Recent studies have drawn attention to the wide range in maximum net photosynthesis attained by single leaves of different genotypes at light saturation and normal carbon dioxide concentration (e.g. Wilson and Cooper, 1969). However, information concerning the extent of genetic variation in biochemical activities in higher plants has been notably lacking. Biochemical studies have been devoted principally towards establishing the qualitative nature and operation of factors which influence the photochemical steps and the component enzymes involved in the subsequent fixation of carbon dioxide.

Populations of ryegrass, selected by Wilson and Cooper (1967) to exhibit a range of photosynthetic activity, were investigated in terms of chloroplast activity. Hill-reaction and PMS-mediated phosphorylation of isolated chloroplasts were compared with photosynthetic activity of the leaves, determined both by a closed-system manometric technique (Wilson et al., 1969) and infrared gas analysis (De Jager, 1968). Chloroplasts were isolated from leaves of plants grown at 15°C in a 16 h photoperiod of 70 Wm$^{-2}$ irradiance in the wavelength interval 300–700 nm and photochemical activities were determined. The data, shown in Table I, revealed

**Table I**

Variation in photosynthesis and chloroplast activity of *Lolium* populations. Plants grown at 15°C, 16 h, 70 Wm⁻² irradiance (300–700 nm)

| Population No. | Origin | Leaf Photosynthesis litres $O_2$ min⁻¹cm⁻² | Hill activity mole FeCN h⁻¹ mg⁻¹ chlor | cm⁻² area $10^{-2}$ | PMS-Phosphorylation mole ATP h⁻¹ mg⁻¹ chlor | cm⁻² area $10^{-2}$ | RuDiPc activity ¹⁴C-dpm min⁻¹ mg⁻¹ protein $10^{-6}$ | cm⁻² area $10^{-4}$ |
|---|---|---|---|---|---|---|---|---|
| Ba 8283 | Spain | 2.00 | 190 | 45.0 | 183 | 43.6 | 34 | 68.2 |
| Ba 8408 | Spain | 1.94 | 159 | 39.8 | 154 | 38.5 | 82 | 67.8 |
| Ba 8319 | Macedonia | 1.82 | 198 | 49.5 | 180 | 45.0 | 84 | 65.0 |
| Ba 8182 | Germany | 1.70 | 191 | 45.5 | 305 | 72.6 | 93 | 55.8 |
| Ba 8169 | Canada | 1.49 | 180 | 42.9 | 367 | 87.4 | 83 | 58.6 |
| Ba 8341/1 | Netherlands | 1.34 | 171 | 46.2 | 188 | 50.8 | 47 | 48.5 |
| Ba 8341/2 | Netherlands | 1.31 | 236 | 63.8 | 136 | 36.8 | 36 | 51.5 |
| L.S.D. 5% | | 0.43 | 42 | 10.1 | 74 | 19.2 | 26 | 9.1 |

a wide range of genetic variation in both Hill activity and PMS-phosphorylation in the populations, when expressed in terms of either chlorophyll content or unit leaf areas. Photosynthetic rates of the leaves of the different populations showed a wide variation (see Wilson and Cooper, 1967) but there was no evident relationship between these *in vitro* chloroplast activities and leaf photosynthesis. Björkman (1968b) has reported differences in the electron transport system of chloroplasts of sun and shade ecotypes of *Solidago virgaurea*, and varietal differences in photophosphorylation in barley (Kleese, 1966) and maize (Miflin and Hageman, 1966) have also been demonstrated, although the latter studies did not include measurements of leaf photosynthesis.

Monteith (1965) suggested that the carboxylating resistance may well assume rate-limiting values when both light and carbon dioxide are abundant. The significant observations of Björkman (1966, 1968a) that the activity of the carboxylating enzyme, ribulose 1,5-diphosphate carboxylase (RuDiPc) (carboxydismutase), was closely related to the rate of light-saturated photosynthesis in *Solidago virgaurea* gave impetus to investigation of the role of the chemical resistances and rate-controlling reactions. Björkman pointed out that careful studies were necessary to determine whether the differences in enzyme activity observed were direct genetic differences in the capacity for enzyme synthesis, or whether these differences were attributable to modifications in enzyme conformation.

Comparative studies of RuDiPc activity were carried out on the ryegrass populations previously investigated in terms of photochemical capacity of the chloroplasts. The data shown in Table I indicate a range in RuDiPc activity of some $40\%$ when expressed on a leaf area basis but almost a factor of 3 in terms of unit soluble protein. The relative pattern of enzyme activity in the different populations varies markedly according to the basis of expression. There is no evident relationship between leaf photosynthesis per unit leaf area and RuDiPc activity per unit of soluble protein, attributable, in part, to variation in composition of the soluble protein of the different populations. A high correlation ($r = 0.94$, $P > 0.001$) was, however, obtained between photosynthetic rate and activity of the enzyme when both were expressed on the same basis, viz. unit of leaf area.

This same relationship was also found in a further study of bred varieties of ryegrass (*Lolium perenne* and *Lolium multiflorum*) and is presented in Fig. 1. A wide range in activity is seen in the *L. perenne* varieties, whereas there was no significant difference within the *L. multiflorum* varieties which had lower photosynthetic activities when expressed in terms of leaf area. RuDiPc activity also correlates highly with light-saturated photosynthesis in seedling leaves ($r = 0.79$, $P > 0.01$) and flag leaves

($r = 0.89$, $P > 0.001$) of different cereal varieties (Treharne, Lloyd and Lawes, unpublished).

Our studies of relationships between leaf photosynthesis and enzyme activities have not been confined to the carboxylation reaction. Six varieties of *Lolium* were selected for further intensive study and are currently being investigated for combined physiological, biochemical and genetic studies of photosynthesis and its component processes (W.P.B.S. Jubilee Report, 1970).

The activities of RuDiPc, phosphoglycerate kinase, triosephosphate

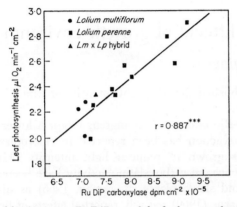

**Fig. 1.** Relationship between RuDiPc and leaf photosynthesis in varieties of *Lolium*.

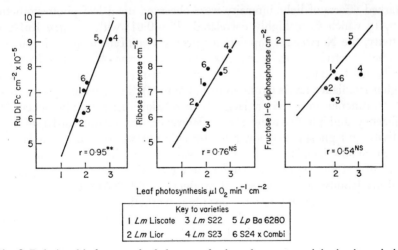

**Fig. 2.** Relationship between leaf photosynthesis and enzyme activity in six varieties of *Lolium*.

dehydrogenase (NADP dependent), fructose diphosphatase, transketolase, ribose-5-phosphate isomerase and phosphoribulokinase were assayed simultaneously from leaf homogenates of the six populations grown at 15 °C in a 16 h photoperiod of 70 $Wm^{-2}$. The relationship between three of the enzyme activities and photosynthesis is shown in Fig. 2 and a high correlation is again evident for RuDiPc. However, although high RuDiPc activity was generally associated with high activity of the other enzymes investigated, no significant overall relationship of these other enzymes with photosynthesis was observed in the populations grown in this particular environment.

# III. Effects of growth environment

## A. Light regime

It is well established that the light intensity at which a plant develops has a marked effect on its photosynthetic characteristics (Böhning and Burnside, 1956; Björkman and Holmgren, 1966). A lower light-saturated rate of the Hill reaction has been reported in chloroplasts of *Teucrium scorodonia* plants grown in reduced light intensity (Mousseau et al., 1967) and differences in carboxylating activity have been clearly demonstrated in sun and shade plants (Björkman, 1966) as discussed earlier. Eagles and Treharne (1969) recently reported effects of light intensity on the photosynthetic components of two contrasting natural populations of cocksfoot (*Dactylis glomerata*), one from Portugal and one from Norway. Marked effects of light intensity were observed upon leaf photosynthetic activity which were highly correlated ($P > 0.01$) with in vitro RuDiPc activity, the Norwegian population showing significant increase in photosynthetic activity with increasing irradiance (from 48 to 144 $Wm^{-2}$), whilst the Portuguese population showed a marked increase only over the higher irradiance levels (from 96 to 144 $Wm^{-2}$). The data analysed across all treatments indicated a lack of correlation between photochemical efficiency and photosynthetic rate. However, the relative order of Hill activity and phosphorylation rates by chloroplasts from the populations grown at low irradiance (48 $Wm^{-2}$) was reflected in the respective patterns of leaf photosynthesis. Under these conditions the limited formation and availability of photochemical products (ATP, NADPH) are likely to impose significant limitations on photosynthetic activity and support Gaastra's (1962) suggestion that the efficiency of light utilization at low irradiance is probably the rate-determining process.

Differential responses to photoperiod are also a feature of these contrasting populations (Eagles, 1967) and we have found a strong relationship between RuDiPc and photosynthesis when photoperiod is the major environmental variable (Treharne and Eagles, unpublished).

## B. Temperature regime

Effects of temperature on photosynthesis in forage grasses have been recently reviewed by Cooper and Tainton (1968) but these effects have been mainly concerned with temperature responses of leaves grown in a single temperature regime. The photosynthetic characteristics of two populations of cocksfoot from contrasting climatic origins, Norway and Portugal, were investigated with two aims in mind (Treharne and Eagles, 1970), (a) to study effects of growth temperature, which could affect both leaf physical properties and photosynthetic capacity at the biochemical level, and (b) to measure short-term effects of analysis temperature which might affect rate of physical diffusion (e.g. stomatal aperture) and would, unquestionably, affect rate of the chemical reactions. Transpiration rates, taken as an indication of "resistance" to physical diffusion, were closely related to leaf photosynthetic rates, but activity of the carboxylation reaction, closely paralleled with the rate of photosynthesis in the two populations at all the analysis temperatures, was, clearly, a factor in determining the photosynthetic activity. Short-term exposure to different temperatures has only a small effect on the rate of the diffusive process (Gaastra, 1959). Marked differences in the efficiency of both Hill reaction and phosphorylation between the two populations were observed. In this growth temperature study, photochemical activities expressed on a unit leaf area basis were highly correlated with the photosynthetic activity of the leaves ($r = 0.92$, $P > 0.001$). A degree of phenotypic plasticity was observed, in that plants responded relatively better when analysed at the temperature at which they were grown, than when analysed at other temperatures. This was reflected in the temperature response curves of the isolated carboxylases, the Norwegian performing relatively better at low temperature than the Portuguese. Similar physiological adaptation in Hill reaction of *Deschampsia caespitosa* has been reported for contrasting climatic races (Tieszen and Helgager, 1968).

# IV. Effects of defoliation and application of hormones

Wareing *et al.* (1968) demonstrated enhanced photosynthetic rates in *Phaseolus vulgaris* and *Zea mays* following partial defoliation treatment. Immediate increases in photosynthesis were also obtained after application of gibberellic acid and cytokinins, and similar effects occur in *Trifolium pratense* (Treharne and Stoddart, 1968). The increases in light-saturated photosynthesis in both these defoliation and hormone treatments were closely paralleled by enhanced specific activity of the photosynthetic carboxylating enzymes, in the respective experiments. The defoliation treatments and application of cytokinins have similar effects and were explained in terms of reduced competition for root cytokinins. Meidner (1969) has subsequently discussed these effects in relation to decreased stomatal resistance following such treatments and concluded "that the rate of carbon dioxide assimilation improves because of an improved carboxylation capacity, which contributes towards increasing stomatal apertures which in turn may further improve photosynthetic rate", thus substantiating the views of Wareing *et al.* (1968). More recently Neales *et al.* (1971) have re-examined the photosynthetic characteristics of *Phaseolus* leaves after defoliation treatment, in terms of both the diffusive resistance and enzyme activity. In a kinetic study carried out for four days after defoliation, a strong association between net photosynthesis and activity of RuDiPc ($r = 0.88$) was again evident, supporting the original findings of Wareing *et al.* (1968). The activities of other photosynthetic and non-photosynthetic enzymes were also affected by defoliation but were not as highly correlated with photosynthetic rate. Using the method of Chartier *et al.* (1970) to separate component resistances, the effect of stomatal resistance under these conditions was negligible, the increase in photosynthetic rate being highly correlated ($r = 0.996$, $P < 0.001$) with the residual resistance which includes the carboxylation and liquid diffusive resistances. Separation of the latter two resistances was not possible, but since Rackham (1967) and Chartier *et al.* (1970) have reported that the liquid diffusive resistance shows relatively little variation in *Impatiens parviflora* and *Phaseolus* respectively, it was concluded that the carboxylation step accounted for the major part of the change in the residual resistance, and, therefore, constituted the rate-determining process in that particular situation. The defoliation treatment delayed the loss in activity of RuDiPc, which normally occurs with the onset of senescence, resulting in a much higher relative photosynthetic activity than in untreated plants. Woolhouse (1967) has also reported increases in photosynthesis following partial defoliation of *Perilla frutescens*, which were paralleled by enhanced RuDiPc activity.

# V. Photosynthesis in plants with the C-4 dicarboxylic acid pathway

A great deal of interest in comparative studies of photosynthesis was stimulated by the discovery of a new pathway, referred to as the $\beta$-carboxylation or C-4 pathway, in certain tropical Gramineae such as sugar cane and maize (Kortschak, 1965; Hatch and Slack, 1966) and in certain species of Amaranthaceae and Chenopodiaceae (Johnson and Hatch, 1968). Whereas the primary photosynthetic carboxylation in temperate (C-3) plants is presumed to be catalysed by RuDiPc with phosphoglycerate as the primary product, in the C-4 plants the enzyme phospho-enol-pyruvate (PEP) carboxylase is implicated in $\beta$-carboxylation photosynthesis and the initial products of C-fixation are oxaloacetate, malate and aspartate rather than phosphoglycerate (Hatch *et al.*, 1967). In the early studies of Hatch's group, the activity of PEP carboxylase in the C-4 plants was shown to be very high, whereas only very low or negligible activity of RuDiPc was reported, leading to the tentative conclusion that the Calvin cycle was inoperative (Slack and Hatch, 1967).

However, in a comparative study of temperature responses in Panicoid and Festucoid grasses, Treharne and Cooper (1969) reported significant activity of RuDiPc in both *Zea mays* and varieties of *Cenchrus ciliaris*, as well as high PEP carboxylase activity. This was subsequently confirmed by Björkman and Gauhl (1969) in six species containing the C-4 pathway, and it was demonstrated by differential extraction techniques that the early reports of absence of RuDiPc were attributable to the compartmentation of RuDiPc in the vascular bundle-sheath cells in these species, with consequent difficulty in extraction of the enzyme. Downton *et al.* (1969) and Björkman *et al.* (1971) have recently reviewed characteristics of $\beta$-carboxylation photosynthesis and have postulated that PEP carboxylase catalyses the initial $\beta$-carboxylation in the mesophyll cells with subsequent transfer of the fixed carbon dioxide to the bundle-sheath cells where the carboxylated compound may be decarboxylated and refixed by RuDiPc. Björkman *et al.* (1970) has suggested that the activity of RuDiPc could limit photosynthetic activity even in plants with the C-4 dicarboxylic acid pathway.

The relative proportions of RuDiPc and PEP carboxylases in a number of species have been studied (Treharne and Neales, 1971) including members of the genus *Panicum* in which different functional patterns in photosynthesis have already been demonstrated (Downton *et al.*, 1969).

Carboxylase activities were assayed at their respective optimal tem-

**Table II**

Activities of ribulose diphosphate (RuDiP) and phospho(enol) pyruvate (PEP) carboxylases in temperate and tropical Gramineae

Plants grown at 25°C, carboxylases assayed at 25° and 35°C

| Species | RuDiP | | PEP | | RuDiP/PEP | |
|---|---|---|---|---|---|---|
| | 25° | 35° | 25° | 35° | 25° | 35° |
| *Zea mays* | 4·9 | 6·3 | 24·5 | 32·6 | 0·5 | 0·2 |
| *Cenchrus ciliaris* | 2·1 | 1·7 | 3·4 | 5·9 | 0·6 | 0·3 |
| *Panicum coloratum* | 0·9 | 0·7 | 4·6 | 13·5 | 0·2 | 0·2 |
| *Panicum miloides* | 4·1 | 3·8 | 8·9 | 22·8 | 0·4 | 0·2 |
| *Panicum meyerianum* | 10·6 | 12·2 | 13·2 | 25·7 | 0·8 | 0·5 |
| *Panicum miliaceum* | 1·4 | 1·7 | 12·2 | 14·9 | 0·1 | 0·1 |
| *Panicum bisulcatum* | 3·8 | 4·5 | 1·0 | 1·1 | 3·8 | 4·0 |
| *Lolium perenne* (S23) | 3·8 | 2·6 | 0·9 | 0·8 | 4·2 | 3·3 |
| *Avena sativa* ("Marvellous") | 5·8 | 5·2 | 2·1 | 3·5 | 2·8 | 1·5 |
| *Triticum aestivum* ("Kolibri") | 4·1 | 3·9 | 1·8 | 2·1 | 2·3 | 1·8 |
| *Hordeum vulgare* ("Zephyr") | 3·1 | 3·0 | 0·8 | 0·9 | 3·9 | 3·3 |
| *Dactylis glomerata* (grown 8°C) | 6·2 | 5·7 | 1·8 | 2·0 | 3·4 | 2·9 |

perature and pH conditions which have been shown to be significantly different (Treharne and Cooper, 1969) and the data are shown in Table II. The tropical (Panicoid) and temperate (Festucoid) species examined all contained significant RuDiPc activity, but the Festucoid species contained relatively less PEP carboxylase than the Panicoid species, and only the latter showed the vascular-bundle sheath anatomy characteristic of plants with β-carboxylation. *P. bisulcatum* was atypical and had the same order of activities as the Festucoid species. These investigations will be described in full elsewhere.

# VI. Endogenous rhythms in chloroplast activity

## A. Photochemical reactions

An endogenous rhythm in Hill-reaction activity of isolated tomato chloroplasts was reported by Hoffman and Miller (1966). The Hill activity of chloroplasts isolated from populations of ryegrass and oats was, therefore, investigated at various intervals during the light period. Seedlings were germinated and maintained in a controlled environment at 15 °C with a photoperiod of 16 h provided by "warm-white" fluorescent tubes giving an incident irradiance of 70 Wm$^{-2}$. Hill activity, in terms of reduction of ferricyanide per unit of chlorophyll, was determined as described previously (Treharne and Eagles, 1969). The data obtained revealed a marked variation during the light period with a significant depression in the rate approximately in the middle of the light period.

Similar studies of rates of *in vitro* phenazine-methosulphate (PMS) mediated photophosphorylation indicated a similar endogenous rhythm in activity of isolated chloroplasts (Treharne, unpublished).

## B. Carbon assimilation

Rhythms in net photosynthesis of higher plants have been demonstrated (Rabinowitch, 1951), and rhythms of considerable magnitude in stomatal aperture (Meidner and Mansfield, 1965) could contribute significantly to these rhythms in carbon assimilation. Intensive investigations (Wilkins, 1959, 1960) have been carried out into rhythms of carbon dioxide fixation in Crassulaceae.

The possible occurrence of a rhythm in RuDiPc activity in two closely related species of ryegrass was investigated. *Lolium perenne* (S23) and *Lolium multiflorum* (S22) were grown in environments where all major factors were held as constant as possible. Two different daylengths, one of

8 h and the other of 16 h, both with incident irradiance of 70 Wm$^{-2}$ and constant 20°C were studied. Activity of RuDiPc was measured at hourly intervals for four days, the activity of the enzyme being determined within 15 min of homogenizing the leaf tissue. Enzyme activity was significantly different in the two populations studied in the shorter day-length, but no difference in rhythm was observed between populations in the respective environments (Fig. 3). The endogenous rhythms in carboxylating enzyme activity however, had different wavelengths but not frequencies, in the two daylengths; in both environments, following an initial peak after the dark period, there was a significant trough in activity which corresponded approximately to the middle of the photoperiods.

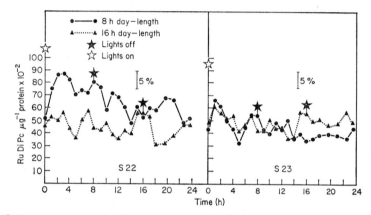

**Fig. 3.** Endogenous rhythm in two varieties of *Lolium* in an 8 h and 16 h daylength.

These rhythms cannot be explained in terms of turnover of enzyme-protein, nor in terms of differences in pH of the system which was adequately buffered in extraction of enzyme (Eagles and Treharne, 1969). They may be ascribed to some form of enzyme activation, possibly attributable to reversible oxidation-reduction of the SH groups known to be associated with RuDiPc (Sugiyama and Azakawa, 1967).

It has been recently observed that RuDiPc activity shows an endogenous rhythm in *Gonyaulax* (Sweeney, 1969) and a similar biphasic rhythm during the photoperiod in RuDiPc activity is also evident in *Phaseolus vulgaris* (Pughe, Treharne and Wareing, unpublished). Furthermore, Jones and Mansfield (1970) have reported a marked circadian rhythm in the carbon dioxide compensation point in *Coffea arabica* grown in a closely controlled constant environment. Interestingly, the level of carbon dioxide compensation point showed a trough in the middle of the light period which was not caused by rhythms in stomatal aperture. It was suggested by

Jones and Mansfield that these rhythms probably arose from a variation in carboxylation efficiency, in photorespiratory activity, or in both. The data discussed would, therefore, seem to implicate the likely role of the carboxylating enzyme in this phenomenon. From a practical point of view, when comparative studies of chloroplast activities are undertaken, especially when different growth regimes are employed, it is clearly necessary, in the first instance, to ascertain possible environment–genotype interactions before selecting suitable sampling times for analysis of activity of various component processes.

Although no simultaneous investigation of enzyme activity and photosynthetic rate of leaves has, as yet, been carried out, Charles-Edwards (unpublished) has made a recent infrared gas analysis study of S22 grown in a 16 h photoperiod. A fairly constant activity, with fluctuations of about 10% was observed over the initial 6 h of the light period followed by a sharp decline in net photosynthesis halfway (8 h) through the light period. Since no significant variation in stomatal resistance was observed it may well be that the pattern of photosynthesis during the day is significantly determined by rhythms in the carboxylating and photochemical activities.

# VII. Heritability and seasonal fluctuation of RuDiPc activity

The investigations described in the earlier sections demonstrate that genetic variation in photosynthesis between varieties exists, often related to variation in the activity of the carboxylating process. From the point of view of its potential use in a selection programme it is necessary to determine the heritability of the carboxylation enzyme activity and its stability in varying environments.

A 6 × 6 half-diallel cross, performed by Wilson and Cooper (1969) between contrasting genotypes of *Lolium perenne* provided suitable material for a genetic study, including estimation of heritabilities. The relationship between the RuDiPc activity in the $F_1$ progeny and the mid-parent value is shown in Fig. 4(a). A high heritability of enzyme activity ($r = 0.70$) was evident and corresponded with the heritability of light-saturated photosynthesis ($r = 0.71$) found by Wilson and Cooper (1969). A subsequent interpopulation diallel cross involving 3 populations each of *L. perenne* and *L. multiflorum* was also analysed for RuDiPc activity and the corresponding parent-progeny regression is presented in Fig. 4(b). A reasonably high heritability ($r = 0.44$) was obtained for enzyme activity expressed per unit soluble protein, and was of the same order when

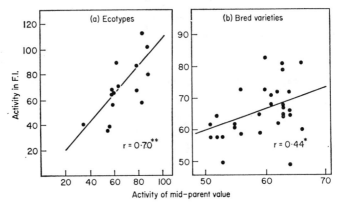

**Fig. 4.** Parent–progeny relationship in *Lolium* F$_1$ RuDiPc activity per unit soluble protein.

expressed on a leaf weight or area basis. The heritability of light-saturated photosynthesis in the interpopulation diallel was also of the same order ($r = 0.50$). The higher value obtained in the first investigation is partly attributable to the use of crosses between clonal parents rather than between outbreeding populations as in the latter study.

The seasonal variation in activity of RuDiPc in a number of grass species grown in field swards was investigated from April 1970 to April 1971. The relative patterns of activity of three of the species, *L. perenne*, *D. glomerata* and *F. arundinacea*, shown in Fig. 5 was very similar in all

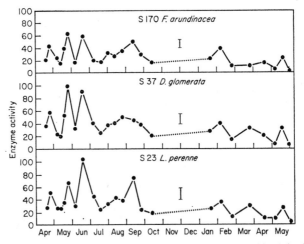

**Fig. 5.** Seasonal variations in RuDiPc (mg$^{-1}$ dry weight $\times$ 10$^{-3}$) in 3 species of Gramineae.

species and the different species maintained their relative order of activity through the season.

Since RuDiPc activity shows significant additive heritability and the differences between species remain relatively stable through the season, it clearly provides a usable criterion for selection. It remains to be seen how far selection for increased activity of the carboxylation step can increase overall photosynthetic activity.

# VIII. General conclusions

In all the investigations described, including those of genetic variation, the effects of growth regimes and effects of defoliation and growth regulator applications, the activity of the carboxylating enzyme ribulose diphosphate carboxylase shows a marked correlation with the photosynthetic rate of the leaf, and would, therefore, seem to constitute a significant rate-controlling factor in the overall process of carbon dioxide assimilation by the plant.

# Acknowledgements

I thank Professor P. T. Thomas, C.B.E., for his interest and for providing the facilities for this research. I am indebted to Dr J. P. Cooper for his constant invaluable advice and to my colleagues Drs C. F. Eagles, J. L. Stoddart and T. F. Neales for their ready collaboration. I also wish to thank Professor P. F. Wareing for his stimulating interest and collaboration, and E. J. Lloyd and Miss J. W. Davies for excellent technical assistance.

# References

BARRS, H. D. (1968). Effect of cyclic variations in gas exchange under constant environmental conditions on the ratio of transpiration to net photosynthesis. *Physiologia Pl.* **21**, 918.

BJÖRKMAN, O. (1966). The effect of oxygen concentration on photosynthesis in higher plants. *Physiologia Pl.* **19**, 618–633.

BJÖRKMAN, O. (1968a). Further studies on differentiation of photosynthetic properties in sun and shade ecotypes of *Solidago virgaurea*. *Physiologia Pl.* **21**, 84–91.

BJÖRKMAN, O. (1968b). Carboxydismutase activity in shade-adapted and sun-adapted species of higher plants. *Physiologia Pl.* **21**, 1–8.

BJÖRKMAN, O. and GAUHL, E. (1969). Carboxydismutase activity in plants with and without β-Carboxylation Photosynthesis. *Planta* **88**, 197–203.

BJÖRKMAN, O. and HOLMGREN, P. (1966). Photosynthetic adaptation to light intensity in plants native to shaded and exposed habitats. *Physiologia Pl.* **19**, 854–859.

BJÖRKMAN, O., NOBS, M. A. and HIESEY, W. M. (1970). Growth, photosynthetic and biochemical responses of contrasting *Mimulus* clones to light intensity and temperature. *Yb. Carnegie Instn Wash.* **68,** 614–620.

BJÖRKMAN, O., PEARCY, R. W. and NOBS, M. A. (1971). Photosynthetic characteristics. *Yb. Carnegie Instn Wash.* **69,** 640–648.

BÖHNING, R. H. and BURNSIDE, C. A. (1956). The effect of light intensity on the rate of apparent photosynthesis in leaves of sun and shade plants. *Am. J. Bot.* **43,** 557–561.

CHARTIER, P. (1969). A model of $CO_2$ assimilation in the leaf. *In Proc. IBP/PP tech. meeting, Trebon, 1969* (I. Setlik, ed.), pp. 307–315. Centre for Agricultural Publishing & Documentation, Wageningen.

CHARTIER, P., CHARTIER, M. and CATSKY, J. (1970). Resistances for carbon dioxide diffusion and for carboxylation as factors in bean leaf photosynthesis. *Photosynthetica* **4,** 48–57.

COOPER, J. P. and TAINTON, N. M. (1968). Light and temperature requirements for the growth of tropical and temperate grasses. *Herb. Abstr.* **38,** 167–176.

DOWNTON, W., BERRY, J. and TREGUNNA, E. B. (1969). Photosynthesis: Temperate and tropical characteristics within a single grass genus. *Science, N.Y.* **163,** 78–79.

EAGLES, C. F. (1967). The effect of temperature on vegetative growth in climatic races of *Dactylis glomerata* in controlled environments. *Ann. Bot.* **31,** 31–39.

EAGLES, C. F. and TREHARNE, K. J. (1969). Photosynthetic activity of *Dactylis glomerata* L. in different light regimes. *Photosynthetica* **3,** 29–38.

GAASTRA, P. (1959). Photosynthesis of crop plants as influenced by light, carbon dioxide, temperature and stomatal diffusion resistance. *Meded. LandbHoogesch. Wageningen* **59** (13), 1–68.

GAASTRA, P. (1962). Photosynthesis of leaves and field crops. *Neth. J. agric. Sci.* **10,** 311.

HATCH, M. D. and SLACK, C. R. (1966). Photosynthesis by sugar cane leaves. A new carboxylation reaction and the pathway of sugar formation. *Biochem. J.* **101,** 103–111.

HATCH, M. D., SLACK, C. R. and JOHNSON, H. S. (1967). Further studies on a new pathway of photosynthetic carbon dioxide fixation in sugar cane, and its occurrence in other plant species. *Biochem. J.* **102,** 417–422.

HEATH, O. V. S. (1969). "The Physiological Aspects of Photosynthesis". Heinemann, London.

HOFFMAN, F. M. and MILLER, J. H. (1966). An endogenous rhythm in the Hill-reaction activity of tomato chloroplasts. *Am. J. Bot.* **53,** 543–548.

HOLMGREN, P., JARVIS, P. G. and JARVIS, M. S. (1965). Resistances to carbon dioxide and water vapour transfer in leaves of different plant species. *Physiologia Pl.* **18,** 557–573.

JAGER, J. M. DE (1968). "Carbon dioxide exchange and photosynthetic activity in forage grasses". Ph. D. Thesis, University College Wales.

JOHNSON, H. S. and HATCH, M. D. (1968). Distribution of the $C_4$-dicarboxylic acid pathway of photosynthesis and its occurrence in dicotyledonous plants. *Phytochemistry* **7**, 375–380.

JONES, M. B. and MANSFIELD, T. A. (1970). A circadian rhythm in the level of the carbon dioxide compensation point in Bryophyllum and Coffea. *J. exp. Bot.* **21**, 159–163.

KLEESE, R. A. (1966). Photophosphorylation in barley. *Crop Sci.* **6**, 524–527.

KOLLER, D. and SAMISH, Y. (1964). A null-point compensating system for simultaneous and continuous measurement of net photosynthesis and transpiration by controlled gas-stream analysis. *Bot. Gaz.* **125**, 81–88.

KORTSCHAK, H. P. (1965). Carbon dioxide fixation in sugar cane leaves. *Pl. Physiol., Lancaster* **40**, 209–213.

LAISK, A. (1968). *In* "Fotosintez i Produktivnost' Rastitiel' nogo pokrova", pp. 5–45. Akad. Nauk. Est. S.S.R.

LAISK, A. (1969). A model of leaf photosynthesis and photorespiration. *In Proc. IBP/PP tech. meeting, Trebon, 1969* (I. Setlik, ed.), pp. 295–306. Centre for Agricultural Publishing & Documentation, Wageningen.

MEIDNER, H. (1967). Further observations on the minimum intercellular space carbon dioxide concentration of maize leaves and the postulated roles of "photorespiration" and glycollate metabolism. *J. exp. Bot.* **18**, 177–185.

MEIDNER, H. (1969). "Rate limiting" resistances and photosynthesis. *Nature, Lond.* **222**, 876–877.

MEIDNER, H. (1970). Effects of photoperiodic induction and debudding in *Xanthium pennsylvanicum* and of partial defoliation in *Phaseolus vulgaris* on rates of net photosynthesis and stomatal conductances. *J. exp. Bot.* **21**, 164–169.

MEIDNER, H. and MANSFIELD, T. A. (1965). Stomatal responses to illumination. *Biol. Rev.* **40**, 483–509.

MEIDNER, H. and MANSFIELD, T. A. (1968). "Physiology of Stomata". McGraw-Hill, London.

MIFLIN, B. J. and HAGEMAN, R. H. (1966). Activity of chloroplasts isolated from maize inbreds and their $F_1$ hybrids. *Crop Sci.* **6**, 185–187.

MONTEITH, J. (1965). Light and crop production. *Field Crop abstr.* **18**, 213–219.

MOUSSEAU, M., COSTE, F. and KOUCHOVSKY, Y. DE (1967). Influence des conditions d'éclairement pendant la croissance sur l'activité photosynthétique de feuilles entières et de chloroplastes isolés. *C.R. hébd. Acad. Sci., Paris* **264D**, 1158–1161.

NEALES, T. F., TREHARNE, K. J. and WAREING, P. F. (1971). *In* "Photosynthesis and photorespiration" (M. D. Hatch, C. B. Osmond and R. O. Slatyer, eds), pp. 89–96. Wiley Interscience, N.Y.

PENMAN, H. (1942). Theory of porometers used in the study of stomatal movements in leaves. *Proc. Roy. Soc. B.* **130**, 416.

RABINOWITCH, E. T. (1951). "Photosynthesis and Related Processes". Vol II, part I. Interscience, New York.

RACKHAM, O. (1967). Radiation, transpiration and growth in a woodland annual. *In* "Light as an ecological factor" (R. Bainbridge *et al.*, eds), pp. 167–185. Blackwell, Oxford.

SLACK, C. R. and HATCH, M. D. (1967). Comparative studies on the activity of carboxylases and other enzymes in relation to the new pathway of photosynthetic carbon dioxide fixation in tropical grasses. *Biochem. J.* **103**, 660–666.

SLATYER, R. O. and BIERHUIZEN, J. F. (1964). Transpiration from cotton leaves under a range of environmental conditions in relation to internal and external diffusive resistances. *Aust. J. biol. Sci.* **17**, 115–130.

SUGIYAMA, T. and AZAKAWA, T. (1967). Structure and function of chloroplast proteins. I. Subunit structure of wheat Fraction I protein. *J. biol. Chem.* **62**, 474–482.

SWEENEY, B. M. (1969). Transducing mechanisms between circadian clock and overt rhythms in *Gonyaulax*. *Can. J. Bot.* **47**, 299–308.

TIESZEN, L. L. and HELGAGER, J. A. (1968). Genetic and physiological adaptation in the Hill-reaction of *Deschampsia caespitosa*. *Nature, Lond.* **219**, 1066–1067.

TREHARNE, K. J. and COOPER, J. P. (1969). Effect of temperature on the activity of carboxylases in tropical and temperate Gramineae. *J. exp. Bot.* **20**, 170–175.

TREHARNE, K. J. and EAGLES, C. F. (1969). Effect of growth at different light intensities on photosynthetic activity of two contrasting populations of *Dactylis glomerata* L. *Prog. Photosynthesis Research* **1**, 377–382.

TREHARNE, K. J. and EAGLES, C. F. (1970). Effect of temperature on photosynthetic activity of climatic races of *Dactylis glomerata* L. *Photosynthetica* **4**, 107–111.

TREHARNE, K. J. and NEALES, T. F. (1971) (in preparation).

TREHARNE, K. J. and STODDART, J. L. (1968). Effects of gibberellin on photosynthesis in red clover (*Trifolium pratense* L.). *Nature, Lond.* **220**, 457–458.

WAREING, P. F., KHALIFA, M. M. and TREHARNE, K. J. (1968). Rate-limiting processes in photosynthesis at saturating light intensities. *Nature, Lond.* **220**, 453–457.

WILKINS, M. B. (1959). An endogenous rhythm in the rate of carbon dioxide output of Bryophyllum. I. Some preliminary experiments. *J. exp. Bot.* **10**, 377–390.

WILKINS, M. B. (1960). An endogenous rhythm in the rate of carbon dioxide output of *Bryophyllum*. II. The effects of light and darkness on the phase and period of the rhythm. *J. exp. Bot.* **11**, 269–288.

WILSON, D. and COOPER, J. P. (1967). Assimilation of *Lolium* in relation to leaf mesophyll. *Nature, Lond.* **214**, 989–991.

WILSON, D. and COOPER, J. P. (1969). Diallel analysis of photosynthetic rate and related leaf characters among contrasting genotypes of *Lolium perenne*. *Heredity* **24**, 633–649.

WILSON, D., TREHARNE, K. J., EAGLES, C. F. and JAGER, J. M. DE (1969). A manometric technique for determination of apparent photosynthesis of *Lolium*. *J. exp. Bot.* **20**, 373–380.

WOOLHOUSE, H. W. (1967). The nature of senescence in plants. *Symp. Soc. exp. Biol.* **21**, 179–213.

# Discussion

**Treharne** had shown in his paper the high correlation between RuDiP carboxylase activity of certain grasses and their rates of photosynthesis. **Lake** doubted whether cause and effect could be distinguished; it might be that high rates of photosynthesis induced high enzyme content. Treharne pointed out that Meidner's kinetic studies on defoliated plants supported the primary role of the enzyme, and his own work showed enzyme activation—deactivation by light and dark and possibly by oxygen, but no apparent activation by level of carbon dioxide substrate: plants grown in the absence of carbon dioxide in the atmosphere had slightly *higher* carboxylase activity than the controls whilst others grown at elevated carbon dioxide concentration had only slightly more enzyme than controls and there was no detectable increase in rate of enzyme synthesis. This was not to say that diffusive resistances in the leaf were irrelevant, it was also true that the liquid diffusive resistance, as normally calculated, included the effect of carboxylating enzyme activity; the physical and chemical components are separable only on theoretical grounds as discussed earlier by Chartier. The possibility of enzyme limitation of photosynthesis is discussed elsewhere in the Symposium by Chartier and Wareing.

# IV.3. The relationship between photosynthesis and respiration

L. J. LUDWIG

*Glasshouse Crops Research Institute, Littlehampton, Sussex, England*

## I. Introduction

Recent research indicates that plant photosynthetic and respiratory processes are closely linked, both metabolically and through environmental and internal controls. This close relationship exists not just for the complex interactions occurring in photosynthetic tissue in the light, i.e. photorespiration, but also for the dark respiratory processes occurring in non-photosynthetic plant parts and in leaves at night.

A number of reports in the literature indicate that the dark respiration rate of a plant is largely determined by the rate of photosynthesis during the immediately preceding light period, the respiration rate being greater after periods of rapid photo-synthesis (McCree and Troughton, 1966a, b; McCree, 1970). A similar form of respiratory regulation appears to occur in shaded leaves (Ludwig *et al.*, 1965; King and Evans, 1967).

Little is known about the physiology of this response. It has been suggested that dark respiration is normally regulated by the pace of synthetic processes (i.e. growth) via feedback control systems involving cellular levels of ADP/ATP and NAD/NADH (Beevers, 1970). This might suggest that the synthetic processes leading to growth are directly linked to changes in the level of recent photosynthate and that changes in respiratory metabolism are induced by the synthetic events rather than by changes in the level of respiratory substrate.

The lack of physiological information on these complex but important interactions contrasts with the current wealth of information on the respiratory changes which occur when leaves are illuminated. Recent studies have established that photosynthesis in $C_3$-pathway (Calvin cycle) plants is accompanied by photorespiration, a special type of respiratory process, operative only in the light and closely linked at the chemical level with the photosynthetic carbon reduction cycle. In $C_4$-pathway plants, where carbon dioxide is initially fixed by the $C_4$-dicarboxylic acid pathway of photosynthesis, there is no direct evidence for the operation of photo-respiration. If it does operate to any extent, then apparently all the carbon dioxide released is immediately refixed by internal recycling (Hatch, 1970; Walker and Crofts, 1970).

Until more is known about the biochemistry of photorespiration its function in the plant must remain a mystery. At present it is generally believed to be a wasteful process because the substantial loss of recently fixed carbon, evolved as carbon dioxide, does not appear to be linked to the production of energetically useful compounds such as ATP or NADH as in dark respiration. The total energy cost cannot be accurately estimated until all the reactions of the process are known, but it has been suggested that the loss is at least 5 ATP and 2 NADPH molecules per molecule of carbon dioxide evolved (Hatch, 1970).

Estimates of the rate of carbon dioxide production by photorespiration in the $C_3$-pathway plants have varied considerably, ranging from 10% to 50% of the gross rate of photosynthetic carbon dioxide fixation.

To determine the importance of photorespiration in crop productivity it is essential that the magnitude of the carbon loss is determined accurately, and that the biochemistry of the process is clarified. If it can be firmly established that the process is energetically wasteful and that the process serves no essential function in the plant, then the reduction of photorespiration by environmental or genetic manipulation becomes a worthwhile objective for the crop physiologist and plant breeder.

The precise measurement of photorespiration is difficult because the evolution of carbon dioxide is usually masked by photosynthesis. Various methods have been devised for calculating or measuring the rate of carbon dioxide production in photorespiration but they all suffer from various limitations and errors. In spite of the limitations, experiments using these techniques have provided considerable information on many of the important factors which influence photorespiration and control its rate (see comprehensive reviews by Goldsworthy, 1970; Hatch and Slack, 1970; Jackson and Volk, 1970; Walker and Crofts, 1970; Ludlow and Jarvis, 1971).

For this Symposium, rather than provide yet another review of the literature on photosynthesis and photorespiration, I wish to present some results from recent experiments where radioactive carbon dioxide ($^{14}CO_2$) has been used in an open gas-exchange system to measure the rate of photorespiration under conditions of steady state photosynthesis and to investigate further the relationship between photorespiration and photo-synthesis.

# II. Experiments using $^{14}CO_2$ to measure photosynthesis and photorespiration

## A. Methods

The third pair of leaves on 22–26 day old sunflower plants (*Helianthus annuus* L., cv. 'Mennonite') was used for the gas exchange measurements. Part of an attached leaf was enclosed in a small "Perspex" chamber constructed in two symmetrical halves which clamped each side of the leaf. The experiments were carried out in a controlled environment cabinet illuminated by 30 cool-white fluorescent lamps (General Electric F48 T10/CW). The light flux density on the upper surface of the enclosed leaf was 116 W m$^{-2}$ (400–700 nm). The leaf temperature, measured by fine wire thermocouples placed against the lower surface of the leaf, was maintained at 25 °C.

While the leaf chamber was continuously flushed with a gas mixture containing a constant amount of $^{14}CO_2$, $^{12}CO_2$ and oxygen, the $^{14}CO_2$ and $^{12}CO_2$ differential between the inlet and outlet of the chamber was continuously measured using a flow ionization chamber and electrometer and an infrared carbon dioxide analyser. Details of the gas supply system, the measuring system, the experimental procedure and methods of calculation have recently been published (Ludwig and Canvin, 1971a). Measurements were made under steady-state conditions at three carbon dioxide concentrations (approximately 50, 150 and 300 vpm) and two oxygen concentrations (1 and 21%).

## B. The $^{14}CO_2$ exchange

When a leaf is flushed with a gas mixture containing a constant amount of $^{14}CO_2$, the initial $^{14}CO_2$ uptake measurements should represent the steady-state gross uptake of $^{14}CO_2$ in photosynthesis because the fixed $^{14}C$ will require a finite time to move into the substrate(s) for photorespiration. However, $^{14}C$ will eventually move into these substrates and $^{14}CO_2$ will be evolved from the leaf in increasing amounts until the substrate(s) equilibrate with the $^{14}CO_2$ being fixed. This evolution of $^{14}CO_2$ will result in a progressive decrease in the measured rate of $^{14}CO_2$ uptake.

A typical $^{14}CO_2$ recorder tracing is shown in Fig. 1. In 21% oxygen, at all three carbon dioxide concentrations, the rate of $^{14}CO_2$ uptake was greatest immediately after the $^{14}CO_2$ was supplied to the leaf and then steadily decreased. The change from gross uptake to net uptake was

CPCE—X

extremely rapid, occurring approximately 30–40 sec after the $^{14}CO_2$ was first supplied.

This was in direct contrast to experiments in 1% oxygen where the measured rate of $^{14}CO_2$ uptake was constant with time (Fig. 1) suggesting that there was no $^{14}CO_2$ evolution at this low oxygen concentration. At all three carbon dioxide concentrations gross $^{14}CO_2$ uptake in 21% oxygen was considerably lower than in 1% oxygen, indicating a direct inhibitory effect of oxygen on photosynthesis (Björkman, 1966; Forrester et al., 1966; Tregunna et al., 1966; Heber and French, 1968).

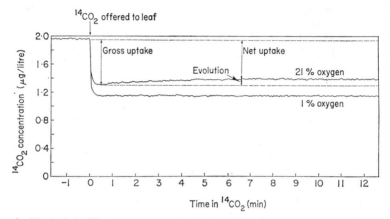

**Fig. 1.** Typical $^{14}CO_2$ recorder tracings showing the uptake of $^{14}CO_2$ by an illuminated sunflower leaf from a gas stream containing 300 vpm carbon dioxide and 1% or 21% oxygen. After Ludwig and Canvin (1971a).

## C. The carbon dioxide exchange

The rate of gross carbon dioxide uptake was calculated from the initial gross $^{14}CO_2$ uptake and the specific activity ($\mu g$ $^{14}CO_2/\mu g$ total carbon dioxide) of the $^{14}CO_2$ in the leaf chamber. The rate of carbon dioxide evolution was then estimated from the difference between the calculated gross carbon dioxide uptake and the measured net carbon dioxide uptake. Because of possible discrimination against $^{14}CO_2$ and dilution of the $^{14}CO_2$ within the leaf by carbon dioxide from respiratory sources, gross carbon dioxide uptake and consequently the calculated rate of carbon dioxide evolution must be underestimated by this method (Samish and Koller, 1968; Ludlow and Jarvis, 1971).

It is clear from the $^{14}CO_2$ exchange that if $^{14}CO_2$ is to be used to estimate gross photosynthesis, the $^{14}CO_2$ uptake measurements must be made within seconds of supplying the $^{14}CO_2$ to the leaf, otherwise the rates of gross carbon dioxide uptake and carbon dioxide evolution will be further underestimated. In 300 vpm carbon dioxide, for example, if the initial $^{14}CO_2$ uptake measurements are delayed for 2 min, gross photosynthesis will be underestimated by about 10% and photorespiration by more than 50%. This may explain why many previous workers using the isotope method (Weigl *et al.*, 1951; Krotkov *et al.*, 1958; Lister *et al.*, 1961; Ozbun *et al.*, 1964; Bidwell *et al.*, 1969) have estimated low rates of photorespiration.

The rates of gross and net carbon dioxide uptake determined from a series of experiments are shown in Fig. 2. Net carbon dioxide uptake in 21% oxygen showed the usual linear response to carbon dioxide at low concentrations. The carbon dioxide compensation point was approximately 45 vpm. The estimated rate of gross carbon dioxide uptake in 21% oxygen was consistently $15.9 \pm 0.8$ ng $CO_2$ cm$^{-2}$ sec$^{-1}$ higher than the rate of net carbon dioxide uptake at comparable carbon dioxide concentrations. The rate of carbon dioxide evolution, represented by this difference, was therefore independent of the external carbon dioxide concentration and the rate of photosynthesis. This is an important finding because it is commonly assumed that the rate of photorespiration is proportional to the rate of photosynthesis. It should be noted, however, that the carbon dioxide concentrations used in these experiments were all rate-limiting for photosynthesis. Because of various diffusion resistances within the leaf (Gaastra, 1959; Lake, 1967; Jarvis, 1971) the carbon dioxide concentration at the carboxylation site would be low and would not change greatly with changes in the external carbon dioxide concentration until non-limiting concentrations were reached. Since there is considerable indirect evidence which suggests that photorespiration is suppressed by higher, non-limiting carbon dioxide concentrations (Zelitch and Walker, 1964; Jolliffe and Tregunna, 1968; Ellyard and Gibbs, 1969; Jackson and Volk, 1970) it seems that the rate of photorespiration in 21% oxygen may be directly related not to the external carbon dioxide concentration or to the rate of photosynthesis but to the carbon dioxide concentration at the site of carboxylation.

## D. The effect of oxygen on the carbon dioxide exchange

In 1% oxygen the carbon dioxide compensation point was very low (Fig. 2) and there was little difference between gross and net carbon dioxide uptake indicating that photorespiration was almost absent at this low oxygen concentration.

It is well established for $C_3$-pathway plants (Turner and Brittain, 1962; Björkman, 1966; Forrester *et al.*, 1966; Tregunna *et al.*, 1966; Egle and Fock, 1967; Hesketh, 1967; Downes and Hesketh, 1968; Jolliffe and

Tregunna, 1968) that the net rate of photosynthesis in 21% oxygen is considerably lower than the rate in 1% oxygen. In 250 vpm carbon dioxide there was a 40% inhibition of net photosynthesis by atmospheric oxygen concentrations (Fig. 2) and the inhibition increased as the carbon dioxide decreased (see Fig. 5, Jackson and Volk, 1970). Forrester *et al.* (1963) and Tregunna *et al.* (1966) suggested that this inhibition by oxygen was due to two separate effects, a stimulation of photorespiration and an inhibition of gross photosynthesis. From the data in Fig. 2 it is possible for the first time to quantitatively separate these two effects. In 250 vpm

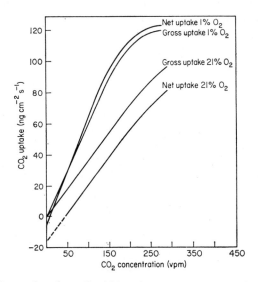

**Fig. 2.** The effects of carbon dioxide and oxygen concentration on the rate of gross photosynthesis, net photosynthesis and photorespiration of sunflower leaves. (Ludwig and Canvin, 1971b.)

carbon dioxide, for example, 68% of the total inhibition could be ascribed to an inhibition of gross photosynthesis and only 32% to a stimulation of photorespiration. It is therefore not valid to assume that the difference between the rate of net photosynthesis in 1% and 21% oxygen is entirely due to photorespiration (Hesketh, 1967; Hesketh and Baker, 1967; Fock *et al.*, 1969).

There is considerable evidence (Zelitch, 1964, 1966; Goldsworthy, 1966, 1970; Egle and Fock, 1967; Jackson and Volk, 1970) that the effect of oxygen on photorespiration is due to the oxidation of glycollate by the enzyme glycollate oxidase (see Fig. 5). Oxygen is the electron acceptor and glyoxylate and hydrogen peroxide are the products. The enzyme is a flavoprotein with a comparatively low affinity for oxygen so that high oxygen concentrations are necessary for its saturation.

On the other hand there is no general agreement as to the cause of the inhibitory effect of oxygen on photosynthesis. A number of mechanisms have been proposed but few appear to explain adequately the effect (see reviews by Turner and Brittain, 1962; Jackson and Volk, 1970).

One hypothesis which has received considerable support suggests that oxygen suppresses photosynthesis by interfering with one or more components of the electron transport system. There is considerable evidence that in isolated chloroplasts, oxygen can participate as a Hill oxidant when other oxidants are absent (Mehler, 1951a, b; Mehler and Brown, 1952; Whitehouse et al., 1971). The main product of the oxidation is hydrogen peroxide. Various sites for this interaction with oxygen have been suggested but most evidence suggests that the main site is at the reducing end of the electron transport chain, beyond photosystem I (Heber and French, 1968). Reduced ferredoxin, the most reduced product of photosystem I so far identified, is known to be auto-oxidizable although in the presence of NADP and oxygen, NADP is the preferred oxidant (Gibbs et al., 1968). Mehler (1951b) and Coombs and Whittingham (1966) suggested that at low carbon dioxide concentrations the rate of turnover of NADP/NADPH would be low, reduced ferredoxin would accumulate and react with oxygen. Thus, increasing the oxygen concentration would increase the rate of the Mehler reaction. At high carbon dioxide concentrations, with a rapid carbon dioxide fixation rate, the rate of turnover of NADP/NADPH would be high, reduced ferredoxin would be maintained at a low level and little reaction with oxygen would be expected. Thus, oxygen and carbon dioxide are assumed to compete for reductant, carbon dioxide being the preferred electron acceptor.

It has frequently been observed (Wilson and Calvin, 1955; Coombs and Whittingham, 1966; Gibbs et al., 1967, 1968) that the inhibition of photosynthesis by oxygen at low carbon dioxide concentrations is associated with a depletion of photosynthetic cycle intermediates and an increase in the formation of glycollate. Since the conditions which favour the Mehler reaction (low carbon dioxide, high oxygen and high light) also favour the production of glycollate, Coombs and Whittingham (1966) suggested that hydrogen peroxide formed in the Mehler reaction might be responsible for the oxidation of certain intermediates of the photosynthetic cycle, resulting in the production of phosphoglycollate or glycollate. This loss of carbon from the photosynthetic cycle would result in a depletion of most intermediates of the cycle, including RuDP, the carbon dioxide acceptor, and thus decrease the rate of carbon dioxide fixation. At high carbon dioxide or low oxygen concentrations the Mehler reaction would be suppressed, little hydrogen peroxide would be formed and glycollate production would cease.

Shain and Gibbs (1971) using a reconstituted system containing fragmented chloroplasts have recently provided experimental evidence to support this hypothesis. They demonstrated that a glycoaldehyde-transketolase addition product derived from fructose-6-P, an intermediate of the photosynthetic cycle, could be oxidized to glycollate by an oxidant generated in photosystem II or by hydrogen peroxide formed by photosystem I.

If, as suggested above, oxygen is responsible either directly, or indirectly via hydrogen peroxide, for the production of glycollate from intermediates of the photosynthetic cycle, and if the subsequent oxidation of this glycollate is responsible for the observed effect of oxygen on photorespiration, it follows that the two separate oxygen effects shown in Fig. 2 are probably closely linked, unless there are alternative mechanisms for the formation of glycollate. It is suggested that if the primary interaction with oxygen in photosynthesis could be prevented, glycollate production would be diminished or possibly cease and photorespiration would be suppressed.

## E. The specific activity of $^{14}CO_2$ evolved during photosynthesis in $^{14}CO_2$

Only the initial $^{14}CO_2$ uptake measurements were required to estimate rates of gross photosynthesis and photorespiration. However, by continuing the $^{14}CO_2$ measurements it was possible to obtain information about the substrate(s) for photorespiration.

In 21% oxygen, changes in the measured rate of $^{14}CO_2$ uptake soon after the $^{14}CO_2$ was supplied to the leaf (Fig. 1) indicated that labelled carbon had moved rapidly from the photosynthetic cycle into the substrate(s) for photorespiration and that $^{14}CO_2$ was being evolved from the leaf. The specific activity of this evolved $^{14}CO_2$ could be calculated from the rate of $^{14}CO_2$ evolution and the rate of total carbon dioxide evolution (see Ludwig and Canvin, 1971a). So that experiments could be compared this specific activity was expressed as a percentage of the specific activity offered to the leaf. This value was termed the relative specific activity.

The effect of carbon dioxide concentration on the relative specific activity of $^{14}CO_2$ evolved from the leaf is shown in Fig. 3. In 290 vpm carbon dioxide the specific activity of the evolved $^{14}CO_2$ increased rapidly and within 7 min it had approached the specific activity of the supplied $^{14}CO_2$ indicating that almost all the substrate for photorespiration was derived directly from the photosynthetic cycle.

At lower carbon dioxide concentrations the specific activity of the evolved $^{14}CO_2$ also increased rapidly but appeared to equilibrate at a lower relative specific activity (approximately 60% in 53 vpm carbon dioxide and 80% in 150 vpm carbon dioxide). The rapid initial labelling together with these apparently different equilibration levels suggest that there were at least two different substrates for photorespiration at low carbon dioxide concentrations; one highly labelled, indicating that it was derived directly from photosynthesis, and one relatively unlabelled.

At the end of the $^{14}CO_2$ uptake period the leaf chamber was flushed with carbon dioxide-free air and the specific activity of the evolved $^{14}CO_2$

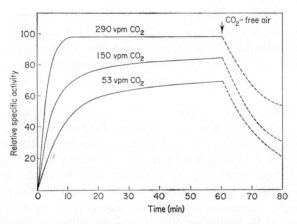

**Fig. 3.** The effect of carbon dioxide concentration on the relative specific activity of $^{14}CO_2$ evolved by sunflower leaves during photosynthesis in $^{14}CO_2$ (Ludwig et al., 1969).

measured directly in light and darkness. These flushing experiments provided considerable additional information on the substrates for photorespiration (Ludwig et al., 1969; Ludwig and Canvin, 1971b) and the results are used in the following discussion.

Most of the specific activity data can be explained in terms of the scheme shown in Fig. 4 (p. 316) which attempts to represent the carbon flow and relationships between the carbon compounds of photosynthesis $(P_G)$ photorespiration $(R_P)$ and dark respiration $(R_D)$. The main carbon dioxide fluxes within the leaf together with the various diffusion resistances (r) have also been shown.

The specific activity of the $^{14}CO_2$ evolved in 290 vpm carbon dioxide (Fig. 3) showed that when carbon dioxide fixation was adequate almost all the substrate for photorespiration was derived from the photosynthetic cycle. Isotopic equilibration was rapid, indicating small pools of intermediates with high turnover rates. Intermediates of the glycollate pathway are known to be rapidly labelled during photosynthesis in $^{14}CO_2$ (Hess and Tolbert, 1966) and the above results are therefore consistent with the view that the glycollate pathway provided the substrate for photorespiration.

Little carbon dioxide was derived from unlabelled substrate. This suggests that $R_D$, which evolved carbon dioxide at approximately 4·7 ng $CO_2$ cm$^{-2}$ sec$^{-1}$ in the dark, was largely suppressed in the light since there is evidence that the substrates for dark respiration are only very slowly labelled from $^{14}CO_2$ fixed in photosynthesis (Benson and Calvin, 1950; Pederson et al., 1966).

On the other hand, when photosynthesis was reduced considerably by low carbon dioxide concentrations (150 and 53 vpm) there appeared to be two different substrates for photorespiration, one which was highly labelled and therefore derived directly from the photosynthetic cycle and one which was not readily labelled from photosynthesis. The origin of the unlabelled carbon was not clear in that it could have come from either $R_P$ or $R_D$. Ludwig and Canvin (1971b) suggest that if dark respiration continued in the light, and all $^{14}CO_2$ was derived from $R_P$, the $^{14}CO_2$ evolved from the leaf after the substrates for $R_P$ have saturated with $^{14}C$ could be expected to have a relative specific activity of 80% (see experiments in 150 vpm $CO_2$, Fig. 3). However, it is then difficult to explain why the "saturated" relative specific activity should be different at other carbon dioxide concentrations. For the experiments in 53 vpm carbon dioxide it could be that after 60 min photosynthesis in $^{14}CO_2$ the substrate(s) for $R_P$ were still not saturated with $^{14}C$ although the labelling kinetics (Fig. 3) suggest saturation occurred after 30 min.

The different relative specific activity levels could also be explained if the rate of $R_D$ in the light changes with the carbon dioxide concentration. This seems unlikely because in 53 vpm carbon dioxide the rate of $R_D$ in the light would have to be at least 8·5 ng $CO_2$ cm$^{-2}$ sec$^{-1}$, almost twice the dark rate, to account for the observed relative specific activity at saturation. If $R_D$ did evolve carbon dioxide at a significant rate in the light, an evolution of carbon dioxide should have been observed in the 1% oxygen experiments since it is known that the rate of $R_D$ is not affected by oxygen concentrations as low as 1% (Forrester et al., 1966). No such evolution was observed (Fig. 2).

The evidence therefore suggests that $R_D$ was largely suppressed in the light at all carbon dioxide concentrations and that most of the unlabelled carbon dioxide as well as the labelled was evolved from $R_P$. If the assumption is made that the highly labelled substrate was saturated with $^{14}C$ at all three carbon dioxide concentrations (i.e. isotopic equilibrium was reached) and that the second substrate was unlabelled, the different relative specific activities at saturation (Fig. 3) suggest that approximately 40% of the carbon dioxide evolved in the light was derived from the unlabelled substrate in 53 vpm carbon dioxide, 20% in 150 vpm and less than 5% in 290 vpm.

The unlabelled carbon could have been derived from relatively remote storage pools either by a direct pathway to $R_P$ or indirectly via the glycollate pathway and possibly the photosynthetic cycle (Fig. 4). It is difficult to envisage two independent oxygen-sensitive pathways providing substrate for $R_P$. It seems more likely that glycollate is produced from both highly labelled and unlabelled sources at low carbon dioxide concentrations.

In carbon dioxide free air following a period of photosynthesis in $^{14}CO_2$, the specific activity changes were complex and a second highly labelled substrate could be identified (Ludwig et al., 1969; Ludwig and Canvin, 1971b). Carbon dioxide fixation in carbon dioxide free air was restricted to internally recycled carbon dioxide and the highly labelled substrate derived from photosynthesis was soon exhausted. However, carbon dioxide evolution from $R_P$ continued so that all substrate must have been derived from storage pools. When previous photosynthesis in $^{14}CO_2$ was high, one of these storage pools was highly labelled (the immediate storage pool, Fig. 4) and supplied substrate to $R_P$ for a considerable period. Eventually, this pool was also exhausted and all substrate was then derived from more distant unlabelled carbon (the remote storage pool, Fig. 4).

All these results indicate that the derivation of substrate for photorespiration at low carbon dioxide concentrations is complex. It seems reasonable to suggest that under both high and low carbon dioxide conditions, all substrate for $R_P$ is derived from the chloroplast via the glycollate pathway. However, until more is known about the mechanism of glycollate synthesis it is not possible to explain the origin of unlabelled substrate and the apparent regulation of the various substrates in response to the carbon dioxide concentration.

If all glycollate is derived directly from an intermediate of the photosynthetic cycle it seems necessary to postulate that at low carbon dioxide concentrations carbon enters the photosynthetic cycle from various storage pools. The photosynthetic cycle, or part of it, would then assume a "respiratory" function, generating substrate for $R_P$ from stored sugars (Fig. 4). In Chlorella it has been shown that exogenous glucose can be fed into the photosynthetic cycle and converted to glycollate in the light (Whittingham et al., 1963). The rate of conversion increased as the carbon dioxide concentration was decreased or the oxygen concentration increased.

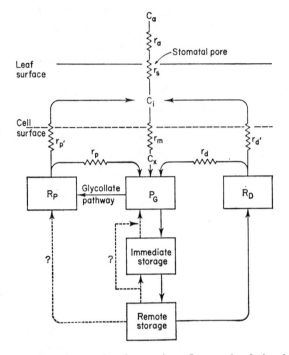

**Fig. 4.** Diagrammatic scheme showing carbon flow and relationships between the carbon compounds of photosynthesis ($P_G$), photorespiration ($R_P$) and dark respiration ($R_D$). For explanation, see text.

# III. The stoichiometry of photorespiration

In an attempt to relate the observed carbon dioxide exchange to the biochemistry of the glycollate pathway as it is currently envisaged by many workers, the flow of carbon in photosynthesis and the glycollate pathway has been followed quantitatively (Fig. 5).

The reaction sequence for the glycollate pathway is still uncertain but it is generally thought to be glycollate, glyoxylate, glycine, serine and then to sucrose via hydroxypyruvate, glycerate, 3-phosphoglycerate and triose phosphate.

An oxygen uptake is associated with the oxidation of glycollate by glycollate oxidase and this is one of the known sites where oxygen concentration regulates the flow of carbon in photorespiration.

The reactions leading to the release of carbon dioxide are not clearly understood. Zelitch (1966) suggested that carbon dioxide was produced from the non-enzymatic decarboxylation of glyoxylate by hydrogen peroxide generated in the glycollate oxidation. It has since been shown, however, that glycollate oxidase is located in the peroxisomes, organelles which contain high levels of catalase (Tolbert et al., 1968). The hydrogen peroxide produced from the oxidation of glycollate is therefore probably rapidly destroyed.

Current evidence suggests that glyoxylate is converted to glycine in the

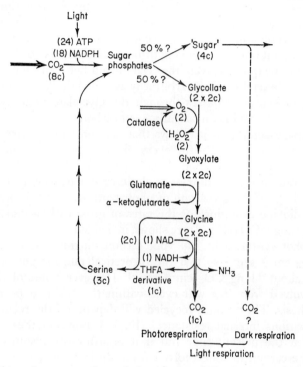

**Fig. 5.** Schematic presentation of the biochemical reactions of the glycollate pathway in relation to the carbon dioxide produced in photorespiration. After Goldsworthy (1970) and Kisaki et al. (1971a).

Figures in brackets indicate the quantitative relationships for eight carbon dioxide molecules fixed in photosynthesis. For further explanation, see text.

peroxisomes by a glutamate/glyoxylate amino transferase (Kisaki and Tolbert, 1969) and that the decarboxylation of glycine, associated with the synthesis of serine, is the main source of carbon dioxide in photorespiration (Kisaki and Tolbert, 1970; Kisaki et al., 1971a, b). The reaction mechanism proposed by Kisaki et al. (1971a, b), is shown in Fig. 5. One molecule of glycine is split by the enzyme glycine decarboxylase to form carbon dioxide, ammonia and a $C_1$ complex with tetrahydrofolic acid which is subsequently transferred by the enzyme hydroxymethyl-transferase to a second glycine molecule, forming one molecule of serine. Thus one molecule of serine is synthesized from two molecules of glycine with the release of one molecule of carbon dioxide. Both enzymes appear to be located in the mitochondria. The serine may be utilized directly in protein synthesis but most is thought to be remetabolized to sugar via hydroxypyruvate, glycerate, 3-phosphoglycerate and triose phosphate.

The overall stoichiometry of the glycollate pathway, as outlined in Fig. 5, indicates that one molecule of carbon dioxide would be evolved for every four carbon atoms, i.e. two glycollate molecules, entering the pathway. The amount of carbon passing through glycollate is not known but in order to examine quantitatively the relationship between photorespiration and photosynthesis it has been arbitrarily assumed that 50% of the carbon fixed in photosynthesis passes through the glycollate pathway and that all glycollate is derived from recently fixed carbon.

With these assumptions it follows that one molecule of carbon dioxide would be evolved from $R_P$ for every eight carbon atoms entering the photosynthetic cycle as carbon dioxide (Fig. 5). Expressed in different terms, the rate of carbon dioxide evolution from $R_P$ should be approximately 12–13% of the gross rate of photosynthesis. The theoretical rates of carbon dioxide evolution for the rates of gross carbon dioxide uptake measured using $^{14}CO_2$ (Fig. 2) are shown in Table I.

Gross photosynthesis in 290 vpm carbon dioxide was approximately 88 ng $CO_2$ cm$^{-2}$ sec$^{-1}$ so that the theoretical rate for photorespiration would be about 11 ng $CO_2$ cm$^{-2}$ sec$^{-1}$. However, some of the carbon dioxide evolved from $R_P$ will cycle within the leaf and be refixed by photosynthesis. The amount recycled will depend on the relative magnitudes of various internal resistances (Fig. 4). Some of these cannot be estimated at the present time but if it is arbitrarily assumed that one third of the carbon dioxide evolved from $R_P$ is refixed, then one would expect to measure external to the leaf a rate of carbon dioxide evolution of approximately 7·3 ng $CO_2$ cm$^{-2}$ sec$^{-1}$. In the $^{14}CO_2$ experiments described earlier the measured rate of carbon dioxide evolution during photosynthesis was 15·8 ng $CO_2$ cm$^{-2}$ sec$^{-1}$, a rate over twice that predicted by the scheme shown in Fig. 5. In this calculation no allowance has been made for carbon dioxide evolved from $R_D$ because the specific activity data (Fig. 3) indicated that in 290 vpm carbon dioxide almost all respired carbon dioxide was derived from recent photosynthetic products. Even if $R_D$ continued to evolve carbon dioxide in the light, its contribution would not be sufficient to account for the observed discrepancy (Table I).

At lower carbon dioxide concentrations where the specific activity data suggest that unlabelled carbon from storage pools is also utilized as substrate for photorespiration, the discrepancy appears to be even greater.

In 53 vpm carbon dioxide, for example, Table I shows that according to the scheme depicted in Fig. 5, recent photosynthate would contribute only 1·6 ng $CO_2$ cm$^{-2}$ sec$^{-1}$ to the measured rate of carbon dioxide evolution. Unlabelled storage pools would therefore have to contribute the remaining 14·2 ng $CO_2$ cm$^{-2}$ sec$^{-1}$ either through $R_P$, or $R_D$ or both. It is clear that the relative specific activity of this carbon dioxide would only be 10% (1·6 × 100/15·8) as opposed to the measured relative specific activity of 65% (Fig. 3).

### Table I

Comparison of the "theoretical" rate of photorespiration with the rate of carbon dioxide evolution measured during photosynthesis in 21% oxygen

| | Carbon dioxide concentration (vpm) | | |
| --- | --- | --- | --- |
| | 290 | 150 | 53 |
| | ng $CO_2$ cm$^{-2}$ sec$^{-1}$ | | |
| Measured gross photosynthesis[1] | 88·0 | 48·0 | 19·4 |
| Photorespiration[2] | | | |
| no refixation | 11·0 | 6·0 | 2·4 |
| 33% refixation | 7·3 | 4·0 | 1·6 |
| Dark respiration[3] | | | |
| no refixation | 4·8 | 4·8 | 4·8 |
| 33% refixation | 3·2 | 3·2 | 3·2 |
| Measured carbon dioxide evolution[4] | 15·8 | 15·8 | 15·8 |

[1] Gross photosynthesis values taken from Fig. 2.
[2] Photorespiration rate calculated from gross photosynthesis using scheme shown in Fig. 5.
[3] Dark respiration rate in light assumed for this purpose to equal rate measured in darkness.
[4] Measured carbon dioxide evolution values taken from Fig. 2.

From these calculations it can be concluded that the scheme generally proposed for photorespiration (Fig. 5) does not account for the observed release of carbon dioxide from recent photosynthetic products. This seems to indicate that the present stoichiometry of the glycollate pathway is incorrect or that other unknown oxygen-sensitive processes also contribute carbon dioxide from recent photosynthate. The alternative non-enzymatic decarboxylation of glyoxylate by hydrogen peroxide proposed by Zelitch (1966), although presumably contributing one carbon dioxide molecule for every two carbon atoms entering the pathway, also seems inadequate as a possible mechanism at low carbon dioxide concentrations where up to 65% of the carbon dioxide fixed in photosynthesis appears to be rapidly re-evolved in photorespiration.

# IV. Photorespiration and crop production in glasshouses

All glasshouse crop plants exhibit photorespiration and therefore appear to assimilate carbon inefficiently. Previous sections indicate that in spite of considerable recent interest in photorespiration much of the biochemistry of the process is still unknown. It is therefore difficult to predict the carbon and energy losses involved and it cannot be stated with any certainty that the process serves no useful function in the plant. Even the magnitude of the carbon dioxide evolution associated with photorespiration is not accurately known because of the inadequacy of current measuring techniques.

It is known, however, that photorespiration can be suppressed by changing the concentration of oxygen or carbon dioxide in the plants' gaseous environment. Data were presented in Fig. 2 which showed that net photosynthesis at low and atmospheric carbon dioxide concentrations could be dramatically increased by decreasing the oxygen concentration. More extensive data for the same plant material (sunflower) are shown in Fig. 6. When the oxygen concentration was reduced from atmospheric (21%) to 1%, there was a 60% increase in the rate of net photosynthesis at normal atmospheric carbon dioxide concentrations (300 vpm). Similar increases have been observed in many other C3-pathway plants (Forrester et al., 1966; Hesketh, 1967; Downes and Hesketh, 1968; Jolliffe and Tregunna, 1968). Furthermore, Björkman et al. (1967) have demonstrated that growing plants in low oxygen results in a considerable increase in the rate of dry matter accumulation or growth. In 300 vpm carbon dioxide, the increase in total dry weight of young bean plants over a six-day period in 2·5% oxygen was about twice that in 21% oxygen.

Growing crops in low oxygen in the glasshouse would not be practical but the data shown in Fig. 6 suggest that similar results can be achieved by carbon dioxide enrichment. At high carbon dioxide concentrations the inhibitory effects of oxygen on net photosynthesis are largely overcome; reducing the oxygen concentration results in very much smaller increases in carbon assimilation. These and other results (Zelitch and Walker, 1964; Jolliffe and Tregunna, 1968; Ellyard and Gibbs, 1969; Jackson and Volk, 1970) suggest that photorespiration is suppressed by high carbon dioxide concentrations.

It is of considerable interest that photosynthesis in low oxygen did not respond to carbon dioxide enrichment (Fig. 6). Atmospheric carbon dioxide concentrations were sufficient to saturate the photosynthetic process in relatively high light (116 W m⁻², 400–700 nm) indicating that stomatal and other internal resistances to carbon dioxide transfer were low. These results suggest that the main effect of carbon dioxide enrichment at atmospheric levels of oxygen is to decrease the sensitivity of the photosynthetic process to oxygen. This would result in an increase in gross carbon dioxide uptake and a suppression of photorespiration (see earlier discussion for a possible mechanism).

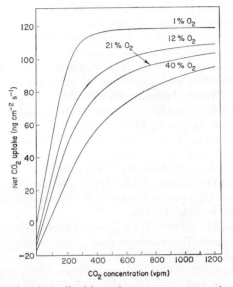

**Fig. 6.** The effects of carbon dioxide and oxygen concentration on the rate of net photosynthesis in sunflower leaves.
(25 °C; light flux density 116 W m$^{-2}$, 400–700 nm)

Further research on the primary effects of oxygen on photosynthesis and photorespiration eventually coupled to a plant breeding programme could possibly result in the development of crop plants which have a very much reduced sensitivity to oxygen. The data presented in Fig. 6 suggest that such plants would have a high photosynthetic potential in atmospheric carbon dioxide concentrations; carbon dioxide enrichment would then be of little benefit and could be discontinued with a consequent reduction in crop production costs.

# Acknowledgements

The experimental work on which this paper is based was carried out in collaboration with Dr D. T. Canvin, Queen's University, Kingston,

Ontario and was supported by grants from the National Research Council of Canada.

# References

BEEVERS, H. (1970). Respiration in plants and its regulation. *In* "Prediction and Measurement of Photosynthetic Productivity" *Proc. IBP/PP technical meeting, Trebon, 1969* (I. Setlik, ed.), pp. 209–214. Centre for Agricultural Publishing & Documentation, Wageningen.

BENSON, A. A. and CALVIN, M. (1950). The path of carbon in photosynthesis. VII. Respiration and photosynthesis. *J. exp. Bot.* **1**, 65–68.

BIDWELL, R. G. S., LEVIN, W. B. and SHEPHARD, D. C. (1969). Photosynthesis, photorespiration and respiration of chloroplasts from *Acetabularia mediterrania. Pl. Physiol., Lancaster* **44**, 946–954.

BJÖRKMAN, O. (1966). The effect of oxygen concentration on photosynthesis in higher plants. *Physiologia Pl.* **19**, 618–633.

BJÖRKMAN, O., HIESEY, W. M., NOBS, M. A., NICHOLSON, F. and HART, R. W. (1967). Effect of oxygen concentration on dry matter production in higher plants. *Yb. Carnegie Instn Wash.* **66**, 228–232.

COOMBS, J. and WHITTINGHAM, C. P. (1966). The mechanism of inhibition of photosynthesis by high partial pressures of oxygen in *Chlorella. Proc. Roy. Soc. London. Ser. B.* **164**, 511–520.

DOWNES, R. W. and HESKETH, J. D. (1968). Enhanced photosynthesis at low oxygen concentrations: Differential response of temperate and tropical grasses. *Planta* **78**, 79–84.

EGLE, K. and FOCK, H. (1967). Light respiration—correlations between $CO_2$ fixation, $O_2$ pressure and glycollate concentration. *In* "Biochemistry of Chloroplasts" (T. W. Goodwin, ed.), Vol. II, pp. 79–87. Academic Press, New York.

ELLYARD, P. W. and GIBBS, M. (1969). Inhibition of photosynthesis by oxygen in isolated spinach chloroplasts. *Pl. Physiol., Lancaster* **44**, 1115–1121.

FOCK, H., KROTKOV, G. and CANVIN, D. W. (1969). Photorespiration in liverworts and leaves. *In* "Progress in Photosynthesis Research" (H. Metzner, ed.), Vol. I, pp. 482–487.

FORRESTER, M. L., KROTKOV, G. and NELSON, C. D. (1966). Effect of oxygen on photosynthesis, photorespiration and respiration in detached leaves. I. Soybean. *Pl. Physiol., Lancaster* **41**, 422–427.

GAASTRA, P. (1959). Photosynthesis of crop plants as influenced by light, carbon dioxide, temperature and stomatal diffusion resistance. *Meded. Landb-Hoogesch. Wageningen* **59** (13), 1–68.

GIBBS, M., BAMBERGER, E. S., ELLYARD, P. W. and EVERSON, R. G. (1967). Assimilation of carbon dioxide by chloroplast preparations. *In* "Biochemistry of Chloroplasts" (T. W. Goodwin, ed.) Vol. II, pp. 3–38. Academic Press, New York.

GIBBS, M., ELLYARD, P. W. and LATZKO, E. (1968). Warburg effect: Control of photosynthesis by oxygen. *In* "Comparative Biochemistry and Biophysics of Photosynthesis" (K. Shibata, A. Takamiya, A. T. Jagendorf and R. C. Fuller, eds), pp. 387–399. Univ. Tokyo Press.

GOLDSWORTHY, A. (1966). Experiments on the origin of $CO_2$ released by tobacco leaf segments in the light. *Phytochemistry* **5,** 1013–1019.

GOLDSWORTHY, A. (1970). Photorespiration. *Bot. Rev.* **36,** 321–340.

HATCH, M. D. (1970). Chemical energy costs for $CO_2$ fixation by plants with differing photosynthetic pathways. *In* "Prediction and measurement of photosynthetic productivity". *Proc. IBP/PP technical meeting, Trebon, 1969* (I. Setlik, ed.), pp. 215–220. Centre for Agricultural Publishing & Documentation, Wageningen.

HATCH, M. D. and SLACK, C. R. (1970). Photosynthetic $CO_2$-fixation pathways. *A. Rev. Pl. Physiol.* **21,** 141–162.

HEBER, U. and FRENCH, C. S. (1968). Effects of oxygen on the electron transport chain of photosynthesis. *Planta* **79,** 99–112.

HESKETH, J. D. (1967). Enhancement of photosynthetic $CO_2$ assimilation in the absence of oxygen, as dependent upon species and temperature. *Planta* **76,** 371–374.

HESKETH, J. D. and BAKER, D. (1967). Light and carbon assimilation by plant communities. *Crop Sci.* **7,** 285–293.

HESS, J. L. and TOLBERT, N. E. (1966). Glycolate, glycine, serine and glycerate formation during photosynthesis by tobacco leaves. *J. biol. Chem.* **241,** 5705–5711.

JACKSON, W. A. and VOLK, R. J. (1970). Photorespiration. *A. Rev. Pl. Physiol.* **21,** 385–432.

JARVIS, P. G. (1971). The estimation of resistance to carbon dioxide transfer. *In* "Plant Photosynthetic Production. Manual of Methods" (Z. Sestak, J. Catsky and P. G. Jarvis, eds), pp. 566–631. W. Junk, The Hague.

JOLLIFFE, P. A. and TREGUNNA, E. B. (1968). Effect of temperature, $CO_2$ concentration and light intensity on the oxygen inhibition of photosynthesis in wheat leaves. *Pl. Physiol., Lancaster* **43,** 902–906.

KING, R. W. and EVANS, L. T. (1967). Photosynthesis in artificial communities of wheat, lucerne and subterranean clover plants. *Aust. J. biol. Sci.* **20,** 623–635.

KISAKI, T. and TOLBERT, N. E. (1969). Glycolate and glyoxylate metabolism by isolated peroxisomes or chloroplasts. *Pl. Physiol., Lancaster* **44,** 242–250.

KISAKI, T. and TOLBERT, N. E. (1970). Glycine as a substrate for photorespiration. *Pl. Cell Physiol.* **11,** 247–258.

KISAKI, T., IMAI, A. and TOLBERT, N. E. (1971a). Intracellular localization of enzymes related to photorespiration in green leaves. *Pl. Cell Physiol.* **12,** 267–273.

KISAKI, T., YOSHIDA, N. and IMAI, A. (1971b). Glycine decarboxylase and serine formation in spinach leaf mitochondrial preparation with reference to photorespiration. *Pl. Cell Physiol.* **12,** 275–288.

KROTKOV, G., RUNECKLES, V. C. and THIMANN, K. V. (1958). Effect of light on the $CO_2$ absorption and evolution by *Kalanchoe*, wheat and pea leaves. *Pl. Physiol., Lancaster* **33,** 289–292.

LAKE, J. V. (1967). Respiration of leaves during photosynthesis. II. Effects on the estimation of mesophyll resistance. *Aust. J. biol. Sci.* **20**, 487–493.

LISTER, G. R., KROTKOV, G. and NELSON, C. D. (1961). A closed-circuit apparatus with an infrared $CO_2$ analyser and a Geiger tube for continuous measurement of $CO_2$ exchange in photosynthesis and respiration. *Can. J. Bot.* **39**, 581–591.

LUDLOW, M. M. and JARVIS, P. G. (1971). Methods for measuring photorespiration in leaves. *In* "Plant Photosynthetic Production. Manual of Methods" (Z. Sestak, J. Catsky and P. G. Jarvis, eds), pp. 294–315. W. Junk, The Hague.

LUDWIG, L. J. and CANVIN, D. T. (1971a). An open gas exchange system for the simultaneous measurement of the $CO_2$ and $^{14}CO_2$ fluxes from leaves. *Can. J. Bot.* 49, 1299–1313.

LUDWIG, L. J. and CANVIN, D. T. (1971b). The rate of photorespiration during photosynthesis and the relationship of the substrate of light respiration to the products of photosynthesis in sunflower leaves. *Pl. Physiol., Lancaster* **48**, 712–719.

LUDWIG, L. J., SAEKI, T. and EVANS, L. T. (1965). Photosynthesis in artificial communities of cotton plants in relation to leaf area. *Aust. J. biol. Sci.* **18**, 1103–1118.

LUDWIG, L. G., KROTKOV, G. and CANVIN, D. T. (1969). The relationship of the products of photosynthesis to the substrates for $CO_2$-evolution in light and darkness. *Prog. Photosynthesis Research* **1**, 494–502.

McCREE, K. J. (1970). An equation for the rate of respiration of white clover plants grown under controlled conditions. *In* "Prediction and measurement of photosynthetic productivity". *Proc. IBP/PP technical meeting, Trebon,* 1969. (I. Setlik, ed.), pp. 221–229. Centre for Agricultural Publishing & Documentation, Wageningen.

McCREE, K. J. and TROUGHTON, J. H. (1966a). Prediction of growth rate at different light levels from measured photosynthesis and respiration rates. *Pl. Physiol., Lancaster* **41**, 559–566.

McCREE, K. J. and TROUGHTON, J. H. (1966b). Non-existence of an optimum leaf area index for the production rate of white clover grown under constant conditions. *Pl. Physiol., Lancaster* **41**, 1615–1622.

MEHLER, A. H. (1951a). Studies on reactions of illuminated chloroplasts. I. Mechanism of the reduction of oxygen and other Hill reagents. *Archs Biochem. Biophys.* **33**, 65–67.

MEHLER, A. H. (1951b). Studies on reactions of illuminated chloroplasts. II. Stimulation and inhibition of the reaction with molecular oxygen. *Archs Biochem. Biophys.* **34**, 339–351.

MEHLER, A. H. and BROWN, A. H. (1952). Studies on reactions of illuminated chloroplasts. III. Simultaneous photoproduction and consumption of oxygen studied with oxygen isotopes. *Archs Biochem. Biophys.* **38**, 365–370.

OZBUN, J. L., VOLK, R. J. and JACKSON, W. A. (1964). Effects of light and darkness on gaseous exchange in bean leaves. *Pl. Physiol., Lancaster* **39**, 523–527.

PEDERSON, T. A., KIRK, M. and BASSHAM, J. A. (1966). Light dark transients in levels of intermediate compounds during photosynthesis in air-adapted *Chlorella*. *Physiologia Pl.* **19**, 219–231.

SAMISH, V. and KOLLER, D. (1968). Photorespiration in green plants during photosynthesis estimated by use of isotopic $CO_2$. *Pl. Physiol., Lancaster* **43**, 1129–1131.

SHAIN, Y. and GIBBS, M. (1971). Formation of glycollate by a reconstituted spinach chloroplast preparation. *Pl. Physiol., Lancaster* **48**, 325–330.

TOLBERT, N. E., OESER, A., KISAKI, T., HAGEMAN, R. H. and YAMAZAKI, R. K. (1968). Peroxisomes from spinach leaves containing enzymes related to glycolate metabolism. *J. biol. Chem.* **243**, 5179–5184.

TREGUNNA, E. B., KROTKOV, G. and NELSON, C. D. (1966). Effect of oxygen on the rate of photorespiration in detached tobacco leaves. *Physiologia Pl.* **19**, 723–733.

TURNER, J. S. and BRITTAIN, E. G. (1962). Oxygen as a factor in photosynthesis. *Biol. Rev.* **37**, 130–170.

WALKER, D. A. and CROFTS, A. R. (1970). Photosynthesis. *A. Rev. Biochem.* **39**, 389–428.

WEIGL, J. W., WARRINGTON, P. M. and CALVIN, M. (1951). The relation of photosynthesis to respiration. *J. Am. chem. Soc.* **73**, 5058–5063.

WHITEHOUSE, D. G., LUDWIG, L. J. and WALKER, D. A. (1971). Participation of the Mehler reaction and catalase in the oxygen exchange of chloroplast preparations. *J. exp. Bot.* **22**, 772–791.

WHITTINGHAM, C. P., BERMINGHAM, M. and HILLER, R. G. (1963). The photometabolism of glucose in *Chorella*. *Z. Naturf.* **18b**, 701–706.

WILSON, A. T. and CALVIN, M. (1955). The photosynthetic cycle $CO_2$ dependent transients. *J. Am. chem. Soc.* **77**, 5948–5957.

ZELITCH, I. (1964). Organic acids and respiration in photosynthetic tissues. *A. Rev. Pl. Physiol.* **15**, 121–142.

ZELITCH, I. (1966). Increased rate of net photosynthetic carbon dioxide uptake caused by the inhibition of glycolate oxidase. *Pl. Physiol., Lancaster* **41**, 1623–1631.

ZELITCH, I. and WALKER, D. A. (1964). The role of glycolic acid metabolism in opening of leaf stomata. *Pl. Physiol., Lancaster* **39**, 856–862.

# Discussion

**Hughes** asked whether the effect of carbon dioxide on the inhibition of net photosynthesis by oxygen only applied at high light intensities. **Ludwig** confirmed that all his experiments were carried out at relatively high light intensities and that comparable experiments had not been performed at low light levels. **Tregunna** said that his experiments showed that the percentage inhibition due to oxygen was independent of light intensity and the effect of carbon dioxide on the inhibition was also the same, on a percentage basis, at high and low intensities. Hughes thought that this was an important question because glasshouse crops are frequently grown under low light conditions. He indicated that $C_3$-plants had a lower light compensation point than $C_4$-plants and should therefore be more efficient at low light. Ludwig pointed out that he had not suggested that it was desirable to select for $C_4$-characteristics in $C_3$-plants. He thought it would be better and probably easier to produce $C_3$-plants with a decreased sensitivity to oxygen. Such plants should be more efficient than those with a $C_4$-pathway of photosynthesis at all light levels because of the lower energy requirement for carbon dioxide fixation.

Tregunna suggested it might also be advantageous to breed plants with wider stomata to reduce the carbon dioxide gradient from outside; any increase in transpiration could be balanced by raising the glasshouse humidity.

# IV.4 Respiration and growth

F. W. T. PENNING DE VRIES

*Department of Theoretical Production Ecology, Agricultural University, Wageningen, The Netherlands*

## I. Introduction

As early as 1922 it was observed that the uptake of glucose by *Aspergillus niger* is related to its growth (Terroine and Wurmser, 1922). Under a range of conditions the weight of the mycelium formed is about 45% of the weight of the carbohydrates consumed. From the observation that this percentage decreases with the age of the culture, it was concluded that another energy-requiring process occurs to keep the organism functioning. This process was calculated to require about 1% of the mycelium dry weight per hour. Tamiya (1932) and Tamiya and Yamagutchi (1933) were among the first to use and quantify the concepts "growth respiration" and "maintenance respiration" by measuring glucose uptake, mycelium dry weight, oxygen consumption and carbon dioxide production of a growing *Aspergillus niger* culture. These workers presented some interesting ideas about basic phenomena of dry matter production. This kind of study is continued in microbiology (Rippel-Baldes, 1952; Bauchop and Elsden, 1960; Payne, 1970), but is very scarce in literature about higher plants.

Another approach to the relation between respiration and dry matter production considers the energy contents of compounds and the reactions by which these compounds are formed. It is used in animal physiology (Brody, 1945; Blaxter, 1962; Needham, 1964), but is also to be found in the older literature of microbiology (Terroine and Wurmser, 1922; Tamiya, 1932) and in more recent work. Forrest and Walker (1971) provide detailed information about the energy requirement during the synthesis of bacteria.

Since the forties much research and study has been devoted to respiration rates of organs and organisms as influenced by temperature, oxygen and carbon dioxide tension, concentration of micro-elements, uncoupling agents and in relation to metabolism. Biochemical investigations have supplied detailed information about glycolysis, the TCA cycle, electron transfer and phosphorylation in mitochondria and related processes (Ducet and Rosenberg, 1962; Beevers, 1970).

Recently the fascinating topic of photorespiration has received much attention. Biochemical mechanisms have been suggested, but the meaning of this process for the plant is still uncertain (Jackson and Volk, 1970; Walker and Crofts, 1970).

Of the many aspects of plant growth only change in dry weight will be considered. Other aspects of growth (fresh weight increase, change in form or volume) have at the most only a small direct influence on carbon dioxide production.

Since simulation models of crop growth have been developed, it has become increasingly evident that quantitatively little is known about respiration involved with crop growth (Canvin, 1970). In the model of de Wit *et al.* (1970) an approach was adopted in which respiration associated with synthesis of dry matter was calculated using biochemical knowledge on the conversion of glucose into plant constituents, and that concerned with maintenance was estimated from plant protein content and temperature. There have been previous attempts to link dry matter production and respiration to substrate use based on molecular conversions (Tamiya, 1932; Krebs and Kornberg, 1957; Schiemann, 1958; Blaxter, 1962), but their results were not detailed and cannot be applied in quantitative estimates of crop and plant respiration. It is, however, this approach that will be extended in this paper in order to elucidate problems concerned with respiration of plants and crops.

Little attention will be paid to the efficiency of energy transfer in the plant. The main reason is the very much easier way in which information is obtained (Krebs and Kornberg, 1957) and calculations are performed, using weights of compounds.

# II. Respiration and synthetic processes

Increase in plant dry matter is nearly always due to synthetic processes. Only where minerals are taken up or glucose accumulates in cells as an end product is dry weight increase not the result of synthesis other than photosynthesis. It is therefore logical to study synthetic processes in detail.

Biochemical pathways for the synthesis of the majority of organic constituents are known (Bonner and Varner, 1965; Dagley and Nicholson, 1970). From such knowledge the weight of a certain compound synthesized from 1·0 g of a particular substrate was established theoretically. Both material conversions occurring during synthesis and the chemical energy to be supplied to the reactions in the form of ATP were taken into account. Results of such calculations are given in Table I. The theoretical derivation of these values will be considered elsewhere. The factor by which the weight of the organic substrate is multiplied in order to achieve the weight of a particular end product formed via a particular conversion pathway will be called the "production value" or "weight

## Table I

Some characteristic values for the conversion of 1·0 g of glucose into plant components, using the most efficient biochemical pathways.

| End product | Weight of end product (p.v.) | Carbon dioxide production factor (c.p.f.) | Oxygen requirement factor (o.r.f.) | Energy efficiency | N and S supplied as |
|---|---|---|---|---|---|
| Amino acids | 0·80 | 0·11 | 0·047 | 0·79 | $NH_3$ and $H_2S$ |
| Amino acids | 0·54 | 0·55 | 0·003 | 0·68 | $NO_3^-$ and $SO_4^{2-}$ |
| Proteins | 0·67 | 0·16 | 0·081 | 0·78 | $NH_3$ and $H_2S$ |
| Proteins | 0·45 | 0·58 | 0·036 | 0·67 | $NO_3^-$ and $SO_4^{2-}$ |
| Nucleic acids | 0·77 | 0·33 | 0·394 | — | $NH_3$ and $H_2S$ |
| Nucleic acids | 0·57 | 0·62 | 0·081 | — | $NO_3^-$ and $SO_4^{2-}$ |
| Lipids | 0·36 | 0·47 | 0·035 | 0·88 | |
| Cellulose and Starch | 0·855 | 0·07 | 0·051 | 0·93 | |
| Sucrose | 0·915 | 0·053 | 0·0385 | 0·96 | |
| Carboxylic acids | 1·43 | −0·25 | 0·13 | 0·6 | |

efficiency" for this conversion (p.v.). Each combination of substrate, pathway and end product has its own p.v., but it appeared in most cases that the resulting p.v. depends little on the pathway chosen. It is therefore unlikely that the p.v. varies between species. The factor by which the weight of the organic substrate is multiplied to give the weight of the $CO_2$ produced will be called the "carbon dioxide production factor" (c.p.f.). The factor necessary to calculate the weight of oxygen required in the conversion of the initial weight of substrate will be termed the "oxygen requirement factor" (o.r.f.). To compare the "weight efficiency" (p.v.) of the conversions with the "energy efficiency" (the combustion value of the end product per decrease of the combustion value of the substrate used) approximate values for the latter are presented in Table I. These are considerably more uniform than the p.v. of the conversions.

For the composition of the amino acid mixture and proteins in Table I, data for alfalfa (Mertz *et al.*, 1952) were used. Nucleic acids are assumed to consist of equal amounts of RNA and DNA. The lipid fraction was taken to be merely glycerine tripalmitate. Carboxylic acids are assumed to consist of equal weights of malic and citric acid. As the *in vivo* pathway of synthesis of carboxylates is not well established it is assumed that the carboxylation of pyruvate is an intermediate reaction, so that during their synthesis carbon dioxide is taken up instead of being produced.

From Table I it is seen that the p.v. of glucose for carbohydrates and carboxylic acids is considerably higher than its p.v. for lipids, amino acids, proteins and nucleic acids. The p.v. for synthesis of nitrogenous compounds is higher when reduced nitrogen and sulphur are supplied instead of nitrate and sulphate, due to the relatively large amount of energy required for reduction. The p.v. for protein synthesis depends upon the composition of its amino acid mixture. For 13 different plant and animal proteins the p.v. for synthesis from glucose and nitrate was calculated to vary between 0·446 (arachin) and 0·496 (gliadin), the c.p.f. being 0·588 and 0·522 and the o.r.f. 0·028 and 0·013 respectively.

The figures in Table I depend little on the assumptions made, the most important ones being that the plant uses what are believed to be the most efficient biochemical pathways, that these are common for all species at any time and that the P/O ratio of ATP production is 3 (Beevers, 1961, p. 127; Hadjipetrou *et al.*, 1964).

Provided that the chemical composition of the plant is known, the p.v.'s of Table I allow the amount of glucose required to synthesize 1·0 g of plant material to be calculated. An example of this is given in Table II, where the chemical composition refers to 25-day old maize plants. The fraction "organic N compounds" is assumed to consist of proteins (75%) and amino acids (20%), having a composition similar to alfalfa (Mertz *et al.*, 1952), and nucleic acids (5%). "Carbohydrates" consist of starch and cellulose (80%), sucrose (15%) and glucose (5%). For "lipids" and "carboxylic acids" the same suppositions as in Table I were made. Nitrogen and sulphur are taken to be supplied in the oxidized form.

Plant tissue contains minerals, which are taken up actively into cells with energy derived from glucose. It may be assumed from data collected by Beevers (1961) and Stein (1967) that 1·0 g of minerals can be taken up actively into cells with energy achieved from approximately 0·05 g glucose. Lehninger (1965) derived similar values on a thermodynamic basis.

As a rule a source of glucose is not present in growing cells and therefore carbohydrates have also to be imported. Assuming that all import is active, that passage of two cell membranes requires the energy of 2 ATP molecules per glucose molecule and that costs of translocation over distances less than 1 m are negligible (Weatherley and Johnson, 1968), it was calculated that for both the unloading and loading of the phloem by 1·0 g of glucose 0·05 g has to be respired. Costs of intracellular transport

**Table II**

The amount of glucose required to synthesize 1·0 g of plant material

| Compound or process | Weight of compounds (g) | p.v. | Glucose required (g) | c.p.f. | Carbon dioxide produced (g) | o.r.f. | Oxygen consumed (g) |
|---|---|---|---|---|---|---|---|
| Organic N compounds | 0·23 | 0·48 | 0·478 | 0·57 | 0·272 | 0·031 | 0·0148 |
| Lipids | 0·025 | 0·36 | 0·070 | 0·47 | 0·033 | 0·035 | 0·0025 |
| Carbo- hydrates | 0·64 | 0·87 | 0·735 | 0·064 | 0·047 | 0·047 | 0·0345 |
| Carboxylic acids | 0·04 | 1·43 | 0·028 | −0·25 | −0·007 | 0·13 | 0·0036 |
| Mineral uptake | 0·065 | 20 | 0·003 | 1·47 | 0·005 | 1·07 | 0·0035 |
| Glucose uptake | — | — | 0·070 | 1·47 | 0·103 | 1·07 | 0·0750 |
| Total | 1·00 | — | 1·384 | — | 0·453 | — | 0·1339 |

are neglected. The membrane transport mechanism of ionic and non-ionic compounds is not clear (Kaback, 1970), so that these figures are estimates.

The result of the refinements included in Table II is that the maximum relative yield of 1·38 g glucose available from the phloem is 1·0 g of tissue and that 0·453 g of carbon dioxide is produced and 0·134 g of oxygen consumed.

Table III presents the results of an experimental test of the above hypothesis. Kandler (1953) cultivated maize embryos in darkness on a solution containing glucose and nitrate. Dry weight increase and glucose consumption were measured. The chemical composition of the young plant was estimated from the observed amount of nitrogen in the embryo.

The requirements for glucose and ion uptake were taken to be two times higher than the ones in Table II to account for uptake by the roots and transport into growing cells from vascular tissue. The lower p.v. for "organic N compounds" compared with Table II was calculated assuming that all amino acids are synthesized in the roots and that half of them are translocated to support shoot growth.

The experimentally established glucose consumption (75·4 mg) is 10% higher than was expected (68·0 mg). Causes of this discrepancy may be

## Table III

The amount of glucose required to synthesize 47·5 mg maize embryo. Measured glucose uptake: 75·4 ± 2·4 mg

| Compound or process | Weight of compounds (mg) | p.v. | Glucose required (mg) | c.p.f. | Carbon dioxide produced (mg) | o.r.f. | Oxygen consumed (mg) |
|---|---|---|---|---|---|---|---|
| Organic N compounds | 5·6 | 0·44 | 12·8 | 0·60 | 7·7 | 0·080 | 1·0 |
| Lipids | 2·4 | 0·36 | 6·6 | 0·47 | 3·1 | 0·035 | 0·3 |
| Carbo-hydrates | 34·7 | 0·87 | 39·9 | 0·062 | 2·5 | 0·045 | 1·8 |
| Carboxylic acids | 2·4 | 1·43 | 1·7 | −0·25 | −0·4 | 0·13 | 0·2 |
| Mineral uptake | 2·4 | 10 | 0·2 | 1·47 | 0·3 | 1·07 | 0·2 |
| Glucose uptake | — | — | 6·8 | 1·47 | 10·0 | 1·07 | 7·3 |
| Total | 47·5 | — | 68·0 | — | 23·2 | — | 10·8 |

an incorrect estimation of the chemical composition of the dry matter. It is also possible that the neglect of maintenance respiration or redistribution (p. 342) is not warranted because of the relatively unfavourable culture conditions, evident from its low nitrogen content (1·9% compared with 3–5% normally observed). This suggestion is supported by the observation that the relative yield of the glucose consumed decreases rather rapidly with increasing age of the plant. A maintenance respiration rate of 5% of the dry matter per day (three times the normal value) may cover the difference between experiment and hypothesis completely. It is also possible that a certain rate of turnover of the synthesized compounds occurs, increasing the amount of substrate required for dry matter production. If this takes place it ought to be included in the calculation of the p.v.

A similar correspondence between theory and experiment was not observed in bacterial cultures where the experimental yield is about 0·3–0·5 of the theoretical value. The cause of this difference between higher and lower organisms is discussed by Forrest and Walker (1971).

# III. Respiration and synthesis from photosynthate

Photorespiration will not be discussed because it does not affect processes after production of photosynthate; that it decreases the rate of photosynthate formation is not relevant here. Heath (1969) has given a review about the interrelationship of photosynthesis and respiration.

Except under laboratory conditions, the substrate for plant growth is not merely glucose and nitrate. The substrate for dry matter production in roots, stems and young leaves is phloem translocate, more mature leaves utilizing their own photosynthetic products. In both cases the substrate for growth is complex: photosynthesis generates a wide variety of compounds (Gibbs *et al.*, 1967) and phloem contains a mixture of carbohydrates and amino acids (Kursanov, 1963).

It was measured in maize plants that from the daily net carbon dioxide uptake about 0·62 g dry matter per g carbon dioxide was formed, or 0·90 g when carbon dioxide fixation is expressed in g $CH_2O$. In *Helianthus annuus* these values are 0·64 and 0·94 respectively (Eckhardt *et al.*, 1971). This ratio is determined by the chemical composition of the plant, which does not depend on the photosynthetic rate. However, it does not matter what part of the carbon dioxide assimilated by leaves in the light ends up in plant material and what part is lost by respiration of leaves in darkness and in the other plant organs. Important questions in understanding plant production are therefore, first: how much photosynthate is required to produce 1·0 g of plant dry matter, and second: how much carbon dioxide uptake by adult leaves corresponds with this. It will be derived that from 2·027 g (carbon dioxide) gross assimilate a maize plant may produce 1·0 g of plant dry matter, and a bean plant this same quantity, but with different chemical composition, from 1·923 (carbon dioxide) gross assimilate. The conversion respiration is 0·430 and 0·368 g carbon dioxide respectively.

For the derivation of the above figures it is assumed that the plant is separated into a photosynthesizing part with hardly any permanent dry matter accumulation, and a non-photosynthetic growing part. The substrate for the formation of dry matter has to be transported from the productive sites to leaves that are not yet able to photosynthesize, to roots and to other organs. Figures 1 and 2 represent an organ converting phloem translocate into new structural material and a photosynthesizing leaf respectively. In both Figures the types of compounds involved are given in blocks and the numbers represent the corresponding weights in grams.

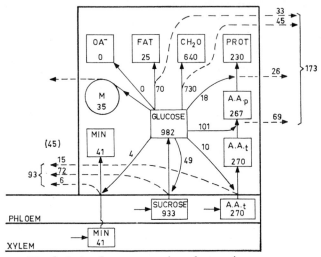

**Fig. 1.** A simple representation of a growing organ.

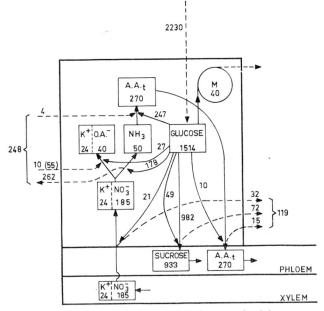

**Fig. 2.** A simple representation of a photosynthesizing organ.

Full drawn lines represent conversion and transport processes, dashed lines represent carbon dioxide exchange, and oxygen is not considered. The chemical composition of vegetative maize plants and the data of Table I were the basis for the calculations.

It is shown (Fig. 1) that $(230 + 640 + 25 + 41 =)$ 936 g tissue may be synthesized from 41 g of minerals (MIN) supplied by the xylem, and $(933 + 270 =)$ 1203 g phloem translocate, consisting of 77·5% of sucrose, and 22·5% of a mixture of amino acids (A.A.$_t$), including 4·7% amides. After uptake, some sucrose is transformed via glucose into lipids (FAT), carbohydrates ($CH_2O$) and some is used to provide energy for uptake processes and protein (PROT) synthesis from amino acids. Glucose is also a source of carbon and energy for the transformation of amino acids of the translocated mixture (A.A.$_t$) into a mixture (A.A.$_p$) ready to synthesize the plant proteins. The composition of A.A.$_t$ was chosen to be the sum of the amino acids usually not formed via aspartic and glutamic acid and a large enough quantity of aspartic and glutamic acid to produce the amino acids synthesized from these. The carbon dioxide production amounts to $(33 + 45 + 26 + 69 =)$ 173 g due to conversions and $(15 + 72 + 6 =)$ 93 g due to membrane transport. The circle with M represents the maintenance processes and the number in it an estimation of its daily glucose requirement. It is not included in the calculations.

Figure 2 shows very simply what may be formed by a photosynthesizing leaf when it is supplying the substrate for the organ of Fig. 1. Considerable amounts of energy are involved in $NO_3^-$ reduction ($NO_3^-$ stands for both $NO_3^-$ and $SO_4^{2-}$). Some carbon dioxide is taken up during amino acid and carboxylic acid synthesis. Not all dry weight increase occurs in the "growing" organ: the formation of $(40 + 24 =)$ 64 g of carboxylates takes place in the adult part and is coupled with $NO_3^-$ reduction (Dijkshoorn, 1962). Like perennial ryegrass (Dijkshoorn et al., 1968) maize exports most of its carboxylates formed to the roots, where the carboxylate group is exchanged with $NO_3^-$. The carboxylate remaining in the leaf consists of an organic anion (OA$^-$) and an inorganic cation (K$^+$), the latter being part of the plant mineral content. It should be mentioned that in Figs 1 and 2 the net process of carboxylate formation is represented. Some non-photosynthetically absorbed carbon dioxide is transported to the roots as carboxylic acid and exchanged. The carbon dioxide involved in this process is given within parentheses in both figures. It appears that approximately 3% of the leaf carbon dioxide uptake is "pumped" from the air into the root medium, the exact percentage depending upon the mechanism of carboxylate formation. Part of the carbon dioxide uptake during photosynthesis is therefore not related to carbon dioxide reduction.

There is evidence that in a well fertilized crop the bulk of the $NO_3^-$

reduction occurs in the leaves during photosynthesis (Beevers and Hageman, 1969). This means that the source of $NADPH_2$ for $NO_3^-$ reduction (from carbohydrate oxidation or active chloroplasts) is irrelevant to this study because a certain measured photosynthetic carbon dioxide uptake would result in both cases in the same amount of reduced nitrogen and reduced carbon. The problem of channelling of energy may be of interest for a plant production approach because, if $NO_3^-$ reduction is competitive with carbon dioxide reduction or utilizes carbohydrates, plants suboptimally supplied with $NO_3^-$ may have a higher carbohydrate production rate. It is also questionable whether the energy for both transport and maintenance is always channelled via carbohydrates, or whether it is directly available from active chloroplasts as suggested by Ried (1970). The value of 2230 g carbon dioxide in Fig. 2 represents the total of carbon dioxide to be reduced if all hydrogen for nitrate reduction and energy for the considered processes is derived from glucose. This value for carbon dioxide reduction is merely given to illustrate the relative magnitude of sinks of carbon and energy during photosynthesis, and not to suggest that glucose is the intermediate in these processes. Photorespiration, like nitrate reduction, could have been represented in Fig. 2 by an additional amount of carbon dioxide that is reduced and subsequently re-oxidized.

Gross carbon dioxide assimilation may be defined as the sum of assimilation in light and dissimilation as measured shortly after a period of long enough duration to establish an equilibrium between photosynthesis and respiration; the leaf should have a normal rate of nitrate reduction. The gross carbon dioxide assimilation, equal to the apparent gross photosynthesis, of the above maize leaf during production of (936 + 64 =) 1000 g biomass is 2230 + 4 + 55 − 262 − 119 (assimilation in light) + 119 (dark respiration) = 2027 g, while the plant dissimilation amounts to 430 g carbon dioxide, of which (119 + 93 =) 212 g due to transport, 173 g due to conversions and 45 g due to exchange. The overall net carbon dioxide uptake by the entire plant is (2027 − 430 =) 1597 g, which does agree with the expected value of (1000/0·62 =) 1610 g. In this calculation it is assumed that nitrate reduction and carboxylate formation occur in light only, and that export continues still at the same rate when dissimilation is measured; maintenance is neglected. It can be concluded that of a gross assimilation of 1·00 g carbon dioxide, equivalent to 0·68 g $CH_2O$, 0·49 g maize plant dry matter can be synthesized.

This set of calculations is evidently oversimplified. The calculated yield of the conversion may be slightly too low, as cells in nearly adult leaves supply substrate for their own growth, for which no translocation costs are incurred. In maize plants the factor 0·51 may therefore be used to calculate vegetative dry matter production from the gross assimilation expressed in g carbon dioxide, or the factor 0·75 if expressed in g $CH_2O$.

For species not exchanging the carboxylate group with nitrate in roots it was calculated in a similar manner that of an apparent gross photosynthetic carbon dioxide uptake of 1923 g carbon dioxide 1000 g biomass may be synthesized, consisting of 46·5% carbohydrates, 22·0% proteins, 15·6% carboxylates, 12·1% minerals and 3·8% lipids; the associated respiration is 191 g carbon dioxide due to transport and 177 g due to conversion. Similar values of carboxylate and mineral content are reported by van Egmond and Houba (1970) in sugar beet plants. Thus in these plants, from 1 g of $CH_2O$ apparent gross photosynthesis (1·47 g carbon dioxide), 0·77 g of plant dry matter may be synthesized. As in the previous

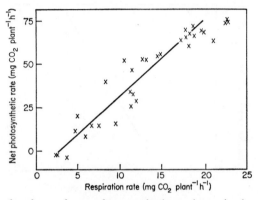

**Fig. 3.** Measured values of net photosynthetic and respiration rate of maize plants. The slope of the line is determined theoretically.

analysis this is probably an underestimate and the factor 0·80 may be more appropriate to calculate dry matter production from apparent gross photosynthesis expressed in $CH_2O$.

The highest relative yields from photosynthetic products observed in rapidly growing plants are about 0·8 (Warren Wilson, 1967). More direct evidence for the reliability of the calculations is presented in Figs 3 and 4. The slope of the line relating net photosynthetic rate to respiration rate of 10-day old maize plants (Fig. 3) and of 17-day old bean shoots (*Phaseolus vulgaris*, Fig. 4) will be derived theoretically. Both correspond well with the experimental data (crosses).

In the maize experiment plants were exposed to a regime of 7 h light followed by 1 h darkness in an assembly as described by Louwerse and van Oorschot (1969). At the third repetition of the light cycle, an equilibrium was reached between the net photosynthetic rate and respiration rate and only measurements of these situations are represented. After the third cycle another value of light intensity in the range from 0 to 300 W m⁻² visible radiation was applied. Assuming that synthetic processes in the growing organs and transport continue at the same rate in light and darkness because of a buffering capacity of the producing leaves, it was calculated from Figs 1 and 2 that a carbon dioxide production rate of 430 g per unit of time should correspond with a net photosynthetic rate of (2027 × 8/7 — 430 =) 1890 g carbon dioxide per unit of time. The factor 8/7 is introduced to take into account that photosynthesis occurs during only a fraction of the time and respiration continuously. When the maintenance respiration rate is independent of the rate of dry matter production the theoretical relationship between net photosynthetic rate

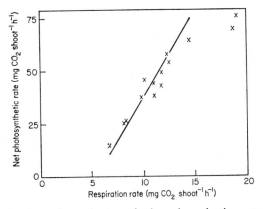

**Fig. 4.** Measured values of net photosynthetic and respiration rate of bean shoots. The slope of the line is determined theoretically.

and conversion respiration rate of maize is given by the line in Fig. 3. Only the intercept of the line, representing maintenance respiration, is adjusted to the position of the crosses.

A corresponding relationship for bean shoots was computed in a similar manner and is presented in Fig. 4 with a line. The experimental conditions were slightly different.

In Figs 3 and 4 there is a good correspondence between theory and experiment, although the experiment is not sensitive enough to detect minor changes in the assumptions. At the highest light intensities this correspondence does not hold. It is not clear in these cases whether substrate (carbohydrate) induced respiration occurs or that a shift of processes takes place to the dark period due to water stress in the light. Figs 3 and 4 do not support the suggestion (p. 332) of an intensive turn over of compounds during synthesis.

# IV. Respiration and maintenance

Maintenance consists of processes to compensate for the degradation of existing structures and organization. The respiration originating from energy production for maintenance is called maintenance respiration. Resynthesis of hydrolysed proteins is likely to be part of maintenance processes, but also dry matter accumulation on one level of organization may sometimes be seen as a part of maintenance on a higher level, e.g. the formation of a new leaf on a plant when it replaces a lost one. It may be stated that maintenance very often comprises synthesis, but also other kinds of processes may participate. Both the factors causing and those influencing the rate of degradation processes, and thus the rate of re-growth, are still largely unknown. It is therefore as yet not possible to derive the rate of maintenance respiration theoretically.

According to Pirt (1965), Ducleaux (1898) was the first to distinguish energy for maintenance and energy for growth. Terroine and Wurmser (1922) estimated it to cause 26% of the fungi mycelium dry weight per day to be combusted. Tamiya (1932) and Tamiya and Yamagutchi (1933) reported similar high values and Pirt (1965) even higher ones for bacteria. McCree (1970) estimated by extrapolation maintenance respiration rates of intact clover plants to be as low as 1·5% of the plant dry matter per day, which is in close agreement with the author's measurements (Table IV). Maintenance respiration has been taken to be the rate constant during 12 h at the end of a dark period which lasted from 1 to 4 days, depending on plant type and pretreatment. De Wit et al. (1970) concluded from results obtained with a simulation model for crop growth that this maintenance respiration rate is a reasonable estimate for vegetative tissue. The respiration rate of storage tissue (Norton, 1963) and woody tissue (Yoda et al., 1965) is much lower. Maintenance respiration rates appear to be more uniform when expressed on the basis of soluble nitrogenous compounds, which suggests a direct or indirect relationship.

It is questionable whether turnover rates of proteins, as measured by Holmsen and Koch (1964) are caused only by maintenance processes or also by redistribution of amino acids in the plant. It is therefore not realistic to calculate the maintenance respiration rate from these figures, giving a protein half-life time of seven days for tobacco plants.

It should be investigated whether the excess ATP produced during photosynthesis (Ried, 1970) or rapid growth (Forrest and Walker, 1971) may be used in processes such as maintenance, thereby reducing the amount of substrate required for these purposes. Uncoupled and idling respiration (Beevers, 1970; Tanaka, 1971) are not considered because of the lack of experimental information.

**Table IV**

Some maintenance respiration rates. Accuracy: $\pm 20\%$

| Object | Respiration rate | |
|--------|---------------------------------|-------------------------------|
|        | g $CH_2O$ g$^{-1}$ day$^{-1}$ | g $CO_2$ g$^{-1}$ day$^{-1}$ |
| Maize, adult leaf, 25°C | 0·011 | 0·015 |
| Maize, adult leaf, 25°C[1] | 0·008 | 0·012 |
| *Phaseolus vulgaris*, adult leaf, 25°C[2] | 0·012 | 0·017 |
| Maize, 20 day old plant, 15°C | 0·013 | 0·019 |
| Maize, 20 day old plant, 20°C | 0·011 | 0·015 |
| Maize, 20 day old plant, 25°C | 0·013 | 0·019 |
| Maize, 10 day old plant, 25°C | 0·013 | 0·019 |
| Maize, 10 day old plant, 25°C | 0·022 | 0·032 |
| *Lolium perenne*, 40 day old plant, 25°C | 0·014 | 0·021 |

[1] Alberda, unpublished results
[2] Louwerse, unpublished results

# V. Respiration and temperature

No observations are known where temperature influences the pathway by which a compound is synthesized or the P/O ratio of energy production. In other words, p.v., c.p.f. and o.r.f. are expected to be the same in the range of temperatures normally encountered. It is therefore concluded that temperature affects the conversion respiration rate only indirectly, the rate of synthesis being intermediate.

The conclusion that the p.v. is independent of temperature is supported by the results of experiments with young organisms growing on glucose solution and seeds germinating at temperatures ranging from 11 to 38°C, presented in Table V. The relative yields of the growth processes are given in g plant formed per g substrate used and in some cases also in heat of combustion of the material formed per decrease in heat of combustion of the substrate used. The number of replicates and individuals per replicate are indicated. Significant differences in relative yield are not caused by temperature variation, but by differences in the chemical composition of the substrate. The different values in Table V for the relative yields within one species will at least partly be caused by the variable chemical composition of seeds. Kaufmann (1952) concluded that the relative yield of *Saccharomyces cerevisiae* depends on temperature but this does not agree with his data.

## Table V

The influence of temperature and chemical composition of seed or substrate on the relative yield of growth processes

| Species | Main storage compounds | Temp. (°C) | Relative yield g g⁻¹ | Relative yield cal cal⁻¹ | Number of exp. and individuals | Duration of the experiment (days) | Reference |
|---|---|---|---|---|---|---|---|
| Rice | carbohydrates | 26 | 0·57 | 0·65 | 1 (50) | 10 | 1 |
| Rice | ,, | 30 | 0·60 | 0·73 | 4 (25) | 9 | 2 |
| Rice | ,, | 20–30 | 0·60 | — | 1 (1000) | 5–15 | 3 |
| Barley | ,, | 22 | 0·64 | — | 8 (100) | 3–7 | 4 |
| Sorghum | ,, | 17 | 0·78 | 0·74 | 2 (45) | 12 | 2 |
| Sorghum | ,, | 33 | 0·54 | 0·74 | 3 (45) | 4 | 2 |
| Maize | ,, | 22 | 0·60 | — | 2 (10) | 10 | 5 |
| Maize | ,, | 15 | 0·50 | — | 1 (100) | 17 | 6 |
| Maize | ,, | 25 | 0·51 | — | 2 (100) | 13 | 6 |
| Maize | glucose + NO₃⁻ | 27 | 0·62 | 0·70 | 2 (16) | 5 | 7 |
| Lentils | carbohydrates and proteins | 11 | 0·56 | 0·63 | 2 (3) | 10 | 2 |
| Lentils | ,, | 18 | 0·57 | 0·63 | 3 (3) | 6 | 2 |
| Lentils | ,, | 30 | 0·57 | 0·62 | 7 (3) | 7 | 2 |
| Peas | ,, | 18 | 0·54 | 0·62 | 5 (3) | 8 | 2 |
| *Vigna sesquipedalis* | ,, | 30 | 0·48 | — | 1 (?) | 3 | 8 |
| *Phaseolus vulgaris* | ,, | 18 | 0·63 | — | 1 (50) | 13 | 6 |
| *Phaseolus vulgaris* | ,, | 25 | 0·73 | — | 2 (50) | 7 | 6 |
| *Brassica napus* | lipids | 11 | 0·83 | 0·52 | 2 (45) | 17 | 2 |
| *Brassica napus* | ,, | 21 | 0·92 | 0·52 | 3 (45) | 9 | 2 |
| Groundnut | ,, | 17 | 0·88 | 0·52 | 6 (1) | 15 | 2 |
| Groundnut | ,, | 30 | 0·86 | 0·54 | 8 (1) | 2–10 | 2 |
| Groundnut | ,, | 20 | 0·96 | — | 1 (50) | 22 | 6 |
| Groundnut | ,, | 27 | 0·95 | — | 2 (50) | 16 | 6 |
| *Aspergillus niger* | glucose + NH₃ (aerobic) | 22–38 | 0·45 | 0·72 | 7–16 (—) | 1–4 | 9 |
| *Escherichia coli* | ,, | 30 | 0·37 | — | 4 (—) | 1–5 h | 10 |

References:
1 Tang et al., 1965
2 Terroine et al., 1924
3 Tanaka, 1971
4 calculated from Barnell, 1937
5 Cooper and MacDonald, 1970
6 Penning de Vries, unpublished data
7 Kandler, 1953
8 calculated from Oota et al., 1953
9 Terroine and Wurmser, 1922
10 calculated from Siegel and Clifton, 1950a, 1950b

It should be noted that "relative yield" includes the integrated maintenance requirement (Pirt, 1965). The relative yield is therefore not an accurate measure of the p.v. of a conversion process. The duration of the experiments is given in Table V.

The presumption that under unfavourable conditions synthesis proceeds less efficiently was rejected by Terroine and Wurmser (1922). Shemikatova (1970) explains the lower relative growth rate and yield observed in these cases as due to a stimulation of maintenance processes. Rippel-Baldes (1952) and Forrest and Walker (1971) suggested that microorganisms do not operate at the theoretical maximum efficiency in converting material and energy. It might be useful to investigate whether the low relative yield of micro-organisms as compared with higher plants is caused only by a lower p.v. of synthetic processes or also by a higher maintenance requirement.

# VI. Respiration and net dry matter production

From the foregoing considerations about respiration ($R$, g carbon dioxide), apparent gross photosynthesis ($P$, g $CH_2O$), dry matter production (DMP) and maintenance, a formula can be given for respiration:

$$R = aP + bW$$

and also one for dry matter production, similar to the empirical one of McCree (1970):

$$DMP = cP - 30/44bW$$

in which $a$ is approximately 0·31 or 0·28, and $c$ is 0·75 or 0·80, depending on the plant type (p. 337). $b$ is 0·0225 day$^{-1}$ and $W$ represents plant dry weight. The variables $a$ and $c$ are determined by the chemical composition of the material synthesized, which may change considerably with time, and $b$ is likely to depend upon tissue protein content and temperature.

Plant dry matter production is the resultant of dry matter production of organs and of various kinds of losses. In the above equation only increase has been considered, except for decreases due to maintenance. An analysis of weight decrease due to loss of organs is beyond the scope of this paper. A third cause of weight loss is redistribution, consisting of breakdown, membrane passage, translocation and resynthesis of complex compounds. This process needs consideration especially during the reproductive phase of plant growth, but it occurs also within the vegetative plant. It is estimated that breakdown, conversion into transportable products, translocation and resynthesis may reduce the weight of the translocate by 15% when it consists of sucrose and by 30% when the translocate consists of amino acids (70%) and sucrose (30%). The substrate for the corresponding respiration is taken from the translocate. Thus respirational losses of crops may be 5 to 10% larger than those calculated from the above formula. From unpublished investigations carried out by the author it appeared that in a continued dark period redistribution in maize may be quite considerable, but little is known about the field situation.

# VII. Concluding remarks

Not all processes concerning physiological aspects of respiration have been considered or even mentioned. An important and essentially un-solved problem in what is discussed remains the nature and intensity of maintenance processes, which were here only empirically treated. This process, however, is of crucial importance in understanding crop pro-ductivity. Data about the chemical composition and accurate methods to determine it are scarce. Such data as are usually reported concern special tissues or chemical fractions of the plant.

Respiration has been considered so far in a steady state. To understand and predict the conversion respiration rate of plants under non-steady-state conditions more information should be available about the effects of factors such as temperature, the relative amount of substrate for growth and the relative water content, on the rates of conversion processes.

# Acknowledgements

The author wishes to express his gratitude to Prof. Dr. Ir. C. T. de Wit for many stimulating and valuable discussions, to Mr J. N. Gallagher for correcting the English text and to Miss H. van Laar for performing numerous computations. Preliminary calculations were performed by Mr A. Brunsting.

# References

BARNELL, H. R. (1937). Analytical studies in plant respiration VII. *Proc. Roy. Soc. Ser. B.* **123,** 321–342.

BAUCHOP, T. and ELSDEN, S. R. (1960). The growth of micro-organisms in relation to their energy supply. *J. gen. Microbiol.* **23,** 457–469.

BEEVERS, H. (1961). "Respiration metabolism in plants." Harper and Row, New York.

BEEVERS, H. (1970). Respiration in plants and its regulation. *In* "Prediction and measurement of photosynthetic productivity". *Proc. IBP/PP technical meeting, Trebon, 1969* (I. Setlik, ed.), pp. 209–214. Centre for Agricultural Publishing & Documentation, Wageningen.

BEEVERS, L. and HAGEMAN, R. H. (1969). Nitrate reduction in higher plants. *A. Rev. Pl. Physiol.*, **20**, 495–522.

BLAXTER, K. L. (1962). "The energy metabolism of ruminants." Hutchinson, London.

BONNER, J. and VARNER, J. E. (1965). "Plant Biochemistry." Academic Press, London.

BRODY, S. (1945). "Bio-energetics and growth" Reinhold, New York.

CANVIN, D. T. (1970). Summary Section 3. *In* "Prediction and measurement of photosynthetic productivity". *Proc. IBP/PP technical meeting, Trebon, 1969* (I. Setlik, ed.). Centre for Agricultural Publishing & Documentation, Wageningen.

COOPER, C. S. and MacDONALD, P. W. (1970). Energetics of early seedling growth in corn. *Crop Sci.* **10**, 136–139.

DAGLEY, S. and NICHOLSON, D. E. (1970). "An introduction to metabolic pathways." Blackwell, London.

DUCET, G. and ROSENBERG, A. J. (1962). Leaf respiration. *A. Rev. Pl. Physiol.* **13**, 171–200.

DUCLEAUX, E. (1898). "Traité de Microbiologie." Vol. 1, p. 208. Masson et Cie, Paris.

DIJKSHOORN, W. (1962). Metabolic regulation of the alkaline effect of nitrate utilization in plants. *Nature, Lond.* **194**, 165–167.

DIJKSHOORN, W., LATHWELL, D. J., and WIT, C. T. DE (1968). Temporal changes in carboxylate content of ryegrass with stepwise changes in nutrition. *Pl. Soil* **29**, 369–390.

ECKHARDT, F. E., HEIM, G., METHY, M., SAUGIER, B. and SAUVEZON, R. (1971). Fonctionnement d'un écosystème au niveau de la production primaire. *Oecol. Plant.* **6**, 51–100.

EGMOND, F. VAN and HOUBA, V. J. G. (1970). Production of carboxylates (C-A) by young sugar beet plants grown in nutrient solution. *Neth. J. agric. Sci.* **18**, 182–187.

FORREST, W. W. and WALKER, D. J. (1971). The generation and utilization of energy during growth. *Adv. Microbiol. Physiol.* **5**, 213–274.

GIBBS, M., LATZKO, E., EVERSON, R. G., and COCKBURN, W. (1967). Carbon mobilization by the green plant. *In* "Harvesting the Sun". pp. 111–130. Academic Press, London.

HADJIPETROU, L. P., GERRITS, J. P., TEULINGS, F. A. G. and STOUTHAMER, A. H. (1964). Relation between energy production and growth of *Aerobacter aerogenes*. *J. gen. Microbiol.* **36**, 139–150.

HEATH, O. V. S. (1969). "The physiological aspects of photosynthesis." Heinemann, London.

HOLMSEN, T. W. and KOCH, A. L. (1964). An estimate of the protein turn over in growing tobacco plants. *Phytochemistry* **3**, 165–172.

JACKSON, W. A. and VOLK, R. J. (1970). Photorespiration. *A. Rev. Pl. Physiol.* **21**, 385–432.

KABACK, H. R. (1970). Transport. *A. Rev. Biochem.* **39**, 561–599.

KANDLER, O. (1953). Über den "Synthetischen Wirkungsgrad" in vitro cultivierter Embryonen, Wurzeln and Sprosse. *Z. Naturf.* **8b**, 109–117.

KAUFMANN, W. (1952). Untersuchungen über den Energiehaushalt der Hezefell und die Oekonomie einiger Energiestoffwechseltypen anderer Mikro-organismen. *Arch. Mikrobiol.* **17**, 319–352.

KREBS, H. A. and KORNBERG, H. L. (1957). A survey of the energy transformations in living matter. *In* "Ergebnisse der Physiologie, biologischen Chemie und experimentellen Pharmakologie", Vol. 49, pp. 212–298. Springer-Verlag, Berlin.

KURSANOV, A. L. (1963). Metabolism and transport of organic substances in the phloem. *Adv. bot. Res.* **1**, 209–279.

LEHNINGER, A. L. (1965). "Bio-energetics." Benjamin, New York.

LOUWERSE, W. and OORSCHOT, J. L. P. VAN (1969). An assembly for routine measurements of photosynthesis, respiration and transpiration of intact plants under controlled conditions. *Photosynthetica* **3**, 305–315.

McCREE, K. (1970). An equation for the rate of respiration of white clover plants grown under controlled conditions. *In* "Prediction and measurement of photosynthetic productivity". *Proc. IBP/PP technical meeting, Trebon, 1969* (I. Setlik, ed.), pp. 221–230. Centre for Agricultural Publishing & Documentation, Wageningen.

MERTZ, E. T., SINGLETON, V. L. and GAREY, C. L. (1952). The effect of sulphur deficiency on the amino acids of alfalfa. *Archs Biochem. Biophys.* **38**, 139–145.

NEEDHAM, A. E. (1964). "The growth process in animals." Pitman, London.

NORTON, G. (1963). The respiratory pathways in potato tubers. *In* "The growth of the potato" (J. D. Ivins and F. L. Milthorpe, eds), pp. 148–159. Butterworth, London.

OOTA, Y., FUJII, R. and OSAWA, S. (1953). Changes in chemical constituents during the germination stage of a bean, *Vigna sesequipedalis*. *J. Biochem.* **40**, 649–661.

PAYNE, W. J. (1970). Energy yields and growth of heterotrophs. *A. Rev. Microbiol.* **24**, 17–52.

PIRT, S. J. (1965). The maintenance energy of bacteria in growing cultures. *Proc. R. Soc. Lond. B.* **163**, 224–231.

RIED, A. (1970). Energetic aspects of the interaction between photosynthesis and respiration. *In* "Prediction and measurement of photosynthetic productivity". *Proc. IBP/PP technical meeting, Trebon, 1969* (I. Setlik, ed.), pp. 231–246. Centre for Agricultural Publishing & Documentation, Wageningen.

RIPPEL-BALDES, A. (1952). Die Energieausnützung durch Mikro-organismen in quantitativer Hinsicht. *Arch. Mikrobiol.* **17**, 166–188.

SCHIEMANN, R. (1958). Betrachtungen über den intermediären Energiestoffwechsel im Hinblick auf die Durchführung von Gesamtstoffwechselversuchen. Deutsche Akademie der Landwirtschaftswissenschaften, Berlin **37**, 65–85.

SIEGEL, B. V. and CLIFTON, C. E. (1950a). Oxidative assimilation of glucose by *Escherichia coli*, *J. Bact.* **60**, 113–118.

SIEGEL, B. V. and CLIFTON, C. E. (1950b). Energy relationships in carbohydrate assimilation by *Escherichia coli*. *J. Bact.* **60**, 573–583.

SHEMIKATOVA, O. A. (1970). Energy efficiency of respiration under unfavourable conditions. *In* "Prediction and measurement of photosynthetic productivity". *Proc. IBP/PP technical meeting, Trebon, 1969* (I. Setlik, ed.), pp. 247–250. Centre for Agricultural Publishing & Documentation, Wageningen.

STEIN, W. D. (1967). "The movement of molecules across cell membranes". Academic Press, London.

TAMIYA, H. (1932). Zur Energetik des Wachstums. II. *Acta Phytochim.* **6**, 265–304.

TAMIYA, H. and YAMAGUTCHI, S. (1933). Über die Aufbau- und die Erhaltungsatmung. III. *Acta Phytochim.* **7**, 43–64.

TANAKA, A. (1971). Efficiency in respiration. Proc. Symposium on Rice Breeding, I.R.R.I., Los Banos, Philippines. In press.

TANG, P. S., WANG, F. C. and CHIH, F. C. (1959). Studies on plant respiration. III. *Scient. sin.* **8**, 1379–1392.

TERROINE, F. and WURMSTER, R. (1922). L'energie de croissance, I. Le développement de l'*"Aspergillus niger"*. *Bull. Chim. Biol.* **4**, 519–567.

TERROINE, E. F., BONNET, R., and JOESSEL, P. H. (1924). L'energie de croissance, II. La germination. *Bull. Soc. Chim. Biol.* **6**, 357–393.

WALKER, D. A. and CROFTS, A. R. (1970). Photosynthesis. *A. Rev. Biochem.* **39**, 389–428.

WARREN WILSON, J. (1967). Ecological data on dry matter production by plants and plant communities. *In* "The collection and processing of field data" (E. F. Bradley and O. T. Denmead, eds), pp. 77–122. Interscience, London.

WEATHERLEY, P. E. and JOHNSON, R. P. C. (1968). The form and function of the sieve tube. *Int. Rev. Cyt.* **24**, 149–192.

WIT, C. T. DE (1965). Photosynthesis of leaf canopies. *Versl. landbouwk. Onderz.* **663**, 1–57.

WIT, C. T. DE, BROUWER, R., and PENNING DE VRIES, F. W. T. (1970). The simulation of photosynthetic systems. *In* "Prediction and measurement of photosynthetic productivity". *Proc. IBP/PP technical meeting, Trebon, 1969* (I. Setlik, ed.), pp. 47–50. Centre for Agricultural Publishing & Documentation, Wageningen.

YODA, K., SHINOZAKI, K., OGAWA, H., HOZUMI, K. and KIRA, T. (1965). Estimation of the total amount of respiration in woody organs of trees and forest communities. *J. Biol., Osaka City University*, **16**, 15–26.

# Discussion

**Penning de Vries** was asked if it were possible to measure maintenance respiration of higher plants directly by using growth inhibitors, as had been done in bacteria. He replied that he was not aware of such experiments; photosynthesis can be stopped by removing carbon dioxide but this does not stop growth or the redistribution of products which together utilize much more energy than was likely to be consumed for maintenance purposes. In reply to another question on variation in maintenance respiration levels in different parts of the plant, he replied that maintenance respiration rates may be expected to depend on the amount of readily hydrolysable protein in the tissue. This will vary with the tissue and would change with time and temperature.

**Scott Russell** asked Penning de Vries to elaborate on how he estimated the energy consumption for salt uptake in his model. He replied that in higher plants energy was expended in transporting an ion across membranes at the site of uptake and again at the site of utilization. In animal cells (Stein, 1967) it had been found that the uptake of one ion across a membrane requires the energy of about one ATP molecule so that, extrapolating, in plants two ATP molecules would be required. But only one of the two ions of a salt has to be transported actively, the other entering to maintain electrical equilibrium, hence the uptake of one ion involves one ATP molecule, from which it can be calculated that approximately 8–10 g of minerals could be accumulated per 1 g of glucose. **Sutcliffe** thought that this interpretation was open to argument although these energy requirements were of the same order as calculated by Robertson for the maximum efficiency of ion uptake by the root. Scott Russell felt that the movement of ions throughout the plant would involve further energy expenditure.

# IV.5 Physiological and biochemical responses to wilting and other stress conditions

S. T. C. WRIGHT

*A.R.C. Plant Growth Substance and Systemic Fungicide Unit, Wye College, Kent, England*

## I. Introduction

When plants are allowed to wilt by withholding water there is a rapid accumulation of a growth inhibitor, abscisic acid (ABA), within the tissues (Wright and Hiron, 1970). The amount of inhibitor accumulated is dependent upon the period of water stress, the severity of the wilt and the temperature (Wright, 1969). Seventy species of higher plants have been surveyed and all have shown an increase in an ABA-like substance following a period of wilting (Hiron, 1971). In the four species so far examined (wheat, dwarf bean, cotton and pea) this substance has been confirmed as (+)—abscisic acid by optical rotatory dispersion (Wright and Hiron, 1969).

Evidence will be presented which indicates that this increase in abscisic acid leads to stomatal closure and thereby reduces the transpiration rate. Such a biochemical "safety" mechanism enables plants to survive periods of water stress without suffering serious damage.

## II. The determination of ABA levels in plant tissues

As the method of estimating the ABA content of plant tissues has been reported elsewhere (Wright and Hiron, 1969, 1970), only a brief outline will be given here.

Following treatment, the plant tissue (usually 20 g) was immediately

349

extracted with cold ether for 20 h. The acid fraction, obtained by a bicarbonate fractionation procedure, was further purified in two stages using thin-layer chromatography. The highly purified extract was applied to a paper chromatogram and developed in a mixture of isopropanol, ammonia and water (10 : 1 : 1 v/v). The chromatogram was divided into twenty-one segments and those segments corresponding to the ABA region ($R_F$ 0·4 — 0·75) were each placed in 2 ml of distilled water and bioassayed using the wheat coleoptile straight growth test. A typical set of histograms shown in Fig. 1 illustrate clearly the much larger inhibitory peak (ABA) given by the plants receiving wilting treatment. The total μg equivalents of ABA per histogram was obtained by converting the inhibitory activity of each segment into arbitrary units of ABA from a dosage response curve

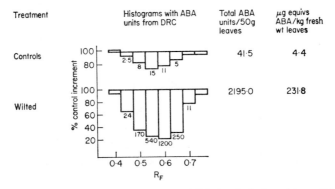

**Fig. 1.** Histograms showing an increase in ABA levels induced by wilting when water was withheld for 66 h from 4-week old Brussels sprout seedlings.

of synthetic ABA and then multiplying the total by a constant to convert the units into μg equivalents of ABA.

# III. Changes in ABA levels in plants during a wilting and recovery cycle

It is well known that stomatal closure may result from water stress, high carbon dioxide concentration or low light intensity and that the rate of response is affected by temperature. To study the effect of water stress on stomatal closure Heath and Mansfield (1962) carried out experiments with *Taraxacum officinale* in which the plants were gradually subjected to an increasing water deficit by allowing the soil in which they were growing to dry out. When the plants had wilted they were rewatered and the effect of recovery on stomatal aperture studied. It was found that prior to and during the early stages of wilting, porometer readings indicated a marked closing response in the stomata. As wilting proceeded the stomata continued to close and it was not until the plants were rewatered that the stomata, very gradually, over a period of three days, returned to their normal daylight opening pattern. Because of the association between a high endogenous ABA level and stomatal closure in dwarf bean plants (Wright and Hiron, 1970) an experiment similar to that of Heath and Mansfield was designed, but in addition to porometer readings ABA levels were determined as well. Porometer readings were made using an Alvim porometer (Alvim, 1965). In this type of porometer the rate of air flow through the leaf is timed with a stop-watch. The leaf resistance is related to the time taken for the pressure, on a sphygmomanometer (blood pressure gauge), to decrease from 60 to 40 mm of mercury.

## A. Brussels sprout seedlings

Four-week old Brussels sprout seedlings (*Brassica oleracea* L., f. *gemmifera* cv. 'Prizetaker') grown in seedtrays containing John Innes potting compost in a glasshouse were thoroughly watered and then allowed to dry out gradually. Within 48 h the seedlings were beginning to show early wilting symptoms (e.g. leaf petioles drooping slightly). The ABA level in these plants was found to have increased 5·8 times and the porometer readings indicated that the stomata were partially closed (Fig. 2). Permanent wilting occurred during the third day and by then the ABA level had increased to about 21-fold the original level. The plants having reached this severely wilted condition (30% leaf water deficit) were rewatered on the fourth day in order to study their recovery. Three hours later the seedlings, as judged visually, were fully turgid and the ABA levels were still very high. There was a close correlation between the ABA levels in the shoots during the wilting and recovery sequence and the leaf resistance readings (Fig. 2). This indicates that with an increasing ABA level the stomata gradually closed and with a decreasing ABA level they gradually opened.

## B. Tomato plants

A similar wilting and recovery cycle was also carried out using 4-week old tomato plants (*Lycopersicon esculentum* Mill. cv. 'Sutton's Best of All') grown in pots (9 cm diameter). This experiment was done under controlled conditions in a growth room (i.e. 14 h photoperiod, 8·6 klx from Atlas "daylight" fluorescent tubes at 25 °C (night temperature 23 °C) and a relative humidity (RH) of 70%). Only ABA levels were determined, since it was thought impracticable to make stomatal measurements with

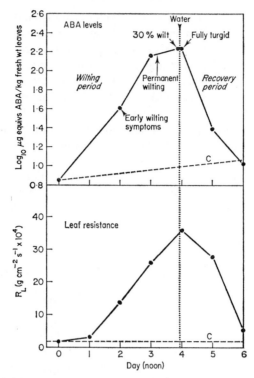

**Fig. 2.** A correlation between endogenous ABA level and leaf resistance during a wilting and recovery experiment with Brussels sprout seedlings (C = ABA level or leaf resistance in non-wilted seedlings).

the Alvim porometer, because of the low density of the stomata in the upper epidermis of the tomato leaf.

When water was withheld, early wilting symptoms appeared on the third day and by then the ABA level had risen 7·4 times, compared with an increase of 5·8 times in Brussels sprout seedlings at a similar stage (compare Fig. 2 with Fig. 3). By the following day the plants were severely wilted (15% leaf-water deficit) and were rewatered at noon. Full turgidity was regained within a period of 4 h. The ABA level of the wilted plants, prior to rewatering, was 16 times higher than the original level. The ABA levels gradually returned to normal over a period of 48 h. At the end of the experiment the mean fresh weight of plants which had not passed through the wilting and recovery cycle was 20% greater than the mean of those which had.

Perhaps the most interesting aspect of these two experiments (Figs 2 and 3) was the rapid increase in ABA during the period leading up to the first wilting symptoms. This increase in ABA level was associated with a partial closure of the stomata in the Brussels sprout seedling experiment. Under high light intensities and optimal growing conditions, this reduction in stomatal aperture might lead to a lowering of the photosynthetic capacity and, moreover, since ABA is also a general growth inhibitor, a slowing down in the growth rate. Apart from the serious effect on growth during the period leading up to wilting, once the ABA levels have built up they can take several days to disperse, the lag period depending upon the ultimate ABA level reached (Wright and Hiron, 1970). During this recovery period the stomata are not functioning normally.

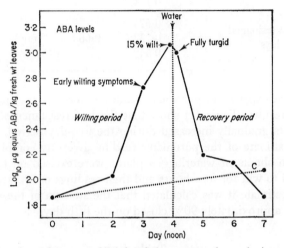

**Fig. 3.** Changes in endogenous ABA levels in tomato plants during a wilting and recovery cycle (C = ABA level in non-wilted plants).

# IV. The effect of waterlogging on ABA levels and stomatal aperture in dwarf bean plants

The transpiration rate of many plant species is reduced by flooding (Parker, 1950). Could this reduction be the result of an increase in the ABA level? To test this hypothesis dwarf bean seedlings (*Phaseolus vulgaris* L. cv. 'Canadian Wonder') were grown in seed trays in a growth room (conditions as for tomato plants above except day temperature 23 °C (night temperature 21 °C)) for nine days. Half the seed trays were then flooded with water for five days. The ABA levels in the waterlogged plants on the fifth day were five times greater than control plants (Table I).

## Table I

ABA levels in waterlogged dwarf bean seedlings

| | Replicate No. | $\mu g$ equivs. ABA/10g fresh wt. leaves | Mean | $\mu g$ equivs. ABA/kg fresh wt. leaves |
|---|---|---|---|---|
| Controls | 1 | 0·147 | | |
| | 2 | 0·126 | 0·131 | 13·1 |
| | 3 | 0·121 | | |
| Waterlogged 5 days | 1 | 0·623 | | |
| | 2 | 0·732 | 0·668 | 66·8 |
| | 3 | 0·649 | | |

In a repeat experiment porometer readings were taken at noon on four days. The results (Table II) show that the leaf resistance of the water-logged plants gradually increased during the five-day period. In order to obtain an estimate of the porometer reading given by completely closed stomata, ten shoots of waterlogged plants were excised on the fifth day and allowed to wilt for four hours and then readings taken (see Table II). From this estimate it was calculated that the stomata of the waterlogged plants were approximately 90% closed on the fifth day.

## Table II

Changes in leaf resistance (readings taken at noon) during a five-day period of waterlogging in dwarf bean seedlings

| Day | Leaf resistance $(R_L)$ g cm$^{-2}$ sec$^{-1} \times 10^4$ | | |
|---|---|---|---|
| | Control $\pm$ 2SE | Waterlogged $\pm$ 2SE | Signif. diff. |
| 0 | 11·3 $\pm$ 2·5 | 12·1 $\pm$ 2·8 | N.S. |
| 1 | 12·4 $\pm$ 2·9 | 16·5 $\pm$ 3·7 | N.S. |
| 3 | 13·2 $\pm$ 2·0 | 23·2 $\pm$ 3·3 | $p = 0·01$ |
| 5 | 9·7 $\pm$ 2·6 | 29·1 $\pm$ 4·1 | $p = 0·01$ |
| 5* | | 42·8 $\pm$ 5·7 | |

5* Estimate of complete stomatal closure (i.e. waterlogged plants with wilted leaves)

At first sight the increase in ABA levels following waterlogging would appear to be incompatible with similar increases resulting from soil water deficits. However, flooding of plants soon leads to an inadequate aeration of the roots, particularly in species not adapted to wet conditions. Consequently there is a decreased permeability of the root tissues to water, an associated decreased absorption and a resulting leaf-water deficit (Kramer, 1969). Thus the increased ABA level of waterlogged plants could have resulted from a leaf-water deficit in the same way as the more obvious wilting conditions studied in the previous experiments. Therefore, it would seem that leaf-water deficits too small to show visible wilting symptoms (i.e. incipient wilting) can lead to an appreciable increase in ABA levels and a resultant reduction in stomatal aperture.

# V. The ABA levels in tomato plants grown under high and low relative humidities

If incipient wilting can lead to significant increases in ABA levels, then plants grown under a low humidity regime might also possess a high ABA level. To investigate this possibility one-month old tomato plants (*Lycopersicon esculentum* Mill., cv. 'Sutton's Best of All') were grown in pots (9 cm diameter) in a growth room (conditions as in previous experiment) and then divided into two groups. One group was transferred to a growth room maintained at 30°C (night temperature 28°C) with an RH of 97% and the other group to a growth room at the same temperatures, but with an RH of 50%. After two days, four samples, each of three shoots, were excised for each treatment for ABA assessment.

The plants which had received the low humidity regime were noticeably smaller than those at the high RH (mean fresh weights of samples were 13·1 g and 14·7 g respectively). This reduced growth of plants kept at 50% RH was associated with ABA levels twice as high as those maintained at 97% RH (Fig. 4). The plants under both treatments had been watered twice daily (0900 and 2100 h) and no wilting symptoms were observed. Therefore, the increase in ABA under the low RH regime was probably due to incipient wilting. However, it must be borne in mind that the soil in the pots of plants at low RH would dry out more rapidly than soil under high RH, despite the twice daily watering routine. Thus one cannot decide whether the incipient wilting was soil- or air-induced. Further experiments need to be done with trickle watering before this question can be answered.

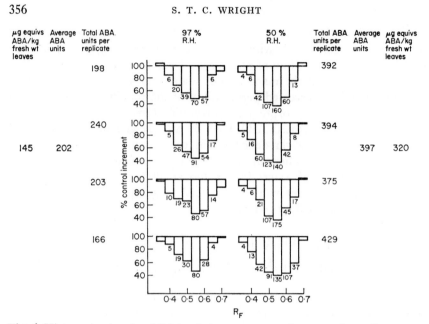

**Fig. 4.** Histograms showing ABA levels in two groups of tomato plants. One group grown at an RH of 97 % and the other at an RH of 50 % for two days.

# VI. The adaptation of dwarf bean plants to a stress-inducing factor

Dwarf bean seedlings (*Phaseolus vulgaris* L cv. 'Canadian Wonder'), when subjected to a continuous stream of warm air (33°–40°C depending on leaf size), have been observed to wilt and then gradually recover their full turgor, despite the continuous passage of warm air. The whole wilting and recovery cycle takes less than 90 min (Wright and Hiron, 1970).

Throughout such an experiment duplicate samples of leaves (10 g) were taken at intervals to determine changes in the ABA levels. Concurrently porometer readings were recorded from three plants. The results (Fig. 5), as well as providing additional confirmation of a strong correlation between ABA increase and leaf resistance (i.e. stomatal closure), help to explain the recovery cycle of these plants. The explanation would seem to be as follows: during the wilting phase (Fig. 5) there is an accumulation of ABA leading to a simultaneous gradual closure of the stomata. Because of the lower transpiration rate the water uptake from the roots must then be in excess of the transpiration losses and the leaves are able to recover their full turgor. Of course if the temperature of the stream of air had been too high, the water loss from the leaves would have been greater than that supplied by the roots, despite stomatal closure. Under such conditions plants continue to show wilting symptoms and eventually become completely desiccated. However, under the specified conditions described, the plants, like those in the waterlogging experiment, were able to adapt to the stress situation.

From the experiments illustrated in Figs 2 and 3 it is clear that when full turgor is restored ABA levels begin to fall. In the continuous stress experiments (i.e. warm air and waterlogging) one would therefore need to

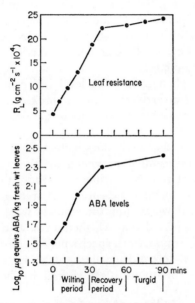

**Fig. 5.** A correlation between leaf resistance and endogenous ABA levels in dwarf bean seedlings subjected to a continuous stress situation (i.e. warm air).

postulate that when full turgor was restored the following sequence commences: the ABA level begins to fall, the stomata begin to open, incipient wilting follows, the ABA level rises again, the stomata close and full turgidity is regained. This cyclical process could be repeated, presumably, throughout the duration of the stress. However, we do know that when ABA disperses during the recovery period after wilting, there is an increase in the level of the glucose ester of ABA (Hiron, 1971). In a continuous stress situation, the recycling process just described would lead to a build-up in this glucose ester and this in turn would slow down the conversion of ABA. As a result, the plant would raise its normal ABA level to a new and higher plateau and in this way become adapted to the stress.

Since ABA is apparently the plant's own anti-transpirant agent, it is of interest to try to estimate the quantitative nature of its action. From the results shown in Figs 2 and 5 one can conclude that when plants are suffering from water stress the degree of stomatal closure is related to the ABA level existing at that particular moment, (assuming daylight and normal carbon dioxide levels).

Presumably, in the fully turgid plant, when the stomata open in response to light, the light response is able to overcome the normal ABA level. However, when a leaf-water deficit sets in and the ABA level increases, the light response is no longer dominant and partial stomatal closure results. Moreover, if the stress continues for long enough the increasing ABA level eventually completely overrides the light effect and the stomata close completely.

What quantitative changes in ABA level will completely override the light response? We can arrive at some approximate estimates; for instance, in Fig. 2, if we assume the stomata of the Brussels sprout seedlings are fully closed at the 30% wilt stage (day 4) and in the control plants fully open (i.e. at noon) then a 17 times increase in the ABA level induced stomatal closure. Using similar reasoning for the warm air dwarf bean experiment (Fig. 5), a nine times increase stimulated stomatal closure. Finally, although no stomatal measurements were made in the tomato experiment (Fig. 3), if we assume the stomata were fully closed during the maximum wilting period (day 4), then a twelve times increase would bring about stomatal closure. Each species may require a different multiple increase in ABA level to override the light response, but these limited results suggest a figure of around 10- to 15-fold may be typical.

# VII. Conclusions

The close correlation between stomatal closure and ABA accumulation during water stress reported for two plant species (i.e. Brussels sprout and dwarf bean) in this paper, when considered in conjunction with the findings of other workers, constitute an indisputable case for believing that ABA levels regulate stomatal closure during periods of water stress. Not only have other workers corroborated the increases found in endogenous ABA levels during water stress (Mizrahi et al., 1970), but they have also reported a reduction in transpiration rate and/or stomatal aperture, as a result of exogenous application of synthetic ABA (Little and Eidt, 1968; Mittelheuser and van Steveninck, 1969; Jones and Mansfield, 1970).

The very sensitive relationship between leaf-water deficit and ABA accumulation in the plant is clearly demonstrated in Figs 2 and 3. In these two experiments the ABA levels had increased 6–8-fold by the time the first wilting symptoms had appeared. Furthermore, the experiments with the different humidities (Fig. 4) and with waterlogging (Table I) illustrate how ABA can increase significantly under conditions where no wilting was apparent and where, presumably, incipient wilting was occurring. These results justify some recent recommendations to growers by Experimental Horticultural Stations such as Fairfield (Anon., 1970), that to maintain maximum growth rate, glasshouse crops should be watered before wilting symptoms appear rather than after.

There has also been some interest shown in recent years concerning the desirability of accurately controlling the humidity in glasshouses to ensure maximum growth. Our results would tend to support this concept but we believe more attention should be given to ways of regulating soil water. Water stress is not easily induced in plants if soil texture, temperature and moisture content are right. Of course humidity control may be essential for crops with low root to shoot ratios, but this low ratio is itself a reflection of high humidity conditions existing during seedling growth. Plants which have experienced periods of water stress are characterized, amongst other features, by a high root to shoot ratio.

Under certain conditions, such as waterlogging, small leaf-water deficits can occur as a result of impaired water uptake by the roots. The waterlogged plants were found to be able to adapt to this situation by increasing their normal ABA level to a somewhat higher one and in this way reducing their transpiration rate and maintaining turgor (Wright and Hiron, 1970). A similar type of adaptation to salinity in soils is believed to involve ABA, (Mizrahi et al., 1970). There are probably many other situations where such adaptation takes place, for instance in evergreens in winter, when the soil is cold and water uptake restricted (Hiron, 1971) or at the top of mature forest trees where water would be limiting. Incipient wilting is believed to be of common occurrence in the field, and temporary adaptation by plants to stress may account for the periods of checked growth observed during drying weather conditions.

Finally, one of the possible practical applications of this work could be the addition of ABA to overhead irrigation water to reduce transpiration. As the calculations have shown there is at least a ten times concentration factor involved in the plant between full stomatal opening and stomatal closure. By using an appropriate dilution of ABA, the disadvantage of a slightly lower photosynthetic capacity might be outweighed by an assured maintenance of unrestricted growth, as well as a large saving in the amount of irrigation water needed per acre.

# Acknowledgements

The author wishes to thank Professor R. L. Wain, F.R.S., for his interest and encouragement in this project and Hoffmann-La Roche & Co. for a generous sample of ($\pm$)—abscisic acid.

## References

ALVIM, P. DE T. (1965). A new type of porometer for measuring stomatal opening and its use in irrigation studies. *UNESCO Arid Zone Res.* **25**, 325–329.

ANON. (1970). Don't wait for plant stress before watering under glass. *Commercial Grower* **3877**, 537–538.

HEATH, O. V. S. and MANSFIELD, T. A. (1962). A recording porometer with detachable cups operating on four separate leaves. *Proc. R. Soc. Lond. B.* **156**, 1–13.

HIRON, R. W. P. (1971). Unpublished results.

JONES, R. J. and MANSFIELD, T. A. (1970). Suppression of stomatal opening in leaves treated with abscisic acid. *J. exp. Bot.* **21**, 714–719.

KRAMER, P. J. (1969). "Plant and soil water relationships: a modern synthesis." pp. 201–207. McGraw-Hill, New York.

LITTLE, C. H. A. and EIDT, D. C. (1968). Effect of abscisic acid on budbreak and transpiration in woody species. *Nature, Lond.* **220**, 498–499.

MITTELHEUSER, C. J. and STEVENINCK, R. F. M. VAN (1969). Stomatal closure and inhibition of transpiration induced by (RS)—abscisic acid. *Nature, Lond.* **221**, 281–282.

MIZRAHI, Y., BLUMENFIELD, A. and RICHMOND, A. E. (1970). Abscisic acid and transpiration in leaves in relation to osmotic root stress. *Pl. Physiol., Lancaster* **46**, 169–171.

PARKER, J. (1950). The effects of flooding on the transpiration and survival of some south-eastern forest tree species. *Pl. Physiol., Lancaster* **25**, 453–460.

WRIGHT, S. T. C. (1969). An increase in the "inhibitor-$\beta$" content of detached wheat leaves following a period of wilting. *Planta* **86**, 10–20.

WRIGHT, S. T. C. and HIRON, R. W. P. (1969). (+)—Abscisic acid, the growth inhibitor induced in detached wheat leaves by a period of wilting. *Nature, Lond.* **224**, 719–720.

WRIGHT, S. T. C. and HIRON, R. W. P. (1970). The accumulation of abscisic acid in plants during wilting and under other stress conditions. *Rep. VII Int. Conf. on Plant Growth Substances, Canberra, 1970* (in press).

# Discussion

In reply to a question **Wright** elaborated current speculations on the mode of action of ABA in his system. He thought that the plant adapted to a continuous stress by gradually building up ABA until a back reaction with its glucose ester precluded any further increase. The biochemistry of the process and the exact site of ABA manufacture were unknown except that synthesis was probably in the leaves since very little was found in the roots and ABA synthesis occurred in excised leaves.

Wright thought it possible that abnormalities in water-culture grown plants when compared with those grown in soil may be related to an increase in their ABA content although he had not measured it; plants grown continuously in water culture probably adapted to that environment. The plants which had been temporarily flooded in his experiments had their roots in anaerobic conditions since aeration of the water diminished the ABA levels reached in the leaves.

**Smith** noted that short-day conditions may also increase ABA contents and he wondered if such plants had greater stress resistance to drought. **Wareing** observed that the cold resistance of short-day plants was increased, although he agreed with **Osborne** that whilst the stress resistance in Wright's beans was acquired within an hour or so, that associated with cold resistance took considerably longer. ABA levels in cold-resistant plants probably increased in parallel with other changes in cell protein etc.

# Some further aspects of control of crop processes

P. F. WAREING

*Botany Department, University College of Wales, Aberystwyth, Wales*

I was invited by the organizers of this meeting to summarize the more important recent advances reported here and to suggest areas in which future research effort might most profitably be directed, but in view of the very wide scope of the meeting I propose to limit my discussion to certain aspects of the subject, and to follow the lead of Dr Warren Wilson in his opening paper, by considering some of the factors affecting source and sink relations.

## I. Factors affecting the rate of supply of assimilates

I do not propose to discuss this subject at length since it has been dealt with by several other contributors to the Symposium but I wish to draw attention to one problem which has emerged during the meeting, namely the question of whether, under field conditions, photosynthesis is limited primarily by the liquid diffusion resistance to carbon dioxide movement within the leaf, as suggested by Dr Chartier, or whether the enzyme-controlled carboxylation step may also be important, as suggested by the evidence presented by Dr Treharne. In his paper, Dr Chartier calculates that the so-called carboxylation resistance has only about one-tenth of the value of the liquid diffusion step, suggesting that the carboxylation process does not constitute an important rate-limiting stage for the overall rate of photosynthesis. On the other hand, Dr Treharne has presented a considerable body of experimental evidence in which a good correlation has been demonstrated between the photosynthetic rate and the activity of the enzyme ribulose, 1–5, diphosphate carboxylase (RuDP carboxylase) within the leaf. Of course, a correlation of this type does not necessarily imply a causal relationship, but if there is, indeed, such a relationship, two alternative situations can be envisaged: either (1) that the enzyme levels are regulated by the rate of photosynthesis, or (2) that the level of enzyme activity is an important factor determining the overall photosynthetic rate. So far as I am aware there is no evidence in support of the first hypothesis and the second seems to me the more likely. If the second hypothesis proves to be valid, then we have to reconcile this fact with the conclusion of those who adopt a more physical approach, that the "carboxylation resistance" is of negligible importance.

There would seem to be several possible explanations of the discrepancy between the results of biochemical experiments and the conclusions arrived at by more theoretical analysis. It is possible that the explanation lies in differences in the conditions under which the experimental plants are maintained; thus the conditions under which theoretical approaches suggest that liquid diffusion resistance is most important are high light intensity and normal (low) carbon dioxide concentrations, and it is possible that, as Monteith (1963) has pointed out, under other conditions the biochemical steps may become more rate-limiting. On the other hand, it is possible that one or more of the premises upon which the theoretical schemes are based is not valid. Indeed, by adopting a kinetic approach, Charles-Edwards (1971) has concluded that diffusive processes do not normally limit the rate of photosynthesis.

Considering the environmental factors which affect the rate-limiting step in photosynthesis under glasshouse conditions, it would seem very possible that under conditions of carbon dioxide enrichment the carboxylation step may become limiting i.e. under these conditions the level of RuDP carboxylase activity may be limiting. This conclusion may well be important in breeding glasshouse crops. Dr Ludwig has suggested that it may be possible to breed plants in which photorespiration is inhibited, and I would suggest that it may be advantageous to breed varieties with an increased content of carboxylating enzymes, for cultivation under conditions of carbon dioxide enrichment in the winter.

The effects of environmental factors, such as light and temperature, on photosynthesis rate are well known, but there have been relatively few studies on the effect of daylength on photosynthesis. Hughes and Cockshull (1965) and Cockshull and Hughes (1969) have studied the effects of "night breaks" of low intensity red light on growth of *Callistephus chinensis* and they obtained a marked increase in dry weight, but this effect appears to have been due to increased leaf area, which enabled the plants to make greater use of the incident light. In his introductory remarks, Professor Schwabe mentioned that he had reached similar conclusions in studies on the effects of low intensity red and far red light on chrysanthemum. He also presents evidence to show that plants of *Xanthium strumarium* maintained under short days are more efficient in the use of incident radiation than plants of this species maintained under long days. The effects of daylength on the photosynthetic rate of plants receiving the same amount of high intensity radiation, other than through effects on leaf expansion, do not appear to have been studied previously, but some observations of Dr D. Lavender, while working at Aberystwyth, appear to be pertinent. He maintained dormant seedlings of Douglas fir under long and short days in a greenhouse during the winter months, both lots of seedlings receiving 8 h of daylight (supplemented by high intensity illumination from mercury vapour lamps), while the long day plants received an additional 8 h of supplementary illumination at a low intensity which would have had negligible effect on photosynthesis. The shoots of both series of plants remained dormant but the roots of both were active and at the end of the experimental period (3 months) the total dry weight of the long day seedlings was twice that of the short day plants, largely due to the difference in root growth. Thus, in this species it would appear that photosynthetic activity is rather directly affected by photoperiod. This effect may be more pronounced in a woody species which shows a marked seasonal periodicity of growth and dormancy than in annual herbaceous species, but it would seem worth investigating the effects of daylength on photosynthetic rate of glasshouse crop plants, which are liable to be exposed to large seasonal variations in daylength under temperature conditions which are favourable for photosynthesis and growth.

Dr Treharne has mentioned in his paper that the rate of photosynthesis can be increased in some species by external application of hormones such as gibberellins and cytokinins and that there is a parallel increase in the levels of certain enzymes, including RuDP carboxylase. These observations raise the question whether photosynthetic rates may be partly under the control of endogenous hormones. Thus it may be significant that Stoddart (1968) has shown that most of the gibberellin in clover leaves is localized in the plastids, where quite high concentrations occur; similar observations have been made for ivy and other species (Frydman, unpublished). It is well known that gibberellin levels are markedly affected by daylength in a number of species (Chailachjan, 1968; Cleland and Zeewaart, 1970; Digby and Wareing, 1966; Lang, 1960; Nitsch, 1963; Stoddart and Lang, 1969) and it seems possible that such variations in hormone levels may affect the photosynthetic rate.

# II. Some factors affecting sink strength

In the past there was an implicit assumption in the classical type of growth analysis that the overall rate of dry matter increase of a plant is determined by (1) the net assimilation rate (over a 24 h period), and (2) the total photosynthetic capacity, as measured by the leaf area; that is, it was assumed that the leaves operate at their full photosynthetic potential for any given set of environmental conditions and that the overall rate of dry matter increase is determined by the potential rate of production and is not limited by the rate of utilization in growth. However, these concepts have now undergone considerable modification and it is now generally agreed that situations may arise in which the overall growth rate is limited by the ability of the growth centres to utilize assimilates in growth, rather than by the "source" strength (Watson, 1971; Warren Wilson, this volume) as, for example, under conditions of high light intensity and cool temperatures such as may prevail outdoors in the spring, when photosynthesis may be very active but growth is limited by low temperatures. However, it is worth examining whether there are other conditions in which sink strength may be limiting.

What determines the rate of growth as measured by the rate of incorporation of assimilates into new tissue? Presumably, in the final analysis, growth rate is determined by the rates of cell division and cell vacuolation, and by the associated biosynthetic processes, including the rates of synthesis of DNA, RNA, protein and cell wall material. However, I would suggest that we should also pay attention to the morphology of the plant. The absolute growth rate of the shoot is clearly dependent upon (1) the rate of production of leaf primordia, (2) the rate of increase in size of these primordia and (3) the final size of the mature leaf; that is to say, the shoot growth rate will be quite profoundly affected by its morphology, as is illustrated by considering the seedlings of some woody plants.

If we compare the growth rate of first-year seedlings of, say, birch with that of a first-year seedling of Scots pine we find that the absolute and relative growth rate of the former is much greater than that of the conifer (van den Driessche and Wareing, 1966). The slower growth rate of the Scots pine seedlings appears to be due to the fact that the individual juvenile needles are small, so that although the apex of the pine seedling initiates new needle primordia at a relatively high rate, the overall rate of leaf area increase in the pine is considerably less than that of the birch. This effect is accentuated by the fact that whereas birch seedlings branch freely, so that there may be a number of apices initiating new leaves, first-year Scots pine seedlings form few lateral shoots. Thus, I suggest that the sink strength of the shoot will be affected by the size and number of leaves and by the branching pattern. If one removes all the lateral shoots of a birch seedling as soon as they appear, so that the plant is restricted to a single stem, it is found that the area of the individual leaves and the net assimilation rate increase, but in spite of these compensating effects the overall relative growth rate of such plants is considerably less than that of naturally branching seedlings (Causton and Wareing, 1967). Thus, one has produced a situation in which the relative growth rate is limited by the rate at which the plant can utilize assimilates in new leaf production. This experiment reminds one, of course, of the practice in tomato growing of removing lateral shoots so that the plants are limited to a single stem. It is possible that this practice limits the overall relative growth rate of the tomato plant and it would seem worth investigating whether production might be increased by growing plants on two or three stems.

Apart from morphological characters of the type just described, obviously the overall growth rate will be determined by a large number of different physiological and biochemical processes, and from the evidence presented by Dr Osborne it is natural to think of endogenous hormones as possible factors affecting growth rate. This is certainly true, for example, of certain types of genetic dwarf varieties, which show markedly increased growth and dry matter production when hormones, such as gibberellins, are applied externally. In such plants it seems clear that the overall growth rate is limited by some genetic block in gibberellin biosynthesis (Phinney, 1961). Again, it has been shown that in certain species leaf growth is markedly affected by root temperatures (Brouwer and de Wit, 1969). It is of interest, therefore, that Atkin (unpublished) has shown that the levels of cytokinins in the root exudate of maize seedlings are greatly reduced by cool root temperatures. It is well known that older generations of gardeners stressed the beneficial effects of "bottom heat" in glasshouses, and I would venture to suggest that this piece of horticultural lore may well have a sound physiological basis.

# III. The mobilizing ability of sinks

Returning now to the question of sink strength, as Dr Warren Wilson has pointed out, this parameter depends both upon the size of the sink and on "sink activity". However, I would suggest that we also need to take into account the competitive ability of a sink. There is no doubt that there is normally competition between the various growth centres and storage regions of the plant for available assimilates. There is a great deal of evidence for such competition and it is sufficient to cite only two examples. Thus, Cockshull and Hughes (1968) showed that when young flowers of chrysanthemum were removed, there was a re-distribution of assimilates, with a resulting increase in dry weight of the roots and leaves. A second example is provided by the observation that root growth is greatly depressed by the presence of developing fruits, but if the fruits are removed then root growth is resumed (Leonard, 1962). Thus, the share of available assimilates which any plant region receives is the result of competition with other growth regions. This conclusion would seem to imply that the differential distribution of dry matter is determined either (1) by the characteristics of the transport system, or (2) by the competitive ability of the growth regions themselves. It seems very probable that the vascular system of the plant is an important factor affecting the pattern of distribution of assimilates. However, if the partition of dry matter were determined solely by characteristics of the vascular system in the plant as a whole, so that the supply of assimilates to any given growth region was not controlled by the region itself, there would seem to be little flexibility for variation in the pattern of distribution to meet varying needs within the plant. Strategically, this seems to me to be a less advantageous situation than one in which the distribution of assimilates can be regulated according to the changing needs of the plant at different stages of development, and circumstantial evidence suggests to me (1) that the pattern of distribution is largely determined by active competition between the various growth centres and (2) that an important factor in this competition is the "mobilizing ability" of the growth centres. Thus, I would prefer to substitute "mobilizing ability" in place of Dr Warren Wilson's "sink activity" (by which I assume he means activity in utilizing assimilates in metabolism and growth), since I suspect that the uptake of assimilates from the transport system is not determined directly by the rate of their utilization in the synthesis of structural material, for reasons which are given below.

We know very little about what controls the mobilizing ability of a growth centre, but I suggest that hormones may play an important role. Some years ago, Mothes and his co-workers (Mothes *et al.*, 1959) showed that when kinetin was applied locally to a tobacco leaf, various metabolites, including amino acids, moved from surrounding regions towards the point of application; this movement was not primarily determined by the utilization of the metabolites, since even unnatural amino acids, such as γ-amino butyric acid, which are not incorporated into proteins, were accumulated in response to kinetin application.

We have carried out a series of studies which show that application of auxins to a non-growing region of the plant will lead to the accumulation of $^{14}$C-sucrose at the point of application (Davies and Wareing, 1965). Here again, the movement of the sucrose cannot be directly determined by its utilization in growth and metabolism since a high proportion of the

[14]C was still present as [14]C-sucrose (Patrick, unpublished). The importance of such "hormone-directed transport" in the normal distribution of assimilates remains to be demonstrated. Moreover, it is not clear whether this phenomenon is equally important in both shoot and root, since the level of endogenous auxins in the roots appears to be very low.

# IV. Root–shoot interactions

The distribution of assimilates between root and shoot has a profound effect upon the overall rate of dry matter production by the plant, since it affects the leaf/weight ratio and hence the relative growth rate. It appears that the partition of assimilates between root and shoot is rather tightly controlled. For example, if one disturbs the root/shoot ratio in birch seedlings by partial defoliation of mature leaves, then it is found that in the ensuing few days the dry matter increment is taken up entirely by new leaves and stem, with a corresponding depression in the growth rate of the root, so that the normal root/shoot ratio is rapidly restored (Wareing, 1970). This type of observation suggests that there is a rather effective homeostatic mechanism which restores the root/shoot balance when it is disturbed. Of course, this balance is affected by a variety of external conditions, including mineral nutrient conditions and water regime, but within any given set of conditions it appears that the root/shoot balance for a given genotype represents a dynamic equilibrium.

If we consider what sort of control mechanisms may be involved, it is clear that there are quite complex interactions between root and shoot in the exchange of metabolites and nutrients; not only does the shoot supply assimilates to the root, but it is known that the root is dependent upon the supply of vitamins, including thiamin, from the leaves. It is also known from the work of Pate (1966) that roots specialize in the synthesis and export of amino acids confined almost entirely to the glutamate and aspartate families of amino acids, whereas the leaves synthesize a range of amino acids (serine, glycine, etc.) complementary to that formed by the root system.

There also appears to be an exchange of hormonal substances between root and shoot. I have already referred to the fact that cytokinins formed in the roots appear to be transported to the leaves in the transpiration stream (p. 367). Gibberellins appear to be formed in both shoots and roots, but Crozier and Reid (1971) have recently published evidence suggesting that in bean plants gibberellin $GA_{19}$ is formed in the shoot and is transported to the root, where it is converted to $GA_1$, which in turn is retransported to the shoot. Thus, there appears to be a re-cycling of gibberellins from shoot to root and back again to shoot. The study of this type of complex interaction clearly calls for a correspondingly sophisticated type of approach, and an attempt has been made to construct a mathematical model to simulate the functional balance between the growth of the shoot and the root (Brouwer and de Wit, 1969; de Wit *et al.*, 1971).

# References

BROUWER, R. and WIT, C. T. DE (1969). A simulation model of plant growth with special attention to root growth and its consequences. *In* "Root Growth" (W. J. Whittington, ed.), pp. 224–241. Butterworths, London.

CAUSTON, D. R. and WAREING, P. F. (1967). Influence of leaf-characters and growth habit on the production of dry matter. *Rep. Forest Res., Lond. 1967,* 161.

CHAILACHJAN, M. C. (1968). Internal factors of plant flowering. *A. Rev. Pl. Physiol.* **19,** 1–36.

CHARLES-EDWARDS, D. A. (1971). A simple kinetic model for leaf photosynthesis and respiration. *Planta* **101,** 43–50.

CLELAND, C. F. and ZEEVAART, J. A. D. (1970). Gibberellins in relation to flowering and stem elongation in the long day plant *Silene armeria. Pl. Physiol., Lancaster* **46,** 392–400.

COCKSHULL, K. E. and HUGHES, A. P. (1968). Accumulation of dry matter by *Chrysanthemum morifolium* after flower removal. *Nature, Lond.* **217,** 979–980.

COCKSHULL, K. E. and HUGHES, A. P. (1969). Growth and dry weight distribution in *Callistephus chinensis* as influenced by lighting treatment. *Ann. Bot.* **33,** 367–379.

CROZIER, A. and REID, D. M. (1971). Do roots synthesize gibberellins? *Can. J. Bot.* **49,** 967–975.

DAVIES, C. R. and WAREING, P. F. (1965). Auxin-directed transport of radiophosphorus in stems. *Planta* **65,** 139–156.

DIGBY, J. and WAREING, P. F. (1966). The relation between endogenous hormone levels in the plant and seasonal aspects of cambial activity. *Ann. Bot.* **30,** 607–622.

DRIESSCHE, R. VAN DEN and WAREING, P. F. (1966). Nutrient supply, dry matter production and nutrient uptake of forest tree seedlings. *Ann. Bot.* **30,** 657–672.

HUGHES, A. P. and COCKSHULL, K. E. (1965). Interrelations of flowering and vegetative growth in *Callistephus chinensis* (var. "Queen of the Market"). *Ann. Bot.* **29,** 131–151.

LANG, A. (1960). Gibberellin-like substances in photoinduced and vegetative *Hyoscyamus* plants. *Planta* **54,** 498–504.

LEONARD, E. R. (1962). Inter-relations of vegetative and reproductive growth, with special reference to indeterminate plants. *Bot. Rev.* **28,** 353–410.

MOTHES, K., ENGELBRECHT, L. and KULAJEWA, O. (1959). Über die Wirkung des Kinetins auf Stickstoffverteilung und Eiweissynthese in isolierten Blättern. *Flora, Jena* **147,** 445–465.

Monteith, J. L. (1963). Gas exchange in plant communities. *In* "Environmental Control of Plant Growth" (L. T. Evans, ed.), pp. 95–112. Academic Press, New York.

Nitsch, J. P. (1963). The mediation of climatic effects through endogenous regulating substances. *In* "Environmental Control of Plant Growth" (L. T. Evans, ed.), pp. 175–192. Academic Press, New York.

Pate, J. (1966). Photosynthesizing leaves and nodulated roots as donors of carbon to protein of the shoot of the field pea (*Pisum arvense* L.). *Ann. Bot.* **30**, 93–109.

Phinney, B. O. (1961). Dwarfing genes in *Zea mays* and their relation to the gibberellins. *In* "Plant Growth Regulation" (R. M. Klein, ed.), pp. 489–501. Iowa State College Press, Ames, Iowa.

Stoddart, J. L. (1968). The association of gibberellin-like activity with the chloroplast fraction of leaf homogenates. *Planta* **81**, 106–112.

Stoddart, J. L. and Lang, A. (1968). The effect of daylength on gibberellin synthesis in leaves of red clover (*Trifolium pratense* L.). *In* "Biochemistry and Physiology of Plant Growth Substances" (F. Wightman and G. Setterfield, eds), pp. 1371–1383. Runge Press, Ottawa.

Wareing, P. F. (1970). Growth and its co-ordination in trees. *In* "Physiology of Tree Crops" (L. C. Luckwill and C. V. Cutting, eds), pp. 1–21. Academic Press, London.

Watson, D. J. (1971). Size, structure and activity of the productive system of crops. *In* "Potential Crop Production" (P. F. Wareing and J. P. Cooper, eds), pp. 76–88. Heinemann, London.

Wit, C. T. de, Brouwer, R. and Penning de Vries, F. W. T. (1971). A dynamic model of plant and crop growth. *In* "Potential Crop Production" (P. F. Wareing and J. P. Cooper, eds), pp. 116–142. Heinemann, London.

# Author Index

*Italic figures refer to pages where references are given in full*

# Subject Index

*A guide to the main topics discussed and plant names mentioned*